THE KING WHISPERERS

POWER BEHIND THE THRONE,
FROM RASPUTIN TO ROVE

THE KING WHISPERERS

**POWER BEHIND THE THRONE,
FROM RASPUTIN TO ROVE**   **KERWIN SWINT**

UNION SQUARE
New York

DEDICATION

To Harvey and Ann

STERLING and the distinctive Sterling logo are registered trademarks of Sterling Publishing Co., Inc.

Library of Congress Cataloging-in-Publication Data
Swint, Kerwin C.
  The king whisperers : power behind the throne, from Rasputin to Rove / Kerwin Swint.
      p. cm.
  Includes bibliographical references and index.
  ISBN 978-1-4027-7201-6
  1. Politicians--Biography. 2. Kings and rulers--History. 3. Political consultants--Biography. 4. Spies--Biography. 5. Generals--Biography. 6. Revolutionaries--Biography. 7. Power (Social sciences)--Case studies. 8. Manipulative behavior--Case studies. 9. World politics--Case studies. I. Title.
  D106.S8 2011
  920.02--dc22
                              2010039018
  10 9 8 7 6 5 4 3 2 1

Published by Sterling Publishing Co., Inc.
387 Park Avenue South, New York, NY 10016
© 2011 by Kerwin Swint
Distributed in Canada by Sterling Publishing
c/o Canadian Manda Group, 165 Dufferin Street,
Toronto, Ontario, Canada M6K 3H6
Distributed in the United Kingdom by GMC Distribution Services
Castle Place, 166 High Street, Lewes, East Sussex, England BN7 1XU
Distributed in Australia by Capricorn Link (Australia) Pty. Ltd.
P.O. Box 704, Windsor, NSW 2756, Australia

Sterling ISBN 978-1-4027-7201-6

For information about custom editions, special sales, premium and corporate purchases, please contact Sterling Special Sales Department at 800-805-5489 or specialsales@sterlingpublishing.com.

We thought, because we had power, we had wisdom.

—Stephen Vincent Benet

CONTENTS

⇒ INTRODUCTION ⇐

In the summer and fall of 1503, Niccolo Machiavelli represented his beloved Florence in negotiations with one of the most ambitious and dangerous men in Europe at the time, Cesare Borgia, the son of the pope. Machiavelli was trying to determine whether it was in the interest of the Florentine republic to enter into an alliance with Borgia, or to rely on its shaky relationship with the king of France for protection. It was a crucial decision, for if the Florentines resisted Borgia, Florence could not be certain France would come to their aid. But if they joined Borgia and he was not victorious, they would be in an even worse situation.

For guidance, Machiavelli wrote to his friend Biagio Buonaccorsi and asked him to send a copy, posthaste, of Plutarch's masterpiece, *Parallel Lives*. Why this book? Plutarch compared the lives and careers of some of the great statesmen of the ages, Roman and Greek generals, lawmakers, and rulers. In his series of biographies and analyses, Plutarch explained what these great leaders had in common and probed their major differences. It is one of the most influential works of leadership and philosophy ever written.

Machiavelli wanted to review Plutarch's biographies in order to better understand the motivations and qualities of men like Cesare Borgia. He hoped that by studying the lives of great men of the past, he could decipher Borgia's intentions and advise the leaders of Florence on the best course of action.

It is in that spirit that I undertake this project. Use the past to understand the present. As one of the founders of the science of politics, Machiavelli knew that the actions and motivations of historical figures could yield clues to the behavior of others, even present-day political and military leaders. Political leaders and public figures have always looked to the past for inspiration and guidance.

For example, George Washington was introduced to classical literature as a youth, and absorbed the histories and biographies of Roman heroes and poets, such as Seneca, Cato, and Cincinnatus. He was particularly influenced by the exploits of Cincinnatus, the Roman hero who came to the aid of his country in its time of great need. To a significant degree, English monarchs were greatly influenced by the Romans and the Greeks, as well as by their own illustrious predecessors: Henry VIII was an avid student of the histories of Henry V, for instance.

As a youth, Theodore Roosevelt was captivated by the oratory and the exploits of the famed Roman Cicero. Martin Luther King Jr. followed in the footsteps of Mohandas K. Gandhi, whose teachings he praised as the "only moral and practical way for an oppressed people to struggle against social injustice." In World War II, legendary tank commanders Erwin Rommel of the German Wehrmacht and George S. Patton of the American Third Army had both read the military treatises of Carl von Clausewitz and studied the battlefield strategies of Napoleon. And modern-day political strategist Karl Rove has long admired the success of Mark Hanna at the turn of the twentieth century.

Thus, there is a well-established pattern whereby each generation examines and considers the circumstances, the thoughts, and the achievements of those who came before. Those who are remembered by history will inevitably, for better or worse, leave a lasting impression on those who follow. The King Whisperers—those who were in a position to influence history—have much to offer if we only pay attention. This is primarily a book about the struggle for power in hostile environments, and the political cunning of men and women who shaped political events to their liking. The cases in the book do not focus primarily on heads of state or elected chief executives, but on the power behind the throne—the Machiavellis of history. There have always existed individuals who, through a combination of political instinct, personal ambition, and opportunity, have successfully driven political players and systems in a direction that advanced their own interests, whether those interests were personal, ideological, or altruistic. From the Babylonians and the Romans, through the Middle Ages and the Industrial Revolution to the modern age, some things have changed very little—the nature of humanity, the use of power, and the skillful manipulation of each.

Using case studies and historical analyses, this book will illustrate some of the most dramatic moments in world history and explain how astute political figures were there to seize the day. The examples range from the ancient world to the twenty-first century and cover a wide range of historical events, political cultures, and engaging personal stories. The reader will encounter a number of familiar historical names, but also a few that are less well known. Looking at these historic figures through the prism of both the past and the present gives us more insight into who they were and what drove them. Let us follow Machiavelli's example. By exploring the convergence of biography, intellectual history, and the larger geopolitical context in each person's life, perhaps we can gain a better understanding of our own times. Plutarch himself said of his famous work *Parallel Lives*, "The virtues of these great men serve me as a sort of looking-glass, in which I may see how to adjust and adorn my own life."

The King Whisperers will focus on ten distinct categories in order to illustrate the differences in approach, style, tendencies, and situational context of the men and women profiled. Many of the figures in the book are the official Number Two leader or designated successor to a leader, while others are political advisors, powerful court officials, or ambitious schemers. Some were Number Two on their way to becoming Number One. There are also some sections of the book that compare and contrast two or more figures, and there are a few that profile more than one person—such as the pioneers of Italian independence in the 1800s, or the shadowy figures behind the Nazi Third Reich. But all are devoted to distilling lessons on power and leadership and to capturing the essence of the King Whisperer.

First: *The Machiavellians*. As one of the premier models for this concept of the political player behind the scenes, Niccolo Machiavelli is credited with establishing the school of political realism that has dominated most political thought for five hundred years. Though Machiavelli himself had a mixed record as a force in the Italian political machinations of his age, his philosophy on the use of power, expressed through his best-known works, *The Prince* and *Discourses on Livy*, has influenced political leaders and advisors the world over for centuries. Actually, since the beginning of recorded history, successful leaders and advisors have used the approach encapsulated in *The Prince*.

Second: *Empire Builders*. Certain individuals have played decisive roles in building and supporting powerful institutions of which they were a part. These institutions may take various forms—government, business and commercial, or social and religious. This type of leader tends to be a "visionary" and often tries to implement grand designs. Otto von Bismarck, the chancellor under Kaiser Wilhelm and the architect of modern Germany, is a notable example.

Third: *Kingmakers*. Many powerful figures throughout history have been in positions to determine the course of events in their country or region. Some have played key roles in toppling regimes and in instituting new ones in their place. Often, their motivation was personal or financial; they largely acted out of self-interest. Others had more patriotic or political motivations. For instance, the Indian power broker K. Kamaraj influenced the direction of modern Indian politics for more than thirty years.

Fourth: *Spies*. Some of the most clever and sometimes devious political masterminds engaged in espionage, behind-the-curtain diplomacy, and counterintelligence operations. As with the Machiavellians, their ambition was usually patriotic in nature, with the survival and prosperity of their nation uppermost in their minds. Francis Walsingham, the spymaster for Queen Elizabeth I; Cardinal Richelieu, of Three Musketeers fame; and Omar Suleiman, the current Number Two to Egyptian President Hosni Mubarak, are ideal examples.

Fifth: *Silver-Tongued Devils*. Many political figures in history are known for the "gift of gab," or a charismatic presence that enabled them to succeed in politics and public life. Whether it was due to great oratorical skill, the ability to sweet-talk friends and foes, or a display of diplomatic doublespeak, these individuals moved mountains and swayed nations. The noted Roman orator and political dramatist Cicero is one example. The French diplomat Talleyrand is another.

Sixth: *The Generals*. Military leaders have always carried political influence, some more openly than others. As Machiavelli said, a prince must always be knowledgeable about military affairs and strategy. Throughout history, commanders and generals have been in a position to exploit their power for personal or political gain. Saladin and Oliver Cromwell exemplify this group.

Seventh: *The Rebels*. The flipside of the Generals—those who led movements of rebellion and either toppled or replaced existing regimes. Whether motivated by ideology, religion, or economics, these rebels in many cases altered the landscape of history. Sakamoto Ryoma of Japan and Ernesto "Che" Guevara of Argentina are two notable examples.

Eighth: *The Truly Evil* (or genocidal lunatics). Were monsters such as Hermann Goering and Heinrich Himmler of the Nazi Third Reich, or Tomás de Torquemada of the Spanish Inquisition, truly evil, mentally ill, or both? Historians disagree, and modern-day psychologists will never know.

Ninth: *The Fixers*. This is a uniquely American concept, the political fixer, or specialist, brought in to perform specific functions for a political leader. Professional political consultants are prime examples. "Dollar" Mark Hanna, the moneyman and strategist behind William McKinley, and a string of twentieth-century American politicos, such as Larry O'Brien, Roger Ailes, and Karl Rove, are key examples.

Tenth: *Schemers*. Notable political players throughout history have been known for scheming, scratching, and clawing their way to power. Some were successful, while others were betrayed or caught up in their own web of deceit. Grigori Rasputin was poisoned, stabbed, and thrown in the river by his enemies, while Haman (from the Bible's book of Esther) was merely hanged.

CHAPTER 1

THE MACHIAVELLIANS

The Machiavellians are the "political realists" of history—those who counsel or practice hard-nosed power politics, along with threats, intimidation, and deception, in order to bring stability and prosperity to their society. And when it comes to power plays and raw political maneuvering, Niccolo di Bernardo dei Machiavelli is the gold standard. He is considered by many to be the father of modern political theory, and is particularly noted for helping give birth to the school of political realism that, arguably, has guided the decisions of most nation-states and regional sovereigns for the last five hundred years.

Niccolo Machiavelli is a character many have heard of, but few really know much about. The name itself conjures up images of power-hungry politicians, behind-the-scenes maneuvering, and deceitful, diabolical acts. But we forget that Machiavelli was a real, flesh-and-blood person.

Beyond the stern warnings and lessons about political power was a reserved but very funny guy, who liked to go drinking with his friends, told dirty jokes, and loved to travel. He had a wife, children, a series of lovers, and a tendency to pull pranks on those close to him. In his later years, he was also a bitter and frustrated person. He was of modest birth, and harbored a fair amount of resentment toward those born into wealth and power. When he wrote *The Prince,* his most famous work, he was an out-of-work government bureaucrat trying to get on the good side of people he detested.

Some years later, resigned to his fate, he wrote *The Discourses,* in which he extols the virtue of republican, or representative, forms of government over absolutist, or autocratic, dictatorships. Based on the totality of his life and his writings, this is probably much closer to how Machiavelli truly felt about leadership and representative government. But it is *The Prince* that the world remembers.

That's because *The Prince* is a handy little manual on how to win. It is a guide to acquiring and keeping power. In essence, Machiavelli advises those who seek power and influence to divorce themselves from ethical considerations and focus on pragmatism and political expedience. In contrast to Plato and Aristotle, the ideal society is not the aim. In fact, Machiavelli emphasizes the need for the exercise of brute power, when necessary, and a carrot-and-stick approach to preserving the status quo. Most often, the aggressive style of leadership he advocates is in pursuit of security and stability for the regime. Machiavelli advises kings and princes that a strong hand is necessary to guide a people to a prosperous and strong society; and that a leader who is successful in accomplishing this will be loved and esteemed by the populace.

The reason Machiavelli's words have survived over the centuries, and his approach to politics has in fact thrived, is that they are timeless. The principles he established and the lessons he dispensed are not tied to a particular era, but are rooted in the ability of a leader—any leader—to assess a situation and then act decisively. He believed that success or failure depended largely on whether leaders' talents and imagination, and their subsequent actions, were well or poorly suited to their times and events. Thus, different courses of action in different periods under a different set of circumstances may yield the same results. This theory of political realism has been the default setting of most world leaders for centuries. Machiavelli and others have laid out the basic principles of how power works. It is up to those individuals who lead, or wish to lead, to apply those principles to their own times. The Greeks, the Romans, the Holy Romans, the French, the British, the Americans, the Russians, the Chinese, and numerous others have adapted the principles of power politics, similar to those enumerated by Machiavelli, to their own unique situations.

"Old Nick"

Machiavelli was born in Florence in 1469 during a time of intense political and cultural turmoil, both on the Italian peninsula and across Europe. During the Renaissance, Italy was the scene of savage political conflict involving the dominant city-states of Florence, Venice, Milan, and Naples, plus the papacy, France, Spain, and the Holy Roman Empire. Each city and region attempted to protect itself by playing the larger powers against one another. The result was massive political intrigue, blackmail, and violence. *The Prince* was written against this backdrop, and in its conclusion Machiavelli issued an impassioned call for Italian unity and an end to foreign intervention.

The Medici family was one of the wealthiest and most powerful dynasties in Europe at the time, ruling Florence for various periods from the 1400s to the 1800s. But Machiavelli, contrary to his modern image, was a passionate believer in republican rule. When the invading French army forced the Medicis to flee in the 1490s, the Florentines established a republic, governed by a council and allied with the French king, Charles VIII. Machiavelli was named by the council as secretary of the Second Chancery, which handled relations with foreign leaders and diplomatic affairs. He held this post until the fall of the republic in 1512.

It was during this time that Machiavelli traveled widely throughout Europe, representing the Florentine government, negotiating agreements with foreign leaders, and trying to ensure his city's survival in the face of the onslaught of invasions, political treachery, and the ambitions of the pope and the Holy Roman emperor. This was also the time when he came into contact with the kings, princes, diplomats, professional soldiers, and court-watchers that formed the core of his political philosophy, and would later serve as the basis of his writings.

Ultimately, the alliance with the French failed the Florentines, as they were outflanked both politically and militarily by the pope, in concert with Spain and Venice. At the urging of the pope and over the objections of Florence's council of leaders, the Medici rulers were restored to power in November 1512. Within days, the foundations of Florentine republican liberty were dismantled and its official roles and offices were abolished.

Machiavelli was in a very dangerous position. He had been a vital player in the life of the republic and was not seen as a friend of the Medicis. His only hope of political survival was to persuade the returning Medici rulers that he had something to offer them; namely, his experience in politics and diplomacy. But it was to no avail. In fact, worse was to come. In the chaotic days of postrepublic rule and the reemergence of the old Medici power base, Machiavelli and a host of others were named in a plot to overthrow them.

There was no direct evidence against him, but Machiavelli was imprisoned in the city he had served as chief diplomat. During his imprisonment he was tortured, but did not admit to a role in the conspiracy. Several months later, he was pardoned and released due to lack of evidence, and also due to the fact that a Medici had just been elected pope (Leo X). Massive celebrations ensued, and in an act of clemency, the Medici government pardoned a number of their perceived enemies.

Machiavelli spent the rest of his life attempting to reestablish himself as a legitimate public official. He was no longer in prison, but he was barred from public life. He had spent his entire career in the study, pursuit, and practice of civic affairs, foreign policy, and the administration of government policy, but he was now in political exile.

It was in this state of "exile" that he wrote *The Prince,* or, as Machiavelli himself referred to it, *Il Principe.* He had been in a position to witness some of the most galvanizing political and diplomatic events of European history, and as he wrote to his friend Francesco Vettori, it is "evident that during the fifteen years I have been studying the art of the state I have been neither asleep nor fooling around, and anybody ought to be happy to utilize someone who has had so much experience at the expense of others."

According to Maurizio Viroli, one of his many biographers, Machiavelli's fondest wish was that this short work might be read and understood by the Medicis, lords of Rome through Pope Leo X and lords of Florence through Lorenzo the Magnificent. Viroli believes Machiavelli hoped that "if they read it, they would realize that he knew better than anyone else what a prince should do to consolidate power, especially a prince who was 'new'—as were the Medicis in 1513. He hoped, in short, that they would entrust him with an office, even the lowliest office . . ."

Many of the sections of *The Prince* are dedicated to Lorenzo de Medici, the young prince of Florence. But when Francesco Vettori presented Lorenzo with Machiavelli's masterpiece of statecraft, he barely glanced at it, showing much more interest in two stud dogs someone had sent him. A shame, for within the pages of *The Prince* are some of the most valuable leadership lessons a prince could ever hope for. (However, Lorenzo's daughter, Catherine de Medici, would later become one of Machiavelli's most ardent admirers.)

Though Machiavelli never made his way back into power in Italy, his writings (mainly *The Prince* and *The Discourses*) have influenced leaders and revolutionaries the world over for centuries. No modern scholar is truly qualified to paraphrase Machiavelli, but it is helpful to distill some of his key lessons.

Many of Machiavelli's lessons are military in nature, but carry political and civil analogies that are relevant to many political situations of the last several hundred years. For example, he emphasized pragmatism. A leader must be clearheaded, he said. Don't be too distracted by ideological teachings, religious doctrine, or altruism. Stay focused on what has to be done in order to secure the regime and, ideally, provide prosperity for the citizens. Don't govern by emotion; make decisions coldly, based on judgment and experience.

Machiavelli also minimized the importance of ethics. This is the primary reason some have considered Machiavelli and his work dark, undemocratic, or even evil. But that reaction is based on a misunderstanding of his intentions. He never said that, to be an effective leader, one must be unethical or act dishonorably. What he said is that the practice of politics and ethical considerations are unrelated to each other. A prince cannot afford to be overly concerned with always acting ethically, for that will lead to his (and his society's) downfall. The success and security of the state come first; ethics second.

A leader must establish a reputation of strength, and always endeavor to maintain that image with his people and with his enemies. If one is able to accomplish this, Machiavelli said, he will be less likely to face revolt to his rule from within. Kings and princes must establish this reputation, sometimes through brutality, or harsh punishments that discourage opponents from rising up. One example he used to illustrate this was Agathocles the Sicilian, who came to dominate Syracuse after organizing the brutal murder of the ruling elite and their families. "After their death," he writes, "Agathocles held rule over the city without any civil strife." Now, obviously, the lesson there was not to go around constantly murdering rivals and opponents, but that when enemies are dealt with harshly and an image of resolute strength is established by a leader, it often produces a period of relative peace and calm. The price of revolution or conspiracy becomes too high.

Machiavelli thought very highly of the ideals and administration of the Romans, as he makes clear in both *The Prince* and *The Discourses*. Again, pragmatism rears its ugly head. Sometimes, as the Romans demonstrated, a state is much better off getting rid of imminent threats rather than negotiating with or placating its foes.

> The Spartans held Athens and Thebes by creating within them a government of a few; nevertheless they lost them. The Romans, in order to hold Capua, Carthage, and Numantia, ravaged them, but did not lose them. They wanted to hold Greece in almost the same way as the Spartans held it, but

they did not succeed; so that they were compelled to lay waste many cities in that province in order to keep it, because in truth there is no sure method of holding them except by despoiling them. And whoever becomes the ruler of a free city and does not destroy it, can expect to be destroyed by it.

With his emphasis on raw power, and vanquishing one's foes, it is easy to see why Machiavelli's writings have been criticized and cast in a dark light. For example, although America's founding fathers had all read *The Prince* and *Discourses on Livy,* and were very impressed by Machiavelli's grasp on leadership, for them his approach put too much emphasis on the power of the state and too little emphasis on the power of the people.

One of the greatest lessons from *The Prince,* according to Machiavelli, is that the most powerful human motivation is fear, and that princes and leaders must use this very human emotion to achieve their goals. "From this arises the question whether it is better to be loved more than feared, or feared more than loved," said Machiavelli, ". . . It is much safer to be feared than loved, if one of the two has to be wanting." He went on to explain that men are much more likely to challenge one who is loved than one who is feared: "for love is held by a chain of obligation which, men being selfish, is broken whenever it serves their purpose; but fear is maintained by a dread of punishment which never fails."

Machiavelli also said that the most important knowledge a prince must possess is military knowledge. "A prince who is ignorant of military matters cannot be esteemed by his soldiers, nor have confidence in them. He ought, therefore, never to let his thoughts stray from the exercise of war; and in peace he ought to practice it more than in war." World history has certainly taught the value of this lesson, from the Norman invasion of England through the Napoleonic Wars, the age of empires, through the bloody twentieth century, right up to Osama bin Laden and al Qaeda.

Machiavelli's cold-eyed view of politics was instantly controversial, especially because of the stance the Catholic Church took toward his writing. *The Prince* was condemned by Pope Clement VIII, and for years was on the Vatican's list of prohibited books. The low opinion was mutual. Machiavelli blamed much of what was wrong with European society and government on the Catholic hierarchy. He was not antireligious or anti-Christian—far from it. But he believed that the church in his time was corrupt; instead of working for people's souls, it was merely another political institution, and a power-hungry one at that.

While Machiavelli emphasized how important it was for a prince and a state to be strong, he believed the church was responsible for "making the world weak, and therefore, easy prey for evil men." The Christian religion, he said, "at least in its current state, teaches men to be humble . . . and asks that you be capable more of suffering than of doing something strong." He said that the church persuaded the multitudes of faithful that "it was evil to say evil of evil," that it was good to live under obedience to the church, and that if priests did wrong they should be left for "God to punish." He blamed the political ambition of the church for preventing "Italy from being united under the rule of a prince or a republic, and therefore from being independent and secure."

Considering Machiavelli's strong statements on the negative role played by the church, it is not surprising that the church fought back. To church leaders, Machiavelli's *Prince* was a work of "evil." In fact, the centuries-old use of the name "Old Nick" as a name for the devil himself is thought to be a direct reference to Niccolo Machiavelli—some evidence can be found for this in the *Catholic Encyclopedia*.

Machiavelli has been widely misinterpreted by other critics as well. *Machiavellian* is used as a pejorative synonymous with *ruthless* or *heartless*. *Machiavellianism* is also a psychological diagnosis for a personality disorder characterized by manipulativeness. Behavioral clinicians Richard Christie and Florence Geis developed a test that purportedly measures a person's level of Machiavellianism, or deviousness and lack of ethics.

But Machiavelli's advice to rulers was meant to produce a secure, successful, and prosperous state. He did countenance duplicity and treachery, but only to further the political goals of the state, not for the personal aggrandizement of the ruler, nor for the sake of acting cruel or inhumane. Indeed, his work in *The Discourses* emphasizes the value that public input and participation has on the long-term success of a state.

So then, what does it mean to be Machiavellian? Machiavelli's work was groundbreaking and revolutionary. His thinking was unconventional and challenged the political and social orthodoxy of his day. As author Maurizio Viroli explains, Machiavelli said very plainly that the ideas set forth by thinkers who had written political tracts and advice for leaders "were simply wrong." To him, Plato's ideal of a philosopher king ruling through virtue and good works was dangerously naive. Other noteworthy writers—for example, the Roman author and political commentator Cicero—had maintained that a prince who wishes to keep power and win glory must always follow the path of virtue; he must be prudent, just, strong, and moderate; and must possess those qualities proper to princes, specifically mercy, generosity, and fairness. Machiavelli, on the other hand, said that a prince who followed this advice under all circumstances would not only fail to maintain his power, but was sure to lose it. He knew his ideas were controversial, and were contrary to the advice of many illustrious writers and thinkers. But he also knew that he was right. "I hope I shall not be considered presumptuous," he writes in *The Prince,* "but I must offer advice based on reality, not on imagination." Much of the advice from previous writers imagined "republics and principalities that have never been seen or been known to exist in truth" and have insisted on teaching princes how to be good in their actions, forgetting that a prince who is always unfailingly good amid so many who are not good will inevitably lose his realm. "It is necessary," he said, for a prince who wants to keep his realm "to learn to be able not to be good" and to use this or not use this, "according to necessity."

Shakespeare couldn't have said it better himself. In fact, the Bard did use a similar line in *Hamlet,* addressing his mother, "I must be cruel only to be kind." A debate has long raged over whether Machiavelli inspired some of Shakespeare's characters, particularly Henry V and Richard II. There is no doubt of Machiavelli's influence on Shakespeare's friend and rival, Christopher Marlowe, who created the character of Machiavel for his play *The Jew of Malta.*

To be Machiavellian is, in a sense, self-contradictory, or at least very difficult. It means favoring policies of brute force and intimidation, sometimes in an authoritarian sense, but at the same time acting in a way that benefits the citizenry. History, both distant and recent, provides us with a plentitude of Machiavellian figures. The most interesting ones, though, are those in a position similar to Niccolo himself—those serving as advisors, counselors, or the power behind the throne.

Pre-Machiavelli: Kautilya and the Origins of Realism

"When Alexander saw the breadth of his domain, he wept for there were no more worlds to conquer." This quote, one of the most famous in literature, is attributed to Plutarch from his work *Parallel Lives*. (For movie buffs, the character Hans Gruber, played by Alan Rickman, made the line famous in the movie *Die Hard* with Bruce Willis.) But after Alexander the Great's death, his empire split apart, and as his kingdom crumbled in East Asia, another rose to replace it—the great Mauryan Empire, ruled by King Chandragupta from 320 to 298 BC.

The guiding hand behind Chandragupta and the rise of the Mauryans was Kautilya, also known in some texts as Chanakya. Iconic figures in India, Kautilya and Chandragupta are less well known in the West. Yet Chandragupta is considered the first unifier of India and its first genuine emperor or king; Kautilya is one of the first great political minds in documented history.

Kautilya developed and managed the strategy undertaken by Chandragupta, who defeated the rival Indian Nanda kings and halted Greek expansion into India. By taking much of western India (the Punjab and the Sindh) from the Greeks, assassinating two Greek governors in the process, and concluding a treaty with Alexander's Greek heir, Chandragupta and Kautilya succeeded in bringing together almost all of the Indian subcontinent. The scope of the Mauryan Empire, which went on to rule India for several centuries, was astonishing. With a population of about 50 million people, the Mauryan Empire encompassed all the land east of present-day Iran and west of the Himalayan Mountains.

In the West, Kautilya is known as the "Indian Machiavelli," because almost two thousand years before Nicolo Machiavelli wrote *The Prince*, Kautilya wrote *The Arthasastra,* the oldest known treatise on the practice of politics. In *The Arthasastra,* Kautilya lays out the "science of politics," intended to teach a wise king how to govern. Kautilya openly discusses his aspirations for his king to become a world conqueror, his analysis of which kingdoms are natural allies and which are enemies, his willingness to make and break treaties according to the needs of the kingdom, and his doctrine of political assassination of foreign kings.

Kautilya's take on the exercise of raw power and political treachery is even harsher than Machiavelli's. In essence, he is more Machiavellian than Machiavelli. *The Arthasastra* is darker and more violent than anything the Florentine diplomat ever proposed. He values cunning, trickery, and violence in his heroes. He outlines the use of secret agents to kill enemy leaders and foreign agents, his view of women as weapons of war, how to employ religion and superstition to bolster his troops and demoralize enemy soldiers, and how to spread disinformation and discord among the enemy.

It is ironic that Machiavelli is the historical figure most associated, wrongly in most cases, with the cynical mantra "The ends justify the means." That philosophy is much more appropriately tied to Kautilya. Indeed, the well-known political sociologist Max Weber famously said that, compared to *The Arthasastra,* Machiavelli's *The Prince* is "harmless." He referred to Kautilya's work as "truly radical Machiavellianism." Thus, Kautilya's *Arthasastra* is first and foremost a book of political realism, an analysis of how the political world actually works, not how it ought to work. It is a book that frequently discloses to a king what calculating and sometimes brutal measures he must carry out to preserve the state and serve the common good. Kautilya was one of the earliest proponents of what has come to be called Realpolitik—in some sense a spiritual forefather of Otto von Bismarck. He assumed that every nation acts to maximize its power and promote its self-interest, and therefore moral principles or obligations figure little, if at all, in actions among nations.

Kautilya is sometimes called Chandragupta's chancellor or prime minister. He composed his *Arthasastra,* or "science of politics," to show a wise king how to defeat his enemies and rule on behalf of the general good. Kautilya instructed kings to use spies to help avoid dissension and promote their political goals. To help spy from within, Kautilya was not above using family, women, and children as spies or even assassins.

Regarding the use of spies, he devised several tests that a king must use to hold on to power internally. These tests were to be used under all circumstances, even against a king's own military leaders and ministers; even when dealing with Kautilya himself. The first was known as the "Test of Fear." In this test, the king would imprison all his ministers, then send in a spy to try to "incite these ministers to agree to kill the king out of fear." If the ministers accepted, the king would then kill them; those who did not would return to their posts.

The next was the "Test of Piety," by which the king would "instigate rebellion on the grounds that the king was impious." Again, those who joined would die or be sent to work in life-threatening jobs, while those who did not would be returned to power. The "Test of Material Gain" would try to entice the ministers "to foment treason with the promise of great wealth." The last test was the "Test of Lust," in which the king would get his spies "to stir a minister to rebellion by telling him that the queen loved him." By performing these internal tests of loyalty, the king would keep his power safe from within.

When it came to civil liberties, Kautilya believed there should be none for the subjects of the king. Arrests could be made of anyone who "spent lavishly, traveled frequently, one devoted to a beloved, and one moving at an odd time in a solitary place or a forest." After arrest, the truly terrible part began. Kautilya recommended torture every other day so the person could be healed and rested for the next round.

"The Indian Machiavelli" also had quite a bit to say about war and peace in *The Arthasastra*. His advice is somewhat reminiscent of Sun Tzu's military treatise *The Art of War*, and also holds some of the same lessons that Machiavelli would later impart in his advice to princes. Kautilya developed a "science" of warfare, presumably part of a larger science of politics. The commandant of the army, he suggested, should be "trained in the science of many different fighting styles and weapons, and also experienced in riding elephants, horses and chariots."

Kautilya's six policies for making war are as follows. His advice to his king was

1. Whoever is inferior to another shall make peace.
2. Whoever is superior in power shall make war.
3. Whoever thinks "no enemy can hurt me, or am I strong enough to destroy my enemy" shall observe neutrality.
4. Whoever is possessed of necessary means shall march against his enemy.
5. Whoever is devoid of necessary strength to defend himself shall seek the protection of another.
6. Whoever thinks that help is necessary to work out an end shall make peace with one and wage war with another.

Following these policies will help a king maintain or acquire more to his empire.

To Kautilya, women were excellent tools of warfare. If a king is trying to undermine a ruling clan, he "should make chiefs of the ruling council infatuated with women possessed of great beauty and youth. When passion is roused in them, they should start quarrels by creating belief [about their love] in one and by going to another." A woman supposedly in love with one leader should go to another, profess her love for him, urge him to murder the first leader, and "then she should proclaim, 'My lover has been killed by so and so.'" Obviously, such tactics create mistrust among leaders of an oligarchy and also bring about the death of key enemies.

Kautilya also notes that "peace can be achieved through various means, but it should be remembered that it is only temporary and is part of a broader policy of lulling the enemy into complacency." This complacency will give the king an advantage when war does come. He was more likely to encourage a king to go to war than either Sun Tzu or Machiavelli, believing that if one could win, then one should fight.

The Medici Family, Act II: Catherine de Medici

There have been many powerful women through the ages, a good number of them quite effective King Whisperers. Catherine de Medici ruled France from behind the throne as regent for three of her young sons in the sixteenth century. Catherine was right in the middle of some of the most contentious, violent, and momentous events of that century. She was connected by blood, marriage, war, or diplomacy to some of the most famous and infamous names of the century—Lorenzo the Magnificent, Mary Queen of Scots, Elizabeth I of England and her spymaster Francis Walsingham, Henri of Lorraine (the duke of Guise), Philip II of Spain, Gaspard de Coligny, and others. She would prove to be one of the most cunning of all the famous names of the century.

Machiavelli's *The Prince* was written largely to curry favor with Lorenzo the Magnificent, patron of the Medici family, freshly returned to power by the pope in 1513. Only, as noted earlier, Lorenzo paid no attention to Machiavelli's treatise—hardly anyone did at the time it was written. But the same cannot be said for his daughter, Catherine, who professed admiration for Machiavelli's political mind. Ironically, this Medici would become one of his most accomplished students.

Caterina de Medici (*Catherine* is the anglicized version) is a very controversial figure, born into power and privilege, yet tossed around in her early years by the reigning religious and political leaders. Both her parents died shortly after her birth. After the Medici rulers were once again ousted from power in Florence, her protector became Pope Clement VII, who was also a Medici, and Catherine was a reviled figure among most Florentines. The pope hired a mercenary army to quell riots in the city and spirited the young Catherine off to Rome. Fortunately for her, she had spent much of her youth in a convent where she at least was well cared for and received a very good education. She was described as "small and slender, with fair hair, thin and not pretty in face, but with the eyes peculiar to all the Medici."

From a very young age Catherine learned the value of political power and the importance of cultivating the right relationships. At first she was nothing more than a pawn for the powers of Europe, but she learned how to play the power game and she played it well. The pope married her off to Henry, duke of Orleans, son of the French king. Though not a Renaissance beauty, she was cultured, fashionable, very bright, and she liked sports. She became a favorite of King Francis, her father-in-law. But most of the French royal family was mainly interested in the money that came with the marriage, not in Catherine herself. After all, though she was connected to money, she was a commoner, and, of course, an Italian! She rarely saw her husband, who preferred his mistress, Diane de Poitiers, twenty years his senior. Catherine did, however, see Henry often enough to bear him ten children, seven of whom lived to adulthood. It seemed that her only purpose in the eyes of the French royal family was to bear sons.

When Henry became king, Catherine was crowned queen, but she had no real influence. Instead, Henry's mistress, Diane de Poitiers, acted as a queen, dispensing patronage and accepting favors. This was unacceptable to Catherine. When Henry died after a jousting accident in 1559—an accident foretold by Nostradamus—Catherine had to come to the fore, since Henry's heir, her son Francis, was only fifteen and suffered from physical ailments. But the marriage of the young Francis to Mary Stuart (Mary, Queen of Scots) severely limited Catherine's influence at court. The Guise family (Mary Stuart's uncles) wielded most of the power behind the scenes, in an attempt to reassert the power of the Catholic nobles. When Francis became ill and died the following year, Catherine acted fast. She made a secret pact with the Protestant Antoine de Bourbon of Navarre, who by previous royal arrangement had rights of regency to the next in line to the throne, Charles IX. Catherine had Bourbon's brother, who the previous year had led a church revolt, released from prison. In exchange, Bourbon renounced his right to act as regent for Charles, clearing the path for Catherine to assume that title. Her position now solidified, she became regent to the next king, her son Charles IX, all of nine years old.

Catherine spent the next thirty years as the guiding hand of France, first during the reign of Charles, then of her favorite son, Henry III. Her main goal was to maintain the power base of her monarchical rule and reconcile the various factions competing for control of French and of

European society. But this was made difficult by the growing division between Catholics and the Protestant French Huguenots. Fiercely Catholic, Spain took issue with Protestant, independent England, and France was caught in the middle. While brought up a Catholic—and related by blood to the papal throne—Catherine had a flexible (some would say naive) attitude toward the Catholic/Huguenot struggle. For example, at the conference of Poissy in 1561 she attempted to bring these two faiths together to discuss their differences, and to try to forge some kind of understanding between them. The conference was a disaster.

The great tragedy of Catherine's reign was the St. Bartholomew's Day Massacre in 1572. The Wars of Religion, as they are called, had festered through the 1560s, as attitudes on both sides of the religious and political dispute hardened. Then came a turning point. In 1567, in an attack called the Surprise of Meaux, Huguenot forces ambushed and attempted to murder King Charles, triggering an escalation of violence on both sides. Though unsuccessful, the Huguenot campaign seems to have led Catherine to abandon her policy of compromise and negotiation for one of increasing repression.

In an ongoing attempt at bringing about peace through marriage, Catherine tried to arrange a marriage between one of her sons and Queen Elizabeth I of England. She successfully pressed for the marriage of her youngest daughter, Marguerite, to the Protestant Henry of Navarre, of the Bourbon family. It was this wedding, and the surrounding climate of suspicion and rancor, that led to the massacre, one of the bloodiest days in European history.

Huguenot leaders had gathered from across Europe for the wedding. It got off to a poor start—Henry of Navarre's mother, Jeanne d'Albret, took ill and died. Huguenot partisans later claimed she had been poisoned. Three days after the wedding, there was an attempt on the life of the Huguenot leader Gaspard de Coligny. He survived the attack, but disaster followed. Huguenot leaders came to the palace to demand justice, while fears in Paris grew that the four-thousand-man Huguenot army—camped just outside the city—would attack.

Catherine met with King Charles and her counselors to discuss the crisis. Historians are divided on who actually advocated for, or ordered, the massacre to begin. But the slaughter of Protestants lasted for weeks, and spread to other cities in France. What began as a targeted campaign to kill Huguenot leaders soon raged out of control, with civilians hunting down and murdering Protestants. Estimates of the number of dead range from a few thousand to upwards of thirty thousand. Many Huguenots were forced to convert to Catholicism, including Henry of Navarre. Other notable Protestants fled the city, barely escaping with their lives, including the ambassador from England's Queen Elizabeth—Francis Walsingham, who is profiled later in the book in chapter 4, "Spies."

Catherine received much of the blame from Protestants, and credit and cheers from many Catholic leaders. And even though he had been dead for half a century, Nicolo Machiavelli received his share of the blame. This view was greatly influenced by the Huguenot writer Innocent Gentillet, who published his *Discours contre Machiavel* in 1576, which was printed in ten editions in three languages over the next four years. Gentillet asserted that Machiavelli's "books were held most dear and precious by our Italian and Italionized [sic] courtiers" and were "at the root of France's present degradation, which has culminated not only in the St. Bartholemew [sic] massacre but the glee of its perverted admirers."The massacre marked a turning point in the Wars of Religion, and in Catherine's reputation across Europe. The Huguenot cause was weakened, and Catholicism's hold on Europe was made stronger, at least in the short term. And Catherine's image as a bloodthirsty Machiavellian queen was solidified.

Ultimately, the French monarchy was unable to control events within its own borders. Charles IX died just two years after the massacre in 1574. His brother, Henry III, ascended to the throne, yet Catherine was still firmly in charge. As she grew older, though, her hold on power grew weaker, and Henry was unable to rally the support of the nobles. After her death in 1589, Henry was murdered, which ended the Medici line of royalty. Henry of Navarre (who had converted to Catholicism) ascended to the throne, beginning the reign of the Bourbon kings, which would last two hundred years until the French Revolution ended the era of the monarchs.

America's Founding Machiavellian: Alexander Hamilton

One of the most Machiavellian figures of the last several centuries was Alexander Hamilton, the most brilliant and the most flawed of America's founding fathers. A tremendous intellect, he was also known for his impatience, his petulance, and for making enemies. He was a "great statesman and a terrible politician . . . He was too honest, too candid," explained historian Karl Walling. He had tremendous influence over George Washington, and he outmaneuvered his main rivals for power, Thomas Jefferson and John Adams, more than once. Adams, his old foe and party colleague, said of Hamilton, "he is the most restless, impatient, artful, indefatigable, and unprincipled intriguer in the United States."

Hamilton was a great supporter of George Washington, often acting as his consultant, his chief policy tsar, and, when necessary, his attack dog. He served as Washington's aide-de-camp in the Revolutionary War, then for the next two decades served at his side through the framing of the Constitution and his two terms as president. Although not personally close to Washington, Hamilton's influence on him was great: He is even credited with writing much of Washington's famous farewell address. Some have dubbed Hamilton the nation's "first and last Prime Minister." Many scholars have noted similarities between Alexander Hamilton and Machiavelli. Both men emphasized national unity and military preparedness; both were concerned with protecting their nation from foreign dominance and intervention; and both were severely criticized for their views on power and statecraft. Though Hamilton certainly did not consider himself a Machiavellian, there are some striking parallels.

Hamilton's background was more modest than Machiavelli's—he was born in the West Indies in the 1750s, the illegitimate son of Scottish trader James Hamilton and Rachel Lavien, of French Huguenot descent. Born out of wedlock and abandoned by his father, he and his mother struggled, often shunned by the church and by family. They operated a small dry goods store until Rachel contracted a fever and died. Orphaned as a teenager, he was sent by his guardian, a successful merchant named Thomas Stevens, to the States for an education. (There is some evidence to suggest that Stevens was Alexander's biological father, which might explain why he and his mother were shunned by James Hamilton.) He enrolled at Kings College, now Columbia University, and was increasingly drawn into the colonial conflict with Great Britain. He enlisted in the New York militia in 1775. His quick thinking and organizational ability earned him a commission as a second lieutenant, where he came to the attention of the most consequential man in his life: General George Washington.

By the age of thirty, Hamilton had a distinguished military career, intimately knew most of the leaders of the American Revolution, was recognized as one of the leading lawyers in the Northeast, and had married well. Talk about the American dream! He was on the fast track to success, something that had eluded Niccolo Machiavelli for much of his life.

John Lamberton Harper, in his book *American Machiavelli,* distills what he sees as the similarities between the two men:

> Both were diplomatic-military advisors in the aftermath of upheavals that gave rise to popular governments. Both struggled with the problem of designing and safeguarding their fledgling republics in the context of internal divisions over the use of force, of controversial alliances, and of constant external peril. Both towered over most of their contemporaries intellectually, but were unable, partly because of their suspect origins, to attain the highest offices. Despite, or rather because of, their extraordinary abilities, they suffered the slings and arrows of vindictive enemies and the myopia of ordinary mortals. Each was driven by a vision of national greatness, but destined for personal disenchantment and defeat.

Hamilton could be hot-tempered, arrogant, and vindictive. His battles, both political and personal, with Thomas Jefferson, James Madison, and John Adams are legendary. The essence of his disagreements with Jefferson and Madison boils down to state power versus national power.

Hamilton understood the power of policy making. As the nation's first secretary of the treasury, and as President Washington's most trusted advisor, he constructed much of the country's fiscal infrastructure; and he did so in a way that favored national power. For example, he proposed to pay the nation's debts in full and to also assume the unpaid debts of the states. That may sound magnanimous, but his real goal was to diminish the importance of the states from a fiscal standpoint and to cement the loyalty of wealthy commercial interests to the national government. Washington also supported Hamilton's controversial "Whiskey Tax" of 1791. The goal was to centralize the production and distribution of spirits and to raise revenue for the fledgling central government. Though a political headache for the new president, it demonstrated the resolve of ardent nationalists like Hamilton to establish a strong national government.

His plan to establish a national banking system was vigorously opposed by Jefferson on the grounds that it would subvert the rights of the states, decrease the role of agriculture, and lead to stronger trading ties with Great Britain, still the dominant force in worldwide trade. Hamilton openly pushed for a closer relationship with Britain, while Jefferson favored closer ties with France. President Washington supported Hamilton's plan, and helped win a congressional majority for its passage.

Hamilton's disputes with the second U.S. president, John Adams, were even fiercer than those with Jefferson. In the 1790s, the disastrous XYZ Affair, in which the French foreign minister, Talleyrand, essentially tried to extort American officials sent by President Adams, brought America to the verge of war with France. Hamilton goaded President Adams into pushing for passage of the notorious Alien and Sedition Acts—ostensibly an effort to root out foreign troublemakers (French agents) bent on subverting American foreign policy, but in reality a political ruse by the Federalists to hound their opponents and threaten them with jail. The controversy surrounding the acts contributed to Adams's political downfall in the election of 1800.

But on a more personal level, Hamilton and Adams simply did not like each other. They were from different walks of life and had trod very different paths to political power. To Hamilton, Adams was a snob. After all, Adams had written that the first of New England's advantages over the rest of America was that its people "are purer English blood;

less mixed with Scottish, Irish, Dutch, French, Danish, and Swede . . . descended from Englishmen too, who left Europe in purer times than the present, and less tainted with corruption." Hamilton, the illegitimate son of a Scottish trader from the West Indies, could not help but take offense. Actually, there was plenty for Hamilton to be offended by—Adams had privately called Hamilton "the bastard brat of a Scotch peddler." But it is also true that Hamilton's harsh, knockabout upbringing left him with an inferiority complex, irritated by bluebloods such as Adams and Jefferson. He had a lifelong chip on his shoulder.

To Hamilton, the most important thing was his view that Adams was simply not up to the task of leading the country—at least in the way Hamilton thought it should be led. President Adams, Hamilton thought, was insufficiently committed to America's relationship with Britain and failed to act decisively in meeting the threat posed by France and its sympathizers in the States. He derided Adams as "hopeless." His distaste for John Adams led him to work behind the scenes to deny him a second term as president in 1800—pretty amazing considering that they belonged to the same political party.

According to most historians, Hamilton hatched a scheme that would have delivered more electoral votes to the Federalist nominee for vice president, Charles Pinckney, than to Adams himself. In a letter to Federalist members, Hamilton wrote that Adams "does not possess the talents adapted to the administration of government, and there are great and intrinsic defects in his character which make him unfit for the office." Adams responded that Hamilton was a man "devoid of every moral principle—a Bastard!"

Aaron Burr certainly thought so. Hamilton's penchant for making enemies caught up with him, this time fatally. Not only had he blocked an attempt during the election controversy in 1800 to make Burr a compromise candidate for president, but he worked against his candidacy for governor of New York four years later. The two had feuded since 1791, when Burr successfully captured a U.S. Senate seat from Philip Schuyler, Hamilton's powerful father-in-law. Hamilton, then treasury secretary, would have counted on Schuyler to support his policies. When Burr won the election, Hamilton fumed. Hamilton considered Burr dishonest and dishonorable, and he didn't keep these sentiments a secret. Remarks he made about the "despicable Burr" at a New York dinner party were reported days later in the *Albany Register*. Burr demanded an apology and Hamilton refused. So, as gentlemen did in those days, they settled their disagreement with a pistol duel, along the banks of the Hudson River in New Jersey. Aaron Burr went home that day; Hamilton didn't.

The Perfect Machiavellian: Richard B. Cheney

Dick Cheney was born to play this role. A hero to the political right, and Darth Vader to the political left, Cheney has influenced American policy and politics over the last thirty-five years perhaps more than any other single person. He believes in conservative Republican principles as the path to preserving American freedom and prosperity every bit as much as Alexander Hamilton believed in Federalism and as Catherine de Medici believed in the divine providence of the French crown.

Cheney worked for four American presidents: Richard Nixon, Gerald Ford, George H. W. Bush, and George W. Bush. In the 1980s, he was a leading member of the Republican delegation in the U.S. House of Representatives, famously running interference for Reagan administration officials during the Iran-Contra hearings.

Cheney is a Wyoming native, and, like many politicians from the western United States, he has a deeply ingrained mistrust of the federal government. Although at first a political moderate in the GOP, Cheney became more conservative as the years went by, as he rose higher in the service of Republican presidents. In his twenties, he dropped out of Yale, drifted back to Wyoming, and worked as a lineman while he decided what he wanted to do with his life. His interest in politics led him to the University of Wisconsin, where he pursued an advanced degree in political science. Unlike the time he spent at Yale, he was an avid student in Wisconsin and a quick learner, with a particular interest in government policy making. He became a student of politics and ideas, reading Machiavelli, Plato, Alexis de Tocqueville, and John Locke.

In 1969 he worked as an intern on Capitol Hill, where he caught the eye of someone who would become very important in his life—Donald Rumsfeld, who was running Richard Nixon's Office of Economic Opportunity. Rumsfeld was impressed with Cheney's intelligence and drive, and he brought him into the Nixon administration as his assistant. Several years later, Cheney followed Rumsfeld into the Ford administration, and it was there that he began to make his mark on politics and policy.

Dick Cheney is the perfect Machiavellian because he fits "Old Nick's" mind-set like a glove. He is a pragmatist. He is a very good diplomat; he is cool, calculating, and patient. A story from the Ford years illustrates this point very well: As assistant chief of staff to Gerald Ford, Cheney once came across a handwritten note from a former Nixon aide who kept his job under Ford. The note was scrawled in the margin of a copy of the president's daily schedule next to an entry indicating a meeting with "assistant chief of staff Dick Cheney." It read: "Can you believe this crap?" Some Ford staffers who had served under Nixon were scornful of Rumsfeld and the starring role he gave to the thirty-something Dick Cheney. The note was meant for an aide to former chief of staff Alexander Haig, who the day before had vacated his office to make room for Cheney. It was the kind of mistake that could cost someone his job, but Cheney chose to sit on it. He didn't confront the author of the note, or go to Ford or Rumsfeld. He just kept it. A few months later, Cheney dropped by the man's office and in the course of the conversation, told him that he had seen his note. "He was cooperative from then on," Cheney told his biographer.

He is also a good Machiavellian because he knows when to seize an opportunity and, when necessary, to go for the jugular. A good example is what came to be called the "Sunday Morning Massacre." Rumsfeld and Cheney had urged President Ford to make sweeping changes in his administration. In the words of veteran journalist T. D. Allman, "Rumsfeld and Cheney staged a palace coup. They pushed Ford to fire Defense Secretary James Schlesinger, tell Vice President Nelson Rockefeller to look for another job, and remove Henry Kissinger from his post as national security advisor. Rumsfeld was named secretary of defense, and Cheney became chief of staff to the president." And just a decade before this, Dick Cheney had been a lineman for a Wyoming power company. Not too shabby.

In the Ford years, Cheney developed a reputation as a savvy political operator. As good staffers do, he avoided the limelight whenever possible. Increasingly, it came to be felt by the Washington media that Cheney was pulling strings from behind the scenes. ". . . Few men have risen so high with so much anonymity," wrote Charles Mohr in the *New York Times* on November 5, 1975. Tellingly, Cheney's Secret Service code name during the Ford years was "Backseat."

It was also during the Ford administration that Dick Cheney began pushing the envelope of presidential power and prerogative. After Watergate and Vietnam, the "imperial presidency" was in decline, with a more assertive Congress, more active congressional oversight committees, and a more hostile media. Cheney was interested in protecting the power of the president and limiting the erosion of executive authority. And he was willing to go to considerable lengths to do so. Once, when *New York Times* investigative reporter Seymour Hersh wrote an article about American submarines spying in Soviet waters that came too close to the truth, Dick Cheney wrote a memo proposing "an FBI investigation of the *NY Times,* Seymour Hersh, and possible govt. sources; Grand Jury indictments of Hersh and the *Times;* A search warrant to go after Hersh papers in his apt" as possible responses to the information leak. Ultimately, President Ford decided to do nothing, but it is a revealing look at Dick Cheney's mind at work, his preference for executive power, and his willingness to play hardball when necessary— very Machiavellian. It also foreshadows some of the tendencies displayed by Cheney and others close to him a quarter-century later, when, as vice president, he played a leading role in pushing for warrantless wiretaps under the USA Patriot Act and aggressive intelligence gathering. "He's had the same idea for the past 30 years," said author Kathryn S. Olmsted. "His philosophy is that the president and the vice president decide what's secret and what's not."

Machiavelli was a master bureaucrat, and so is Dick Cheney. Cheney's talent for working the bureaucracy rivals that of Alexander Hamilton's days at the Treasury Department. Both men understood government backwards and forwards, and knew where the bodies were buried, so to speak. During the presidency of George W. Bush, the president and others were often accused of living inside a "bubble"—listening only to government insiders and shunning input from other sources. But this is largely by design. Cheney and Rumsfeld did much the same thing during the Ford years, surrounding Gerald Ford with a close-knit group of insiders dedicated to pushing the administration's viewpoints and heading off alternative suggestions.

After the Democrats took the White House with Jimmy Carter, Dick Cheney was elected to represent Wyoming in Congress, where he served from 1978 until he was named George H. W. Bush's defense secretary in 1989. He rose quickly through the ranks of the House GOP. It was in Congress in the 1980s that Cheney became more demonstrably conservative, and a key leader in the national Republican Party. Many remember the leading role he played as the ranking Republican on the Iran-Contra investigative committee in 1987. Cheney believed that the Democrats would take the opportunity to undermine President Reagan, and saw his role as defending the president and the administration. No doubt, it was the skill and bravado he displayed in the Iran-Contra hearings, as well as his experience in the Ford White House, that made him a leading candidate for a spot in George H. W. Bush's administration. Cheney's tenure as defense secretary was one of the highlights of the Bush presidency.

One of Machiavelli's most important lessons for princes was that their thoughts and their training must always emphasize military strategy and preparedness. In this capacity, Cheney excelled, bringing in the sharpest and best-prepared military minds to execute a very dangerous and risky international military mission in Operation Desert Storm (the first Gulf War). Cheney's bureaucratic expertise served him well at the Pentagon and with the Joint Chiefs. After all, the American military is one of the largest and most complex bureaucracies in the world.

But it is Cheney's role as vice president that has defined him for the ages. It is no exaggeration to say that there has never been a vice president as powerful as Dick Cheney was in the Bush White House. That, too, was by design. Cheney accepted the post of VP with the understanding that his role would be significantly different than that of previous vice presidents. George W. Bush approved an arrangement that gave Cheney access to "every table and every meeting," making his voice heard in "whatever area the vice president feels he wants to be active in," according to former Bush Chief of Staff Josh Bolten. And Cheney used that authority with singular force of will. Other recent vice presidents have enjoyed a standing invitation to join the president at "policy time." But Cheney's interventions also came in the president's absence, at Cabinet and sub-Cabinet levels where his predecessors were seldom seen.

Authors Barton Gellman and Jo Becker, in their book about Cheney called *Angler: The Cheney Vice Presidency,* attest to the historic nature of Cheney's tenure: "In roles that have gone largely undetected, Cheney has served as gatekeeper for Supreme Court nominees, referee of Cabinet turf disputes, arbiter of budget appeals, editor of tax proposals." Unlike any of his predecessors, he exercised "direct and indirect power over the federal budget—and over those who must live within it."

But it is through the U.S. response to the War on Terror and the conduct of American foreign policy since 9/11 that Dick Cheney truly made his presence felt. It was Cheney, along with his old mentor Donald Rumsfeld (George W. Bush's defense secretary) and so-called neocon policy advisors Paul Wolfowitz and Richard Perle, who pushed for some of the more controversial Bush-era policies on warrantless wiretapping, prisoner detainment, and the definition and sanctioning of torture. Gellman and Becker contend that these policy developments often resulted from Cheney making end runs around President Bush, announcing, for example, in a speech to the U.S. Chamber of Commerce that terrorists do not deserve to be treated as prisoners of war before Bush had actually made that decision. "Ten weeks passed, and the Bush administration fought one of its fiercest internal brawls, before Bush ratified the policy that Cheney had declared: The Geneva Conventions would not apply to al-Qaeda or Taliban fighters captured on the battlefield."

Other Machiavellian tendencies were also apparent in the vice president's office. Across the board, he went to unusual lengths to avoid transparency—declining to disclose the names or even the size of his staff, generally releasing no public calendar, and ordering the Secret Service to destroy his visitors' logs. His general counsel asserted that "the vice presidency is a unique office that is neither a part of the executive branch nor a part of the legislative branch," and is therefore exempt from rules governing either one. Cheney refused to observe an executive order on the handling of national security secrets, and he proposed to abolish a federal office that insisted on auditing his compliance.

Contrary to some analyses, Cheney was not a copresident. George W. Bush went in different directions on some policies and even overruled Cheney on occasion. But Dick Cheney was a masterful behind-the-scenes player who got his way on most issues he cared about. Love him or hate him, in an almost four-decade-long career, he made his mark on American government policy, and on history, more than many elected American presidents. Machiavelli would probably laugh.

CHAPTER 2

EMPIRE BUILDERS

The main goal of the Machiavellians was political survival. Theirs was primarily a quest for power—how to attain it, how to keep it, how to pass it on. They became known largely for their tactical skills and gamesmanship, as well as for duplicity and treachery. Machiavellians often acted to benefit the citizenry, but did so mainly because that is what kept them in power.

The figures in this chapter had grander plans. They dedicated themselves—their lives and their careers—to something larger than themselves. There are certain individuals throughout history who have played decisive roles in building and supporting powerful institutions of which they were a part. These institutions may take various forms— government, business and commercial, or social and religious. This type of leader tends to be a "visionary" and often tries to put in place grand designs.

Empire Builders see themselves as servants to a cause: They work to achieve progress for some "greater good"—something bigger and more important their own personal political situation. Unlike the Machiavellians, many Empire Builders are willing to sacrifice, in some cases even die, to achieve their goals. They are different because they are able to take the long view, as opposed to most Machiavellians, who tend to focus on the short term. In many cases they have little choice but to take a long-term perspective, sometimes thinking in terms of "generations" in order to accomplish their goals. Needless to say, their scope and their vision are broader than that of, say, a Cesare Borgia or a Catherine de Medici. Eventual victory for their cause is their motivation, not necessarily the drive to accumulate political power.

The Holy Warrior: Bernard of Clairvaux

St. Bernard of Clairvaux, the twelfth-century French abbot, theologian, poet, and papal counselor, devoted himself and his followers to an ideal—a life totally dedicated to the word of God and the victory of Christendom. An early force behind the shadowy and mysterious Knights Templar, he played a key role in cultivating political support for the Second Crusade, as he built a monastic empire in western Europe that rivaled any the church had seen up to the 1300s.

He is a stark and curious figure—today he would be considered a religious fanatic. Actually, even at the time he was considered a religious fanatic! Upon joining the Cistercian monastery at Citeaux, France (near Dijon) in 1113, which was founded to restore monastic worship to a more primitive and austere state, Bernard began a practice of highly regimented austerity—strict fasting, sleep deprivation, self-flagellation—that severely impaired his health. As a result, throughout his adult life he suffered from anemia, migraines, gastritis, and hypertension, as well as an atrophied sense of taste.

Yet he was one of the most successful and revered religious leaders of his or any age. In addition to a reputation as a man of deep devotion and commitment to the church, Bernard was known for his charisma and persuasive powers of speech. He was descended from Burgundian nobility, and was very well educated, with a natural gift for literature and poetry. He was also a natural leader, and soon became to many a striking example of life in the service of God. Three years after arriving at Citeaux, he and twelve other monks moved to the nearby Valley of Wormwood, renaming it the Valley of Light, or Clairvaux, and built a chapel and monastery. There, Bernard built his monastic kingdom, which became a magnet for zealous young churchmen from across Europe.

What was his secret? At least part of it was charisma. We get an idea from historian Piers Paul Read: His biographer considered him good-looking; he was slim and fragile, with soft skin, fair hair and a reddish beard. But clearly, says Read, his power over others came from the force of his personality and his conviction. "His face radiated with a bright splendor, which was not of earthly, but of heavenly origin . . . even his physical appearance overflowed with inner purity and an abundance of grace." Benedictine historian Dom David Knowles writes, "As a leader, as a writer, as a preacher, and as a saint his personal magnetism and his spiritual power were far-reaching and irresistible." Bernard's influence within the church gave him political power, which he used to further the interests of the Cistercian order. Through his leadership, Citeaux became the spiritual center of Europe. Religion and politics became intertwined: Bernard included among his ex-monks a pope, the archbishop of York, and cardinals and bishops throughout Europe.

In part, Bernard's ascent to prominence had much to do with his relationship with the Knights Templar, the mysterious and very powerful Christian military order that had formed after the First Crusade to protect European interests in the Holy Land. Some find it curious that a revered religious leader was the primary patron of this shadowy group, which, in recent years, through books and Hollywood movies, has been tied to, among other things, the legend of the Holy Grail, Solomon's treasure, the *Gnostic Gospels,* the rise of freemasonry, and religious heresy.

But Bernard's ties with the order went deep—one of the founders of the Templar order, André de Montbard, was his uncle on his mother's side. Bernard was asked by Hugh of Payns, the central founder of the Templars, to sanctify the mission of the order, which strongly appealed to Bernard. The Templars had adopted the beliefs and customs of the Cistercian order and its strict regimen of worship, which convinced Bernard that they were truly committed to doing the work of God.

At the Council of Troyes in 1128, Bernard, who was called to serve as secretary for the council, appealed to the envoy sent by Pope Honorius II to make the Knights Templar an official order of the Catholic Church. In an unusual request, Bernard asked that the new order be answerable only to the pope himself. Bernard had come to see the Templar Knights as holy warriors, dedicated to protecting the church's interests. The threats posed to the survival of the church in the Holy Land convinced the pope that Bernard's request was in the best interests of all Christians, and he duly affirmed the status of the new military order. Bernard himself wrote the rules and charter of the Knights Templar. When he returned to the Clairvaux abbey, he wrote an official treatise, *De Laude Novae Militae* (In Praise of the New Knighthood). There was no doubt in Bernard's mind that the Holy Land was the patrimony of Christ, unjustly seized by the Muslims; his treatise emphasized to the Templars that it would enhance their spiritual life if they trod the same ground as their savior—it was a constant reminder that they, too, would conquer death. For better or worse, Bernard became their champion and their protector within the church.

Bernard's growing influence in the church, and on European politics in general, was soon to be felt. According to the *Catholic Encyclopedia,* he took up the banner of the papacy and "defended the rights of the church against the encroachments of kings and princes." Upon the death of Pope Honorius II in 1130, a schism broke out in the church, when there were two claimants to the papal crown—Innocent II and Anacletus II. Anacletus was the favored candidate of the Roman clergy and had been elected by a narrow margin, but many of the more influential cardinals from France, England, Spain, and Germany favored the election of Innocent II. Bernard, too, supported Innocent because he was more open to the monastic reforms advocated by the Cistercians. The French king, Louis VI (Louis the Fat), convened a conference to sort out the controversy. Due to his experience in church affairs and his reputation for wisdom, Bernard was summoned by the bishops at the conference to act as judge. Arguing that Innocent II would be a pope for all the world and not just for Rome, Bernard was able to successfully assert the claims of Innocent II, who was duly elected the new pope. Bernard became a very powerful advisor to the new pope and traveled with him often.

Now one of the most powerful figures in Europe, Bernard spent much of the next decade alternating between Clairvaux Monastery, where he could devote himself to prayer and spiritual scholarship, and traveling throughout western Europe, combating heretics, preaching the Cistercian philosophy, and working to consolidate Innocent II's claims to the papacy. In 1132, he traveled to Liege (in modern-day Belgium) to consult with the Holy Roman emperor, Lothiar II. The next year, Bernard was in Italy persuading the Genoese to make peace with Pisa, because Innocent needed the support of both principalities in his struggle with Anacletus. Bernard traveled to Bavaria and convinced Frederick, head of the house of Hohenstaufen, to join forces with Innocent II and the Holy Roman emperor. With the political support arranged by Bernard, Anacletus was officially excommunicated at the Council of Pisa in 1135. Anacletus died in 1138, ending the schism and sealing the victory of both Innocent II and of Bernard of Clairvaux.

Bernard's political influence began to rival that of the pope. Writing in the 19th century, the historian Henry Hart Milman asserts that Bernard was arguably the leading figure of all Christendom. "He runs alike the monastic world," wrote Milman, "in all the multiplying and more severe convents which were springing up in every part of Europe, the councils of temporal sovereigns, and the intellectual developments of the age."One result of Bernard's growing fame was the rise of the Cistercian order in Europe. Between 1130 and 1145, no fewer than ninety-three monasteries connected to Clairvaux were either founded or affiliated from other orders. By the middle of the twelfth century, Cistercian monasteries were established in Germany, Sweden, England, Ireland, Portugal, Switerland, Denmark, Italy, and Austria. One of the more politically influential Cistercian orders was found in Rome, the Abbey of the Three Fountains. It was administered by a former monk from Clairvaux, Bernard of Pisa—a close friend and ally of Bernard of Clairvaux. Innocent II died in 1143, and in 1145 Bernard of Pisa was elected Pope Eugenius III, owing largely to the influence of Bernard of

Clairvaux. Bernard had built a monastic empire that stretched the length of Europe, extending his power base to virtually all the political capitals of the continent.

The next phase in Bernard's public career is a controversial one: his role in the Second Crusade. In 1145, all of Christian Europe was shaken by news from the Holy Land: Christian forces had been defeated at the Siege of Edessa and most of the country had fallen into the hands of the Muslim Turks. The sacred kingdom of Jerusalem, Antioch, and other Crusader states was under imminent threat. In response, Pope Eugenius III appealed to the young king of France, Louis VII, to take up the cross and fight for Christ's kingdom in the Holy Lands. The French king, all of twenty-five years old, was extremely ambitious. He had married Eleanor, daughter of William, the duke of Aquitaine, and Louis saw for himself a noble future as the savior of Christian Europe. But many of the French nobility, wary of the young king's ambitions, were lukewarm to the idea.

Louis turned for help to the one man in Europe who had both the spiritual authority and the political clout to lend credibility to the campaign—Bernard of Clairvaux. Bernard was sympathetic to the need for a campaign to save the Holy Land, but was opposed at first to a spiritual venture being led by a secular lord like Louis. But Pope Eugenius endorsed the French king's campaign to save the honor of Christendom, and gave Bernard the task of promoting it across Europe.

Bernard dutifully obeyed and threw his full weight behind the effort, meeting with great success. In a series of church meetings and public declarations, Bernard's charismatic appeal and his famed powers of persuasion were on full display. His eloquence and his reputation for powerful speaking were such that it was said "mothers hid their sons, wives their husbands, companions their friends," in case they were led away, pied piper–like, by this persuasive witness to the faith.

His first address was to a large gathering in Vezelay, France. Bernard's intention to preach was widely publicized and nobles and villagers came from far and wide to hear the great man. When he had finished his address, thousands were ready to take up the cross. Bernard wrote to the pope: "You ordered; I obeyed; and the authority of him who gave the order has made my obedience fruitful . . . villages and towns are now deserted."

Bernard preached the Crusade to multitudes of eager listeners: He traveled to northern France, then to Flanders, and he wrote letters to the English people. He then went on to Germany, where he eventually persuaded a reluctant King Conrad to lead the German crusaders. Finally, in January 1147, the pope convened a "solemn and magnificent occasion" in Paris to officially sanction the Crusade. It was very likely here that Pope Eugenius gave the Crusaders the sacred right to wear a scarlet cross over their hearts, signifying the red blood of the Christian martyr—now the well-known symbol of the Knights Templar.

But for all the hallowed talk of saving Christ's kingdom, and for all the noble words spoken on its behalf and all the revenue raised by the church and by the monarchs of Europe, the Crusade was doomed by political differences, egos, and the collapse of Louis VII and Eleanor of Aquitaine's marriage. The journey to the Holy Land was very costly, as the Crusaders were unaided by Byzantine Christians. Whole legs of the army were damaged or destroyed by the Turkish army as the crusaders marched through Anatolia. When the French reached Antioch, Eleanor, who had been traveling with the French army, had become very critical of her husband's venture. The reigning prince of Antioch was Raymond of Poitiers, a distant uncle to Eleanor, and she struck up a friendship with her uncle that greatly irritated the French king. When Louis, in a rage, marched for Acre against Raymond's advice, Eleanor announced that she was staying to prepare an annulment of their marriage—but Louis took her and her entourage with him by force. The consequent assault on Damascus, which turned out to be well fortified by Muslim troops, ended in humiliation for the Crusaders.

The reverberations were felt across Europe and throughout the Christian world. The Second Crusade, sanctified by the pope and promulgated by Bernard of Clairvaux, had ended in disastrous failure. There was plenty of blame to go around, and no shortage of scapegoats. Inevitably, some of the responsibility fell on the shoulders of Bernard of Clairvaux, who had so feverishly worked to build support for the Crusade. Bernard believed the debacle to be God's punishment for men's sins. He defended himself and explained his viewpoints in his second book, *De Consideratione.*Though his legacy was partially tainted by the failure of the Second Crusade Bernard of Clairvaux remains a pillar of Christian faith and a loyal soldier in Christ's army. After his death, his reputation only grew, particularly within the Catholic Church. His writings on loving God and living a Christian life are widely read today. But it is his political legacy and secular influence that are remembered here, for scholars, both secular and religious, continue to be inspired by this most intrepid of Empire Builders.

The Most Beautiful Man in the Empire: Ibrahim Pasha

In a role similar to that of Bernard of Clairvaux, Pargali Ibrahim Pasha was a visionary and powerful grand vizier (chief minister) to the sultan considered to be the greatest ruler of the Ottoman Empire, Suleiman the Magnificent. A natural leader who exerted great influence over the sultan, Ibrahim Pasha is celebrated as one of the engineers of the empire and the most powerful of the imperial grand viziers. On the diplomatic front, Ibrahim's work with Western Christendom in the sixteenth century helped bring the Ottomans to the precipice of world power. As a military strategist, he led the sultan's forces to encircle and confront their main adversaries, the Holy Roman Empire. During his reign, he was reverently known as "The Most Beautiful Man in the Empire."

Ibrahim Pasha played a significant role in pushing the early boundaries of Ottoman imperial rule. As a slave of the sultan (the two had known each other since childhood), Ibrahim was totally dedicated to Suleiman and to what could be called the "Manifest Destiny" of the Turkish kingdom. His fervor in pursuit of victory for the Ottoman Turks rivaled Bernard of Clairvaux's passion for protecting the empire of God on earth. He enjoyed a meteoric rise, attaining the position of vizier before the age of thirty, a fascinating career as a diplomat, a general, and a royal governor.

Ibrahim Pasha was a Greek Christian from the town of Parga on the Ionian Sea. The historical record is not clear on precisely how he came into the service of the Ottoman royal family. One account suggests he was taken captive by pirates and sold into slavery. Or he may have been part of an

Ottoman custom of taking "tribute" boys from around the empire to serve the royal family as slaves, laborers, scholars, government officials, or even husbands. The Ottomans took these boys regardless of region, ethnicity, or religion, and trained them to serve the Muslim Ottoman system. These recruits were "as long as they lived, at once slaves, proselytes, students, soldiers, nobles, courtiers, and officers of government."

Ibrahim was educated in the palace school in Istanbul and soon attracted the attention of the royal family. He was very intelligent and talented, speaking Italian, Turkish, and Persian as well as Greek, and he was also an accomplished musician. It's easy to imagine that he was very popular—charismatic, tall, and thin. He and Suleiman were near the same age and became good friends. After he became emperor, Suleiman made him his chief falconer, then chief of the sultan's bedchamber—one of the most important posts in the Ottoman hierarchy. The slave who held that position was in constant contact with the emperor, guarded him in his sleep, and accompanied him everywhere. The two men became very close. Some historical accounts suggest an intimate relationship between the sultan and Ibrahim. Historian André Clot, writing in the nineteenth century, relates the experiences of foreign visitors, including the Venetian ambassador:

> When they were not together, they sent each other letters from one pavilion to another. They would go for walks together, unescorted, in the palace gardens or take boat trips with a single oarsman. Such intimacy between a Sultan and one of his slaves had never been seen before. Indeed, it was considered such a scandal that chroniclers kept silent about a relationship which, in their view, tarnished the Sultan's glory . . . the Sultan's intimacy with Ibrahim was considered by public opinion to go too far.

No matter the relationship between Suleiman and Ibrahim, all accounts agree that Ibrahim was promoted through the system very fast, and his appointment as grand vizier was unusual and controversial. Even Ibrahim himself was anxious about the rapidity of his rise through the ranks. According to the seventeenth-century historian Michel Baudier, Ibrahim asked the sultan not to promote him to such an important position so as not to arouse jealousy among others. Suleiman praised his modesty, but insisted on honoring him and his abilities.

The word *vizier* means "burden-bearer," an official appointed to help bear the burdens of state, relieving the sovereign of administrative and managerial duties. During Suleiman's rule, there were normally four viziers, the chief counselors to the sultan for peace and war, administration, and justice, for example. All viziers carried the title pasha, which was sparingly used in the sixteenth century, but came into wider use after Ibrahim's reign. Suleiman elevated the office of grand vizier from simply the chief of the viziers to an exalted, very powerful status, effectively the sultan's right hand.

Ibrahim's appointment as grand vizier made him essentially the prime minister of the Ottoman government—the chief administrator and also the head of the army. It was the most powerful post in the kingdom and it brought with it many opportunities for material wealth. Ibrahim built for himself a magnificent palace, according to historians one of the finest ever seen in Istanbul. As "chief slave" of the sultan, Ibrahim received honors and respect almost equal to those of Suleiman himself. The sultan also conferred on him the title of beylerbey, which gave him authority over all Turkish territories in Europe and, in time of war, the command of all troops in the region.

One of the greatest honors Suleiman bestowed on Ibrahim was the gift of his own sister, Hanim, in marriage. Ten days of festivities celebrated the wedding, as Ibrahim and Hanim received offerings and gifts from around the kingdom. Ibrahim was now not only the closest and favorite of the sultan's advisors, but a member of his family. And yet, legally, he was still a slave.

Very soon, Ibrahim had the opportunity to prove himself worthy of all this trust and adulation. There were a series of uprisings in Egypt and Syria. Egypt had only recently been conquered by the Ottomans and was particularly unstable. Suleiman sent an army of two thousand foot soldiers and five hundred palace guards to the rebelling territories, with Ibrahim in charge. Ibrahim took control of the territories of Aleppo and Damascus and reorganized the government, executing most of the top officials and dignitaries. Then the forces made their triumphal entry into Cairo—with Ibrahim leading the way, mounted on a richly decorated horse sent by the sultan. The procession was meant to impress and intimidate the local authorities, and it did. Ibrahim's authority was recognized and respected by most of the regional tribes and prominent officials. Those still in revolt were tracked down, brought to Cairo, and beheaded. As he had done in Damascus, Ibrahim instituted a new regime to govern Egypt, which proved to be very successful. Both Egypt and Syria remained secure for most of the next three hundred years. Ibrahim returned to Istanbul a conquering hero.

Ibrahim Pasha had a nuanced understanding of symbolism, imagery, and statecraft. During his reign as grand vizier, he effectively staged and publicized Suleiman's image as *sahib-kiran*—the ruler of a new, universal empire. Ibrahim portrayed Suleiman to the empire, and to Europe, as the new world conqueror, the new Alexander the Great, who was one of the sultan's heroes. Ibrahim's rhetoric bordered on the messianic. Like Bernard of Clairvaux, Ibrahim believed that both history and divine providence were guiding his actions and those of his master, Suleiman.

Ibrahim and Suleiman proved to be quite a headache for Holy Roman Emperor Charles V and his brother Ferdinand. The Ottoman Turks' 1532 raid to battle Charles's army for the conquest of Europe was at least as much a show of bravado, orchestrated largely by Ibrahim, as it was true military strategy. The parades and demonstrations of power staged by Ibrahim demonstrated that the Ottoman court was familiar with the language and symbols of how power was displayed in contemporary Europe. The Turks proved adept at using the same language of propaganda and symbols of imperial display to counter them, and in 1533 Ibrahim Pasha successfully turned Charles V's Hungary into an Ottoman vassal state.

Ibrahim Pasha's power and influence was at its height. But perhaps that was the problem. Had he accumulated too much power, too much wealth, too much influence for his own good? In March 1536, the courts and palaces of Europe and Asia were amazed to learn of the execution of the man who was so close to the sultan and who had grown so powerful in his kingdom.

Ibrahim's troubles began with the Persian campaign of 1534. The enmity between the Sunni Ottomans and the Shiite Iranians had torn apart the region for centuries. Turkish trade relationships were threatened by the new leaders of the Persian empire, the Safavids. The ambition of the Persians also blocked a path for the Ottomans to the Indian Ocean. Thus, Suleiman engaged in a two-year campaign against the Safavids, and Ibrahim Pasha was the head of the spear.

The official explanation for Ibrahim's execution was that he had committed blasphemy against Islam and against Suleiman during the Persian campaign by referring to himself in negotiations and in official documents as "Sultan" Ibrahim Pasha. He had already been given all the power that Suleiman had to give, but by calling himself sultan, Ibrahim had tried to equate himself with the emperor. Suleiman, therefore, had no choice under Ottoman law but to execute his old friend and close advisor.

But there is more to the story. Ibrahim had enemies. During the Persian campaign, for example, Suleiman had increased the authority of Iskender Celebi, his minister of finance, with direct control of preparations and supplies for Turkish armed forces. This brought him into conflict with Ibrahim, and the two became fierce rivals. Ibrahim managed to convince Suleiman that Iskender should be removed from office due to incompetence, and since it would be dangerous to let him live, to execute him. He was hanged in the public marketplace. But before he was hanged, he accused his rival Ibrahim of plotting with the Persians and against Suleiman. Did the sultan find evidence to validate the claims of Iskender Celebi? Or did he get rid of his grand vizier on the off chance that Iskender might have been telling the truth?

Then there is the matter of the Sultan's wife, Roxelana. After the Hungarian campaign against Charles V and Ferdinand, the sultan had added another girl to his harem. *Roxelana* means "the Russian woman," but due to her playful temperament, she was quickly given the nickname

Hurrem, meaning "the merry woman." She was apparently very intelligent and crafty, she sang and played the guitar, but the prime source of her hold over the sultan was that she bore him four sons. Hurrem became chief of Suleiman's harem and one of his closest personal confidantes.

And one thing is clear from historical accounts: She detested Ibrahim Pasha. It may have been that she was jealous of their close relationship. Suleiman and Ibrahim spent a great deal of time together, Suleiman trusted him completely, and Roxelana had invested a great deal of time and energy gaining the sultan's trust while edging aside her other rivals. Another possibility stems from the support Ibrahim had for Mustafa, the son of one of Roxelana's rivals in the sultan's harem.

In any case, one major obstacle to eliminating Ibrahim was removed in 1534 with the death of the sultan's mother, Hafsa, who had been a supporter of Ibrahim. So when the time came, reluctantly according to most sources, Suleiman ordered the execution of his best friend. But it's not quite as shocking as it sounds. Remember, Ibrahim was the sultan's slave, and therefore bound to fulfill his every wish and command. Every slave knew that "the sword could come down" anytime the sultan so chose, even for the smallest error or misjudgment. And Suleiman did not hesitate to rid himself of potential threats to his reign, even executing two of his sons for alleged treason.

Perhaps the story of Ibrahim Pasha is a cautionary tale. One can scale great heights and achieve great things under the service of powerful kings, and yet lose everything in a flash. Talent, creativity, and dedication took him a long way; but his legal status as a slave and the enmity of his detractors eventually brought him down.

The Kingdom of Spice: Jan Pieterszoon Coen

The casual visitor to the Rijksmuseum in Amsterdam might miss the portrait of the tall, sullen man with the deep-set eyes and a defiant glare. But this painting of Jan Pieterszoon Coen, with his flowing waistcoat, Elizabethan collar, and look of absolute confidence, captures in many ways the risk, the dangers, and the rewards of seventeenth-century economic expansion and the Spice Wars between Holland, Portugal, and England.

Jan Coen is the rare historical example of someone who was both a swashbuckler and a bookkeeper, equally comfortable leading a raid to sink English ships and performing management reviews. Under his guidance, the Dutch East India Company (the VOC) built one of the premier economic and financial empires of the seventeenth and eighteenth centuries. Coen is a national hero in the Netherlands for providing the drive and initiative that set the VOC on the path to dominance in the Dutch East Indies. A quote of his from 1618 is well known: "Despair not, spare your enemies not, for God is with us."

Aside from his reputation as an adventurer and a skilled military commander, he is considered the first European official to figure out how to make the spice trade profitable. It was Jan Pieterszoon Coen, according to the *Far Eastern Quarterly,* who resolved the problem of profitability and devised a system whereby his company would be assured of an adequate return on its investments in the East Indies. Coen served two terms as governor-general of the VOC at a time when the spice trade meant huge profits, violence, warfare, and espionage. Spices were, after all, a comparatively rare and valuable commodity, not unlike oil in today's marketplace. Exotic spices, such as nutmeg, mace, and cloves, were treasured in the kitchens and pharmacies of sixteenth- and seventeenth-century Europe. Nutmeg was even believed to be an effective remedy against plague.

The spice market had been dominated by Venice, with its close trading links with Istanbul. But in the 1600s the new maritime powers—Spain, Portugal, the Netherlands, and England—set out to break the Venetians' hold on the spice trade by going directly to the source. This meant sailing to Indonesia, specifically to the Moluccas, where subtropical conditions produced some of the rarest fruits and spices on earth.

Jan Coen was driven by a fanatical belief in the destiny of the Dutch trading empire. In fact, his overall aim was the creation of a commercial empire of the East, controlled by the Dutch East India Company and centered on the Indonesian spice corridor. Like most Empire Builders, he believed in what he was doing enough to shed blood for it. He eventually subjugated much of the eastern Indonesian islands, establishing a chain of fortified posts in the Indonesian Archipelago, displacing the Portuguese, and preventing penetration by the English. His dream of a vast maritime empire stretching from Japan to India was never fully realized, but his energetic administration and militarization of the Indies established Dutch rule in Indonesia, where it remained for four centuries.

Coen was born in Hoorn, the Netherlands, in 1587 and at the age of thirteen went to Rome, where he worked with Dutch merchants, learning bookkeeping, commercial trade practices, and foreign languages. In 1607, he sailed to Indonesia with the fleet of Pieter Verhoeff as assistant merchant of the Dutch East India Company, which had received from the Dutch government exclusive shipping and trading rights in the area from the Cape of Good Hope to South America. While on this journey, the young Coen learned firsthand the dangers of early commercial expansion, as Verhoeff and fifty of his men were killed during negotiations with the chiefs of the Banda Islands. Upon his return to Holland in 1610, Coen submitted to the company's directors a report on trade possibilities in Southeast Asia. As a result of this report, he was again sent overseas, in 1612, with the rank of chief merchant. After establishing contacts in the Moluccas, he was appointed head of the company's post at Bantam, in Java. Soon after he became director-general of the company's commerce in Asia.

Coen was raised a strict Calvinist, but more importantly was a ruthless businessman. He was convinced of the necessity of strict enforcement of contracts entered into with tribal rulers in Asia. He often aided Indonesian princes against their indigenous rivals or against other European powers, and was given commercial monopolies for the company in return. Through Coen's aggressive policies, the Dutch, at the cost of heavy military and naval investment, gradually gained control of the area's rich spice trade. Between 1614 and 1618, Coen secured a clove monopoly in the Moluccas and a nutmeg monopoly in the Banda Islands. When the sultan of Bantam resisted his attempts to control the spice trade, Coen transferred his headquarters to present-day Jakarta, to be freer to pursue his aims. Jakarta became the Dutch headquarters, and Coen fortified this strategic trade location with arms and battlements. In

October 1617, he received news of his appointment as governor-general of the Dutch East Indies.

In the meantime, relations had deteriorated with the English, who threatened the Dutch monopoly in the Indies. The English had their eyes on the nutmeg trade and the treasure of other spices of the Indonesian islands. They refused to abide by the contracts the Dutch had established, maintaining that they were free to trade in the islands, which were not under Dutch sovereignty. The Dutch, and especially Coen, had no intention of allowing the English to reap the benefits of Dutch labor and Dutch blood. Conflict was inevitable.

Coen had numerous conflicts with English merchants and vessels, telling one English commander, John Jourdain, that under no circumstances would Holland allow foreign interference in Dutch trade rights. Though both men aspired to control the spice trade, Coen was willing to use far bloodier methods. He swore to establish a Dutch presence in the region, even if it meant conquering the islands by force, which eventually he did. Following several incidents at sea, Coen issued a proclamation warning the English that any further logistical or advisory military support to the people of the islands would not be tolerated, and that armed force would be used against anyone who meddled in Dutch affairs.

But the English were defiant. At the end of 1618, an English force, with a fleet commanded by Sir Thomas Dale, arrived at Jakarta and tried to establish a foothold there. The rulers of Jakarta, fearful of full Dutch control of their lands, made an alliance with the English. Big mistake. An inconclusive naval battle followed in which Coen had only a few ships at his disposal, and these were loaded with precious cargo. He gave orders to defend the Dutch fort as well as possible against the English and the Jakartans and left for Ambon, a port in the Moluccas, to reorganize his fleet. The English could have pursued them and finished them right then and there. But their commander, Thomas Dale, chose the cautious route and decided to fortify their positions at Jakarta instead.

Fortune continued to shine on Coen's plans. In separate incidents, both Dale and John Jourdain were killed in running battles with the Dutch, depriving the English of seasoned leadership and splintering their forces. By May 1619, Coen's forces had been reinforced with additional ships and troops. Retribution was swift. The Dutch fleet sailed for Jakarta, which Coen seized, burned to the ground, and renamed Batavia, after the first tribe to settle the Netherlands.

The stage was now set for the gradual consolidation of the VOC's main objectives in Asia. But Coen was more ambitious and less conciliatory than his overlords. No sooner had Coen attained total victory than he was informed by courier that Holland and England had reached an agreement, whereby hostilities against the English must cease at once. Called the Treaty of Defense, it was the result of an Anglo-Dutch conference that had been called to discuss the deteriorating conditions in East Asia. The treaty granted the English one-third of all trade in the Spice Islands, in return for English agreement to help defend the region from the Spanish and Portuguese. Many historians believe that if the VOC officials had known the full extent of Coen's plans for Asia, or the nature of his accomplishments in Jakarta, they would never have signed the treaty.

Coen was furious. In a letter to his Dutch employers, he was biting and sarcastic: "The English owe you a debt of gratitude, because after they have worked themselves out of the Indies, your Lordships put them right back again . . . it is incomprehensible that the English should be allowed one-third of the cloves, nutmeg, and mace since they cannot lay claim to a single grain of sand" among the islands.

Yet Coen remained calm, and pursued his overall plans under new and different conditions. He had learned to bide his time and seize the opportunities when they came along. Coen knew better than anyone that the English could not uphold their end of the treaty—they simply did not have the ships, the manpower, and other resources needed for full-scale expeditions and maritime defense against foreign fleets. He sensed an opportunity. With his main goal establishing Dutch dominance in the entire region, Coen set out to crush his old enemies, now inhabiting the Banda Islands and still negotiating with the Spanish. He invited the English to join him, knowing full well that they could not. When English commanders informed him they did not currently have the resources, Coen accused them of backing out of the defense treaty, then proceeded to strike out on his own.

In the spring of 1621, he assembled the largest force yet seen in the Banda Island chain, including thirteen large ships, thirty-six barges, and an army of sixteen hundred men, including eighty Japanese mercenaries. There were a handful of English still living in the Bandas, and Coen invited them to join the mission, also knowing they too would refuse. Actually, Coen's spies had told him that some English were training and equipping some of the native Banda tribes. Coen had known for some time that the inhabitants of Banda had been selling spices to the English in violation of contracts with the VOC, as well as entertaining offers from the Portuguese. When he arrived in Banda, Coen learned that the English had opened a factory at the town of Lonthor and had presented a battery of four guns to the Bandanese, in spite of the recently signed defense treaty and English obligations. Coen used the guns as a pretext to invade. He asserted that the safety of all involved, including the English, was best served by bringing the islands under Dutch control as soon as possible. A bloody assault ensued, during which thirteen thousand Bandanese were slaughtered, and countless others deported.

Thus, the Banda Islands and English claims on the territory were all brought under the control of the Dutch, with Coen marshaling his forces to control access to its ports. Content with his accomplishments in the region, Coen handed his post as governor-general over to Pieter de Carpentier, and he returned to Holland in 1623, receiving a hero's welcome off the coast of Texel. Well compensated by the VOC for his accomplishments in Asia, he became a director of the trade office in Hoorn. The troubles with the English did not go away, however, and Jan Coen was once again pressed into service. He was asked by his employers to return to the Indies, but his departure was delayed by official protests from English trade officials, who considered him an outlaw.

Finally, in 1627 he and his family were smuggled secretly to the Indies and he assumed command of Dutch forces there. For two years, Coen and other VOC officials fended off invasions of Batavia from neighboring local tribal leaders. The Dutch successfully defended their holdings, but Coen was stricken ill in 1629 and died in Batavia.

The years between 1614 and 1624 served as a transition period, during which the foundations of the VOC were definitively laid, owing very much to Coen's firm hand and capacity for strategic leadership. Starting from a loose confederation of Dutch ships sailing the waters of East Asia, having little coordinated planning, Coen built a new professional organization with fixed procedural rules and a series of fortified factories. The VOC was one of the great success stories of commercial empire building, and Jan Pieterszoon Coen was its guiding light. And, consistent with many King Whisperers throughout history, he was prepared to defend his empire with blood.

Iron and Blood: Otto von Bismarck

No look at Empire Builders would be complete without considering Otto von Bismarck, duke of Lauenburg, one of the most famous names in European history. He shares with Bernard, Pasha, and Coen a vision for "empire" and a missionary zeal in pursuing "greatness"; in Bismarck's case, for the German people, or, more precisely, the Prussian state. Bismarck is credited with the unification and founding of modern Germany. His astute, cautious, and pragmatic foreign policies finally brought the German people what many had tried for decades, even centuries, to accomplish—the consolidation of its various principalities and regions into a sovereign German nation.

Serving under Wilhelm I, the king of Prussia and later the emperor of Germany, Bismarck was the driving force behind German politics for three decades, from 1862 to 1892. During most of his thirty-year-long tenure, Bismarck held nearly undisputed control over the government's policies. With the assistance of his allies, Helmuth von Moltke, the army chief of staff, and Albrecht von Roon, the minister of war, Bismarck guided Kaiser Wilhelm through a series of military confrontations and diplomatic maneuvers that literally changed the map of Europe.

It is only a slight exaggeration to say that Bismark's one true love was his home state of Prussia, in eastern Germany. The richest and most powerful of the Germanic states, Prussia had been the dominant player in German politics for over a century, since the days of Frederick the Great. Bismarck was a proud Junker, a descendant of the landed aristocracy of

Germanic nobility. He was also a royalist, dedicated to the traditional monarchy of Prussia and maintaining its base of power in Europe.

He is most often associated with his motto: "Not by orations and resolutions of a majority are the great questions of the time decided . . . but by iron and blood." Blood and iron—that combination is what he is remembered for, and that was the basis of his later nickname, "the iron chancellor." Although less well known, another motto of his is equally telling: "The Prussian eagle shall spread its wings from the eastern to the western boundaries of its domain, free and independent; not fettered by the influences of the federation." One might say that he worshiped on the altar of the Prussian state.

For centuries, Germany had been intentionally kept weak and divided by its neighbors, the French, the Russians, and the Holy Roman Empire. Prior to 1871, Germany had consisted of thirty-eight separate principalities, loosely bound together as members of the German Confederation. With the beginning of his tenure as prime minister of Prussia in 1862, Bismarck used both diplomacy and the Prussian military to achieve unification, and to end Austrian and French domination of Germany. Not only did he maintain Prussia's status as the most powerful and dominant component of the new Germany, but he also ensured that Prussia would remain an authoritarian state, rather than a liberal parliamentary regime, as in England.

His quest to ensure that Prussia stayed in the forefront of German political rule meant dealing with Prussia's biggest competitor in the region, Austria. As Prussian delegate to the legislature of the German Confederation in the 1850s, he had worked to check Austrian influence with other German states, and also played off Russian interests against those of Austria.

Bismarck faced both a diplomatic crisis and an opportunity when the king of Denmark died in November 1863. Succession to the duchies of Schleswig and Holstein was disputed—they were claimed by Christian IX (heir to the throne of Denmark) and by Frederick von Augustenburg (a German duke). German public opinion strongly favored Augustenburg's claim, as Holstein and southern Schleswig were (and are) German-speaking. But Bismarck, ever the Prussian royalist, wanted Prussian control of these duchies, and if a German duke took possession of them, that would never happen. So he took the unpopular step of insisting that the territories legally belonged to the Danish monarch under the London Protocol signed a decade earlier. Nonetheless, Bismarck did denounce Christian's decision to completely annex Schleswig to Denmark. With support from Austria, he issued an ultimatum for Christian IX to return Schleswig to its former status; when Denmark refused, Austria and Prussia invaded, forcing Denmark to cede both duchies.

At first this seemed like a victory for Augustenberg, but Bismarck had no intention of letting Schleswig or Holstein out of the grasp of the Prussians. While some Germans and Austrians pushed the Diet of the German Confederation (in which all the states of Germany were represented) to determine the fate of the duchies, Bismarck delayed while he negotiated behind the scenes. He induced Austria to agree to a power-sharing arrangement in which Prussia would be responsible for Schleswig and Austria would control Holstein. Bismarck's long-term plan to control both duchies was working.

In 1866, Austria once again took the issue to the German Diet to push for a final agreement on the duchies. Bismarck now saw an opportunity to grab control of Holstein and to diminish Austrian influence in Germany. In the view of Bismarck and Moltke, war with Austria was inevitable, even desirable. The Austrians were too late in realizing this. Bismarck used the crisis as an excuse to start a war by charging that the Austrians had violated the terms of the power-sharing agreement. Bismarck sent Prussian troops to occupy Holstein. Provoked, Austria called for the aid of other German states, which quickly became involved in the Austro-Prussian War. With the aid of Albrecht Roon's army reorganization, the Prussian army was nearly equal in numbers to the Austrian army. And with the organizational genius of Moltke, the Prussian army prevailed. Bismarck had also made a secret alliance with Italy, which coveted Austrian-controlled Venetia. Italy's entry into the war forced the Austrians to divide their forces and fight a two-front war.

To the surprise of the rest of Europe, Prussia quickly defeated Austria and its allies at the Battle of Königgrätz. The Prussian king and his generals wanted to push on, conquer Bohemia, and march to Vienna, but Bismarck, worried that Prussian military luck might change or that France might intervene on Austria's side, advised otherwise.

The Prussian victory produced sweeping changes. As a result of the Peace of Prague (1866), the German Confederation was dissolved; Prussia annexed Schleswig, Holstein, Frankfurt, Hanover, Hesse-Kassel, and Nassau; and Austria promised not to intervene in German affairs. To solidify Prussian hegemony, Prussia and several other German states chartered the North German Confederation in 1867; King Wilhelm I served as its president, and Bismarck as its chancellor. This marks the start of what historians refer to as "The Misery of Austria," in which Austria served as a mere vassal to the more powerful Germany, a relationship that was to shape history up to the two world wars.

Bismarck, who by now held the rank of major, wore this uniform during the campaign, and was at last promoted to the rank of major-general in the cavalry after the war. Although he never personally commanded troops in the field, he usually wore a general's uniform in public for the rest of his life, as seen in numerous paintings and photographs. He was also given a cash grant by the Prussian Landtag, which he used to buy a new country estate, Varzin, larger than his existing estates combined.

Military success brought Bismarck tremendous political support in Prussia. In the elections to the House of Deputies in 1866, liberals suffered a major defeat, losing their large majority. The new, largely conservative House was on much better terms with Bismarck than previous bodies; at the minister-president's request, it retroactively approved the budgets of the past four years, which had been implemented without parliamentary consent.

Prussia's victory over Austria exacerbated tensions with France, which was just fine with Bismarck. The French emperor, Napoleon III, justifiably feared that a powerful Germany would change the balance of power in Europe. At the same time, Bismarck did not avoid war with France. As with the Schleswig-Holstein affair, he had a long-range strategy in mind. He believed that if the German states perceived France as the aggressor, they would unite behind the king of Prussia. In order to achieve this end, Bismarck kept Napoleon III involved in various intrigues whereby France might gain territory from Luxembourg or Belgium—France never achieved any such gain, but was made to look greedy and untrustworthy. German author Erich Eyck notes sarcastically that if one reads Bismarck's memoirs, one is led to believe that Germany and Prussia were minding their own business when they were reluctantly drawn into war by France. Of course, the reverse is true—France was suckered into conflict by Bismarck, who used the crisis to rally the German states in support of Prussian political and military goals.

A suitable premise for war arose in 1870, when the German prince, Leopold, a Hohenzollern related to the Prussian monarchs, was offered the Spanish throne, which had been vacant since a revolution in 1868. At first reluctant, Leopold's family was lobbied by Bismarck and Roon to accept the throne. There was no way France would accept the arrangement—they would be faced with Hohenzollern monarchs in both Prussia and Spain. So France complained loudly and acted to block Leopold's candidacy, demanding assurances that no member of the house of Hohenzollern would ever become king of Spain.

On July 13, 1870 King Wilhelm was taking a morning stroll in Ems, a resort town near Koblenz, when he was approached by Count Vincent Benedetti, the French ambassador to Prussia. Benedetti had been instructed by the French government to insist on assurances from Wilhelm that he would never approve the candidacy of a Hohenzollern to the Spanish throne. The meeting was informal and took place on the promenade with the king's entourage at a discreet distance. The king refused to agree to the French demand in strong but polite language, and the meeting soon ended. The king's secretary wrote a report about the encounter, which was passed on to Bismarck in Berlin. The king gave permission to Bismarck to release an account of the events. The result was what became known as the "Ems Dispatch," and led directly to the Franco-Prussian War. In a titanic act of chutzpah, Bismarck took it on himself to edit the report, sharpening the language. He cut out Wilhelm's conciliatory phrases and emphasized the real issue. The French had made certain demands under threat of war, and Wilhelm had refused them. This was no falsification; it was a clear statement of the facts. The telegram was released to the media and foreign embassies, and implied both that Benedetti was more demanding and that the king had been exceedingly abrupt. It was designed to give the French the impression that King Wilhelm I had insulted Count Benedetti; likewise, the Germans interpreted the modified dispatch as a case of the count insulting the king.

By editing the telegram, Bismarck intended to give France an opportunity to declare a war as part of his plan to unify Germany. Indeed, he remarked, "The Ems Telegram should have the desired effect of waving a red cape in front of the face of the Gallic [French] Bull." The edited telegram was to be presented henceforth as the cause of the war.

France mobilized and declared war just five days after the dispatch was published in Paris. France was seen as the aggressor and the German states, swept up by nationalism and patriotic zeal, rallied to Prussia's side and provided troops. The war was a great success for Prussia. The German army, under nominal command of the king but controlled by Chief of Staff Helmuth von Moltke, won a quick series of stirring victories. The major battles were all fought in one month (from August 7 through September 1), and both the French armies were captured: the first at Sedan and the other at Metz. Napoleon III was taken prisoner and kept in Germany for a while, in case Bismarck needed him to head a puppet regime; he later died in England in 1873.

Bismarck acted immediately to secure the unification of Germany. He negotiated with representatives of the southern German states, offering special concessions if they agreed to unification. The negotiations succeeded; while the war was in its final phase, King Wilhelm of Prussia was proclaimed "German emperor" on January 18, 1871 in the Hall of Mirrors at Versailles. The new German Empire was a federation: Each of its twenty-five constituent states (kingdoms, grand duchies, duchies, principalities, and free cities) retained limited autonomy under the king.

In the end, France had to surrender Alsace and part of Lorraine, because Moltke and his generals insisted that it was needed as a defensive barrier. Bismarck initially opposed the annexation because he did not wish to make a permanent enemy of France. France was also required to pay an indemnity.

As chancellor of a unified Germany, Bismarck did not have free rein, but he did have enormous political power. His influence over the German king was very strong. Wilhelm I rarely challenged the chancellor's decisions; on several occasions, Bismarck obtained his monarch's approval by threatening to resign. When confronted with organized opposition, Bismarck took steps to silence or restrain political opponents, as evidenced by laws restricting the freedom of the press, the Kulturkampf,* and the antisocialist laws.

However, after the death of Wilhelm I in 1888, Bismarck's days in the political sun were numbered. He had less influence over Wilhelm II, even coming into open conflict with the new monarch on a number of matters. Bismarck was finally forced out in 1892 and replaced as chancellor. Wilhelm II and his chancellors favored a much more aggressive foreign policy, compared to the cautious and calculating Bismarck. His successors as chancellor were much less influential, as power was concentrated in the emperor's hands, culminating in World War I, a disaster (for Germany).

---

*Literally, "culture struggle," this amounted to Bismarck's efforts to subject the Catholic Church to state controls.

CHAPTER 3

KINGMAKERS

On occasion, powerful figures who arise through a political or military system do not seek the top leadership post for themselves, either because they are unable or unwilling to do so, but because they are in a position to strongly influence who does get to rule. Some have played key roles in toppling regimes and in instituting new ones in their place. Oftentimes, their motivation was personal, political, or financial, and they acted largely out of self-interest. Others had more patriotic or nationalistic motivations. Kingmakers may wield a sword, a pen, or the power of the ballot box.

The term *Kingmaker* has come into wide use in the twentieth and twenty-first centuries to describe various sorts of power brokers, whether they are in politics, the world of business, or similar kinds of organizations and settings. The term is used so often, to describe so many different kinds of individuals and circumstances, that its meaning has become diluted. It is helpful, therefore, to consider the lives and actions of the very people in history who gave us this concept.

"A Direction That History Did Not Take": Sir Richard Neville

The logical place to start this analysis is with the very man whose life and times originated the term. The phrase *Kingmaker* was coined in England in the 1400s, in reference to Richard Neville, the 16th earl of Warwick. Neville was the fifteenth century's wealthiest and most powerful English noble, with political connections that went well beyond the English border. He was instrumental in the deposition of two kings and the reemergence, however brief, of Henry VI, a fact that later earned him the moniker "Warwick the Kingmaker."

He might have been king himself—at a couple of points, he probably held the power to ascend to the throne. But through circumstances of birth, he was not in the proper line of succession to inherit the throne. His great-grandfather had been King Edward III, but Richard's connection to the royal line was through his grandmother, Joan Beaufort, who was the illegitimate daughter of John of Gaunt, Edward III's youngest son.

Though he himself could not legally become king, Richard Neville believed he could rule through others, and he literally died trying. It helped immensely that he married into one of the richest and most powerful families in Europe. At a very young age, he wedded the sister of the duke of Warwick, Anne Beauchamp. And with the death of Warwick in 1446, Richard and Anne inherited the titles, estates, and privileges of the Warwick line.

It is interesting to note that there is no reliable likeness that exists today of Richard Neville. At a time when earls, lords, barons, and dukes sat for paintings to record their majesty and greatness for everyone to admire, Neville either did not bother, or the drawings and paintings of him and his family simply did not survive the ravages of time. In any case, we moderns are robbed of his face—we are not sure what he looked like. But that may be entirely appropriate for a man who is a bit of a conundrum in English and European history. Was he a hero or a villain? Noble or selfish? Did he labor on behalf of a national identity and set of principles, or merely to establish a reign of supremacy for his family? In his popular biography of Neville from 1957, Paul Murray Kendall asserts that Neville was destined to become the enigmatic figure that he is because "he represents a direction that history did not take. He was molded by an age of endings and beginnings, the collapsing reign of Henry VI; and though he helped to create a new monarchy which would rule England until 1688, he soon revolted against his own handiwork."

His career could be considered a gigantic failure, both because he ultimately could not control the course of English politics and because he poisoned his own character and legacy in the wake of his overreaching. And yet, many see magnanimity in him, a sort of greatness, almost like that of a tragic protagonist.

Neville was one of the central characters in the famed War of the Roses, the series of bloody dynastic civil wars fought out between supporters of the rival houses of Lancaster and York over the English throne between 1455 and 1487. The name of the conflict stems from the banner colors that represented the two houses: red for Lancaster and white for York (although neither house marched under a rose banner). The conflict was not known as the "War of the Roses" until the publication of *Anne of Geierstein* by Sir Walter Scott in the 1800s. Scott relied on a fictional scene from a Shakespearean play in which the two armies marched under banners featuring red and white roses.

Richard Neville had family ties to the Yorks—his aunt Cecily was married to Richard Plantagenet, the duke of York. Originally, young Richard; his father, the earl of Salisbury; and Richard, the duke of York, were all in the service of King Henry VI. But it was an uneasy alliance. Henry was a weak leader, emotionally unstable, prone to bouts of depression and rage, and never in complete control of his affairs. The duke of York struggled for influence at court with rivals, such as the duke of Somerset. Here York was at a disadvantage, because Somerset was a favorite of both the king and his queen, Margaret of Anjou, the nominal leaders of the house of Lancaster. Then in 1453 the Nevilles were given very practical reasons to turn against the king when he granted control of territory owned by the Neville estate to Somerset, his chief minister.

In 1454, due to Henry's incompetence, the royal council named the duke of York "protector of the realm." But the next year Henry rallied his supporters, spurred on by Somerset, and removed York from his position. Almost immediately, York, Richard Neville, and his father returned to their estates and began raising troops. When York rose in rebellion against Henry VI, both of the Nevilles—father and son—joined him. Neville and his father were instrumental in the Yorkist victory over the Lancasters at St. Albans in 1455. King Henry was captured and Somerset was killed. For his service, Neville was appointed captain of the garrison at Calais, which had been captured from the French in 1347 and was a vital strategic military post for the English army. In the late 1450s, Neville used his time in continental Europe to establish ties with Charles VII of France and other European power brokers.

The Lancasters and the Yorks continued to struggle for supremacy, with Henry VI and his supporters maintaining a tenuous hold on the monarchy. In September 1459, rising tensions led once again to a clash between the two houses, this time at Ludlow in the north of England. Neville had crossed over from Calais to join the fight. But this time, the Lancasters were victorious, and the York forces were scattered. The duke of York fled to Ireland, while Neville and his father returned to Calais, accompanied by York's son, Edward, the future King Edward IV.

By this time, Richard Neville, earl of Warwick, had become the de facto leader of the York rebellions, by virtue of his command of the forces at Calais and his strategic leadership in battle. In 1460, Neville returned from Calais and pressed the fight, alongside York and his son, Edward. Later that year, York was killed in battle, along with Neville's father, the earl of Salisbury. Warwick was now the undisputed leader, and his goal became to place York's son, Edward, on the throne of England. That opportunity came in March 1461 after the decisive battle of Towton, near Yorkshire. The Yorkist forces routed the Lancasters, forcing Henry and Margaret to flee to Scotland. Neville stayed with the bulk of the army to secure the North, while Edward took a contingent of forces back to London, where he was proclaimed King Edward IV.

Richard Neville had brought down a king and put another in his place. His victory was now complete. Or was it? Machiavelli constantly reminded aspiring princes that maintaining power was different from attaining it. Initially, Neville was at the apex of his power, as King Edward named him admiral of England, and his estates grew, making him the wealthiest man in the kingdom. His brothers John and George also benefited, acquiring titles and land throughout central and northern England. But all was not well.

Neville spent considerable time trying to build alliances with the French. In 1464, he even tried to arrange a marriage between King Edward and Louis XI's sister-in-law, strongly hinting that Edward had expressed interest in such an arrangement. But what Neville did not know—in fact, what no one at the time knew—was that King Edward was already married. Earlier that year, Edward had married Elizabeth, daughter of Richard Woodville. When this became public, Neville was enraged. He had been embarrassed—he had unknowingly deceived the French into thinking a royal match with England was in the offing. He was also greatly offended by the secrecy with which the king had acted, keeping Neville totally in the dark. Some historical accounts speculate that Edward was wary of his dependence on Neville and was cultivating a separate base of support with the Woodville family.

Relations between the king and Neville worsened over the next two years, partly due to foreign policy differences. Neville favored closer relations with France, while Edward was influenced by his father-in-law, Richard Woodville, to pursue closer ties with the Burgundians. In October 1466, King Edward signed a pact with the Burgundians without informing Neville, who at the time was still negotiating with the French. Neville was caught off guard, once again made to feel like a fool. It became increasingly clear that he had lost his influence at court, as the real power was now held by the Woodvilles.

By the late 1460s, Richard Neville was reconsidering his allegiances and was even open to the possibility of working with his old adversaries, the Lancasters. There was still considerable opposition to Edward's reign, opposition that Neville could exploit. He increasingly turned his attention to Edward's younger brother, George, the duke of Clarence. George was nineteen years old, very ambitious, and a little dense. Could Neville place the young George on the throne, as he had done with his older brother? He certainly seemed to think so.

George married Neville's daughter, Isabel, in 1469, as secret preparations were made for fresh uprisings against Edward's reign. Neville and his agents began to spread the rumor that King Edward was actually a bastard, and that George was the legitimate heir to the duke of York and the rightful ruler of England. The historian Paul Murray Kendall supposes that Neville believed that his daughter Isabel "offered him the chance of becoming the founder of a royal dynasty; and he would unquestionably find it easier to rule in the name of his weak son-in-law than through a revengeful, if helpless, Edward."

King Edward had ventured north to investigate word of a rebellion organized by Robin of Redesdale. Not suspecting a mass insurrection, he took with him only a modest number of soldiers. But unbeknownst to him, Richard Neville decided to use all the forces he could muster to support the rebellion, not to help put it down. With the help of his brother, the archbishop of York, and the soldiers marching under Robin of Redesdale, Neville was able to encircle the king's company and force his surrender.

Neville had once again won the day. He had hoodwinked and outmaneuvered the king, who was now, for all intents and purposes, his prisoner. But once again, he was not able to make his victory complete. He dared not execute Edward and try to seize the throne, either for himself or in the name of George, for he and his forces would have been overwhelmed by the fury of the populace. And he could not galvanize support in London to proclaim a new regime in place of Edward, try as he might. Eventually, by the fall of 1469, support for Edward forced Neville to allow him to return to London. His coup had failed.

But Neville didn't give up his quest. A man of his wealth, prestige, and ingenuity would find new partners and forge new alliances. Enter the king of France, Louis XI. Louis offered his old friend refuge in Paris. But the French king also had an ulterior motive. He arranged a reconciliation between Neville and his old foe Margaret of Anjou. Part of the arrangement committed Neville's youngest daughter, Anne, to marry Margaret and Henry VI's youngest son. Louis wanted to support Neville in vanquishing their common enemy, Edward IV, and place Henry VI, still a prisoner in the Tower of London, back on the throne of England. Irony of ironies, the earl of Warwick, the destroyer of the Lancaster king Henry VI, had pledged with every ounce of his being to restore the house of Lancaster.

Once again, Neville launched a rebellion in the north. This time, however, he was supported by his brother John Montague, who had not taken part in the earlier rebellion, but was disappointed when his loyalty to Edward was not rewarded with the restoration of his lands. King Edward's forces were cut off from reinforcements and resupply from London, and Edward was forced to flee, taking refuge in Burgundy among his allies. Henry VI was restored as monarch, but had no real power. The Kingmaker Richard Neville would once again be the real power behind the throne, just as he had been in the early days of Edward's reign.

But then international politics seized the stage. Louis XI of France declared war on the Burgundians. Charles, the duke of Burgundy, responded by helping Edward raise and supply an invasion force to retake England. In this climactic battle, two things happened that swung fortune toward Edward. First, his brother George, duke of Clarence, who might have been king but was shunted aside in favor of Henry VI, switched sides—taking his forces and joining his brother in battle. Second, the battle groups Neville expected from Margaret of Anjou and Louis XI were unavoidably detained on the continent by bad weather.

When they clashed at the Battle of Barnet in 1471, Neville's army, outmanned and outgunned, met with disaster. Fog shrouded the battlefield, and his forces became entangled, attacking their own troops with "friendly fire." Edward's forces attacked from the center and cleared the field. Neville's brother, Montague, was killed during the fighting, and then Neville himself, age forty-three, was struck down while attempting to reach his horse. It was finally over—the Kingmaker was dead, long live the king.

The War of the Roses and the dynastic battle for succession to the

English throne wasn't settled until 1485, when forces loyal to Henry Tudor, the Lancaster claimant to the throne, were victorious over the army of the unpopular and controversial Richard III. Henry Tudor was proclaimed Henry VII and began a Tudor family reign that would last well into the seventeenth century. He solidified his hold on the throne by executing rivals and opponents at the slightest indication they might be a threat—a policy his more famous son, Henry VIII, would continue.

Warwick the Kingmaker failed to build and secure a family dynasty that would rule England in his name. But he was successful in altering the course of English and European history—several times, in fact. He may have been forgotten by much of the world, but historians find him valuable as a representative of the spirit of the age of kings. He represents a bridge between two different epochs—one medieval and one modern. His roots and his traditions lie in the Middle Ages, but the causes and movements he persuaded much of Europe to support were in a way a harbinger of what was to come in English, then later in European political struggles: Who has the right to rule and why?

The Duke of (New) York: James "Big Jim" Farley

In the modern era, Kingmakers do not necessarily make use of swords and armies, but instead wield power through political organizations, protest movements, and democratic elections. Some of the same character traits apply, however, including strategic judgment and a knowledge of how to use both friends and enemies.

In the dying days of the famed New York City Tammany Hall political machine, James A. "Big Jim" Farley became the most powerful force in New York state politics. For several decades, beginning in the 1920s, Farley was one of the foremost Kingmakers in American political history. As chair of the New York state Democratic Party, and then later as Franklin Roosevelt's campaign manager and the chair of the Democratic National Committee, Farley helped mold the direction of New York state politics, then national politics.

He was a key force in the resurrection of the Democratic Party in the early twentieth century, building a modern political organization and serving as a national political strategist. He helped to secure the governorship of New York first for Al Smith and then for Franklin Roosevelt. He then managed Roosevelt's presidential campaigns of 1932 and 1936. Farley was a key strategist in pulling together the New Deal coalition of Catholics, labor unions, blacks, and farmers for FDR. He presided over the administration's patronage machine, helping to fuel the social and infrastructure programs of the New Deal. He was also a key advisor to Harry Truman, and remained a prominent national figure and confidant to popes, dignitaries, and sitting presidents until his death in 1976. He is remembered as one of America's greatest campaign managers, politicians, business minds, and political bosses.

Farley came from humble beginnings in upstate New York, the grandson of Irish Catholic immigrants. After the death of his father, Farley worked in his mother's grocery store, working his way through high school, then a bookkeeping course at the Packard Commercial School of New York City. But from a young age he had been interested in politics—he had followed political events, particularly election news, with the same fervor and interest with which he followed the New York Yankees and other sports teams.

He entered elective politics at the age of twenty-three, winning the office of town clerk in his hometown of Grassy Point, New York. He then became chair of the Rockland County Democratic Party several years later and began rebuilding the organizational strength of the long-moribund Democratic Party in upstate New York. The state of New York, indeed most of the country, was firmly in the hands of the Republicans in the first quarter of the twentieth century, and many Democrats had given up trying for statewide office, particularly in the northern part of the state.

But Farley believed that the right Democrat could be competitive in the race for governor, especially if he had the right kind of organization behind him and the right kind of packaging as a candidate. He believed that candidate was Alfred E. Smith, head of the New York City Board of Aldermen. Farley reasoned that Smith had served with distinction in the State Assembly and had built a record that was appealing to both Democrats and Republicans, giving him an opening to crack the ceiling that had hung over Democratic candidates in New York state for years. It also helped that Smith had maintained an image of honesty and forthrightness, a break from the Tammany image so ingrained in the minds of Americans at the time. So in early 1918, the thirty-year-old chair of the Rockland County Democratic Party went to see Al Smith, told him that he should run for governor, and explained why he could win.

Smith was impressed, but noncommittal. He told Farley to run it by Commissioner Murphy and then get back to him. "Commissioner Murphy" meant Charles F. Murphy, head of the Tammany Hall political machine. At that time, Tammany Hall didn't hold nearly the power it did at its height in the late 1800s, but it was still the ticket to patronage jobs and elected office for Democrats in and around New York City. Armed with voter data, Farley managed to convince Murphy and other top party leaders that Smith would indeed have a chance. At the state party convention in 1918, young Jim Farley placed Smith's name in nomination, and with Tammany's machine in New York City, combined with Farley's vote-getting strategies upstate, Smith prevailed.

Like Farley, Smith was an Irish Catholic and a progressive. As governor, and later as a presidential candidate, he fought for legislation granting workers' compensation, women's pensions, and civil service reform; focusing on children's and women's labor issues; and establishing national parks. Though he lost the governorship in 1920 to the Republican candidate Nathan Miller, due to the national strength of the Republican Party, he regained the office in 1922, 1924, and 1926; all those campaigns were managed by Farley. The 1922 campaign for governor featured a knock-down, drag-out fight between Smith and the renowned newspaperman William Randolph Hearst, who was attempting to reenter politics, with an eye toward the White House. Farley helped Governor Smith navigate these treacherous waters and regain the Democratic nomination.

By the mid-1920s, Jim Farley had become known as a top political mind, both in New York and nationally. Though he had met Franklin D. Roosevelt on a couple of business occasions, he only got to know him personally while he was a delegate at the 1924 Democratic National

Convention. Roosevelt had placed Smith's name in nomination for the presidency, coining his famous "Happy Warrior" phrase in a speech on behalf of Smith. Though Smith did not win the nomination—the party was in chaos that year, torn apart by the issue of Prohibition—Smith, Roosevelt, and Farley formed an association that would prove to be highly successful over the next decade.

Al Smith did get the presidential nomination in 1928, with the assistance of Farley and other party stalwarts. Farley was then recommended by Smith to serve on the executive staff of the state Democratic Party. Their first topic of discussion was finding a candidate to replace Smith as New York governor. It was important to find a candidate capable of winning, and someone who could also help Smith capture New York's forty-five electoral votes in the presidential election. And because Smith was Catholic, a Protestant was preferable. It didn't take the party very long to realize that the perfect man for the job was Franklin Roosevelt.

Roosevelt asked Farley to manage his campaign for governor. Farley gladly obliged, and worked very closely with Roosevelt's top assistant, Louis M. Howe, to find the votes. The year 1928 was a Republican year nationally. Al Smith was trounced by Herbert Hoover in the presidential election—done in largely by support for Prohibition and the freewheeling, pro-business policies of the GOP. But Farley and Howe found the votes for Franklin Roosevelt to win the governorship. With significant support from Farley's stronghold in upstate New York, Roosevelt won the election by a margin of more than 25,000 votes, even though the man at the top of the ticket, Al Smith, lost the state to Hoover.

After the 1928 election, Farley was elevated to state party chairman, where he began the task of reorganizing state party operations into a well-oiled machine, the model for a state political party organization. A number of historians and political analysts later realized that the job of rebuilding the national Democratic Party began in New York state under the direction of James Farley. He was trained as a bookkeeper and a businessman, and those are the skill sets he brought to political organization. "A strong organization can do more than merely assist voters to the polls on election day," he said. "The members distribute propaganda, defend the party position, hold rallies, and carry on other very necessary activities." Farley and Louis Howe labored for two years in a whirlwind organizational effort at party building, making phone calls, setting up meetings, and writing letters. Farley traveled to as many as twenty states in 1931 and 1932 to help build a party infrastructure.

In looking ahead to the 1932 presidential election, Farley believed that the logical candidate to carry the Democrats forward was the popular governor of New York, Franklin D. Roosevelt. Part of his confidence was grounded in history—New York was an important state. It carried a significant number of electoral votes in the presidential election, and there was a strong precedent of New York governors obtaining their party's nomination for president—Grover Cleveland, Theodore Roosevelt, Charles E. Hughes, and Al Smith. But part of Farley's determination also lay in the strength he saw in Franklin Roosevelt. Just as he realized that Al Smith was someone of substance and talent, he recognized FDR's innate sense of himself, his times, and what America needed in 1932. Only this time, Farley wasn't alone—many observers, inside and outside the party, recognized Roosevelt's appeal, including FDR himself.

Fortune also had a hand in Farley and Roosevelt's rise. The Republican Party and President Hoover's inability to stem the tide of poverty and unemployment as the Great Depression took hold gave the Democrats an opening. FDR's reelection as New York governor in 1930 was not unexpected, but what did raise eyebrows was the margin—he won by almost three-quarters of a million votes. Immediately after the election, Farley, as state party chair, wrote a memo to the press:

> I fully expect that the call will come to Governor Roosevelt
> when the first presidential primary is held, which will be late
> next year. The Democrats in the nation naturally want as
> their candidate for president the man who has shown himself
> capable of carrying the most important state in the country by
> a record-breaking majority. I do not see how Mr. Roosevelt can

escape becoming the next presidential nominee of his party,
even if no one should raise a finger to bring it about.

Though Roosevelt was the leading candidate, winning the nomination
wasn't a slam dunk. Farley was instrumental in working the floor, counting
delegates, and negotiating with party leaders to support Roosevelt.
The main obstacle to Roosevelt's path was Speaker of the House John
Nance Garner of Texas, who supported Al Smith, Farley and Roosevelt's
old political mentor. But Farley, with the help of Joseph Kennedy of
Massachusetts, struck a deal with Garner: He would support Roosevelt's
nomination and in return would get the vice presidency. Farley had gone
to the national convention in Chicago as a well-known New York political
boss, but he left the convention a national political figure.

The main factor in winning the presidency in 1932 was, of course,
the Great Depression and the Hoover administration's inability to find
meaningful solutions to this unprecedented economic downturn. But in
that campaign, Roosevelt and Farley also began to bring together what
came to be called the New Deal coalition. This coalition of interests
was built around something very important to the political values of
both men—a commitment to progressivism, which meant reforming
government and society to improve the lives of as many people as
possible, particularly the working classes and lower-income Americans
who struggle to provide for their families. Organized labor; farm groups
and federations; intellectuals; urban voters; racial, ethnic, and religious
minorities; female voters; and white Southerners all supported Roosevelt,
and these groups formed the backbone of Democratic Party support in
national elections for the next thirty-five years.

At that time, it was a political tradition for an incoming president to
name his campaign manager or an influential supporter to the position
of postmaster general. Jim Farley accepted this appointment, but he also
became the chair of the Democratic National Committee, which had more
far-reaching significance for FDR and the Democrats. As chair of the
national Democratic Party during the Roosevelt administration, Farley
had the authority to control federal patronage positions in the government
bureaucracy and within FDR's circle of advisors. He was a key member

of Roosevelt's "brain trust"—a close group of both formal and informal advisors with whom FDR would consult on a range of issues.

Farley used his control of patronage to help ensure that Roosevelt's first hundred days of New Deal legislation was successful. He used his influence in the party, in Congress, and in the bureaucracy to line up votes for the New Deal's reform programs. The energy of the Roosevelt administration in combating the plague of the Great Depression and the implementation of New Deal programs generated a fair amount of excitement and hope across most of the country.

The 1936 presidential election was a cakewalk for the Democrats. FDR's campaign was again managed by Jim Farley. Roosevelt won in a landslide, winning over 60 percent of the popular vote and carrying forty-six of the forty-eight states—the most lopsided presidential win in American history up to that time. He lost only the states of Maine and Vermont. This gave Farley the opportunity to coin one of the most memorable phrases in presidential campaign lore. A popular political saying in the early twentieth century had been, "As Maine goes, so goes the nation." When the 1936 election results were known, Farley quipped, "As Maine goes, so goes Vermont."

But like many good things in life and in politics, the close working relationship between Farley and Roosevelt came to an end. Farley was dead set against Roosevelt serving a third term, which would break the Democratic Party tradition of serving two presidential terms, a tradition set by George Washington and the venerable founders of the party of Thomas Jefferson and James Madison. That, and also because James A. Farley, like many American political figures, looked in the mirror and saw a future president staring back at him. Farley believed that with his experience and his contacts within the Democratic Party, he himself could have been nominated for president in 1940.

When Roosevelt was nominated for a third term, Farley resigned his positions as postmaster general and chair of the Democratic National Committee. But though he left Roosevelt's side, he did not leave politics—far from it. He still held sway over New York politics for years to come. And he continued to support most of Roosevelt's policies, particularly those oriented toward their prized New Deal constituencies.

Farley demonstrated his power in politics and his "kingmaking" ability when in 1942 he engaged in a titanic struggle with the Roosevelt White House over the Democratic nomination for governor of New York. FDR and his men wanted Senator James M. Mead to assume the governorship. Farley supported the attorney general of New York, Jack Bennett. Farley had the votes, but Roosevelt and his team applied intense pressure on delegates to the state convention. Neither side gave an inch, but through several days of arm-twisting and negotiations, Farley's side emerged victorious. In reporting the high-stakes confrontation, *Time* magazine asserted, "Jim Farley was once again the supreme Democratic boss of New York . . . after the nomination, Jim Farley received more handshakes than Bennett himself." Bennett lost the general election to Thomas Dewey, a future presidential nominee himself. But 1942 was a midterm election, and as often happens the party out of power, the Republicans, won all the statewide elections in New York that year.

Jim Farley continued to be a force in politics and private business for the next three decades. He was a particularly valuable advisor to his friend Harry Truman, who ascended to the presidency after Franklin Roosevelt's death in 1944. He became an elder statesman and influential advisor to national Democratic Party officials and politicians, including President John F. Kennedy and Lyndon B. Johnson. He remained active in politics and engaged in public life until his death in 1976 at the age of eighty-eight.

The Kingmaker of India: K. Kamaraj

India is the largest democracy in the world. A country of over a billion people, India has multiple ethnic groups, religions, and political parties competing for influence. The twentieth century was a time of intense change and rapid developments—India started the century as a British colony, obtained independence in 1947, then slowly stabilized its political system and grew to be a world economic power by the end of the century.

Part of India's success involves the creation and maintenance of a relatively open political system, and a commitment to social and economic progress. In the middle of the twentieth century, which was a time of turmoil and chaos in much of Asia, a succession of national and

community leaders steered India toward a brighter future. One of the
most important of these was Kumaraswamy Kamaraj, or K. Kamaraj.
Known as the Kingmaker of Indian politics, his career spans about fifty
years from the 1920s to the 1970s, and cuts across India's colonial period
under British rule and through the years of independence and growth.
He believed that he was following in the footsteps of Mahatma Gandhi in
making India an independent, unified country, capable of taking care of its
citizens. A close ally of Jawaharlal Nehru, the first prime minister of India,
he rose from the ranks of local and regional politics and became involved
in the struggle for Indian independence. He earned the title Kingmaker
because he rarely sought the political spotlight for himself, and was
instrumental in bringing to power two of India's prime ministers in the
1960s, Lal Bahadur Shastri and Indira Gandhi.

Unlike the American Kingmaker Jim Farley of New York, Kamaraj
was not interested in moving up to run for the top spot in government. He
was content to support others if they were willing to work for a stronger,
more equitable system for all. Part of Kamaraj's appeal, and one of the keys
to his success, was his ability to move beyond narrow political and social
interests and work for a united India. This was particularly challenging for
him because of India's traditional caste system. His family heritage did not
belong to one of the upper castes. Kamaraj's low social origins contributed
to his success in bringing low-caste and Harijan ("untouchable") voters
into the political process. He underscored his strong belief in personal
contact by visiting nearly all the villages in his state more than once.

Kamaraj's focus, though, was on the political process and economic
development; he dropped the caste title early in his career and built a
reputation from working with leaders from varied backgrounds. For
example, in his home state of Tamil Nadu, he is remembered for facilitating
the spread of education to millions of the rural poor in the 1950s by
introducing free education and free midday meals in schools.

The power base for his rise in Indian politics was the Indian National
Congress (INC), the party of Gandhi and Nehru. It was the dominant
political organization in India and the party associated with the
independence movement. As a youth, he was able to see Mahatma Gandhi

as he passed through his town, and Kamaraj was inspired to pursue a life of public service. He joined the party at the age of sixteen, organizing meetings, collecting money for party materials, and participating in all forms of political protests.

Kamaraj was known for being unselfish: For years, he was content to remain a rank-and-file Congress volunteer, working hard for the cause of the freedom movement, heedless of his personal comfort or career. He was eighteen when he responded to the call of Gandhi for noncooperation with the British. He was arrested six times for his political activities, spending a total of eight years in British colonial jails. This only endeared him to party leaders and to the rural populations he represented. By his thirties, he was a respected leader in the independence movement and a rising star in Indian politics.

In 1940, he became the president of the Tamil Nadu Congress Party, a post in which he served for twenty-three years. In 1954, he became the chief minister of Madras Province. It was here that Kamaraj established a national reputation for reaching out to all parties and interests for the benefit of social equality and economic progress. His Cabinet included members of opposition political parties and community organizations. During his tenure in Madras Province, the state made immense strides in education and trade. More than fifteen thousand schools were added throughout the state and the percentage of Indian children in school rose from 7 percent to 37 percent. He was also instrumental in expanding electric power generation throughout the state and in bringing new industry to the region, dramatically improving employment opportunities.

During the years of Kamaraj's administration, Tamil Nadu came to be known as one of the best managed states in India. But Kamaraj became increasingly concerned with the long-term health of the party. The growing strength of the opposition party, the DMK (Dravida Munnetra Kazhagan), led him to believe that the most effective way to serve his party was to give up his ministerial post and devote his full energies to rebuilding the regional party organization in Madras. Once relieved of his duties, he believed, he could undertake an extensive tour of the communities in the province. His goal was the revitalization of the party machine. He felt that many Congress members had become preoccupied with positions of power at the parliamentary level. By his example, he hoped to influence the behavior of his fellow party members. In what came to be called the Kamaraj Plan, a number of Congress leaders voluntarily left their government posts and engaged in rebuilding the party at the grassroots level.

The Kamaraj Plan demonstrated his deep commitment to the political principles of service and community. The plan was very popular with some Congress leaders (particularly Prime Minister Nehru) and was seen as instrumental in revitalizing the party at a critical time. Even Nehru offered to resign, but he was assured by practically everyone in the party organization, including Kamaraj, that he was too valuable to the nation to take such a step. Due, in large part, to the success and the notoriety of his initiative, Kamaraj was elected the next president of the Indian National Congress in 1963.

In the 1960s, he provided steady leadership to the national party and became a senior statesman for the country. When Prime Minister Nehru died in 1964, the country and the party faced turmoil. The party had suffered through declining majorities in parliament for several years and India faced a serious foreign policy crisis with China. Nehru had been party leader and prime minister since Indian independence in 1947, and he had no natural heir to the nation's leadership. A power struggle ensued, featuring a strong challenge from the party's right wing, led by Morarji Desai. Kamaraj met with party leaders from around the country and calmly encouraged party unity. He believed that Lal Bahadur Shastri, a committed socialist like himself and Nehru, and a respected figure from the independence movement, could carry the banner of Indian national progress into the future. With his support, Shastri was elected.

During his term as prime minister, Shastri worked closely with Kamaraj to boost India's agricultural productivity, the so-called Green Revolution, and to manage the twenty-two-day war with neighboring Pakistan. However, in 1966, Shastri died suddenly of a heart attack during a state visit to the Soviet Union, where he had signed a cease-fire agreement with the president of Pakistan. The government was once again thrown into turmoil, largely due to the suddenness of the prime minister's death. Some suspected foul play, but nothing was ever proved. In the tense situation, India once again benefited from the guiding hand of Kamaraj, who successfully urged the selection of Nehru's daughter, Indira Gandhi, as Shastri's successor.

The party and Kamaraj suffered political setbacks in the early 1970s and his influence diminished somewhat. But he never abandoned his principles, and he continued to advise Congress Party members until his death from heart failure in October 1975. Though he was a powerful political leader, Kamaraj did not enrich himself through his political activities. He was unmarried and he led a relatively Spartan life, taking pleasure in the simple things. Writing in the *New York Times,* the late Pulitzer Prize-winning journalist J. Anthony Lukas described Kamaraj thus:

> Kamaraj's real achievement, then, has not been in remaking the party but in manipulating the diverse and disputatious elements within it. His genius lies in dealing with men as they are, not in changing them, and this ability is based on a realistic assessment of human nature.

⇒ CHAPTER 4 ⇐

SPIES

Spycraft and political espionage have been some of the most useful tactics of both cold wars and hot wars throughout history, when used effectively. The figures in this chapter are individuals of exceptional talent, creativity, and intelligence, and all of them were vitally important to the survival and prosperity of their respective states at a crucial time in their development.

They are generally not from the ranks of the elites, and therefore are not rivals for the throne or candidates for supreme leader. They tend to be either commoners or educated professionals who rise to positions of influence by a combination of skill, luck, and timing. Normally behind-the-scenes players, their understanding of the flow of information and how to attain it and use it are the keys to their success.

This chapter covers the last six hundred years, a time when espionage and warfare have been in transition from largely voluntary, crisis-driven activities to portfolios handled by highly trained professionals. Many of the early lessons of spying are on display and serve as the basis for the later development of state espionage; for example, the question of whether it is better to crush a spy ring in its infancy or allow it to develop so that one may better follow and eavesdrop on one's enemies. One of the sections that follows looks at a well-known state-sponsored espionage team, while another compares and contrasts the relative success of two wartime spy insurgents. What is clear in each of these cases is that the needs of the state, or the regime, dictate the order and organization of the espionage activity, which has taken many different forms over the centuries.

The Spymaster: Francis Walsingham

Sir Francis Walsingham was one of the most cunning and successful government officials of the second millennium. He was the principal advisor to Queen Elizabeth I during the golden age of England's rise as a world power. Known as the queen's "spymaster," Walsingham is frequently cited as one of the earliest practitioners of modern intelligence gathering, both for espionage and for domestic security.

The spymaster oversaw operations that gathered intelligence from across Europe and disrupted a range of plots against the queen, famously engineering the execution of Mary, Queen of Scots. Walsingham was a member of the small professional class who directed the Elizabethan state, overseeing foreign, domestic, and religious policy, as well as the subjugation of Ireland. A Renaissance man, his foreign policy demonstrated a new understanding of the role of England as a maritime, Protestant power in a global economy. He was an innovator in exploration, colonization, and the use of England's maritime power.

Walsingham the man stood out; he was different. A conservative Protestant—a Puritan, to be more specific—he looked austere, usually dressed in black, ordinary clothing at a time when Elizabeth's court was filled with preening social climbers in raspberry reds, canary yellows, and deep blues. He also acted and sounded austere. Reading historical accounts, one gets the sense that his serious manner and intense focus on business drove Queen Elizabeth a little crazy at times. She made light of his constant seriousness and rather dour persona, referring to him as her "moor," or her "Ethiopian," perhaps because of his long, pointed face, dark beard, and sallow complexion, but more perhaps because of his dark moods and stark warnings. Walsingham had a dry, self-deprecating sense of humor about the whole situation. In giving her unblemished advice or confronting an uncomfortable truth, he might start by saying: "In my native land of Ethiopia . . ."

Elizabeth needed Walsingham. He was right to be dour; there was plenty to be anxious about at the time he was advising the queen. England faced myriad enemies, both within England's borders and from across the sea. Elizabeth had come to power at a time of intense religious conflict in Europe between Catholicism and Protestant reformers. Her half-sister, "Bloody" Mary Tudor, who reigned before her, had been Catholic, but Elizabeth and her closest advisors were Protestant.

The religious conflict in Europe and the resentment it generated within England was at the heart of the very real threats facing Elizabeth's reign as queen and the security of the English nation. Walsingham's combative instinct prompted him to confront enemies at times, a trait that created conflict with Elizabeth, who strove to find a middle ground and often avoided confrontation until it was absolutely necessary. But confrontation was inevitable. Relations with France were tattered and very difficult. The French monarch, Charles IX, and his mother, Catherine de Medici—the real power in France—thought it was only a matter of time until England became theirs, both for reasons of religion and for reasons of imperial expansion and trade power. And the growing rift with Spain—driven partly by the hatred of King Philip II (Mary Tudor's husband and Elizabeth's brother-in-law) for the Protestant "heretic," Elizabeth—represented nothing less than a holy war that saw England as a trophy destined to belong to Philip and to the pope.

The reality was that England was extremely vulnerable to practically any opponent who dared invade the island nation. As Walsingham biographer Stephen Budiansky put it, England was virtually "powerless, utterly naked against the threat of invasion should any of these ancient enemies and rivals decide once again that war and conquest were more to their interests than peace. England was an eerily empty land, barely

3 million people in a country that in the fourteenth century, before the great plague, had had twice as many. In sheer numbers Spain and France simply overwhelmed England: Spain's population was three times that of England, France's five times."

What England did have were some very clever, very wise officials in charge of the government, starting with Elizabeth herself, but including Walsingham's predecessor Sir William Cecil, later referred to as Lord Burghley. Cecil recognized the threats, but Walsingham, who replaced him as principal secretary to the queen in 1573 when Burghley became lord treasurer, was the one who mobilized Elizabeth's court and engineered England's triumph over her persistent enemies by the end of the 1580s.

Walsingham had a flair for espionage that was grounded in his personal character traits. Basically, he knew how to keep his own mouth shut, and, for that, people trusted him. "No one ever heard Walsingham let a stray word slip," according to Budiansky, his biographer. "In the perpetual intrigue of the court, boasts of influence and intimate knowledge of goings-on were the common currency of power . . . In an age of braggarts and swagger and public lamentations, a man with the self-assurance to keep his own counsel stood out." It was said by his contemporaries that his confidence was "distinctly unnerving." He was a man who "knew excellently well how to win men's minds unto him, and to apply them to his own uses."

One of the earlier services Walsingham provided to Elizabeth was serving as England's ambassador to France in the early 1570s, before becoming principal secretary to the queen. This was a dangerous assignment, given the tensions between the two nations at that point in history, and it was made worse by the growing religious conflict. But Walsingham distinguished himself, jousting expertly at the French court with the old Machiavellian herself, Catherine de Medici. Walsingham is probably the only man in history to have traded barbs with both the French queen mother and with Elizabeth I without finding himself hanged or beheaded.

His post in France enabled him to see firsthand the dangers faced by Protestant Europe, and, by extension, England and Queen Elizabeth herself. The St. Bartholomew's Massacres of 1572 shook all of Europe to the core. Catholic leaders, including the pope, cheered, while Protestant officials recoiled in horror. Walsingham, a dyed-in-the-wool Protestant, remained calm. He was probably safe, he thought, from both the king's men and from the crowds because of his official presence in Paris as the representative of a sovereign government. However, he did risk that safety by offering sanctuary at the English ambassador's residence to a number of Protestants fleeing the murderous mob—one of them, Philip Sidney, later became his son-in-law. Walsingham's experience in France at the hands of Catherine de Medici and the French crown would later prove invaluable to him, as it taught him that there would be no way out of England's dilemma through compromise or negotiation, but only through cold, deliberate action.

The hallmark of Walsingham's career and the linchpin of his fame was his use of spies. As the renowned Chinese strategist Sun Tzu might have said, one good spy is worth ten thousand soldiers, and Walsingham more or less proved that. He practically created modern spycraft, and is certainly one of the best examples in history of planning and utilizing a program of state-sponsored espionage to achieve political goals for his country. In reviewing his elaborate strategies, one marvels at the patience and discipline it must have taken to see his web of deceit through to the end. These were long-term spy programs, some taking years before bearing fruit.

There were the obvious sources of information and security—port officers who checked ships and queried travelers, as well as mounted patrols at the Scottish border. But the most valuable information was obtained from a network of informants cultivated by Walsingham from his perch at the queen's side. Some of these sources lived on the fringes of society, while others were well known and moved about freely—an ever-changing mix of travelers, merchant adventurers, Scottish exiles living in Italy, Portuguese exiles living in London, double-agent priests and church leaders, English soldiers of fortune in the pay of the Dutch, ships' captains, expatriate traders, and even some famous men of letters and science—possibly including the playwright Christopher Marlowe.

They kept their eyes and ears open, listening for court gossip, trade news, naval preparations, movements of troops, names of prisoners, anything that might prove useful. Some were high-minded and acted out of a sense of religious or national duty, but most were motivated by the usual suspect: money. The right amount of money would make normally reasonable men risk their lives. Those who lived a more shadowy existence would gladly take the risk; others looked at it more as a business proposition—what was the information worth? The trouble is that those who are motivated by money can't always be trusted. So how does one know if the information they are providing is truthful and accurate? That is why Walsingham cultivated so many sources from such varied backgrounds—to allow him to pick and choose what to believe; to consider the information from a variety of perspectives; and to evaluate the information's veracity before choosing a course of action.

Walsingham the Puritan was not above using torture to extract information from reluctant sources. When enemy spies fell into his hands or prisoners in the Tower had information he needed, he would order them to be put on "the rack." Contrary to popular opinion, torture was not routine—using the rack, for example, required official permission. Walsingham did not favor torture for its own sake, or used in a gratuitous manner. But use it he did, to great effect.

From the late 1570s through the better part of the next decade, many of Walsingham's espionage efforts were aimed at one target: Mary Stuart, Queen of Scots. One might even say she was his obsession. She certainly recognized it, writing on more than one occasion to her supporters to be wary of her "mortal enemy," Secretary Walsingham.

Why the obsession? Mary, and her Catholic supporters across Europe, constituted the most direct threat to the survival of England as a free and independent nation as it had been seen since the days of Henry V. A cousin of Queen Elizabeth I, she was next in the line of succession to the throne of England. But many Catholics insisted that Elizabeth was not the legitimate heir to the throne—the marriage of her parents (Anne Boleyn and Henry VIII) had been annulled. To the pope, and also to France and Spain, this made Mary Stuart of Scotland the legitimate heir—which, of course, would mean that Catholicism would return to rule England.

Pro-Catholic groups had openly advocated Elizabeth's overthrow for years, and some had acted in secret to get rid of her as far back as 1569. The pope had made the intentions of the Catholic powers crystal clear with the formal excommunication of Queen Elizabeth from the Catholic Church in 1570. The papal bull issued by Pope Pius V in May 1570 read in part:

> Having taken possession of the kingdom, she monstrously usurps the chief authority in the church and fills the royal Council with heretics. We declare the said Elizabeth a heretic, and that all who adhere to her incur the sentence of anathema and are cut off from the unity of the Body of Christ. Moreover, that she has forfeited her pretended title to the aforesaid kingdom, and is deprived of all dominion, dignity, and privilege. We declare that nobles, subjects, and peoples are free from any oath to her, and we interdict obedience to her monitions, mandates, and laws.

The Florentine banker Roberto Ridolfi hatched a plot in 1571 that would have assassinated Elizabeth and placed Mary Stuart on the throne as the husband of the duke of Norfolk, Elizabeth's second cousin. The plot was discovered, Ridolfi fled, and the duke of Norfolk was executed. After the Ridolfi Plot, it became clear to Walsingham that Mary Stuart was enemy number one—the focus of all that threatened Elizabeth and her realm; sooner or later she would have to be dealt with, as would the power of Catholic France and Spain. Mary became "a rallying point for resurgent Catholicism everywhere; if ever Scotland and England were brought back to the old religion, the Protestants of the continent would be isolated and soon exterminated," wrote Walsingham. As proof, he needed look no further than his own experiences in Paris during the St. Bartholomew's Massacres. So he laid a trap—an elaborate and dangerous trap, years in the making.

Elizabeth's court at least knew where Mary was—since 1568 she had been held in England, at first for her protection from the Scottish nobility, who had turned against her and forced her abdication from the Scottish throne. But after her complicit involvement in the Ridolfi Plot against Elizabeth, Mary's confinement became more of an imprisonment. During Mary's long years of confinement, there had been one plot after another organized by various Catholic nobles and priests—all aimed at Elizabeth's murder and Mary's elevation to the throne. Walsingham's network of spies and informants were hard at work throughout the 1570s and 1580s, collecting information and disrupting enemy plans.

In 1580, it was discovered by Walsingham's spy network that the French ambassador in London, Michel de Castelnau, Seigneur de Mauvissiere, was orchestrating a new system of secret couriers who were sending coded messages between Mary and her supporters. It wasn't the first time—previous attempts had been discovered and foiled, with the perpetrators arrested and jailed or executed. But this time, Walsingham allowed the intrigue to play out so he could see where it led.

Walsingham had a mole in the French ambassador's office (the identity of this mole is still not certain today). Suffice it to say that this bit of state espionage turned the tide of events decidedly in favor of Walsingham and Elizabeth. Through watching, waiting, and listening, by 1584 Walsingham was able to learn the identity of the secret courier delivering the messages between ambassador Mauvissiere and Mary—it was Francis Throckmorton, an Oxford-educated gentleman from a well-known Catholic family. Throckmorton was watched for weeks and then caught in the act of coding one of the letters to Mary. He was arrested, sent to the Tower, and put on the rack. After several days of torture, Throckmorton cracked. He told everything he knew—an invasion force of five thousand men would be led by the French head of the Catholic League, the duke of Guise; Elizabeth would be executed and Mary Stuart crowned the new sovereign of England. The big bombshell was the direct involvement in the plot of King Philip II of Spain. Throckmorton had met numerous times with Philip's ambassador to London, Bernardo de Mendoza. The plan, approved by Philip, called for the duke of Guise's invasion force to be supplemented by a second force of twenty thousand Spanish troops in the North. Francis Throckmorton was hanged, drawn, and quartered; the Spanish ambassador, Mendoza, was forced to leave the country, and the French ambassador, Mauvissiere, was effectively blackmailed by Walsingham into cooperation; Mauvissiere was replaced as ambassador the following year.

Walsingham had by now made it a sport to place spies in the Tower of London, who would ingratiate themselves with Catholic agents doing time there, learn key names and facts, then be sent to France to infiltrate Catholic spy networks. The reverse was also true—he had been able to "turn" some of the Catholic spies he held in the Tower—they began working for him, trying to expose Mary and her cohorts.

The most successful of these Catholic spies was Gilbert Gifford. In 1586, Gifford became the new courier between Mary and her supporters both inside England and back on the continent. He was one of the first, and one of the most successful, double agents in modern history. There had been couriers working on behalf of Catholic agents before, but this time all correspondence to and from Mary crossed Walsingham's desk—he saw everything. One of the plots uncovered through this tangled web of deceit involved a man named Anthony Babington—a young, handsome English gentleman, a Catholic—who was in league with agents of the Spanish king.

In July 1586, Babington wrote to Mary and detailed the entire plot—the Spanish invasion, Mary made the new queen, Elizabeth's execution. The note, of course, first went to Walsingham before being sent on to Mary—Walsingham awaited Mary's reply to Babington. When it came, Walsingham knew the trap had been sprung. Mary had received Babington's news with great excitement, she had approved of the plans, including Elizabeth's murder. Now, for the first time, Mary Stuart had implicated herself, in writing, in the overthrow of the English monarchy and the murder of the queen.

In September of that year, Babington and his fellow conspirators were arrested and hanged. Walsingham formally pressed for Mary Stuart to be brought to trial. Queen Elizabeth was hesitant—all along she had been slow to call for her cousin Mary's downfall, for fear of setting a precedent for executing monarchs. On this point, she and

Walsingham disagreed, and it caused some rancor between them.But Elizabeth eventually relented because the evidence against Mary was so compelling. Late in the fall of 1586, Mary was found guilty by a special tribunal of the "compassing, practicing, and imagining of her Majesty's death." In February 1587, Mary, Queen of Scots, was led to the great hall of Fotheringay Castle, where she had been tried, "mounted the three steps to a wooden stage that had been erected, and placed her head upon the block, where it was severed with three blows from the executioner's axe."

A great enemy of England was now gone, but Walsingham dared not celebrate, at least not openly. Although he had been triumphant, and had been vindicated by the series of events that unfolded, his unrelenting pressure on Elizabeth to bring Mary to trial and seek her execution had strained their relationship. He stayed away from court for a while. His health, always precarious, had also taken a turn for the worse.

There was still the small matter of Spain and King Philip. But here, too, Walsingham's network of spies and informants had helped pave the way. By early 1587, England was openly at war with Spain in the Netherlands. Walsingham had counseled such a course, bringing him into conflict with his old friend and mentor William Cecil, Lord Burghley. Elizabeth, true to character, had sought a middle course to avoid open warfare, but the deteriorating situation of the Dutch Protestants, at the hands of the Spanish, had forced her hand.

Leading up to the conflict in the mid- to late 1580s, Walsingham pursued a number of secretive strategies, some bearing fruit; others not. One of the more successful tactics to harass the Spaniards and keep them at bay was the use of privateers to attack, sink, or rob Spanish vessels. In fact, he called the plan his "Plat for the Annoying of the King of Spain." Sir Walter Raleigh was used for such purposes, and Sir Francis Drake struck major blows against Spain, both before and during open war. Walsingham's spies in Italy reported that such raids had shaken King Philip's credit with Genoese bankers.

From time to time, Walsingham would receive tips from overseas informants about Spanish preparations for a major naval invasion of

England—it was said they were building an "armada." But many of the reports were conflicting and some were unreliable. The more reliable information came from diplomatic sources in Italy. When King Philip signed an agreement with the pope to back his invasion, the College of Cardinals leaked the information to friends and colleagues like a sieve.

One particular source cultivated by Walsingham provided the most useful intelligence. Anthony Standen, an English Catholic, had switched his allegiance since Mary's execution and begun working for England's national interests. Standen was very well connected; his close friend, the Tuscan ambassador to Spain, kept him apprised of Spanish naval preparations. Standen was able to give Walsingham details about the movement of vessels in and out of ports, the number of soldiers boarding ships, and their intended destinations.

By April 1588, the reports of Standen and other informants convinced Walsingham, as well as Lord Burghley and several of Elizabeth's other advisors, that England's defense preparations needed to commence immediately. In May, Elizabeth finally agreed to launch English ships in the direction of the oncoming Spanish. Sir Francis Drake led one of the task forces and overall command was held by Lord Admiral Charles Howard. In running battles up the English Channel, the English tried to hold off the numerically superior Spanish. One particularly effective and dramatic battle involved the use of fire ships— the English packed eight merchant ships with wood, cloth, and oil; set them on fire; and sent them drifting toward the Spanish fleet.

The English defense had been enough to disrupt the plans of the Spanish fleet: They were unable to coordinate their ships to attack England's coast and were forced to sail north. After rounding Scotland, they sailed into violent storms off the coast of Ireland, losing half their fleet. The war was over. All the money, political muscle, and religious fervor thrown into the Spanish Armada and the holy war to take England had been for naught. Pope Sixtus was eventually convinced that it was God's will. King Philip of Spain never recovered, either politically or emotionally.

Walsingham did receive his due, at least from some in Elizabeth's court. Vice-Admiral Lord Henry Seymour wrote him at his home, saying "I will not flatter you, but you have fought more with your pen than many have in our English navy fought with their enemies." But Walsingham had little time or opportunity to savor his latest triumph, aside from rejoicing at England's salvation. His health continued to deteriorate, and he was forced to spend more and more time away from court. He passed away in early spring 1590.

Walsingham was certainly an example of man and a moment coming together propitiously. His rare ability to think strategically in the long term and organize intelligence networks, the likes of which had never been seen before, may have saved England. His position as principal secretary to the queen was also at its height of power during his tenure in that office. He and William Cecil had made it a powerful position, but after Walsingham's time it faded in importance. But his legacy is secure as one of history's great power players, a unique blend of insight, determination, and administrative ability that saw his country through one of its most trying times.

Eminence Rouge and Eminence Grise: Cardinal Richelieu and Father Joseph

The celebrated French clergyman, noble, and statesman Cardinal Armand Jean du Plessis de Richelieu was one of the most successful political minds of the last thousand years. He was also a very practiced spymaster. Consecrated as a Catholic bishop in 1617, Richelieu soon rose in both church and state, becoming a cardinal in 1622, and King Louis XIII's chief minister in 1624. The 1844 work *The Three Musketeers* by Alexandre Dumas, in which Cardinal Richelieu is one of the primary antagonists, initially gave rise to the popular image of the cardinal; later works by other authors and later stage and movie productions reinforced the image of a villainous Richelieu.

Real life is much more nuanced, however. The Cardinal de Richelieu was authoritarian and oppressive, but his political influence also helped transform France into a strong, centralized state. He came to be known by the title of the king's "chief minister" or "first minister." As a result, he is sometimes considered the world's first prime minister in the modern sense of the term. He sought to consolidate royal power under the crown and to crush domestic political and religious factions. Meanwhile, his chief foreign policy objective was to check the power of the Austro-Spanish Habsburg dynasty.

He is one of those rare figures in history—a churchman dedicated to God, but at the same time a political leader dedicated to empowering the state. He had qualities similar to those of Bernard of Clairvaux: He was dynamic, intelligent, determined, and immensely influential. But whereas Bernard fought to protect the kingdom of God, Richelieu fought to expand the kingdom of France. Though he devoutly believed in the mission of the Roman Catholic Church, he sought to assign the church a more practical meaning in the politics of the day. Thus, under Richelieu, the church often became a tool for the promotion of state policy and the consolidation of royal power.

His political ideas and philosophy were evident early in life. In his early writings, he viewed authoritarianism as essential to political stability. He believed in the divine right of the king, and envisioned a well-defined, divinely ordained authority at all levels of society. He had a clear view of the way society was supposed to function: Everyone played a specific role in and made their contributions to the system—the clergy through their prayers, the nobles with their arms under the control of the king, and the people through their obedience to the state. The monarchy was the divinely appointed mechanism that made it all work; its purpose was peace and order in society, every subject contributing to the life of the whole.

Richelieu's tenure in office coincided with a crucial period of reform for France. Earlier, the nation's political structure was largely feudal, with powerful nobles and a wide range of laws in different regions. Nobles periodically conspired against the king, raised private armies, and allied themselves with foreign powers. This system gave way to centralized power under Richelieu, as he worked to restrain the power of the nobility. Richelieu's successes were extremely important to Louis XIII's successor, King Louis XIV. He continued Richelieu's work of creating an absolute monarchy; in the same vein as the cardinal, he enacted policies that further suppressed the once-mighty aristocracy.

Part of Richelieu's dark legacy stems from the fact that he was clearly an authoritarian who believed that power flowed from the top, not the other way around. He was adept at using government power to enforce that belief. He censored the press, established a large network of internal spies, forbade the discussion of political matters in public assemblies such as the court of justice in Paris, and had those who dared to conspire against him prosecuted and executed. The Canadian historian and philosopher John Ralston Saul has referred to Richelieu as the "father of the modern nation-state, modern centralized power and the modern secret service."

He created an administrative apparatus with men totally dependent on himself, which facilitated tremendously the implementation of his policies. He established a church utterly loyal to the French monarchy. In fact, the French state had far more extensive control over the revenue of the church than in any other Catholic country. Most importantly, he had the skills and intellect to find a way to deal with the conspiracies and plots against his regime—selective revenge, counterattacks, and the use of the crown to track down political opponents. He was also able to diminish the role of the Parliament when it became an obstacle to his plans for centralization of authority and the construction of an absolutist state.

Many see the roots of absolutism on display in Richelieu's France—he was among the first to make use of mass communication as a tool of government propaganda, for example. The government published a weekly newspaper, whose stories were approved by the cardinal, some even written by him or members of the royal circle. Richelieu also made use of the arts for political purposes. He was known as a great patron of the arts, founding the Academie Française and supporting many artistic and cultural endeavors. But he also used these institutions to officially sanction acceptable literature, painting, architecture, and so on.

Born in 1585 into an impoverished Parisian family, Richelieu began his climb to power as an advisor to the queen mother, Marie de Medici, who was acting as the nominal ruler of the French territories until her son, Louis XIII, came of age. When Louis did take the throne, however, a power struggle ensued, and he banished his mother from court, Richelieu along with her. But Richelieu continued to ingratiate himself with the king and his advisors, providing information about the queen mother's activities and about other threats to Louis's authority. Although King Louis did not like him personally, Richelieu became a powerful political voice in his court, and by the late 1620s, the dominant voice.

The next two decades saw Cardinal Richelieu transform the French system of government and influence the direction of political events in all of Europe. Like Francis Walsingham, the key to Richelieu's success—and survival—was one of the most extensive systems of espionage the world had ever known. The intelligence network he put in place across Europe gave him crucial information about the intentions of rival powers and about plots against him personally. His spies also enabled him to spread disinformation, sending opponents in false directions, and on a few occasions his agents influenced the foreign and military policies of the enemies of France, the Habsburgs in particular.

He recruited an army of royal spies, men of confidence, and pamphleteers who disseminated Richelieu's ideas in advance of their implementation. His informants reported any word of dissent heard in the territories. Punishment was swift and cruel. Richelieu once boasted, "If you give me six lines written by the most honest man, I will find something in them to hang him." All the while he remained one step ahead of would-be usurpers and assassins, jealous of his influence. The smallest whisper of disloyalty was detected. When a young courtier said, in the privacy of confession, that she thought Richelieu was ungodly, the priest hearing her confession notified the cardinal and the unfortunate woman was banished to a convent.

One of his espionage tools was the growing use of intendants—officers sent directly by the crown for a specific purpose. Originally used as troubleshooters (for tax collection or to root out corruption), his intendants increasingly became spies. They were given authority over the judicial officials and subjects of the crown, with the power to resolve and decide affairs of state at the local level. By the mid-1630s, he had spies everywhere—both within France and throughout Europe—listening in on diplomatic conversations, tracking the movements of foreign officials, and watching for signs of domestic political problems in France.

Royal officials sent out into the field were routinely ordered to keep their eyes and ears open and to report back secretly. Ambitious officials began creating their own local networks of spies to provide intelligence they could then provide to Richelieu. There were also special commissions created to investigate political opponents, apply pressure on French nobles, and interrogate local officials. All intelligence reports went directly to Richelieu, who created a special staff to handle the information—the beginnings of a secret service, or a state police.

As with Walsingham, the cardinal made special use of prisons, particularly the Bastille, which was loaded with political prisoners, informants, and double agents. It was difficult to prove treason in court, so many of those arrested simply languished in a cell. Hardest hit were nobles involved in suspicious groups or activities—which very likely formed the basis of the classic Alexandre Dumas novel *The Man in the Iron Mask.*

One of Richelieu's premier weapons in the web of espionage he created was his friend and confidant Father Joseph. His real name was François Leclerc du Tremblay. Known simply as Father Joseph, or sometimes Père Joseph, he was a capuchin friar, a papal envoy, and an agent provocateur in Richelieu's campaign against the Habsburgs. He and Richelieu had a long association—it was Father Joseph who first brought Marie de Medici's attention to the youthful Richelieu's administrative talents in 1615. He was Richelieu's right hand for most of his tenure in French government. As such, Father Joseph himself spawned quite a few legends in the history of Europe, and in the art of political espionage. He became known as "his Gray Eminence" (*Eminence Grise*), for his common grayish brown robe; this in contrast to Cardinal Richelieu, who was "his Red Eminence" (*Eminence Rouge*). He was the subject of Aldous Huxley's 1941 book *Eminence Grise,* a look at the roots of the political skullduggery of modern Europe. The phrase *Eminence Grise* has since come to mean a powerful political advisor working in the background, à la Dick Cheney to George W. Bush.

Father Joseph was a visionary—he dreamed of a new crusade led by Christian Europe against the Ottoman Turks. But his grand plans were disrupted by the Thirty Years' War: the religious and political struggle that preoccupied much of Europe for the first half of the seventeenth century. He then subordinated himself to working for Richelieu's ambitions of a French-dominated Catholic Europe. Richelieu and Father Joseph orchestrated the victory over the Protestant Huguenot stronghold at La Rochelle in 1628, greatly enhancing Richelieu's prestige at the French court. The victory at La Rochelle stood out not as one of Catholicism over Protestantism, but as a triumph over the political threat posed by the independent Huguenots. To Richelieu, they had to be brought under the yoke of the French crown, thus reducing the possibility of rebellion against the king.

On their return to Paris, Father Joseph was entrusted with the organization of the cardinal's espionage network against both his domestic and foreign enemies. Richelieu's main foreign policy goal was to defuse the military and political threat to France represented by the Habsburg states, Austria and Spain. During French involvement in the Thirty Years' War, Father Joseph demonstrated incomparable skill. While the cardinal had to remain in France to advise King Louis XIII and defend his policies against his enemies, Father Joseph, his trusted agent, worked abroad making alliances with the foreign princes in Germany and Italy. For example, some accounts credit Father Joseph with the subterfuge leading to the Habsburg Emperor Ferdinand sacking his chief military advisor, Albrect von Wallenstein, at the same time that Richelieu was negotiating with the Protestant leader of Sweden, Gustavus Adolphus, to invade Austria from the north. Richelieu had no problem conspiring with Protestant powers if it meant furthering the goals of the French crown.

In his 1941 biography of Father Joseph, *Eminence Grise,* Aldous Huxley drew parallels between the authoritarian regime of Richelieu and Joseph and the contemporary dangers posed by Nazi Germany. He emphasized the fanaticism of the two men, focusing on Father Joseph's mystical tendencies, his devious political methods, and his attraction to nationalism. "The road trodden by those bare horny feet (Joseph eschewed shoes and most other luxuries) led [through the Thirty Years' War] to August 1914 and September 1939." A *Time* magazine review of *Eminence Grise* speculated that what fascinated Huxley about Father

Joseph was "the moral dilemma of a mystic who is also a power politician, and whose whole active life is an illustration of Author Huxley's (and many other people's) pessimism about politics and history . . ."

In truth, Father Joseph did become a very powerful behind-the-scenes player in the power politics of the time, and he was Richelieu's closest confidant. He wandered about Europe, from all appearances a poor itinerant, but actually the center of a sophisticated espionage ring, whose designs on its neighbors he furthered through countless contacts and intrigues. According to Huxley, "His friars were in every part of the world, from Persia to England, from Abyssinia to Canada. In the midst of his wearisome and questionable political activities, the thought that he was helping to spread the gospel of Christ must often have been a source of strength and consolation. True, his enemies in Spain and Austria and at the Roman Curia accused him of using his missionaries as French agents and anti-Habsburg fifth columnists. And, alas, the charge is not entirely baseless."

Father Joseph died in 1638, just three years into French involvement in the Thirty Years' War, and before he was to have been named a cardinal by the Vatican. He was also to have been Richelieu's successor as chief minister to the king. But the trappings of state security and the network of informants he and Richelieu had established allowed the cardinal to soldier on.

Richelieu himself died four years later, and then King Louis XIII passed on the following year. Cardinal Richelieu's legacy is clear: He took a medieval, feudal state, splintered by the competing interests of the nobles, and turned it into a strong, centralized regime capable of extending its power well beyond its borders. Richelieu formed a model upon which the ideal of nationalism could frame itself. He centralized political power and worked toward a more uniform legal system. Richelieu built for France the stable and powerful monarchy that gave it a long preeminence among nations and contributed to overall European development. The foundation of monarchical power and state security he built was put to great use by Louis XIII's successor, Louis XIV, the self-proclaimed "sun king," and was instrumental in France's rise as a world power.

Spy vs. Spy: Lawrence of Arabia vs. Wassmuss of Persia

In examining the role of spycraft and wartime strategy, it is often helpful to compare and contrast the activities of two rivals for the same prize. T. E. Lawrence, also known as Lawrence of Arabia, is famous the world over as the British intelligence officer who helped organize and engineer the great Arab revolt during World War I, opening a new front in the war and weakening Germany's ally, the Ottoman Empire. But Wassmuss of Persia? No, it's not a joke—there really was a Wassmuss of Persia. He is known in some circles as the "German" Lawrence. Wilhelm Wassmuss was a German diplomat and intelligence official who attempted to bring Iran into World War I on the side of the Germans, thereby driving a wedge into the British force structure in the Middle East. Both Lawrence and Wassmuss were covert field agents, working on behalf of their governments to destabilize an enemy regime during the biggest war the world had ever seen. One was successful, and went on to become a celebrity; the other wasn't, and has been largely forgotten by history.

What is often forgotten, or overlooked, about Thomas Edward Lawrence is that he was a scientist. Before he was an intelligence officer, before he was the instigator of a great political and military revolt, he was an archaeologist. In fact, what made him valuable to the British army in World War I was the knowledge of Syria, Turkey, Iraq, and Palestine he had accumulated doing archaeological fieldwork. An Oxford man, Lawrence had studied medieval castles and architecture—his academic thesis was titled "The Influence of the Crusades on European Military Architecture."

While in college, he had traveled to France and Syria, conducting research and making architectural drawings. After graduating, he traveled throughout the Middle East working as an archaeologist for the British Museum. His work in the region gave him an intimate knowledge of railroads, transportation routes, seaports, and market centers—information that would later prove invaluable to British military intelligence. While there he learned Arabic. Thus, when war came, T. E. Lawrence had the makings of the perfect intelligence agent: He spoke the language, knew the region, had local contacts, and had been trained to survive in hostile environments. He was an archaeologist and an adventurer; he was an Indiana Jones before there was an Indiana Jones.

Of course, he would love that characterization. His classic book, *The Seven Pillars of Wisdom,* his retelling of his experiences in the Middle East leading up to and including the Arab Revolt, is sometimes seen as vainglorious and self-aggrandizing. And yet, independent descriptions of the Arab Revolt do not contradict the broad outlines of Lawrence's manuscript. Major General Sir Edmund Allenby, commander of the Egyptian Expeditionary Forces and the key liaison between Lawrence and the Arab forces of Prince Feisal, accepted virtually all of Lawrence's strategic recommendations. Allenby said after the war, "I gave him a free hand. His cooperation was marked by the utmost loyalty, and I never had anything but praise for his work, which, indeed, was invaluable throughout the campaign." And British military archives, made available for research in the 1970s, back up most of Lawrence's key claims.

But there has always been a romanticization of Lawrence and his achievements. For one thing, the public needed heroes. The death and carnage resulting from World War I, particularly the gruesome tales of trench warfare in Germany and France, were heartrending to European audiences. By contrast, the heroic, swashbuckling Arabian epics of Lawrence and Prince Feisal were welcome and refreshing.

The Lawrence of Arabia legend was born almost immediately after the war. Much of the credit for that goes to the American journalist Lowell Thomas. A war correspondent during the conflict, Thomas riveted audiences across Europe in 1919 and 1920 with his dramatic rendering of the exploits of T. E. Lawrence and General Allenby, complete with slide show and photos. The performance in London in September 1919 was delivered to an audience studded with Cabinet members and ambassadors at London's Covent Garden. "It was a rousing occasion; the Welsh Guards played background music, and an Irish tenor rendered the Muslim call to prayer. The lecture, which was repeated around the world over the next four years by Thomas, was seen and heard by over a million. Lurking in the darkened rear of the auditorium on several occasions was Lawrence himself, blushing to the roots of his hair, some thought with pleasure."

So Lawrence the myth was a rousing success. Lawrence the man is a bit more complicated. He was highly intelligent, no doubt, very creative, and it seems somewhat insecure and easily frustrated. He stood 5 feet 5 inches (165 cm) and weighed around 145 pounds (66 kg) soaking wet. But he was intensely focused and driven to succeed—partly as a result of his Oxford education. Part of his insecurity may have been due to his upbringing. He was one of five illegitimate sons of Sir Thomas Robert Chapman and Chapman's daughter's governess, Sarah Junner. Lawrence had a difficult childhood, and claims to have run away for several weeks as a teenager, serving as a boy soldier for a time with an artillery unit at Cornwall. There is no doubt, however, that he grew to be an upright, patriotic Englishman, dedicated to Victorian ideals of God and country.

Another part of the mystery surrounding Lawrence, perhaps part of the mystique, are the questions—accusations, really—about his sexuality. There is no evidence that he was homosexual. There is plenty of evidence, though, that he enjoyed being whipped. In fact, he routinely hired soldiers to whip him, a compulsion he picked up, he claimed, from his many beatings in childhood. By Lawrence's own account, he was briefly taken prisoner by the Turks early in the war, questioned, beaten, and then sodomized by guards before being released. His friends insist he was not homosexual, only that he had no interest in sex at all. Some point to his strict and literal interpretation of Victorian standards of morality, encouraging purity outside marriage, and discouraging carnal pleasures. But there is at least one arguably homoerotic passage in *The Seven Pillars of Wisdom*—the dedication to someone called S.A.:

I loved you, so I drew these tides of men into my hands
and wrote my will across the sky in stars
To earn you Freedom, the seven-pillared worthy house,
that your eyes might be shining for me
When we came.

Death seemed my servant on the road, till we were near
and saw you waiting:
When you smiled, and in sorrowful envy he outran me

and took you apart:
Into his quietness . . .

No one knows who S.A. is, and Lawrence never said. Some sources
propose that S.A. is Selim Ahmed, a young Arab boy who worked with
Lawrence at an archaeological dig before the war. More than one observer
has speculated as to the relationship between Lawrence and Prince Feisal.
Lawrence was clearly enchanted with the dashing prince, and wrote
admiringly of him. Ultimately, his sexuality is ambiguous, and, many
would no doubt say, irrelevant.

What is relevant, and much less in doubt, are his achievements in
the Middle East. At the outset of the war, the interests of the British
government and those of Arab nationalists, led by Sharif Hussein, were
aligned: They both wanted to wage war against the Turkish Ottoman
government. The Arab groups were striving for independence; Britain
sought to undermine Germany's ally in the region and to secure British-
held territories in the Arab world.

In October 1916, Lawrence was sent as the British liaison officer to
work with Arab nationalist forces. Together with Arab irregular troops,
commanded by Hussein's son, Feisal, he plotted an insurgency aimed
at tying down Ottoman troops and resources. His most important
contribution was in convincing Hussein and Feisal to coordinate their
actions with those of the British. What resulted were extended guerrilla
actions against the Ottomans that made it impossible to carry out their
war aims in support of Germany. For example, Lawrence persuaded the
Arabs not to make a frontal assault on the Ottoman stronghold in Medina,
but to allow the Turks to stockpile troops and weapons in the city garrison.
That left Arab forces free to attack the Turks' weak point, the Hejaz railway,
which supplied the garrison at Medina. Thus, the battlefield was widened,
which preoccupied more Turkish troops, hindered their movements, and
prevented their use in other battle theaters of the Middle East.

In July 1917, Lawrence led Arab forces in a surprise attack and capture
of the strategically important port city of Aqaba in Palestine. The port was
heavily defended, but the approach from the rear across the desert was

thought to be an unlikely invasion route, and was lightly defended. Due to Lawrence's experience with the geography of the area, and the ability of Feisal's irregular troops to move swiftly in desert terrain, they were able to catch the Aqaba garrison almost totally by surprise. Aqaba was the only Ottoman port on the Red Sea, and could have threatened General Allenby's expeditionary force preparing to advance into Palestine. Arab troops then attacked Ottoman positions in support of General Allenby's advance on Gaza; those British forces were able to take Jerusalem by Christmas 1917.

By 1918, the tide was turning decisively in favor of the British and the Arabs. More British forces were made available, as well as shipments of rifles, explosives, and machine guns. Lawrence and several other British officers led raids against Ottoman forces on the Hejaz railway, destroying Turkish trains and cargo, capturing supplies, and tying down thousands of Turkish troops. In the final weeks of the war, Lawrence played a role in the capture of Damascus, the final crushing blow against the Ottomans.

Lawrence and Feisal dreamed of establishing an independent Arab state with its capital at Damascus, and Feisal as king. But it was not to be. In the aftermath of the war, Britain and France divided up the Middle East among themselves, supporting friendly pro-Western governments: Such an arrangement had been discussed during negotiations under the Sykes-Picot Agreement in 1916. France gained control of Syria, and Britain maintained its influence over Palestine and Iraq.

After the war, Lawrence continued to call for an independent Arab state, serving in the British delegation at the Paris Peace Conference of 1919, in which he worked closely with Feisal. In the early 1920s, he served as an advisor to Winston Churchill, who had been appointed to the British colonial office in Iraq. Working with Churchill, Lawrence was instrumental in the accession of Feisal to the throne of Iraq, and he encouraged the foundation of the kingdom of Transjordan, now Jordan. It wasn't the independent Arab state he and others had long sought, but he knew it was likely the best that could be achieved at the time.

He also spent his postwar years writing and editing *The Seven Pillars of Wisdom*. But then he began to run from the limelight—wearied by years of war, then international politics. In late 1922, he resigned from the

colonial office and enlisted in the Royal Air Force under the assumed
name of John Hume Ross. He had wanted to avoid publicity and begin
work on other literature while undercover in the service. But he was soon
exposed and forced out of the RAF. He then joined the Royal Tank Corps
in 1923, this time as T. E. Shaw. But he was unhappy there, and petitioned
to join the RAF under his real name, finally being admitted in 1925 due
to the political influence of close friends.

He spent the late 1920s at various international postings in the RAF,
and continued to work on other books, including *The Mint*, which was a
critical look at recruiting and training practices in the RAF. In 1928, he
was required to return to England, due to false rumors about purported
espionage activities. He left the service in 1935 and set about starting a
private press to produce limited editions of his and other works. In May
of that year he was killed in a motorcycle accident—he had swerved to
avoid two youths on the road, crashed into a ditch, and suffered severe
head trauma. It was an untimely end to one of the great romantic figures
of the twentieth century.

The story of Wilhelm Wassmuss is altogether different. Though
Lawrence and Wassmuss shared a certain charisma and a flair for the
dramatic, British success in the region doomed Germany's ambitions there,
so Wassmuss's activities haven't been immortalized the way Lawrence's
have. And in contrast to Lawrence's unequivocal success, Wassmuss not
only failed in his strategic goals, but he accidentally handed the British and
the Americans an intelligence bonanza by losing a German codebook.

While Lawrence worked for British military intelligence, Wassmuss
was a diplomat, working in German consular offices in the Middle
East. Like Lawrence, he had spent considerable time in the region. He
had formed an attachment to the peoples of the Middle East and had
developed an intimate knowledge of their customs, history, and language.
And, like Lawrence, he would often don the flowing robes of a desert
tribesman as part of his cover.

The German government desperately wanted to end English
domination of India and Mesopotamia, and to blunt Russian influence
in the Middle East. The region was strategically important to British

foreign policy interests, but oil had also begun to flow from the Persian Gulf to Abadan, greatly increasing the value of the area. Wassmuss's grand plans included fomenting a holy war in Iran against the British and eventually supporting an uprising that would threaten British colonial India.

Before the war, Wassmuss had been based in Bushehr on the southwestern coast of Persia (Iran), where he had befriended tribal leaders who resented British interference in their arms-smuggling operations. In spring 1915, Wassmuss was sent to Shiraz in southern Iran as German consul. Wearing Persian garb and pretending to be a Muslim convert, he began to stir up local tribes in a campaign of violence and sabotage aimed at driving the British from the gulf, or at least diverting badly needed troops to contain the uprising. He made extravagant claims, such as that the German kaiser had also converted to Islam and had ordered his ministers and subjects to do likewise. He told them that the kaiser had even traveled to Mecca and had adopted the name Haji Wilhelm Mohammad. He even went as far as to tell them he had a secret wireless form of communication directly with the kaiser, and he would put on an elaborate show using a set of headphones and a steel antenna, producing sparks to simulate a secret conversation he had just held with Kaiser Wilhelm. If these fantastic claims were not enough, he also promised local tribesmen German financial support and political independence after the war.

Like Lawrence, his knowledge of the area was invaluable, and his plans showed early potential for success. However, in the town of Behbahan, a local chieftain he knew invited him and two of his German diplomatic colleagues to dinner and promptly arrested them. The British had been aware of Wassmuss's covert activities as early as 1914 when communications from German consular officials in Bushehr were captured, implicating Wassmuss in the anti-British resistance. British officials had offered a cash reward for Wassmuss's capture, and the Behbahan chief had planned to turn him in. He sent a messenger to inform the British—they came, but by the time they arrived in Behbahan, Wassmuss had managed to escape. How he escaped is not clear. According to one account, he told his guard that he was concerned about his sick horse, kept going to the stable to check on it throughout the night, and was eventually able to slip away undetected. In any case, he made a very costly mistake that provided a great boost to British intelligence. One of the items he left behind when he escaped was his copy of a German codebook. The codebook found its way to London and helped the British crack the German codes used in World War I, possibly shortening the war.

Nevertheless, during the following three years, Wassmuss was able to cause such widespread mayhem that he became known as the "German Lawrence." In November 1915, he led a coup in Shiraz, in Fars Province, together with pro-German officers of the newly created Gendarmerie, in the course of which the British consul and eleven other British subjects were apprehended. The women were later released, but the men were incarcerated in the fortress of Ahram, near the Persian Gulf, which belonged to a pro-German sheikh.

Wassmuss's triumph was short-lived, for his support came mostly from coastal tribes, which were too far from Shiraz to be of much help. In February 1916, the pro-British governor-general of Fars Province, who had fled to British-occupied Bushehr during Wassmuss's coup, set out for Shiraz with his British-supplied private army. Although he was killed in a hunting accident on the way, his son, who inherited the title, completed the journey, and, together with pro-British officers of the Gendarmerie and Persian troops, recaptured the provincial capital. A new, British-led Persian force, the South Persia Rifles, was then organized to prevent any further pro-German coups.

After that, Wassmuss focused most of his energies on forming new tribal alliances, such as with the Tangistanis, who viewed the formation of the South Persia Rifles as a British plot to further increase their power. In May 1918, a large Tangistani force attacked a detachment of the South Persia Rifles on the Bushehr-Shiraz road. As British troops rushed to the rescue, a major battle took place. Though Tangistani forces far outnumbered those of Great Britain, they were nonetheless decisively defeated. Wassmuss was running out of room in Persia.

As the war was winding down and his local support was dwindling, he fled to the Persian city of Qom, where he was finally captured by the British in 1919. After months of questioning, his use to the British government was exhausted and he was released in 1920, after which he made his way back to Berlin. But the postwar German government was in no position, either politically or financially, to honor pledges Wassmuss had made to Persian tribes during the war. He made a valiant effort to honor the personal commitment he had made to his Persian allies. Wassmuss returned to Bushehr in 1924, determined to rebuild relationships and to repay local tribesmen. He bought farmland and tried to launch an agricultural exchange, but it failed. He returned to Berlin in 1931, reportedly a broken man.

A Spymaster for the Twenty-First Century: Omar Suleiman of Egypt

On June 26, 1995, Egyptian President Hosni Mubarak was on his way from Addis Ababa International Airport to a meeting of the Organization of African Unity when his armor-plated limousine came under intense attack from rocket-propelled grenades, armor-piercing machine gun bullets, and explosives. A number of Mubarak's presidential bodyguards were killed or injured while riding in escort vehicles during the attack. President Mubarak survived because the man sitting next to him, General Omar Suleiman, the head of the Egyptian General Intelligence Service, had insisted that the president's specially designed, armored Mercedes be flown to the Ethiopian capital to ensure the president's safety.

A normal vehicle would have been totally destroyed in the deadly attack. Only the day before, General Suleiman had ordered the armored vehicle to be shipped to Addis Ababa, over the objections of President Mubarak's foreign policy advisors, who worried that it would offend the conference's Ethiopian hosts. The attack had come from eleven members of the militant Islamist group Gama'a al-Islamiya. The group was led by Shawqi al-Istanbuli, who happens to be the brother of Egyptian President Anwar Sadat's killer, Khalid al-Istanbuli.

Within a year of the attack, the general's intelligence network had rounded up hundreds of members of the militant group, had imprisoned most of them, and had tortured more than half of them for information. General Suleiman went to war inside Egypt against militant Islam.

By 1998, his Egyptian intelligence service had crippled virtually all of Egypt's main Islamic extremist groups. Those successes were the opening salvo of a campaign against Islamic extremism by a man who has become known as perhaps the most powerful intelligence chief in the world, and a power behind the throne in contemporary Egypt.

The general's insistence on maximum security for President Mubarak saved the leader's life, and Suleiman's success in rooting out militant Islam in Egypt cemented the bond between the two men. Mubarak began spending more and more time with his intelligence chief, according to journalists and other observers in Egypt. "He tells Mubarak everything that's happening," said one retired general. After decades in power, "the gerontocracy that surrounds the president tells him what they think he wants to hear. Suleiman tells Mubarak the way it is."

Omar Suleiman has become one of the most powerful men in the Middle East, and is a possible successor to President Mubarak, who is in his eighties. This is a pretty remarkable rise for a man who only became known to most Egyptians in 2000, seven years after he became the director of general intelligence. Suleiman's influence in Egypt and in international politics is not typical of most government intelligence chiefs. He holds a rank in the Egyptian Cabinet not held by an intelligence official since the reign of Gamal Abdel Nasser in the 1960s. While serving in a government in which the president and most of the senior officials are from the Delta region, Suleiman is from Qena in Upper Egypt—ironically a poverty-stricken stronghold for Islamic fundamentalism. In fact, it is the region that produced many of the extremists that Suleiman and Mubarak have been battling for over a decade.

In a 2003 profile of General Suleiman in the *Atlantic Monthly,* Mary Ann Weaver wrote that growing up in Qena, there were only two routes to upward mobility: become a soldier or a sheikh. Suleiman chose the military. He excelled as a soldier and as a leader, rising to national prominence through the armed services. The arc of his career in the military to a large degree has followed the arc of Egypt's political history. After attending Egypt's prestigious military academy, he was sent to the Soviet Union's Frunze Military Academy in the 1960s, just as Mubarak was, becoming an infantryman. He took part in the 1967 and 1973 Arab-Israeli wars; his role in these conflicts is not well known, or at least not well publicized. By the mid-1980s, he had received bachelor's and master's degrees in political science from Ain Shams University and Cairo University. He was then transferred to military intelligence, where he began his climb to the top of the security apparatus. When Egypt switched its strategic alliance from Moscow to Washington in the 1980s, Suleiman received training at the John F. Kennedy Special Warfare School at Fort Bragg, North Carolina. His relationship with the United States was reinforced during numerous political conflicts with Iraq and Iran, and also through the liberation of Kuwait from Iraqi control in 1991. He continues to have privileged contacts with U.S. intelligence and military officials, with whom he has been dealing for more than twenty-five years. He is considered a moderate in the West, but is seen as a fierce defender of Egyptian sovereignty and security inside Egypt and throughout the Middle East.

According to Noam Amit, an Israeli journalist, "at first glance, he looks like a classic spy—balding, chubby, of medium height, a person who draws no particular attention. On second glance, people who met him said, 'You notice his dark eyes and piercing gaze.' He does not speak much, but when he does, his voice is quiet and restrained and his words are thought out. 'He is an impressive man,' an official who met him said. 'He has what the Arabs call Hava—meaning dignity. He has presence.' He conducts himself in a presidential kind of way, demonstrating a sense of self-importance that is rare in the milieu of other senior position holders in the Arab world."

Weaver, in her *Atlantic Monthly* profile of the general, is reminded of Anwar Sadat: "He is tall and slim, with the kind of upper Egyptian, Nubian looks that Sadat had." All who have met him come away impressed with his demeanor and his air of resolve and self-confidence, according to Weaver.

As head of Egypt's general intelligence service (GIS), known as the Mukhabarat, the general's political and military portfolio is vast. The GIS combines the intelligence-gathering elements of the American CIA, the counterterrorism role of the FBI, the protection duties of the Secret Service, and the high-level diplomacy of the State Department. It also includes some functions unique to authoritarian regimes common in the region, such as monitoring Egypt's security apparatus for signs of internal coups. It is an elite institution, with a long reach inside the government as well as abroad. It also crosses over the military and civilian worlds; thus, the general holds a rank in the military and in President Mubarak's Cabinet.

Another thing that makes Suleiman's position in Egyptian government unique is his nearly seamless and relatively rapid crossover from secret spy chief to prominent public official. Traditionally, the very identity of the head of the GIS is kept secret. But in 2001 he began to take over key responsibilities from the Egyptian foreign ministry and his name and photo began to appear in the government-owned daily newspaper *Al-Ahram*. Since then, his influence in Egypt and in the Arab world has become one of the defining political realities of the Middle East. He has intervened in civil wars in Sudan, patched up a rift between Saudi Arabian King Abdullah and Libyan leader Muammar Qadaffi (especially difficult considering that Qadaffi tried to have Abdullah assassinated), and put pressure on Syria to stop meddling in Lebanon and to distance itself from Iran. But most important, Suleiman has mediated the Israeli-Palestinian conflict, which has become Egypt's most significant national security priority.

Quickly and quietly, he has become a central figure in what used to be called the "global war on terrorism." The Egyptians, led by Mubarak and Suleiman, share with the United States, Great Britain, and most other Western nations a common enemy: militant Islam. This does not make Suleiman a friend of Israel or, for that matter, pro-American. The most accurate description for Suleiman is pro-Egypt and pro–Hosni Mubarak. He sees the Egyptian state and modern Arab society as a whole endangered by what he regards as the dangerous fanaticism of the mullahs. One Israeli intelligence official emphasizes that Suleiman is "first and foremost an Egyptian patriot, and his primary task, perhaps his only one, is to defend the regime and protect the life of the president."

He is a devout Muslim, but despises the militant Islamic movement that seeks to destabilize governments throughout the region and funds campaigns of murder and terror. He is particularly sensitive to its role in Egypt because some of the leaders of radical international groups are, in fact, Egyptian (for example, Ayman al-Zawahiri, the lieutenant to Osama bin Laden). This is the worldview that spurred him to help the CIA and place at its disposal Egyptian interrogators to help question al-Qaeda detainees. For that, the CIA is grateful and has come to consider Egyptian intelligence services to be as valuable as those of Israel's Mossad.

Naturally, Suleiman's Egypt also shares with the West a marked dislike for the radical clerics who run contemporary Iran. Iran's role as a major state sponsor of terrorist organizations makes it an enemy of most Arab states in the region, which are the central target of Iran's terrorism links. Since the days of Anwar Sadat, Egypt has been a steady partner in the struggle against the fanatical mullahs.

Since the Hamas Party takeover of the Gaza governing authority in 2007, Suleiman has been a key mediator between Hamas and their domestic political rivals, Fatah. His efforts there are generally supported by the United States and by European Union members. He was responsible for the relative success of the temporary cease-fire agreement between Israel and Hamas in 2008. He is, arguably, the Middle East's most important troubleshooter.

With President Mubarak's advancing age, all eyes are on Suleiman as a potential successor. The only other major contender to succeed the president is his son Gamal Mubarak. Gamal is a close advisor to his father and is an official in the ruling National Democratic Party. But he has no official role in the government, and little direct political or diplomatic experience. He is a sentimental favorite among many in Egypt, and he's a favorite of some Egyptian newspapers. He is also considered a reformer, and for many traditional constituencies in Egypt he is seen as too Western.

There is also significant sentiment inside Egypt against a dynastic family succession of the type in Syria, in which Bashar al-Assad succeeded his father, Hafez al-Assad. Many worry that an inheritance-of-power scenario like that would usher in a period of great instability. Some analysts consider the prospect of such father-to-son nepotism humiliating for a country that has long claimed the mantle of Arab leadership.

On the other side of the spectrum, the opposition movement inside Egypt has emerged as a growing political presence. The opposition's leader, former International Atomic Energy Agency head Mohamed ElBaradei, has promised a vigorous challenge to the Mubarak government. Threatened by the continuation of a Mubarak dynasty on the one hand and rising opposition forces on the other, the military and state security elites that, many argue, run Egypt may close ranks behind Omar Suleiman. In Egypt's modern history, its leaders have come from the military. This puts Omar Suleiman, a modern-day Francis Walsingham, in position to be the next leader of Egypt (as of this writing). But whether or not he ascends to the top job, he has left an indelible mark on modern Egyptian history and Middle East politics.

CHAPTER 5

SILVER-TONGUED DEVILS

According to *Webster's Dictionary*, the term *silver-tongued devil* dates from the late sixteenth century, which was about halfway through the Renaissance and just on the cusp of the Enlightenment. Many of the courts of Europe of the time had been influenced by thinkers, poets, writers, talkers, and quite a few charlatans, which may explain the "devil" part.

Of course, in our modern age of politics, good communication is essential. Television and the Internet have transformed our expectations about leadership, imagery, and verbal expression. Good communicators who know how to touch people's emotions have a decided edge—think John F. Kennedy, Ronald Reagan, and Mikhail Gorbachev. But good communicators have always been able to influence people and events. Sometimes that influence has been through public speaking and other times it has come from behind the scenes in private meetings and conversations, or through letters, pamphlets, books, and newspapers, such as *The Federalist Papers*.

The figures in this chapter are known primarily for their communication skills and their persuasive abilities. They had an enormous capacity to influence those around them, and those chronicled here represent some of the most renowned speakers, writers, leaders, and political agitators in world history. And all of them affected the course of history in very profound ways.

The Righteous Pagan: Cicero

Marcus Tullius Cicero was the prototypical silver-tongued orator. His impassioned and eloquent speeches defending the Roman Republic, as well as his plethora of writings on government, life, and society, are the stuff of legend. There was a time when his work was required reading for high school and college students from New York and Philadelphia to London, Paris, and Berlin. One could not gain a proper understanding of Western civilization and philosophy without regarding the life and times of the celebrated Roman statesman and writer. Cicero's commitment to the ideals of a just society and a republican form of government were particularly important to those who fomented the American and French revolutions in the eighteenth century and to those Britons who spearheaded progressive change in the nineteenth century.

When the Bostonian John Adams spoke out against British colonial tyranny in the 1770s, he may even have imagined himself as Cicero, railing against dictatorship and the conspiracy of power, bringing the Roman Senate to its feet in thunderous applause. And England's William Wilberforce was a great student of the classics, especially Virgil and Cicero, which no doubt served him well when he rose in Parliament in the early 1800s to urge the abolition of slavery.

The fast-moving political and social torrents of the twentieth century seemed to push Cicero and other classics to the rear somewhat, in favor of more contemporary and pragmatic agitators—John Locke, Karl Marx, Max Weber, and Aleksandr Solzhenitsyn. But Cicero's pleas for republican government and a society that seeks to build people up, not tear them down, continue to speak to generations across the centuries. Part of the reason Cicero has stood the test of time is that, compared to most of the ancients, we know quite a bit about him. He left a very long paper trail of commentaries, speeches, poems, and private letters, many of which were circulated so widely that they were not lost to history, but survived in one form or another.

Cicero is generally regarded as one of the great minds of the ancient world. Deeply influenced by Greek culture, he was by temperament still firmly wedded to Roman tradition. A philosopher, linguist, poet, statesman, and, of course, a great orator, Cicero was one of the ancients profiled in Plutarch's famous work *Parallel Lives*. He was declared a "righteous pagan" by the early Catholic Church, and therefore many of his works were deemed worthy of preservation and study. Unluckily for him, his life happened to coincide with the last golden age of the Roman Republic before it was dismantled and became an empire.

Like many of the figures profiled in this book, Cicero was not from a noble family; he wasn't even a native Roman. He held Roman citizenship and was an active participant in Roman society, culture, and politics, but his family roots were from outside Rome—specifically the Volscian tribe, a fledgling city-state on the Tiber River. This fact produced a certain level of insecurity in Cicero that marked his public career. He wasn't a Roman blue blood. He was a political outsider, which meant that he would not have an easy path, as did many Roman statesmen, who could count on family and social connections for advancement. Cicero had to earn his own way.

Therefore, he always felt a need to prove himself to the aristocratic class—the conservative, land-owning families, the patricians. Politically, these elder statesmen were known as optimates, meaning "best people." The optimates controlled most official government posts and were very much associated with republican government, holding sway over the Senate and resisting any changes that would threaten this arrangement. Opposing the optimates during this time were the populares—adherents of a political movement taking up the cause of "the people." This group, which included Julius Caesar, advocated reforms that would loosen the grip of the Senate on Roman policy making.

As Cicero entered public life, he wanted to be tied to neither side politically, but sought to represent the interests of all of Rome. But like many political leaders through history, he would find this to be impossible. He found himself unwillingly at the heart of a hundred-year civil war that pitted the traditional oligarchy of the Senate, the optimates, against a new breed of fiery class-war demagogues, the populares.

Cicero made his reputation as a lawyer, where his skills for oratory were on full display. As a "new man," not of noble or politically connected origin, he was forced to take cases that many other lawyers would not have accepted; but his talent for public speaking won many of those "unwinnable" cases. He began to build a reputation as a skillful and persuasive mind, and was marked by some as a person with a future in politics. This was exactly what he wanted—from a young age he aspired to play a role in the life of the republic and was fully determined to craft a successful political career.

His first public office was as one of twenty annual quaestors, a training post for administrators. A quaestor had no political or military authority, but Cicero campaigned vigorously for the post because it offered him an entry point into politics and the prospect of higher office. As a quaestor in western Sicily in 75 BC, he served with distinction. He proved to be a competent administrator and one who could be trusted by the local population. He also continued to build a reputation as a talented lawyer and orator, taking many cases while in Sicily and building his client list. He also began to build a political following. He returned to Rome at the end of his term in 74 BC feeling very good about his prospects.

The next rung up the political ladder was election as one of eight praetors, who acted as judges in the courts or administered law in the provinces. Only after serving as a praetor could one become eligible to serve as a consul, which was the ultimate prize. As soon as he was eligible, at the age of forty, Cicero was elected praetor, taking office in 66 BC As a praetor, he tried to manage a difficult balancing act, weighing the interests of the optimates against the growing appeal of the reform crusade of the populares.

As soon as his term as praetor was up, he began planning his campaign for the consulship. This process was somewhat akin to election campaigns in today's industrialized world; in fact, Cicero's brother Quintus wrote a "Short Guide to Electioneering" (*Commentariolum Petitionus*), in which he set out a comprehensive campaign strategy. There were two consuls elected by the people (or, at least, by the male citizens of Rome) who had the responsibility of administering the government of Rome. The two consuls alternated power each month, and were advised by the Senate. But, in reality, the consuls were often led around by the nose by the Senate, which is one of the things the populares wanted to change. Interestingly, in his campaign for consul, Cicero, in modern terminology, "went negative." As modern political candidates normally do, he played to his strength, which was public speaking. He delivered ferocious speeches against two of his main opponents for consul, Catiline and Antonius. Catiline turned out to be one of the great antagonists of Cicero's political years, a politician determined to overthrow the existing political order and an early mentor of Julius Caesar. Cicero asked: "Can any man be a friend of someone who has murdered so many citizens? He has fouled himself in all manner of vice and crime. He is soaked in the blood of those he has imperiously slaughtered. He has robbed the provincials. He has violated the laws and the courts." Certainly, modern-day political strategists would have been impressed with his mudslinging, all the more so because it worked. Cicero easily won election to one of the two consulships, taking office in 63 BC.

The other consul position was won by the feeble Antonius, whom Cicero bought off. Not interested in the usual governorship that followed service as a consul, Cicero agreed to give up the rich province he had been allocated, Macedonia, and pass it to Antonius. This would allow Antonius to further enrich himself by controlling access to land and capital. In return, Antonius agreed to give Cicero a free hand during their consulship and agreed to withdraw his support of the troublemaking Catiline. Thus Cicero was, in effect, the sole consul.

Sure enough, within the year Catiline had organized a conspiracy to seize control of the Roman government in a coup, which involved assassinating Cicero and a number of leading senators. This was Cicero's moment. He rallied the republic to stand fast against the threat. In addressing the Senate, Cicero argued in favor of allowing the imposition of a special decree known as the Final Act. This would allow Cicero to declare a state of emergency, giving the government superlegal authority to act to protect the state. In a thundering address to the senate, Cicero proclaimed:

> No king remains, no tribe, no nation who can cause you alarm. No external or foreign threat can infiltrate our Republic. If you wish Rome to live forever and our empire to be without end, if you wish that our glory never fade, we must be on our guard against our own passions, against men of violence, against the enemy within, against domestic plots. But against these evils your forefathers left you a great protection [in the Final Act]. Cherish this pronouncement.

Fortunately for Cicero, and for the Senate, Catiline had fewer allies in Rome than he thought. His secret plans were divulged to Cicero, who confronted him in the Senate, threatening him with exile. The two engaged in a historic argument in front of the Senate, Catiline insulting Cicero as an "immigrant." Knowing his political life was over, Catiline then fled to join the conspirators in the field, who had been building an attack force. But many of the soldiers who had been recruited by the conspiracy slipped away as political support in Rome dried up. The remaining forces, including Catiline himself, who died fighting to the last, were crushed by a Roman garrison.

In the meantime, a debate raged in the Senate over the fate of Catiline's fellow conspirators, who had been rounded up and were being held in various locations around the city. As Roman citizens, they had the right to a trial; but the Senate had voted to invoke the Final Act, which meant in theory that their rights could be suspended; they could be executed immediately as traitors. This was controversial, and created a dramatic rift among the optimates and the populares. Cicero proceeded with the execution orders, but with the knowledge that under Roman law, even a consul could later be held accountable for actions that violated the rights of citizens.

Cicero had stood fast against challenges to the Roman government and to the authority of the Senate. He had decisively put down a plot by a leading populare, albeit a shrill and reckless one. He was victorious, but his victory came at a price. For one, he was now seen as firmly on the side of the optimates, and therefore had lost his political capital with the populares, and with leaders like Julius Caesar. And he had executed Roman citizens, an act for which he would later be made to pay. For the moment, though, he was the hero.

Indeed, he should have remembered the traditional message whispered in the ear of Rome's conquering heroes by slaves riding in their chariot: "Remember, you are human." The next few years would see his political and personal fortunes dramatically reversed. After his term as consul was over, his political enemies held sway over Roman politics. He had refused the offer of Julius Caesar, elected consul in 60 BC, to join him, along with the famous general Pompey and Crassus (a leading populare), in a joint government that would later be called the First Triumvirate.

This made him vulnerable. He did not realize how vulnerable until too late. His criticisms of the Triumvirate and their reform policies produced in Caesar a willingness to allow Cicero's enemies to act against him. A law was passed making it a crime to execute Roman citizens without a trial: This was aimed straight at Cicero for his execution of the Catiline conspirators. Before action could be taken against him, Cicero fled the city and remained in exile for the better part of a year until the crisis had passed.

Upon his return, he was welcomed by friends and his optimate allies, but his political influence was severely diminished. He spent much of the next decade writing his memoirs, essays on political governance, and poetry and philosophy. Still an influential senator, he also kept his eye on politics. The Triumvirate collapsed with the death of Crassus during battle in Parthia, and the vicious struggle for power between Caesar and Pompey. When Caesar defeated Pompey in 48 BC and became the sole leader, he was open to a reconciliation of sorts with Cicero. Though the two had been political opponents, they were both in a sense moderates—Caesar knew he could accomplish more working with friendly senators, and Cicero (naively, it seems) held out hope that Caesar would be open to restoring some elements of the old republic. But the next several years saw very little progress made in repairing relations between optimates and populares. In fact, many optimates grew ever more suspicious of Caesar, and scornful of his pursuit of power.

When Caesar was stabbed to death in full view of the Senate on March 15, 44, no one was more shocked than Cicero. He had not been involved in the plot. But when Marcus Brutus held up his bloody dagger and shouted Cicero's name as he hailed the return of freedom to Rome, Cicero was thrust front and center once again. But unlike his previous achievements, this wasn't planned—he was reacting to events. And as they often do, events began to spin desperately out of control.

Initially, Cicero enjoyed widespread support in Rome. But he had no army, only other politicians from the Senate. Meanwhile, Caesar's killers (Brutus and Cassius) faced off against Caesar's heirs (Mark Antony and Octavian) on the battlefield. Cicero despised the power-hungry Antony, and admired but distrusted Octavian, Caesar's ambitious eighteen-year-old adopted son. Cicero railed against Antony from the Senate, declaring him an enemy of the state. Cicero's rhetorical flourishes were impressive and warmly received in the Senate, but did not change the facts on the ground. He tried to play Octavian off against Antony, but ultimately to no avail. When the pro-Republican forces were defeated in battle and Brutus committed suicide, Octavian joined forces with Antony and formed the Second Triumvirate (along with one of Caesar's generals, named Lepidus).

Cicero was finished. This time there would be no exile—there was nowhere to go. Antony exacted the ultimate revenge. For, despite all of Cicero's oratorical brilliance, military force—not to mention the force of outsize personalities warped by ambition—had brought five hundred years of Roman democracy to an end. The new dictatorship immediately declared hundreds of senators to be public enemies and put bounties on their heads. Not surprisingly, one of them was Cicero himself. Cicero went into hiding. He was still very popular with many Romans, many of whom refused to report that they had seen him. But a freed slave of his brother Quintus tipped off a centurion that Cicero was heading to the seaside, planning to leave on a ship destined for Macedonia. Assassins caught up to him on a wooded trail near the shore. Cicero's last words were reported to be: "There is nothing proper about what you are doing, soldier, but do try to kill me properly." He then lowered his head to his executioner and breathed his last.

Cicero is remembered as an important figure in literature and philosophy, as well as for his political activities. His skill as an orator, rhetorician, and poet accounts for his lasting influence on philosophy and literature. His dedication to the study of philosophy has been of enduring importance for succeeding generations. But it is his love of liberty that is his most important legacy. His commitment to a republican system of leadership has inspired millions and influenced the rise of democratic political movements the world over.

Empress of the East: Theodora of Byzantium

Five centuries later, after the Roman Empire had split into east and west, the Eastern Roman Empire (Byzantium) produced another silver-tongued power broker—Theodora, one of the most powerful and influential women in world history. Theodora had remarkable influence on the Emperor Justinian, and his reign was stamped with her achievements as much as his. She was even more of an outsider than Cicero—at least Cicero started life with Roman citizenship and a relatively well-off family. But Theodora rose to unimaginable heights during her brief life (she died at forty-eight, likely from cancer). Hers is one of the most remarkable rags to riches stories ever told, having risen from poverty and prostitution to empress of the Eastern Roman Empire.

Unlike Cicero, whose life and achievements are very well documented, we know much less about Theodora. One of the primary sources about her life, the *Anekdota,* is the work of the historian Procopius of Caesarea. The *Anekdota,* or Secret History, has been widely read and quoted because Edward Gibbon, in his classic eighteenth-century work *The Decline and Fall of the Roman Empire,* used it as his exclusive source for information on Theodora. Fortunately for history, most of the facts about Theodora's life are not in dispute. Chroniclers of the period generally agree that she had been a dancer and a prostitute and had committed many lurid acts of depravity in her youth. But most historic sources on her life also indicate a turnaround after she converted to Christianity, albeit a heretical form of Christianity called Monophysitism. Taken together, the historical accounts of her life—the famous but less-than-flattering *Secret History of Procopius,* along with that of other historians, notably John of Ephesus— tell an amazing tale of a young girl born into poverty, forced into dancing and prostitution, who, through her travels, gets religion, meets the crown prince, falls deeply in love, becomes empress of the Byzantium Empire, and makes an indelible mark on world history. Cleopatra had nothing on this girl.

The question is this: How did a commoner with a lurid past persuade Justinian, nephew of the Emperor Justin, to court and marry her? It is a remarkable turnaround, but considering all her later achievements, it is consistent with her apparent ability to influence those around her. Theodora's beauty is well documented, and apparently figured prominently in her persuasive abilities. There is some evidence to suggest that she may have met the prince Justinian through political intrigue. She had befriended a dancer named Macedonia, who according to several sources was an informant working for Justinian. It is possible that Macedonia introduced Theodora to Justinian, very likely as a courier of information.

Whatever the exact circumstances of their meeting, Justinian was quite taken with her, and the two of them developed a very strong bond. He had to persuade his uncle, Justin, to change imperial law that at the time forbade a man of senatorial rank from marrying a courtesan. After the death of Emperor Justin's wife, who had strongly objected to Theodora, Justin acquiesced to Justinian's requests and changed the law, allowing truly penitent actresses and courtesans to enter into proper society.

Soon thereafter, the elderly Justin died, and Justinian and Theodora ascended to the throne. Theodora wasn't merely the wife of the emperor, she was the co-leader of the empire. He not only loved her as a wife, but also respected her political judgment. One Byzantine official, Joannes Laurentius Lydus, wrote that Theodora was "superior in intelligence to any man." Justinian himself said that he consulted her on many acts of state, including reforms meant to end public corruption.

Gibbon wrote that Justinian seated her on the throne as an equal and independent colleague in the sovereignty of the empire, and an oath of allegiance was imposed on the governors of the provinces in the joint names of Justinian and Theodora.

It is clear that Theodora greatly influenced the policy direction of the Byzantine Empire under the rule of Justinian, including an end to the repression of Monophysites (the Christian sect she had converted to) and reforms aimed at protecting the status of women.

Theodora was a rock of strength that helped hold the empire together in times of turmoil. During the Nika Revolt, it was Theodora who rallied the empire to stand fast and defend Constantinople. Political factions often clashed at public events, particularly the popular chariot races. Anyone who has been to an English soccer match can testify that large crowds of sports fans can quickly get out of control and cause security problems. During a chariot race in the famous Hippodrome in 532, political demonstrations led to large-scale rioting, which led to a full-scale revolt against imperial rule. Rioters burned buildings, assassinated public officials, and proclaimed a new emperor, Hypatius, the nephew of the former emperor Anastasius.

The resulting chaos led some officials to recommend fleeing the city. In the panicky debate that ensued at the palace, Theodora rose to speak. She said others might flee, but that she would not: "If flight were the only means of safety, yet I should disdain to fly. Death is the condition of our birth; but they who have reigned should never survive the loss of dignity and dominion." She made a dramatic case for staying and fighting, declaring, "If you resolve, O Caesar! to fly, you have treasures; behold the sea, you have ships; but tremble lest the desire of life should expose you to wretched exile and ignominious death. For my own part, I adhere to the maxim of antiquity, that the throne is a glorious sepulchre." She would rather die as a ruler than flee as nothing. Her speech steeled the crowd, and Justinian ordered his troops to attack the rioters. In the ensuing battle, tens of thousands died (over thirty thousand rioters were killed), but the imperial forces were victorious.

Theodora showed her Machiavellian side when she insisted that
Hypatius, whom the rioters had named the new emperor, and his brother
Pompeius be executed. Many had called for mercy, and Justinian was
inclined to spare them. But Theodora convinced him that if the two
of them lived, it would make Justinian look weak, and it would invite
additional rebellions in the future. To Theodora, mercy in this case was
not a viable option because the security of the regime was in question. This
is consistent with the philosophy Machiavelli would set down in *The Prince*
a thousand years later, particularly the story of Agothocles the Sicilian.

Theodora is known for efforts to protect the weak and the poor.
She is associated with Justinian's great building program, which built
or rebuilt housing for the poor, hospices, roads, bridges, aqueducts, and
at least twenty-five churches. Notable among these is the world-famous
Hagia Sophia, considered the epitome of Byzantine architecture and one
of the true wonders of the ancient world.

Her influence on legal reforms involving women is one of her greatest
legacies. During Justinian's reign, numerous brothels were shut down
and prostitutes were housed in convents. Until 528, it was legal to rape
slaves and lower-class women. Justinian and Theodora's legal reforms
made rape a capital crime. Changes in the law also made it illegal to force
any woman onto the theatrical stage (where Theodora spent much of
her childhood and adolescence) without her consent. Thus, the status of
women in the empire underwent a dramatic change due to Theodora's
influence. Justinian ensured that these changes continued even after her
death; for example, putting an end to the practice of imprisoning women
on charges of carrying an outstanding debt.

Under the reign of Justinian, Theodora worked to end the
persecution of minority churches, including her own brethren, the
Monophysites. The official Orthodox Church considered them to be
heretics and promoted their persecution and sometimes their slaughter.
Overcoming Justinian's early opposition, she persuaded him to establish
places of refuge for Monophysites throughout the empire; she advocated
their views on religion openly and publicly. For this she was condemned
by many Orthodox church leaders.

Theodora was later made a saint in the Orthodox Church. Her influence on the emperor Justinian led to historic advances in human rights and social justice in the Byzantine Empire. And her powers of persuasion and her communication ability saved Justinian's crown from the violence of the mob. She is one of the great female leaders of world history, remembered for her efforts to protect religious minorities, provide housing and services for the poor, and improve the status of women.

Citizen Talleyrand: Charles Maurice de Talleyrand-Perigord

Talleyrand, one of the most famous diplomats in history, is the classic image of the charming, sophisticated smooth talker. He was certainly a shameless flatterer, and true to his aristocratic heritage, a gentleman of arresting grace, wit, and style. But he was mostly a survivor—and often a liar. Of course, in order to survive in french politics through the regimes of Louis XVI, the French Revolution, Napoleon Bonaparte, Louis XVIII, Charles X, and Louis-Philippe, one had better be prepared to fib a little. It is astounding that one man not only survived politically through one of the most tumultuous periods in European history, but that he so thoroughly left his mark on that period.

Talleyrand has been described variously as a "womanizer," a "rogue," a "world-class bribe-taker," and even a "traitor." How interesting, then, that he began his career in the service of the church. Like his French predecessor nearly two hundred years before, Cardinal Richelieu, Talleyrand first became a priest and then a bishop. But unlike Richelieu, he had neither the faith nor the patience to serve as a man of God. Talleyrand was from an ancient aristocratic French family, and his natural path to prominence would have been the military. That path had been blocked because he was born with a deformed right foot. His family, encouraged by his tutors, steered him toward the church, believing it might offer him better opportunities.

His family was correct. The church did offer him opportunities, and the fact that his uncle was the archbishop of Reims certainly didn't hurt. He was ordained as a priest in 1779 and the next year became the Catholic Church representative to the French crown, the agent-general of the clergy. Then in 1789, due to the influence of his family and to his own intrinsic political talents, he was appointed bishop of Autun.

Much of Talleyrand's notoriety is due to his outlandishness. According to biographer Robin Harris, it was as a Catholic priest that Talleyrand discovered the joys of sex, boasting at his seminary about his conquests. But it is the contradictions in his life—some might call it brazen, in-your-face hypocrisy—that make him such a colorful historic figure.

What he seems to have been very good at is seeing which way the political winds were blowing, and then getting on the right side; in fact, he made an art of it, and it was key to his survival through so many twists and turns of the French state. He swore allegiance to King Louis XVI and reassured the king of his zeal for the royal cause, yet only months later helped draft the revolution's proclamation of a republic, the Declaration of the Rights of Man. He was sworn to defend the privileges of the church, yet at the onset of the French Revolution, and to the astonishment of his fellow bishops, he participated in the nationalization of the clergy and proposed the national confiscation of church property.

The adoption of this Civil Constitution of the Clergy, without papal approval, completely reorganized the French church on a democratic basis. As the first bishop to take the oath of loyalty to this constitution, Talleyrand also consecrated the first bishops elected according to the new procedure. The resulting excommunication by the pope did not distress him, for he was already planning to leave the church. It no longer offered sufficient scope for his ambition, and, since he had been deprived of his property under the law expropriating church assets, the church could no longer satisfy his monetary needs. Elected administrator of the government of Paris in January 1791, he resigned as bishop of Autun. It was said that after officiating at a Mass celebrating the first anniversary of the fall of the Bastille, he later celebrated at not one, but two casinos in Paris.

Talleyrand was keenly interested in fashion, and he was a great conversationalist, gourmet, and wine connoisseur. For several years during his service to Napoleon, he owned Château Haut-Brion in the Bordeaux region of France, where he employed the renowned chef Antonin Careme, one of the first celebrity chefs of Europe, known as the "chef of kings and king of chefs." Talleyrand's Paris residence on the world-famous Place de la Concorde was bought by the Rothschild family in 1838 and is now owned by the U.S. Embassy.

As one biographer put it, Talleyrand was never happier than when he felt rich. He had a pretty serious gambling habit, and he frequently ran up heavy debts through gaming-table losses. Through it all, living the life of the rich was his guiding principle. "Never be a poor devil," he told a civil servant friend. "I have always been rich."

He had a rare rapport with women—he counted many of the most intelligent, attractive, and influential of them among his friends or lovers. Many seemed to surrender to his allure despite their better judgment. A French noblewoman recalled her response to his compelling charms: "One couldn't help regretting that there were so many reasons for not thinking well of him, and after listening to him for an hour one was compelled to banish the recollection of everything one had heard against him." It seems that, to many in French society, he was as seductive as he was obviously dangerous.

Courting aristocratic women was a key element in his political survival, both because of their political and social influence and because of their ability to cross borders unhindered. One of his lovers, Germaine de Staël, was in a position to assist him greatly, for example, by lobbying French authorities to allow Talleyrand to return during the waning days of the revolutionary government, and then to have him made its foreign minister. And he also grew close to Catherine Worlée, born in India and married there to a British government official, George Grand. The marriage was short-lived. She had traveled much of the world before settling in Paris and developed a reputation as a notorious courtesan in the 1780s. She became Talleyrand's mistress in the late 1790s, and he was eventually pressured by Napoleon to marry her, which he did in order to preserve his political career.

He had seen the coming power of revolutionary forces in 1789 and thus joined the revolution. "I placed myself at the disposal of events," he later wrote. He knew that in terms of power, the monarchy and the clergy were finished. But he favored a constitutional monarchy like England's, not a republic, and certainly not the radical policies espoused by many in the new French National Assembly.

Part of an eight-member committee charged with writing the new constitution, Talleyrand tried to steer a moderate course. He did what he could to encourage democratic reform without completely abandoning the monarchy, and to base a government system on the rights of citizens. The new constitution's prologue, The Declaration of the Rights of Man and of the Citizen, had more than a whiff of American influence. His efforts to balance government power and citizen power were well received by most, and for his efforts he was named the president of the Assembly in 1790.

One serious challenge to revolutionary France was the opposition of the other European monarchs, particularly England. Talleyrand believed that establishing and maintaining good relations with England were essential for France's survival. Of particular concern was the possibility of England joining Austria and Prussia in a coalition against France. His reputation as a clever negotiator was put to the test when, at the close of 1791, Talleyrand was sent by the foreign ministry to London to persuade England to remain neutral.

Though his English wasn't perfect, his skills at flattery and persuasion were good enough to secure a declaration of neutrality from the British government in May 1792. But the worst excesses of the French Revolution—street violence and public executions—were being widely condemned across Europe, thereby making his diplomatic efforts fruitless. Indeed, the revolution was spinning out of control in Paris, and Talleyrand felt the political ground shifting under his feet. He needed to leave France, at least until things cooled down. He managed to secure a passport to return to England on official diplomatic business. But in his absence he had become an enemy of the revolution for his close ties to the monarchy; by then Louis XVI had been executed.

For a time, he became, literally, a man without a country. He could not return to France, and then in 1794 he was kicked out of England. War between France and England had become inevitable, and representatives of the old French regime who had fled to England, the émigrés, had demanded Talleyrand's expulsion from England. So Talleyrand went to—where else?—America. He remained there for two years, engaging in profitable financial speculations that enabled him to rebuild his fortune. While there, he became good friends with a number of American government officials, some of whom had been revolutionary leaders themselves, such as Alexander Hamilton. Talleyrand displayed a portrait of Hamilton over his mantel for years after he was back in France. He stayed in the United States until the worst days of Robespierre and the Terror had passed, and some semblance of stable governance had returned to France with the establishment of the Directory. He returned to Paris in 1796 with the assistance of friends, notably Madame de Staël.

Of course, one of the biggest changes in France at the close of the eighteenth century was the rise of Napoleon Bonaparte. As with the revolution in 1789, Talleyrand saw the winds of change coming and climbed onboard. Made foreign minister of the Directory in 1797, again with the help of Madame de Staël, Talleyrand increasingly tied himself to Napoleon's rising star.

Though he tried to evade responsibility for it, Talleyrand encouraged the attempted colonization of Egypt, and suffered politically when that mission failed. His role in the notorious XYZ Affair—when Talleyrand demanded cash from the Americans in return for altering French foreign policy in their favor—helped undermine the credibility of French government under the Directory, and led to his resignation in 1799. But by then, Napoleon's plans for a coup were well under way, supported, of course, by Talleyrand himself. After Napoleon seized power, he made Talleyrand his foreign minister.

Talleyrand and Napoleon shared a mutual admiration. Though not Louis XVI, Napoleon represented strength and grandeur, the flexed muscle of France. And Napoleon was well aware of Talleyrand's aristocratic background and his talents as a diplomat; he believed he could make use of a man so distinguished in international politics. But Talleyrand, as always, sought a moderate, middle course in making foreign policy; in fact, that is one reason he had been made foreign minister by the Directory in the first place—to restrain Napoleon's "Alexander the Great" tendencies. This would cause differences between the two, and an eventual split.

Talleyrand helped to bring about the Concordat of 1801 with the Vatican, which restored the Catholic Church as the majority church in France and returned much of its civil status. Shortly afterwards, the ban of excommunication against him was lifted. Then in 1803 he was appointed to the lucrative position of grand chamberlain under Napoleon, now the emperor, and in 1806 he was named prince of Benevento.

He was opposed to Napoleon's wars against Austria, Prussia, and Russia in 1805 and 1806, and regretted the draconian peace terms imposed on those countries afterwards. They were now, in his view, humiliated states that could reasonably be expected to oppose Napoleonic France in the future. Napoleon tended more and more to ignore Talleyrand's cautious advice, and the split between the two widened as he tried unsuccessfully to restrain Napoleon's ambitions. Napoleon's moves to annex Spain triggered Talleyrand's resignation in 1807, although he remained in the Imperial Council and continued as grand chamberlain until early 1809. Ironically, Talleyrand was assigned the distasteful duty of keeping the three Spanish princes seized at Bayonne captive in his château.

As Napoleon's excesses started to wear thin and his hold on France started to waver, Talleyrand began to look past the current regime and to his own political future. Relations between the two men continued to deteriorate, as their views on the future landscape of Europe diverged, and Talleyrand was no longer close to Napoleon. For one thing, Talleyrand had suffered financially by the prohibition on trade between England and continental Europe, mandated by Napoleon. This economic blockade had led to the collapse of certain banks in Belgium and Austria to which Talleyrand had entrusted his investments.

Frustrated with Napoleon and convinced of the necessity of a strong Austria to maintain European stability, Talleyrand switched horses once again. He began secretly working with Russia, England, and Austria to destabilize Napoleon. This began in 1808, when he accompanied

Napoleon to the Congress of Erfurt. Talleyrand met secretly with Tsar Alexander of Russia, giving him information on Napoleon's plans and advising him not to make an alliance with France. He also managed to persuade the tsar to oppose Napoleon's designs on Austria. Napoleon surely would have had him killed had he known Talleyrand had become a foreign agent. During the Franco-Austrian War, Talleyrand was receiving thousands of francs from Austria in return for details of French troop movements. No doubt, in his mind, Talleyrand was not a traitor to France, but a traitor to Napoleon.

Napoleon's disastrous attack on Russia in 1812 was the beginning of the end for him and gave Talleyrand yet another opening to remain a political force. After the French army's agonizing retreat from Moscow, Talleyrand had reopened a dialogue with the Bourbons. When the victorious allies entered Paris in 1814 after Napoleon's fall, Talleyrand persuaded them to restore the Bourbon monarchy in the person of Louis XVIII, who in return made him foreign minister. Talleyrand, the master diplomat, was back at work. He negotiated the first Treaty of Paris in May 1814, by which France, despite its defeat, was granted a return to the French borders of 1792. He then represented France at the Congress of Vienna of 1814 and 1815, where he scored his greatest diplomatic triumphs. Winning the European powers to his principle of "legitimacy"—namely, the restoration of Europe to its prerevolutionary status—and shrewdly exploiting the dissension among the allies, he succeeded in taking part in the negotiations on equal terms with the principal victorious powers.

In July 1815, Louis XVIII named him president of the Council, essentially the head of the government. But Napoleon's brief return to power, and his subsequent defeat at Waterloo, led to a much less lenient Second Treaty of Paris late in 1815. Talleyrand was not able to hold the support of the Bourbons through the turmoil, and was forced out of office. He had burned too many bridges and had switched sides too often for many in power to trust him. For most of the next fifteen years, he was restricted to the role of elder statesman, though he did continue to receive an income from the government.

After the revolution of 1830, the incoming regime of Louis-Philippe, whom he had helped bring to power, offered him the portfolio of foreign affairs, but Talleyrand preferred to serve as ambassador to London. He served in this role from 1830 to 1834, and partially regained his old image as a master deal maker. He worked to improve relations between England and France, and played an important role in negotiations that eventually led to an independent Belgium in the late 1830s.

He died several years after his final service to Louis-Philippe, in May 1838 at the age of eighty-four. He very likely saw himself as one of France's saviors—he had saved France from the most radical of revolutionaries, from Napoleon, and from serfdom at the Congress of Vienna. But what he really came to be known for was the art form of political survival—of artful persuasion, and emerging through conflict on the winning side. He told one official during a private conversation: "They think that I am immoral and Machiavellian, yet I am simply impassive and disdainful. I have never given perverse advice to a government or a prince, but I do not go down with them. After shipwrecks, you need pilots to rescue the shipwrecked. I stay calm and get them to port somewhere. No matter which port, as long as it offers shelter."

The Ideologue: Leon Trotsky

In George Orwell's classic 1945 book *Animal Farm,* the character Snowball is a charismatic, fervent ideologue who is a true believer in Animalism—the theory developed by animal thinkers that the animals, not the humans, should be running the farm. Snowball throws himself heart and soul into taking over the farm and spreading the ideas of Animalism. However, his idealism leads to his downfall. Relying on the power of his ideas and his inspirational speaking skills, he is shoved aside by brute force in an authoritarian conspiracy led by a character named Napoleon.

Considering Orwell's history with Trotskyism and the Spanish Civil War, as well as his stated admiration for socialism and his distaste for totalitarianism, Snowball is quite obviously meant to be Leon Trotsky and Napoleon is clearly Joseph Stalin. But Orwell seemed to be of two minds about Trotsky. Although he admired Trotsky's commitment to socialism, he was wary of his judgment. For example, in the book Orwell depicts Snowball in a mostly appealing light (most definitely preferable to Napoleon), but he also introduces some moral flaws. Snowball accepts without question the superiority of the pigs over the rest of the animals. And it is easy to see that his passionate, single-minded enthusiasm for grand projects and grand rhetoric might have erupted into full-blown megalomaniacal despotism had he not been chased from the farm. In the end, Orwell's preference for Snowball might simply have been a matter of choosing the lesser of two evils.

Yet Leon Trotsky was an inspirational figure, and his talent for motivation and public speaking was a tool used to great effect by Vladimir Lenin and the Bolshevik revolutionaries to build support for their movement and to help wrest control of Russia away from their opponents.

Though he certainly did not favor republican government, Trotsky did have some things in common with Cicero. They were both spellbinding speakers with a strong interest in political theory. In addition, they were both assassinated by political opponents. But politically, Trotsky was a revolutionary, more in the mold of Catiline or Caesar. And he was far different from the other Silver-Tongued Devils profiled here, Theodora, and especially the self-interested Talleyrand. Trotsky was first and foremost an intellectual. The power of ideas motivated him and blinded him at the same time. His dedication to an ideal over pragmatic political survival makes him, in a way, anti-Machiavellian.

Trotsky rose from very humble origins in Ukraine to become second in command to Russian communist leader Vladimir Lenin, and then the main rival and antagonist of the dictator and mass murderer Joseph Stalin. Stalin later exiled Trotsky and eventually sent an assassin to fatally bludgeon him with an axe to his skull.

Trotsky became involved in revolutionary activities while still a teenager. At age eighteen, in 1897, he helped organize the South Russia Workers Union, and went to work printing leaflets and distributing revolutionary materials in support of socialism. The next year, he was arrested along with other union members. He spent two years in prison awaiting trial. While there he studied philosophy and started to embrace Marxist principles about society and history.

He was exiled to Siberia, where he spent two years before escaping and fleeing to London. While in England he became acquainted with Lenin and other revolutionary leaders and he joined the staff of the Marxist revolutionary newspaper *Iskra*. He also met his future wife, Natalia Sedova, in London. They married in 1903 and she became his companion and confidante until his death in 1940.

As a political organizer, Trotsky strove to unify the disparate Marxist factions and splinter groups behind a common movement. Unable to do so, that became one of his great frustrations throughout his life and career. This was reflected early on when he split from Lenin in 1904. The party became divided between two factions—Lenin and his supporters, the Bolsheviks, argued for a smaller, more revolutionary party, while the Menshevik faction argued for a larger, more inclusive party. Trotsky sided with the Mensheviks.

He would later admit that he had been wrong in opposing Lenin's more revolutionary path, but in the meantime, he spent the next decade writing and speaking on behalf of revolutionary socialism. He also began developing his theory of Permanent Revolution, which would later lead to serious differences between him and Joseph Stalin. He was arrested numerous times for revolutionary activities and imprisoned or exiled at least twice before World War I. It was at these trials that Trotsky became known as a moving and inspirational speaker. He gave some of the best speeches of his life while on trial for espionage and treason against the Russian state. One gets an idea of the eloquence and philosophical nature of his remarks from some of the early twentieth-century articles he wrote in support of Marxism:

> As long as I breathe I hope. As long as I breathe I shall fight
> for the future, that radiant future, in which man, strong and
> beautiful, will become master of the drifting stream of his
> history and will direct it towards the boundless horizon of
> beauty, joy, and happiness! (On Optimism and Pessimism, on
> the 20th Century, and on Many Other Things, 1901)

In 1908, living in Vienna, Trotsky started a Russian language newspaper to promote socialist and Marxist ideals. Aimed at Russian workers, the newspaper was called *Pravda,* which means "truth." In the years leading up to World War I, the Bolshevik movement adopted the name *Pravda* for its party newspaper, which became the vehicle for distributing news and propaganda to the party faithful for the next seventy-five years. Trotsky became one of its main writers and editors at different points in his career.

The onset of World War I caused various realignments of socialist and revolutionary parties throughout Europe. Some leftist groups opposed the war, while others took a more moderate approach and supported the Russian government in its time of crisis. Trotsky steadfastly opposed the war, but he didn't go as far as Lenin, who advocated a split with the other leftist parties for their support of the war. To avoid becoming politically isolated, Lenin eventually endorsed Trotsky's more moderate approach.

In 1914, Trotsky moved to France as a war correspondent for an international socialist newspaper. But he was deported the following year for revolutionary activities. He was sent by French authorities to Spain, but the Spanish government wanted no part of him, and he was deported to the United States in December 1916. From New York City, he continued writing for various Russian language and other international newspapers, and frequently made speeches at gatherings of leftist political organizations. He was living in New York when the February 1917 revolution overthrew Tsar Nicholas and the imperial Russian monarchy. With the monarchy gone, Trotsky was free to return to Russia.

What awaited him was Aleksandr Kerensky's liberal nationalist government, which took power after the fall of the tsar. Arriving in mid-May, Trotsky plunged himself into workers' revolutionary organizing. After widespread Bolshevik unrest in August, Trotsky and a number of other leftists were arrested. While in prison, he was elected to the Bolshevik Party Central Committee, in recognition of his talent at political organizing. Upon his release from prison the following month, he was elected chair of the Petrograd Soviet, a pro-Bolshevik workers'

council. He then played a leading role in the uprisings that led to the
fall of the Kerensky government and the victory of the Bolsheviks. His
Military Revolutionary Committee secured Petrograd as the Kerensky
government fell in November 1917. Ironically, it was Stalin who wrote
about Trotsky's leading role in the revolution for an article in *Pravda* in
November 1918:

> All practical work in connection with the organization of the
> uprising was done under the immediate direction of Comrade
> Trotsky, the President of the Petrograd Soviet. It can be
> stated with certainty that the party is indebted primarily and
> principally to Comrade Trotsky for the rapid going over of the
> garrison to the side of the Soviet and the efficient manner in
> which the work of the Military Revolutionary Committee was
> organized.

Later, after their falling out, Stalin expunged this portion of his
description of the revolution.

By 1918, Trotsky was the second most important person in the new
communist government. He joined Lenin in defeating proposals for a
coalition government that would have included the Menshevik faction
and other socialist revolutionaries. His official government title was
commissar for foreign affairs, and he led the Soviet delegation at the
armistice negotiations at Brest-Litovsk. Trotsky and other leftists at first
resisted accepting Germany's terms for peace, hoping that they could
encourage an uprising from the workers' movements in Germany and
continue the revolution throughout Europe. But Lenin, always more
pragmatic than Trotsky, realized that a German revolution was not in the
offing and moved to accept the German proposals for peace.

Lenin thought it essential for Russia to be free of the war in Europe
so it could focus on its own defenses and political reform. Trotsky was
named commissar of war and was put in charge of building a new Red
Army. The old army was in shambles and Russia was under immediate
pressure to defend the new communist government from threats of civil
war and foreign intervention. Trotsky focused on building a smaller,

more disciplined command structure. Officers were chosen by the leadership instead of by the rank and file. His abandonment of the old revolutionary army structure brought intense criticism from many in the party, including Joseph Stalin. But his reforms and tactics were ultimately vindicated by the success of the Red Army in repelling the attacks by the anticommunist White armies in 1918 and 1919.

Trotsky distinguished himself as an inspiring and motivational leader during the period of civil war from 1918 to 1920. He dramatically increased the size of the army and introduced into the armed forces the concept of political commissars, who were responsible for ensuring the loyalty of military leaders. Trotsky often spoke to individual units and rallied them to protect the gains made by the revolution. Recounting one experience in which he addressed a group of army deserters who had been rounded up and detained, he reminds one somewhat of Henry V at the Battle of Agincourt:

> The "comrade-deserters" were looking at me with such curiosity that it seemed as if their eyes would pop out of their heads. I climbed on a table there in the yard, and spoke to them for about an hour and a half. It was a most responsive audience. I tried to raise them in their own eyes; concluding, I asked them to lift their hands in token of their loyalty to the revolution. The new ideas infected them before my very eyes. They were genuinely enthusiastic; they followed me to the automobile, devoured me with their eyes, not fearfully, as before, but rapturously, and shouted at the tops of their voices. They would hardly let me go. I learned afterward, with some pride, that one of the best ways to educate them was to remind them: "What did you promise Comrade Trotsky?"

After the years of revolution and civil war, Trotsky came into increasing conflict with some in the party. He was still very popular with the rank-and-file members of the Communist Party, but he had serious differences with some party leaders, notably Joseph Stalin. Stalin had for several years openly criticized Trotsky's handling of key military decisions, but beginning in 1920 the criticism aimed at Trotsky became more heated and public. Trotsky's disagreement with Lenin about the proper role of trade unions was used by Stalin to argue that Trotsky was disloyal to the party. The criticisms began to have an effect. At the Tenth Party Congress in 1921, a number of Trotsky supporters lost their leadership positions in a move orchestrated by Stalin.

Lenin's deteriorating health, and the power struggle to succeed him as party leader, was the beginning of the end for Trotsky. Lenin suffered several strokes in 1922 and 1923, taking him away from party business and undermining his authority. Stalin was elevated to the position of general secretary of the Central Committee, increasing his authority over party personnel and patronage. Echoing back two thousand years to the Roman Triumvirate that eventually doomed Cicero, Stalin formed an alliance, the *troika,* with Grigory Zinoviev and Lev Kamenev. The stated purpose was to better govern in Lenin's absence, but the real reasons were to push Trotsky further from the ranks of party leadership, isolate him, and ensure that he would not be in a position to succeed Lenin.

Though Lenin had a close working relationship with Stalin through years of struggle and sacrifice, he still saw Trotsky as one of the key leaders of the movement. But, more and more, he was being marginalized. As Stalin began to accrue more power in the party, his heavy-handed tactics and increasingly authoritarian party directives disturbed Lenin. Stalin's dismissive and rude treatment of the ailing Lenin and his wife greatly disheartened Lenin, who began to actively suggest that Stalin be replaced as general secretary. Lenin made plans to work with Trotsky to blunt Stalin's takeover of the party, but then Lenin was silenced by a final stroke in March 1923.

Trotsky continued to speak out against what he saw as a power-hungry troika. That October he addressed a wide-ranging critique to the Central Committee, arguing against the party's economic policy and its failure to institute political reforms. But the party leadership used his remarks as an opportunity to launch a blistering counterattack against Trotsky and his supporters—he was accused of factionalism. Complicating matters, Trotsky fell ill and was unable to defend himself for long periods. Lenin's death made Trotsky's isolation complete. Stalin used Lenin's funeral to make Trotsky appear disloyal and uncaring—he sent Trotsky a false date for the funeral, guaranteeing that he would miss it.

Over the next few years, Trotsky's political position grew worse. One of the great disagreements he had with Stalin was philosophical. Trotsky had for years developed and argued for the old Bolshevik ideal, first described by Karl Marx, of a Permanent Revolution. Under this ideal scenario, a true socialist society depended on widespread, ongoing, worldwide revolution that would spread socialism across the globe. But Stalin and others in the party began to develop an alternative vision— Socialism in One Country—the view that the Soviet Union could develop a communist society on its own and compete for power with the rest of Europe. As Stalin's power in the party grew, his supporters denounced Trotsky's ideas as rooted in the past and even counterrevolutionary.

The party's Central Committee was relentless in its attacks on Trotsky. He was forced to resign as commissar of the army and surrender control of the Revolutionary Military Council. Increasingly, he became an opposition figure within the party, and his supporters were gradually removed from leadership positions. From 1926 to 1928, Stalin's means of silencing and removing opposition became more severe. He began using the Soviet secret police to infiltrate and discredit political opponents, including Trotsky.

Finally, in 1927 Trotsky was expelled from the Central Committee and then from the Communist Party. Then early in 1928 he was expelled from the Soviet Union and deported to Kazakhstan, a Soviet republic. After his expulsion, many Trotskyists repented and admitted their "mistakes." Trotsky lived in Turkey for four years, then France. Then, pressured by Soviet authorities, he went to Norway, and finally settled in Mexico in 1936.

As Stalin continued to purge "disloyal" party members and eliminate opposition in the Soviet Union and across Europe using his secret police, there were two assassination attempts on Trotsky in Mexico. The second was successful. Presumably, a Stalinist agent, Ramón Mercader, a Spanish communist, gained the confidence of the

Trotsky household. In August 1940, during a meeting in Trotsky's office, Mercader attacked Trotsky with an axe, plunging the weapon into the back of Trotsky's head. He died of his wounds the following day.

Trotsky was a brilliant intellect, a galvanizing public speaker, and a talented political organizer. He remains one of the best examples of ideologically driven political revolutionaries in history. But he made mistakes. Some consider him arrogant, in that on many occasions he refused to compromise with political rivals, including Lenin himself. He is also accused of putting too much faith in revolutionary ideals and not paying enough attention to political realities. He seemed to be aware of his shortcomings as a politician, even if he was unable to change his approach. In his later years he wrote:

> It is no wonder that my military work created so many enemies for me. I did not look to the side, I elbowed away those who interfered with military success, or in the haste of the work trod on the toes of the unheeding and was too busy even to apologize. Some people remember such things. The dissatisfied and those whose feelings had been hurt found their way to Stalin or Zinoviev, for these two nourished hurts.

CHAPTER 6

THE GENERALS

As Niccolo Machiavelli said in *The Prince,* the most important kind of knowledge that a leader of men must possess is the knowledge of how to make war:

> A Prince should therefore have no other aim or thought, nor take up any other thing for his study, but war and its organization and discipline, for that is the only art that is necessary to one who commands, and it is of such virtue that it not only maintains those who are born princes, but often enables men of private fortune to attain to that rank.

All one has to do is glance at the record of human history to see that military power (and the ability to wield that power) is often the only measure of a society's survival and its ability to influence the world. The last part of Machiavelli's quote above is the essence of this chapter: Knowing how to wage war is such a "virtue" that it enables those who are not born princes or born into power—even those born into the lower rungs of society—to wield real power.

Many leaders through history have come to political prominence through military power. Some were born into royalty and raised to lead by the sword, yet under the right circumstances, even a commoner can rise to the highest ranks of command through superior strategic skills, the ability to lead and inspire men, and an instinct that tells him when to take risks and when to calculate.

The individuals in this chapter represent several different paths to political power, all beginning on the battlefield. Some took advantage of political weakness or discord in their governments, some rose through duty to a sovereign, and some had history thrust upon them by fortune or circumstance. All grew to become leaders of great armies, which, in turn, led to political conquest.

King Arthur's Role Model?: Flavius Stilicho

Little consensus exists about the origins of the legend of King Arthur, first popularized by Geoffrey of Monmouth in the twelfth century. Yet on one thing most historians do agree: The story is not based on a single individual, but is a composite character, drawn from multiple tales of heroism and sacrifice from early western Europe. Some historians tie the inspiration for the King Arthur figure to the declining days of the Western Roman Empire, particularly Roman Britain.

First-millennium Celts and Britons would have been very familiar with the legends and tales of heroism from centuries of Barbarian attacks on and Roman defense of its western territories. One common thread between the Western Roman Empire and post-Roman Britain is a constant struggle against foreign invaders. Indeed, both the British Isles and the Roman garrisons in Gaul and Hispania (the Iberian Peninsula) fought off invasions from some of the same Germanic tribes.

Several Roman defenders of the Western Empire spawned tales of bravery and nobility that became widely known throughout western European culture. One of these was Flavius Stilicho, the half-Roman, half-Vandal military commander who defended the western Roman territories in the late fourth and early fifth centuries AD. Rising to the rank of consul, he expelled Barbarian invaders and influenced a string of weak emperors until he was betrayed by rivals and executed in 408. Stilicho proved to be the last great defender of the empire, for without him the Barbarians finally succeeded in besieging and sacking Rome in 410, marking the end of an almost thousand-year reign. And like Geoffrey of Monmouth's King Arthur, Stilicho met a tragic but noble end, worthy of Shakespeare.

Stilicho's father, who was from a Vandal tribe that had been incorporated into the Roman legions, served with distinction as a cavalry officer in the Roman army. Stilicho's mother was Roman. Though his father was a Vandal, Stilicho clearly considered himself Roman. He was probably a Nicene Orthodox Christian.

His early career included both diplomatic and military experience during the reign of Theodosius I, who was the last emperor to rule both the eastern and western halves of the Roman Empire jointly. In 383, Theodosius sent him as an envoy to the court of the Persian King Shapur III to negotiate a peace settlement relating to the partition of Armenia. Upon his return to Constantinople at the successful conclusion of peace talks, Stilicho was promoted and later given the title of magister militum, meaning senior military commander. The emperor recognized Stilicho's abilities as a commander, and to form a blood tie with him, Theodosius married his adopted niece, Serena, to Stilicho. The marriage took place around the time of Stilicho's mission to Persia, and ultimately Serena gave birth to a son, who was named Eucherius, and two daughters, Maria and Thermantia.

In 392, Stilicho helped raise the army that Theodosius would lead to victory at the Battle of the River Frigidus (the Frigid River). This army included a fair number of Barbarian tribes fighting alongside the Romans. One of Stilicho's allies during the Frigidus campaign was the Visigothic warlord Alaric, who commanded a substantial number of Gothic troops. Alaric, an ally only when it was politically expedient, would go on to become Stilicho's chief adversary during his later career as the head of the Western Roman armies. Stilicho distinguished himself at Frigidus, and Theodosius, exhausted by the campaign, saw him as a man worthy of responsibility for the future safety of the empire.

The last emperor of a united Rome appointed Stilicho guardian of his young son, Honorius, shortly before his death in 395.

Following the death of Theodosius, Honorius became emperor of the Western Roman Empire, and his brother, Arcadius, of the Eastern Roman Empire. Neither proved to be effective emperors, and Stilicho came to be the de facto commander-in-chief of the Roman armies in the West while his rival, Rufinus, became the power behind the throne in the East. The reign of Arcadius in the East was plagued by his weak leadership and by political intrigue. In the West, Stilicho proved to be a skillful leader, although political maneuverings by agents of both of the imperial courts would hinder him throughout his career.

His first brush with such court politics came in 395. The Visigoths had recently elected Alaric as their king. Alaric broke his treaty with Rome and led his people on a raid into Thrace. The army that had been victorious at the Frigidus was still assembled, and Stilicho led it toward Alaric's forces. The armies of the Eastern Empire were occupied with Hun incursions in Asia Minor and Syria, so Rufinus attempted to negotiate with Alaric in person. This resulted in suspicions in Constantinople that Rufinus was in league with the Goths. Stilicho now marched east against Alaric. According to the poet Claudian, who immortalized Stilicho in verse, he was in a position to destroy Alaric and the Goths, when, inexplicably, he was ordered by Arcadius to retreat. Suspicion of betrayal and espionage was rampant. Soon afterwards, Rufinus was hacked to death by his own soldiers.

Two years later, in 397, Stilicho defeated Alaric's forces in Macedonia, although Alaric himself escaped into the surrounding mountains. The same year saw him successfully quell the revolt of Gildo in North Africa. In 400, Stilicho was recognized as defender of the empire and appointed consul—the highest honor in the Roman state.

In 401, two Barbarian leaders planned the joint invasion of the Roman Empire—Alaric and the Ostrogoth leader Radagaisus. Radagaisus attacked first, and invaded Raetia. Stilicho rushed his soldiers to the area, crossed the Danube River, and crushed Radagaisus. Wasting no time, Stilicho turned his attention toward Alaric and his Visigoths, who had invaded Italy. Bravely hastening on in advance of his main body of thirty thousand troops, he led his best fighting units in a surprise night attack against Alaric's position around Milan. One of his chieftains implored him to retreat, but Alaric refused.

On Easter Sunday 402 at Pollentia, Stilicho defeated Alaric and captured his camp, along with his wife. But Alaric managed to escape with most of his men. This battle would be the last victory for the empire celebrated in traditional Roman style—a triumphal march down the city center. In 403 at Verona, Stilicho again bested Alaric, who only escaped by the speed of his horse. After the battle, Stilicho negotiated a truce with his old ally, and allowed Alaric to retreat to the east.

But Stilicho's peace agreement with Alaric, and imperial court rumors of Stilicho's ambition to command both the Eastern and Western armies, gave his political opponents an opportunity. Taking advantage of a rising wave of anti-Barbarian and anti-German feeling, some historians conclude that advisors to Honorius convinced him that Stilicho, only half-Roman, had grown too powerful, had become too ambitious, and was a threat to the emperor. Edward Gibbon, in *The Decline and Fall of the Roman Empire*, asserts that

> The crafty Olympius [a court official], who concealed his vices under the mask of Christian piety, had secretly undermined the benefactor by whose favor he was promoted to the honorable offices of the Imperial palace. Olympius revealed to the unsuspecting emperor, who had attained the twenty-fifth year of his age, that he was without weight or authority in his own government; and artfully alarmed his timid and indolent disposition by a lively picture of the designs of Stilicho, who already meditated the death of his sovereign, with the ambitious hope of placing the diadem on the head of his son Eucherius.

Stilicho, at first unaware of the unfolding political intrigue, retired to the garrison at Ravenna where he was taken into custody. Although it was within his ability to contest the charges, Stilicho did not resist, either because of loyalty to Rome or for fear of the consequences to the already precarious state of the Western Empire. He was executed on August 22, 408. His wife and son, Eucherius, were murdered in Rome shortly afterwards.

In the disturbances that followed the downfall and execution of Stilicho, the wives and children of Barbarian officers in the service of Rome throughout Italy were slain by the local Romans. The natural consequence was that these men (estimates place their numbers as perhaps thirty thousand strong) flocked to the protection of Alaric, clamoring to be led against their cowardly enemies. Accordingly, the Visigothic warlord crossed the Julian Alps and began a campaign through the heart of Italy. By September 408, the Barbarians stood before the walls of Rome.

Without a strong general like Stilicho to control the by-now mostly Barbarian army, Honorius could do little to break the siege, and adopted a passive strategy trying to wait out Alaric, hoping to gather his forces to defeat the Visigoths in the meantime. What followed were two years of political and military maneuvering, with Alaric, king of the Goths, attempting to secure a permanent peace treaty and rights to settle within Roman territory. He besieged Rome three times without attacking, while the Roman Army watched helplessly. But it was not until the deal had fallen through a fourth time that he attacked and sacked the city in August 410. The removal of Stilicho was the main catalyst leading to this monumental event, the first Barbarian capture of the city in nearly eight centuries and a presage of the final collapse of the imperial West.

Charles the Hammer: Charles Martel

Three centuries later, another general fought for conquest of Gaul (modern France and Belgium). But since the days of Stilicho and Alaric, the landscape of Europe and the Mediterranean had changed vastly with the splintering of the old empire, the rise of the Merovingian Franks, and the emergence of Islam. In the early eighth century, the Islamic Moors invaded and subjugated most of Spain and Portugal (Hispania). The Islamic armies then pushed north into Gaul, but were forced back by a Frankish army led by Charles Martel. *Marteau* (*Martellus* in Latin) is the old French word for hammer.

Is this the man who saved Europe from the Muslims? Well, that's the legend. Charles Martel, the bastard son of Pippin II of Herstal (and the grandfather of Charlemagne), led the restoration of the Frankish empire in the eighth century and defeated the invading Muslim armies at the Battle of Tours in 732, preserving Christianity in Europe.

Tradition holds that this was a defining moment in world history, in that it halted the Muslim incursions into Europe that began with the conquest of Hispania, saved Christianity from being swallowed by Islam, and preserved the emerging culture of western Europe that flowered during and after the Renaissance. According to historian Victor Davis Hanson, "most of the 18th and 19th century historians, like Edward Gibbon, saw Tours as a landmark battle that marked the high tide of the Muslim advance into Europe." German historian Leopold von Ranke felt that "Poitiers was the turning point of one of the most important epochs in the history of the world." European schoolchildren learn about the Battle of Tours in much the same way that American students learn about Valley Forge and Gettysburg.

Some historians, however, are less certain that it was a world-altering event, as claimed by Gibbon. Franco Cardini, for example, writes in *Europe and Islam* that the Battle of Tours as a decisive defeat for the Muslims in Europe is a myth propagated by Frankish writers and the Catholic Church. Support for this view may be offered by the contention of some historians that it was later Frankish chroniclers who bestowed the title "the Hammer" on Charles, and that he did not carry that name during his lifetime. Cardini and others view the battle as one of a series of events that led to the withdrawal of Muslim forces from southern Europe. Other historians, such as William E. Watson, claim a middle ground, essentially arguing that even if Tours didn't "save Europe" from Islam, it certainly made the Franks the dominant power in the region and eventually led to Frankish domination of Gaul.

But who exactly was Charles Martel, and what was his significance? Though illegitimate, Charles was born into a Frankish political system whereby the Merovingian kings of the era designated certain public officials to serve as "mayor of the palace," a court office whose duties grew to include presiding over court personnel, commanding the king's armies, and advising the king on the appointment of counts and dukes. Essentially, they became a true power behind the throne.

The Merovingian kings adopted the traditional Roman system by which great landowners of the empire had employed a *maior domus* (mayor, or supervisor, of the household) to supervise the administration of numerous, often scattered, estates. Thus, *maior domus* is the Latin origin of the modern English slang term *major domo.* The Merovingians appointed a *major palatii* (mayor of the palace) to perform a similar function. The mayor gradually acquired further duties and powers: He obtained authority over court personnel, commanded the king's armies, and advised the king on the appointment of counts and dukes— essentially acting as the regent, or viceroy, of the kingdom. The later Merovingian kings were little more than puppets and were enthroned and deposed at will by powerful mayors of the palace.

Pippin II—the reigning mayor of the palace—died in 714, touching off a battle for succession among his heirs. Only a few months before his own death, Pippin's only surviving legitimate son had been assassinated. Having no direct claim to either the throne or the regency, the charismatic Charles recruited followers and took control of several territories in Gaul by force over the span of several years. Both Pippin's designated successor, Theudoald (his grandson), and the Merovingian King Dagobert III were very young. By contrast, Charles was seen by many in the kingdom as a strong and capable leader. His regency was supported by several regions of Gaul, and by 716 he had gathered an army capable of seizing power.

His successes on the battlefield validated his claim to rule. In several major battles, Charles led his forces to victory, sometimes against superior numbers and with military tactics unfamiliar in western Europe at the time—for example, feigning retreat and drawing the enemy troops into a trap. By 718, he had consolidated his hold over most of the Frankish territories of Gaul, he had placed a king favorable to him on the throne, and he had deposed the reigning archbishop, replacing him with an ally.

He then turned his attention to the rest of Gaul and then to Germania. Between 718 and 730, Charles expanded his power with a series of victories over various Germanic tribes, including the powerful Saxons. He also began to lay a political foundation, winning the loyalty of a number of important bishops and abbots by donating land and money for the construction of abbeys. In just over a decade, he had unified the Franks under his banner, solidified his control of Gaul, and incorporated most of Germany into the Frankish kingdom.

The next challenge for the Franks, and for all of Europe, came from the south. The Battle of Tours followed twenty-three years of Islamic Umayyad conquests in Europe that began with the invasion and defeat of the Visigothic Christian kingdoms of the Iberian Peninsula (Spain and Portugal) in 711. These were followed by military expeditions into Frankish and Germanic territories. Umayyad military campaigns had reached northward into Aquitaine and Burgundy, including a major engagement at Bordeaux in 721 and a raid on Autun.

The army of the Umayyad caliphate was under the leadership of Abd-er Rahman, governor of Spain. Abd-er Rahman led a Muslim army numbering in the tens of thousands across the western Pyrenees and toward the Loire River, but they were met just outside the city of Tours by Charles.

Contrary to the intelligence the Muslims had on the Franks at the time, Charles and his army were well prepared for the attack. Martel had trained his forces for a decade for this battle, and was well aware of his opponents' strengths and weaknesses. For their part, the Umayyad forces did not know much at all about the Franks. The invading forces were caught entirely off guard when they found a large force, well disposed and prepared for battle, with high ground, directly opposing their attack on Tours. Charles had achieved total surprise. He then chose to begin the battle in a defensive, phalanxlike formation. According to Arabian sources, the Franks drew up in a large square, with the trees and an upward slope to break any cavalry charge. The invading Muslims rushed forward, relying on the slashing tactics and overwhelming number of horsemen that had brought them victories in the past. However, the

Frankish army, composed of foot soldiers armed primarily with swords, shields, axes, javelins, and daggers, stood its ground. Complicating their assault, the hilly terrain caused difficulties for the Umayyad troops. Their strength lay within their cavalry, armed with large swords and lances, which, along with their baggage mules, limited their mobility. The Franks displayed great strength in withstanding the ferocious attack. It was one of the rare times in the Middle Ages when infantry held its ground against a mounted attack.

The exact length of the battle is unknown; Arab sources claim that it was a two-day battle, whereas Christian sources hold that the fighting dragged on for seven days. In either case, the battle ended when Charles's forces captured and killed Abd-er Rahman. Some chroniclers claim that he was surrounded by Frankish troops as he tried to stop a retreat by some of his forces. The Muslim army withdrew peacefully overnight and even though Martel expected a surprise retaliation the next day, there was none. The death of their leader was a sharp setback for the Muslims, and they had no choice but to retreat back across the Pyrenees.

Despite the defeat at Tours, the Umayyads remained in control of Narbonne and Septimania for another twenty-seven years, though they could not expand further. In 735, the new governor of al-Andalus again invaded Gaul. Antonio Santosuosso and other historians have written how the new governor of al-Andalus, Uqba b. al-Hajjaj, again moved into France to avenge the defeat at Poitiers and to spread Islam. Santosuosso notes that al-Hajjaj converted about two thousand Christians he captured over the course of his career.

In the last major attempt at forcible invasion of Gaul through Iberia, he assembled a sizable invasion force at Saragossa and entered what is now French territory in 735, crossed the River Rhone, and captured and looted Arles. From there, he struck into the heart of Provence, ending with the capture of Avignon, despite strong resistance. Uqba b. al-Hajjaj's forces remained in French territory for about four years, carrying out raids on Lyons, Burgundy, and Piedmont. Again Charles Martel came to Gaul's rescue, reconquering most of the lost territories in two campaigns in 736 and 739, except for the city of Narbonne, which finally fell in 759.

Notable in these campaigns was Charles's incorporation—apparently for the first time in western Europe—of heavy cavalry with stirrups to augment his phalanx. His ability to coordinate infantry and cavalry veterans was unequaled in that era and enabled him to triumph on the battlefield despite his enemy's superior numbers. Some historians, such as Santosuosso, believe the 735 and 736 battles were as important for Charles and the eventual preservation of Christian Europe as the Battle of Tours.

The last period of Charles's life is known as the interregnum. In 737, the last Merovingian king, Theuderic IV, died. As the reigning *maier domus,* Charles did not appoint a new king, and there were no new claimants to the throne. The throne lay vacant until Charles's death in 741. There was no need for a king—it was said that Charles "cared not for name or style so long as the real power was in his hands."

The interregnum was more peaceful than most of Charles's stormy rule had been, and he turned much of his attention to administrative matters, as well as integrating the outlying realms of the empire into the Frankish church. He divided his kingdom among two of his adult sons, Carloman and Pippin. Pope Gregory III later crowned Pippin king, beginning the reign of the Carolingian Kings. In AD 800, the old Western Empire was reconstituted; Pippin's son Charlemagne was named emperor—bringing about the birth of the Holy Roman Empire. Thus, Charles Martel provides us with one of history's great turning points. In the words of Edward Gibbon: "the hero of the age."

The Prophet: Saladin

A number of modern Arab and Muslim leaders have looked in the mirror and have seen the famed Muslim hero Saladin staring back at them. The legacy of Saladin and his victory over the Crusaders in the twelfth century looms large over modern Middle East politics and the search for Arab identity. During the reign of Egypt's Gamal Abdel Nasser in the 1950s and 1960s, for example, the image of Saladin was stamped heavily on Nasser's aspirations of pan-Arabism—the movement to unify the peoples and countries of the Arab world. From the 1980s to 2003,

Saddam Hussein of Iraq saw himself as a modern-day Saladin—even more so because both he and Saladin were born in Tikrit, Iraq. He believed he was building a military framework that would someday enable him to dominate the Arab world and lead them into the future. But Saddam Hussein was no Saladin. And a number of Middle Eastern scholars report that today's radical Islamists—for example, al-Qaeda leader Osama bin Laden and the Taliban's Mullah Muhammad Omar of Afghanistan—see themselves as the heirs of Saladin.

Understandably, the age of Salah ad-Din Yusuf ibn Ayyub (known as Saladin in the West) is considered a golden age to many in the Muslim world. It was Saladin who led the Islamic military forces that conquered the European Christian stronghold of Jerusalem in 1187 and unified the Muslim forces of Egypt, Syria, Iraq, and Yemen—a historic turning point in the development of the Arab world. As such, he is one of the foremost heroes, if not the ultimate one, in the Arab and Muslim worlds.

Yet, in addition to his military prowess, he is also known for his chivalry and humanity, quite unlike Saddam Hussein or Osama bin Laden. Saladin was a devout Sunni Muslim, and despite being the sworn enemy of the Crusaders, his professional and civil behavior was noted by many Christian chroniclers of the age. His approach to dealing with his military opponents won the respect of many of them, including Richard the Lionheart of England.

Christian biographers did as much as Muslim chroniclers to popularize the Saladin legend. The stories of his courtesy and benevolence were brought back to Europe—how, for example, he gave furs to some of his Christian captives to keep them warm in the Damascus dungeons. When the Crusaders took Jerusalem in 1099, they murdered virtually all its inhabitants, boasting that parts of the city were knee-high in blood. By contrast, when Saladin captured the city in 1187 he spared his victims, giving Christian pilgrims safe passage. These stories helped Saladin achieve a reputation in Palestine and in Europe as a chivalrous knight—so much so that by the fourteenth century an epic poem chronicled his exploits, and the writer Dante included him among the virtuous pagan souls in Limbo.

Ironically, he came to power in a way similar to that of the great Christian hero and military leader Charles Martel: He had to fight for it and win it. He was Kurdish, born in Tikrit, Iraq in 1138, and moved with his father to the Syrian capital of Damascus. His father and uncle were in the service of Nur ad-Din, the powerful ruler of Damascus and Aleppo. In the middle of the twelfth century, there was a vicious power struggle for control of Egypt, Syria, and Palestine between the Franks (the Latin-Christian rulers of the states established by the First Crusade—in essence, the descendants of Charles Martel and Charlemagne) and various rival Muslim kingdoms.

Saladin became an important commander in the army led by his uncle, Shirkuh. Both Saladin's father and uncle became Nur ad-Din's most trusted generals. Shirkuh and Saladin led part of Nur ad-Din's army into Egypt to prevent its domination by the Frankish ruler King Amalric. In 1169, Shirkuh's forces established military control over the Muslim forces defending Egypt, effectively displacing the Shiite rulers who had governed Egypt. Shirkuh became vizier—forming a regime allied to Nur ad-Din in Damascus. But Shirkuh died later that year and Saladin inherited his title. When the last Fatimid (Shiite) caliph died in 1171, Saladin began to consolidate a Sunni-dominated military and political movement under his own command.

Over the next several years, he built a separate Muslim power base in Egypt that grew to rival that of Nur ad-Din. Saladin maintained a difficult balancing act: He kept up appearances as a loyal Number Two to his father and uncle's old master, Nur ad-Din, while at the same time he put together a military force loyal to him alone.

First, he had to pacify the Egyptian capital of Cairo and eliminate any signs of Fatimid resistance. His troops slaughtered thousands of men, many of them Sudanese slave-soldiers, who were loyal to the Fatimid caliphate. He then ordered their homes burned and their families exiled to serve as examples to those who would resist Saladin's authority. Many of these soldiers of Egypt were replaced with Sunni troops Saladin called up from Alexandria, where he had commanded part of his uncle Shirkuh's army the previous year.

With his newfound power, he did not challenge Nur ad-Din outright for control, but decided to outlast his old master. Nur ad-Din died three years later in 1174 and Saladin eventually asserted his control over the caliphate, occupying both Damascus and Egypt. In the process, Saladin survived repeated assassination attempts from soldiers hired by rival Syrian chieftans who viewed him as a usurper. His command of the largest Muslim military force in the Middle East and his miraculous survival, despite the myriad assassination plots, put him in a position to assert his leadership.

He claimed legitimacy not from his lineage, but from his dedication to Sunni orthodoxy and from having taken a sacred pledge to impart the faith. With the last of the Fatamid caliphs gone, Saladin abolished the Egyptian Shiite caliphate. He wanted to do more than just build a military power; he was interested in building a thriving civil society dedicated to Sunni Islam. He looked at Egypt as a source of revenue and power for the wars against Christian and European crusades, and also against dissident Muslim sects who challenged his authority. He wanted to make Cairo the center of a Sunni orthodox cultural and ideological revival. Among his most famous architectural contributions were the military fortress known as the Citadel, and the Madrasa—a college-mosque that served as a Sunni religious and cultural center.

Pious, frugal, generous, and merciful, he was also a shrewd and able leader. He is described by historians as small in stature, with a round face, black hair, and dark eyes. Like most members of the Islamic elite, he was literate, cultured, and skilled with the lance and the sword. As a young man, it was said that he had been more interested in religion than combat. Author Piers Paul Read asserts "there is no doubt that his war against the Christian Franks was inspired by a genuine religious zeal," not simply by an appreciation gained from Nur ad-Din that the disparate Islamic states could only be brought together by a jihad (holy war).

The unification of the forces of Islam under Saladin's military command stood in marked contrast to the confusion and disunity of the Frankish administration of the kingdom of Jerusalem in the late twelfth century. In 1186, the child-king Baldwin V died and his stepfather, Guy of Lusignan, took the throne. Raymond III of Tripoli, who had been regent to Baldwin V, objected, but was powerless to act. Raymond was at first a rival to King Guy; however, the threat posed by the Muslim army under Saladin eventually forced their reconciliation. Other power bases in the kingdom were the Knights Templar, the religious/military order chartered by Bernard of Clairvaux, and the Knights Hospitallers, a religious order similar to the Templars.

But the factional nature of the kingdom of Jerusalem led to a chain of events that caused its downfall. There had been an uneasy truce in the 1180s between the Frankish Crusader kingdom and the Muslim caliphate. But that truce was broken by Raynald of Chatillon, an ally of King Guy, who had raided and plundered Muslim caravans and shipping in the early 1180s, killing Egyptian troops in the process. Saladin demanded justice. Raynald became a marked man for Saladin, "whose role as a guardian of the Holy places in Arabia underpinned his authority in the Muslim world."

War came to the Holy Land. Muslim armies from Aleppo, Mosul, Damascus, and Egypt converged near the Jordan River to give Saladin the largest fighting force he had ever commanded. At the same time, King Guy Lusignan called on all available fighting men, including mercenaries, to defend Christian Palestine. He assembled an army of over thirty thousand, virtually all the Christian forces in the region; Latin cities and fortresses were left empty.

The first major conflict was the Battle of Hattin. Here, according to historians, the battle turned on one thing—water. King Guy had been goaded by Raynald of Chatillon and Gerard of Ridefort (the head of the Templar order) into rushing his forces into the desert at the height of summer without adequate supplies. Wells in the region were dry and King Guy's men were becoming deyhdrated. During the night, the Muslim troops advanced closer. At daybreak, Saladin ordered his scouts to set fire to the scrub brush that covered the surrounding hills—the breeze carried the smoke toward the Christian camps, increasing the soldiers' misery in the dry, waterless conditions.

At midmorning, Saladin's army attacked. Guy's forces, maddened by thirst, the heat, and the smoke, had no chance. Some escaped, but most were killed or captured by the end of the day. Among them was the bishop of Acre, who carried with him the sacred relic of the True Cross— reputedly a fragment of the original cross and a cherished Christian relic. King Guy was taken to Saladin's tent, along with Raynald of Chatillon. Tradition holds that Saladin gave the dehydrated King Guy a glass of rosewater. After Guy drank from it, he passed it to Raynald, but Saladin's men grabbed it away.

> Saladin now berated Raynald for all his iniquities and, in obedience to Muhammad's teaching, offered him the choice of accepting Islam or death. Raynald laughed in his face, saying that it was rather Saladin who should turn to Christ: "if you would believe in Him, you could avoid the punishment of eternal damnation which you should not doubt is prepared for you." On hearing this, Saladin took up his scimitar and cut off Raynald's head.

But Saladin spared the life of Guy: "A king does not kill a king," he is reported to have said. The same mercy, however, was not extended to the Knights Templar and the Knights Hospitallers. "I shall purify the land of these impure races," declared Saladin. Only the head of the Templar order, Gerard of Ridefort, was spared. The other knights were given the choice of rejecting Christ and embracing Islam or death, the same deal offered to Raynald. None of them accepted the offer. The next dawn, more than two hundred knights were assembled in front of the camp, on their knees, in a straight line. Behind each knight stood either a Muslim soldier or a cleric holding a scimitar. With a wave of Saladin's hand, they were beheaded.

It was a rare act of cruelty for a man known for his chivalry and justice. The verdict of most historians is that Saladin's well-known reputation for magnanimity was partly a matter of calculation. "When it seemed politic to be cruel, he was cruel: he ordered the crucifixion of Shiite opponents in Cairo and at times the mutilation or execution of his captives. Although he came to respect and even admire the chivalrous code of the Frankish knights, and was assiduous in his courtesy to

Christian princes and kings, he felt an implacable hatred for the military orders," such as the Knights Templar and the Knights Hospitallers.

It seems that although Saladin was a military leader and strategist in the mold of a Charles Martel, his inspiration and motivation stemmed from his religious fervor, much like Bernard of Clairvaux. His mission was political and military—fighting for control of Syria, Egypt, and Palestine—but it was also spiritual.

The backbone of the Christian defenses for the kingdom of Jerusalem had been crushed at Hattin. Thus, the battle for the actual city of Jerusalem was rather anticlimatic; the deed had been done. After Hattin, the Crusader strongholds at Acre, Ascalon, and Gaza were forced to surrender. The main challenge at Jerusalem was breaching the city walls and overcoming the meager defenses left in place before the local population could carry through on its threat to destroy the sacred Dome of the Rock and burn the city.

Saladin negotiated a ransom, paid mostly from the public treasury, to allow the inhabitants of the city safe passage. He and his forces entered the city gates on October 2, 1187, the anniversary of the ascension to heaven of Muhammad from the Temple Mount. The temple was surrendered to Saladin, who then ousted the Templars from their headquarters at the Al-Aqsa Mosque. The Church of the Holy Sepulchre was left under the authority of the Orthodox and Jacobite Christians, but the cross was taken down from the Dome of the Rock, which was then dragged through the city and beaten by exultant Muslims with clubs.

The Latin Christians were not completely defeated in the region: They managed to hold on to the coastal cities of Antioch, Tripoli, and Tyre, as well as several fortresses on the road to Jerusalem. But the symbolism of the loss of Jerusalem was a shocking blow to Christian Europe. Hattin and the fall of Jerusalem prompted a new Crusade. The new pope, Gregory VIII, proclaimed that the capture of Jerusalem was punishment for the sins of Christians across Europe. The cry went up for a new Crusade to the Holy Land.

Spurred by religious zeal, Henry II of England and Philip II of France ended their conflict with each other to lead a new Crusade—both imposing a "Saladin tithe" on their citizens to finance the venture. Henry II's death in 1189 put the English contingent under the command of his son, Richard the Lionheart. The elderly Holy Roman emperor, Frederick I Barbarossa, responded to the call to arms, and led a massive army across Anatolia, but drowned while crossing a river before reaching the Holy Land. The Christian armies had lost a powerful ally—Saladin had dreaded the appearance of Barbarossa's army on the shores of Palestine. His sudden death surely emboldened Saladin: It must have assured him that Allah truly was on his side. Many of Barbarossa's discouraged troops left to go home.

King Guy had been released by Saladin after the fall of Jerusalem. But rather than give up his fight, he broke his pledge to Saladin and rallied thousands of Crusader forces and led a siege on Muslim-controlled Acre. The stalemate lasted over a year, until the Christian armies were joined by Richard and Philip. Perhaps learning from the failure of the Second Crusade, Richard had made sure to raise the funds necessary to acquire sufficient troops, as well as the latest weaponry and technology, to be successful. Led by the kings of England and France, the Christian forces eventually took Acre. However, during negotiations for surrender of the city, Richard grew impatient and, in a historic act of brutality, executed three thousand Muslim prisoners. Saladin retaliated by killing all Frankish prisoners captured during the siege.

Then Richard confronted Saladin's forces at the Battle of Arsuf on September 7, 1191, at which Saladin was defeated. But Richard's goal of retaking Jerusalem was never fulfilled. For one thing, he knew he did not have adequate troops and resources to hold the city, even if he captured it. There were also political complications with the succession of the Christian crown of Jerusalem in dispute. And Richard faced discord back in England: His brother John was attempting to seize power and his Crusader ally Philip II of France was also plotting against him, forcing him to return to Europe.

Much has been written about the relationship between Richard and Saladin. Although at war, with treacheries committed by both sides, the two developed a mutual respect as soldiers. When Richard became ill with fever, Saladin offered him the services of his personal physician. Saladin also sent him fresh fruit chilled with snow, as treatment. At Arsuf, when Richard lost his horse, Saladin sent him two replacements. Richard found that Saladin was not at all what he had expected. The English king developed an admiration for Saladin's commitment to his religion and to his men.

As leaders of their respective factions, Richard and Saladin forged an agreement with the Treaty of Ramla in 1192, whereby Jerusalem would remain in Muslim hands but would be open to Christian pilgrimages. The treaty reduced the Latin Christian kingdom to a strip along the coast from Tyre to Jaffa. Though neither Saladin nor Richard was aware of it at the time, the Crusades were over, and Jerusalem was still in Muslim hands. Saladin died of a fever on March 4, 1193, at Damascus, not long after Richard's departure.

It could be said that Saladin was the Charles Martel of Islam: He defeated the Christians and preserved Arabia and the Middle East for Islam, much as Martel is credited with halting the spread of Islam north into Europe. He is the Muslim archetype of the solider, statesman, and servant of God. His legacy was a united Islam, the capture of Jerusalem, and the establishment of Islamic political control of the Middle East.

The Lord Protector: Oliver Cromwell

The legacy of Oliver Cromwell is quite different from that of Saladin, Charles Martel, or, for that matter, Flavius Stilicho. Cromwell's life— slayer of kings, champion of parliament, and lord protector of the Commonwealth from 1653 to 1658—has always stirred debate. Was he a hero or a villain? Or neither? Was he a defender of his faith and of his people, or was he a power-hungry tyrant? In fact, one could probably still stir up a pretty good pub fight in London over the matter. But in Ireland there would be no debate—Cromwell is a truly hated figure in the land of St. Patrick.

Cromwell's life is somewhat of an enigma. A relative nobody at age forty, in just over a decade he became the most powerful man in Britain. His is one of the most amazing midlife turnarounds in world history—rather like a forerunner to that of George W. Bush of Texas. Though the Bush analogy is mostly satirical, the two men did share a similar life-changing epiphany upon entering middle age, in both cases centered around religion. Cromwell's unlikely rise to power and influence was based on his military prowess, though he had no military training and zero military experience before the English Civil Wars. This is a man who literally remade himself at just the right time to place his stamp on world history.

He was not born poor, but on the lower rungs of English landowning gentry. A distant relative of Thomas Cromwell, a court advisor to King Henry VIII, his family owned a modest house and a small strip of land in Huntingdon, England. Cromwell would later say of his background, "I was by birth a gentleman, living neither in considerable height, nor yet in obscurity." He had little formal education, having to leave college early after the death of his father in order to help care for the family property and his seven young sisters.

What little social status he had was mostly acquired through his wife's family. At age twenty-one, he married Elizabeth Bourchier, the daughter of a London leather merchant. Sir Bourchier owned extensive land in Essex, and had extensive contacts in the English merchant community—these ties would later prove helpful to Cromwell's military and political career. Yet Cromwell himself was not successful in business or in other enterprises in which he was engaged. He had briefly been a member of Parliament, representing Huntingdon in 1628. But he made little impression as a legislator, giving only one speech and having no effect on the proceedings. After King Charles I dissolved the Parliament in 1629, the king ruled for the next eleven years without a Parliament.

There is considerable evidence that Cromwell suffered from depression. In fact, his "melancholia," as it was diagnosed by seventeenth-century doctors, is a recurring motif in Cromwell's life and career. He sought treatment for his depression as early as the 1620s, but it seems to have grown worse in the 1630s as his family and personal fortunes declined. Court records indicate that he become involved in a major dispute over landholdings in Huntingdon and was called before the Privy Council in 1630. The next year, he sold his property in Huntingdon and bought a small farm a few miles away. He was slowly working his way down the ladder of success, and historians speculate that this may have had a major emotional impact on his psyche.

Sometime in the early 1630s—the exact timing is uncertain—he experienced a profound religious awakening that evidently changed the future course of his life and, consequently, that of all Britain. Undoubtedly, he had hit rock bottom in his personal life and fortune. But his religious conversion led to drastic changes in his life and character. By his own admission he had been "chief of sinners," particularly with alcohol. He adopted a much more serious work ethic and a commitment to Puritanism that would inform all his future endeavors.

Cromwell's midlife crisis/religious awakening is what is so reminiscent of the experience of former U.S. president George W. Bush. The young Bush led a knockabout, haphazard existence with no particular direction and an alcohol problem—as he has written about and openly discussed. Around age forty (as with Cromwell), he had hit rock bottom in his personal and professional life. He, too, turned to God for answers and experienced a spiritual and personal awakening that turned his life around, eventually rising to the American presidency.

The depth of Cromwell's spiritual awakening can be seen in his letters to friends:

> Oh, I lived in and loved darkness, and hated the light. I was a chief, the chief of sinners. This is true; I hated godliness, yet God had mercy on me. O the riches of his mercy! Praise him for me;—pray for me, that he who hath begun a good work would perfect it to the day of Christ . . . my soul is with the congregation of the firstborn, my body rests in hope, and if here I may honor my God either by doing or by suffering, I shall be most glad.

The dominant historical narrative of Cromwell's life has been that this religious conversion dramatically altered his life and circumstances, leading to a burning desire to seek reform in church and state alike. Believing that he was doing God's will, he gained the confidence and

energy to drive himself and others forward in pursuit of those goals.
Yet others believe that Cromwell's obscurity up until 1640 has been
overplayed. Still, the record shows that Cromwell's life before and after
his embrace of God and his dedication to the church are two separate and
distinct chapters.

When Charles I faced rebellion in Scotland in 1640—the so-called
Bishops' Wars—he was forced to reconstitute Parliament in order to raise
the necessary funds. By this time, Cromwell had become associated with
reformist elements in Parliament—those who advocated a monarchy
checked by regular parliaments and expansion of social liberty. Charles's
insistence on the powers of absolute monarchy and the denial of rights
and privileges to property owners and merchants produced considerable
ill will among the populace. As Parliament tried to encourage reform,
the king dug in his heels and refused to compromise. Cromwell was
not a galvanizing public speaker, but his passion and conviction were
evident in his denunciation of royalist excess—for example, the arrest and
imprisonment of the Puritan John Lilburne for importing religious tracts
from Holland.

By 1642, the forces supporting Parliament and the king's army were
in open warfare. Oliver Cromwell had never been a soldier. But at the onset
of conflict, at the age of forty-three, he recruited and led a cavalry unit of
two hundred volunteers. After minor skirmishes with the king's soldiers,
Cromwell led the unit in the Battle of Edgehill that fall. Cromwell and his
cavalry then joined the parliamentary forces under the command of the
earl of Manchester. After successfully leading troops into battle in East
Anglia, notably the Battle of Gainsborough, Cromwell was made a colonel
in the parliamentary army, and then rose to the rank of lieutenant general
in 1644. After the victory at the Battle of Marston Moor, Cromwell was
dubbed "Old Ironsides." He took to calling his cavalry unit "the Ironsides,"
and that is how they were known. They were fighting, he told them, for an
England dedicated to God, not dedicated to a king.

Serving under Sir Thomas Fairfax, Cromwell and his Ironsides
were instrumental in the victory at Naseby in 1645. With no military
training, Cromwell had become the premier cavalry commander in

the entire conflict, routing the king's forces in several key battles. His strengths were the moral authority he projected to his men and an instinctive ability to lead and train them. In a war fought mostly by amateur soldiers, this gave Cromwell's men an edge. The First English Civil War came to an end when Charles I surrendered in 1646. Fairfax and Cromwell received the army's formal surrender at Oxford that June. The four-year war had made Cromwell a hero; he had entered the conflict as nothing more than a member of Parliament; at its end, he was one of the primary leaders of Parliament.

But political conflict continued from 1646 to 1648. Negotiations for a new constitution broke down, with Cromwell largely caught in the middle. Parliamentary hard-liners (mostly affiliated with the English and Scottish Presbyterian movement) wanted to immediately abolish the monarchy and establish a system of universal suffrage. Many in Parliament and in the army thought this was premature and would lead to anarchy. The debate became irrelevant when in November 1647 Charles escaped from his imprisonment at Hampton Court. The king immediately organized Royalist uprisings in the West and the North, supported by Scottish Presbyterians disenchanted by Cromwell's religious policy, leading to the Second English Civil War.

Cromwell was appointed commander-in-chief of the army and pursued the Royalist forces with fierce resolve. Historians have noted that his letters and speeches increasingly used biblical imagery and took on the tone of a religious crusade. He urged supporters to read the book of Isaiah, in which only the most godly survive. For him the army was God's chosen instrument to bring justice to Britain. His letters further reveal a firm belief in "providentialism," the notion that God actively directs the affairs of the world through the actions of certain "chosen people." He believed himself to be one of the chosen, and that his army's victories indicated God's approval of his actions.

Led by Cromwell and Fairfax, the army had subdued the Royalists and Scots who were fighting for Charles I by the end of 1648. The king was once again imprisoned. Cromwell now joined those calling for an end to the monarchy and the execution of Charles I. He had come to believe that Charles I had to be eliminated if Britain were to move forward. Charles was found guilty of treason and was beheaded at the Banqueting House of the Palace of Whitehall on January 30, 1649.

Supported by the army, the remaining independent members of Parliament (the Rump Parliament) declared England a Commonwealth, and created the Council of State to govern the country. European governments were horrified at the king's execution and there were rumors of foreign invasions to reestablish the Stuart monarchy. Meanwhile, Scotland declared its allegiance to the teenage Charles II, and much of Ireland had Royalist sympathies. To deal with these threats, the English Commonwealth, led by Cromwell's army, engaged in a campaign to bring Scotland and Ireland under its control. Cromwell's invasion of Ireland is seen by some as a religious crusade—he detested Catholicism and blamed it for the persecution of Protestants across Europe.

The Irish campaign is controversial. Although successful, the English army laid waste to a number of Irish towns and settlements. During the siege of Drogheda in September 1649, for example, Cromwell's troops reportedly massacred up to 3,500 people after the town's capture. This was seen by many in England as revenge for the 1641 slaughter of Protestant settlers in Ulster. But most Irish have long considered Cromwell's actions in Drogheda and in neighboring Wexford to be war crimes. Some historians have suggested that Cromwell did not order the killing of noncombatants and that these campaigns are no worse than most major warfare of the age. Undoubtedly, Cromwell wanted to crush the resistance in Ireland and make an example of those who supported the Royalist cause.

Then in 1650 Cromwell turned his attention to Scotland, crushing the Scottish Royalist/Presbyterian forces at Dunbar, killing four thousand, taking another ten thousand prisoner, and capturing the capital, Edinburgh. In September 1651, Cromwell destroyed the last remnants of the Scot-led resistance at the Battle of Worcester. Thus, throughout the years of the Commonwealth, England, Scotland, and Ireland were ruled by a single government for the first time in British history. Cromwell believed himself to be the instrument of God's work on earth, and the savior of godly Britain. His victories were "a high act of the Lord's providence."

Roughly thirteen years after he had resigned himself to becoming a simple farmer and minor local official, Cromwell was very close to becoming the most powerful man in Britain. He urged the Council of State—the administrative arm of the Rump Parliament—to set up new elections under the Commonwealth, to unite England, Scotland, and Ireland under one united polity, and to establish a broad-based and tolerant national church. But political conflict, spiced with religious disagreements, continued. Little agreement or political progress was forthcoming, and Cromwell—the spiritual godfather of the new Britain—grew increasingly impatient.

Finally, in early April 1653 Cromwell suggested that the Rump Parliament reconstitute itself into a commission that would undertake the task of forming a new government. But his advice was ignored, and business continued as usual. Then on April 20 Cromwell stormed into the chamber, supported by forty armed guards, forcibly cleared the room, and dissolved the Parliament himself on his authority as commander of the army. He is reported to have said, "You are no parliament; I will put an end to your sitting." The key to his political strength throughout the 1650s was the loyalty of the army: It allowed him to threaten or use force when necessary and gave him political cover, as needed. In this regard, Cromwell's growing dominance of English government was not unlike the influence of some twentieth- and twenty-first-century military juntas in much of the developing world.

The successor to the Rump Parliament was the so-called Barebones Parliament—named after one of its members, Praise-God Barbon, a sectarian minister. This assembly was charged with forging a compromise agreement that would establish a constitutional system of government. But by this time—after the many efforts by committees and parliaments and the different iterations of a new constitution—it was decided to create a government around Cromwell himself—the man who had brought England to this point.

Under the proposed system, called the Instrument of Government, executive power was vested in an elected lord protector advised by a Council of State. It represents the first written constitution in the

English-speaking world. Cromwell was named lord protector for life.
He was sworn in at a ceremony at Westminster Hall on December 16,
1653. He wore plain black clothing to the ceremony to emphasize that he
was not a king, but a servant to Britain, though to many the distinction
between a king and a lord protector was hard to see. His ascension to
this high office alienated a fair number of English citizens, particularly
among the clergy, who regarded it as a betrayal of the principles for which
the English Civil Wars had been fought in the first place.

He served as lord protector over a united Britain until his death five
years later in 1658. The most likely cause of death was a urinary tract
infection, possibly related to a bout of malaria. He was succeeded as
lord protector by his son, Richard. But Richard Cromwell was not Oliver
Cromwell. He had no power base in either the civilian government or in
the army, and he was forced out of power in May 1659. The following year,
in one of the greatest ironies of all mankind, a reconvened Parliament
invited Charles II to take the royal throne of England, restoring the
monarchy and the Stuart line of royalty. Invariably, this leads one to ask:
"What was all the fighting about?"

But Charles II wasn't yet through with the man who had signed
off on the beheading of his father and had seized control of his realm.
Cromwell had been buried in an elaborate ceremony at Westminster
Abbey in September 1658. In 1661, the new king ordered Cromwell's
body exhumed, along with that of a few of his ministers. Their corpses
were submitted to ritual posthumous execution on a gallows erected
at Tyburn, near London's Hyde Park today. Cromwell's corpse was
decapitated, his body buried beneath the gallows in a pit, and his head
displayed on a pole outside Westminster Hall for more than twenty
years. Reportedly, his head blew down in a storm, then changed hands
a number of times over the centuries and was finally buried in 1960 at
Sidney Sussex College, in Cambridge, where he had briefly been a student.

Some consider Cromwell a hypocrite for engaging in civil war,
helping to murder the king, then eventually assuming the trappings of
a monarch himself. Others disagree, insisting that he acted honorably
in order to reform a political system badly in need of restructuring

and establish a more just civil government. Indeed, after Cromwell the days of a traditional, absolute monarchy were numbered: The Glorious Revolution in 1688 established a constitutional monarchy, with enumerated parliamentary powers as a check on the monarch—which was one of the original goals of Cromwell and the movement he helped create.

Cromwell's admirers also point to his role in creating a larger degree of plurality and freedom of religion, with tolerance for Protestants outside the Church of England and also for Jews; yet he was virulently anti-Catholic. His policies also helped to unite the British state and develop a stronger and more successful foreign policy, adding to England's prestige in Europe. As a general and a leader of men, his battlefield successes are unquestioned. Most would agree that in the social and religious changes he brought to English society, and in acting to remake England's politics, Cromwell surely believed that he was doing God's will.

The Razor: Hideki Tojo

The final entrant among the generals who greatly influenced the politics of their nation is Hideki Tojo of Japan. Tojo masterfully used his knowledge of the military high command and his considerable political skills to sway Emperor Hirohito and assume primary control of wartime Japan. As with Flavius Stilicho and Oliver Cromwell, Tojo was eventually executed. Of course, Cromwell had been dead for more than three years at the time of his hanging, and the charges against Stilicho were fabricated by his political opponents so they could get rid of him. Hideki Tojo's execution was a different matter altogether.

Unlike Cromwell, and more like Stilicho or Saladin, Tojo was a military man. He was born into a military family, raised to revere military traditions, and graduated from the Imperial Japanese Army Academy at the age of twenty-one. His father had been a lieutenant general in the Imperial Japanese Army, descended from the old samurai warrior class, and his mother was the daughter of a Buddhist priest. Hideki was one of ten children and the oldest son. As a youth, he was steeped in a very traditional, very conservative promilitary environment, and as a young adult he became part of what is now seen as an extremist military-fascist movement that came to dominate Japanese government in the 1920s and 1930s, pushing Japan toward imperialism and war.

He was brought up to be ambitious and combative. Some observers noted that he exhibited a nervous temperament and liked to keep busy. To him, work was pleasure, and he developed a very strong work ethic. He was not a maverick or a rebel, but was very supportive of institutions and tradition—he was tutored to obey orders by his samurai father. In remembering his encounters with Tojo, the American secretary of state, Cordell Hull, wrote that he "was a typical Japanese officer, with a small-bore, straight-laced, one-track mind. He was stubborn and self-willed, rather stupid, hard-working, and possessed a quantity of drive."

As a young officer, Tojo was posted in Germany on two occasions as a military attaché and a resident officer. As he later rose to power, he grew to become very supportive of European fascism and the Nazi Party in particular. Between the two world wars, Japan and Germany experienced somewhat similar social, political, and economic traumas: increasing social and economic polarization, a loss of confidence in existing political institutions, and a fear of the growing threat of socialist workers' movements and communism. As with Germany, economic collapse and the growing communist threat on the left prompted a political reaction on the far right. Tojo and many other Japanese officers were drawn to the Imperial Way Faction, a political movement in the Imperial Japanese Army, active in the 1920s and 1930s. Largely supported by junior officers, the Imperial Way aimed to establish a military government that promoted totalitarian, militarist, and expansionist ideals.

The instability in Japan and the rest of Asia convinced a number of Japanese officers that the military would have to play a leading role in saving Japan and extending its power. This political movement adopted a traditional Japanese spiritual philosophy, Hakkio Ichiu, that Japan was on a divine mission to unify Asia under Japanese rule. For example, the decades-long effort by imperial Japan to subjugate China, culminating with the Sino-Japanese War in 1937, was often referred to in Japan as a holy war. Later, during World War II, Japan's war policy in the Pacific theater was considered part of its divine mission. In a speech to the Japanese Parliament in 1942, Tojo praised the military's efforts to "quickly bring about the fulfillment of our mission in the Holy War."

Tojo enjoyed a steady rise through the ranks of the military in the 1920s, first as an instructor at the Army Staff College. In 1929, he was promoted to the rank of lieutenant colonel. His nickname became "Razor" (*Kamisori*), earned for his reputation as a sharp, legalistic mind, capable of making quick decisions. As he developed his political views in the 1920s, he was also steeped in the anti-Western environment of Japanese nationalism, particularly the strident anti-Americanism of many in the military establishment. Many had become irritated at what they viewed as Western interference in the "normal aspirations" of Japan to grow and prosper. For example, American resistance to Japan's claims on parts of China, Korea, and Siberia was seen as arrogant meddling. Thus, Tojo and most others in the Japanese military later saw the coming conflict with the United States as inevitable, as opposed to the viewpoint in the United States and Britain toward Japanese hostilities (notably Pearl Harbor) as "illegal," and even "cowardly."

In 1933, Tojo was promoted to major general. The following year, he was appointed commander of the army's 24th Infantry Brigade; then, in September 1935, he was made commander of Japan's invading Kwangtung Army in Manchuria. Tojo's leadership in the army and his political position were boosted by a failed coup attempt in February 1936. A rival political faction, the Kodoha, had murdered several top officials and tried to seize power. Emperor Hirohito was outraged. In the aftermath, he gave the order to purge the army of its most radical officers, and the coup leaders were tried and executed. Following the purge, most Japanese nationalists were now unified behind the leadership of Hideki Tojo and others in support of a greater role for the military in policy making and political planning.

In 1937, he was promoted to chief of staff of the Kwangtung Army. As chief, Tojo was responsible for various military operations to increase Japanese penetration into Inner Mongolia's border regions with Manchukuo. In July 1937, he personally led the units of the 1st

Independent Mixed Brigade in Operation Chahar (Battle of the Great Wall). His military and political reputation was enhanced by his command in the field, and Tojo was recalled to Japan in May 1938 to serve as vice-minister of the army.

His political star continued to rise into the 1940s. In October 1941, he was appointed army minister in Prime Minister Fumimaro Konoe's Cabinet. He was a vocal supporter of the Tripartite Alliance between Japan, Nazi Germany, and Fascist Italy, and as army minister he continued to expand the war with China. In order to further isolate China from external aid, Japan had invaded French Indochina in July 1941. In retaliation, the United States imposed economic sanctions on Japan in August, and imposed a total embargo on oil and gasoline exports. The crisis with the West that many in Japan had expected, and that Tojo had openly wanted, was fast approaching.

On September 6, a deadline of early October was fixed in imperial conference for continuing negotiations with the Americans. On October 14, the deadline had passed with no progress. Prime Minister Konoe then held his last Cabinet meeting, but Tojo did most of the talking:

> For the past six months, ever since April, the foreign minister has made painstaking efforts to adjust relations. Although I respect him for that, we remain deadlocked . . . The heart of the matter is the imposition on us of withdrawal from Indochina and China. . . If we yield to America's demands, it will destroy the fruits of the China incident. Manchukuo will be endangered and our control of Korea undermined.

The prevailing opinion within the Japanese army at that time was that continued negotiations were fruitless, and could be dangerous. The emperor thought that he would be able to better control opinions in the army by using the charismatic and well-connected Tojo. It seems that Tojo helped the emperor arrive at the conclusion already reached by the army and navy high commands—that war with the United States was inevitable. On October 16, Konoe, politically isolated and convinced that the emperor no longer trusted him, resigned. Later, he justified himself to his chief Cabinet secretary, Kenji Tomita:

Of course his majesty is a pacifist, and there is no doubt he wished to avoid war. When I told him that to initiate war is a mistake, he agreed. But the next day, he would tell me: "You were worried about it yesterday, but you do not have to worry so much." Thus, gradually, he began to lean toward war. And the next time I met him, he leaned even more toward war. In short, I felt the Emperor was telling me: "My prime minister does not understand military matters, I know much more."

In other words, the emperor needed a wartime consigliere. Following the advice of his closest political advisor, Koichi Kido, he chose Tojo to lead his new government, partly because Tojo was known for his devotion to the imperial institution. The emperor summoned Tojo to the Imperial Palace one day before he took office as prime minister.

Tojo wrote in his diary, "I thought I was summoned because the Emperor was angry at my opinion." He was given one order by the emperor: to make a policy review of what the imperial conferences had sanctioned. Tojo, who privately thought this was a waste of valuable time, nevertheless accepted the order, and carried out the review. On November 2, Tojo and his army staff chiefs reported to Hirohito that the review had been in vain. The emperor then gave his consent to war.

On November 3, chief Osami Nagano explained in detail the Pearl Harbor attack to Hirohito. The eventual plan drawn up by army and navy chiefs of staff envisaged such a mauling of the Western powers that Japanese defense perimeter lines—operating on interior lines of communications and inflicting heavy Western casualties—could not be breached. In addition, the Japanese fleet was under orders from Admiral Isoroku Yamamoto to be prepared to return to Japan on a moment's notice, should negotiations with the Americans succeed.

On November 5, Hirohito approved in imperial conference the operational plan for a war against the West and had a number of meetings with the military and Tojo through the end of the month. On December 1, another imperial conference finally sanctioned the "[w]ar against the United States, England and Holland." The attack on Pearl Harbor came six days later.

During the war, control of most of the Japanese government was in Tojo's hands. He continued to hold the position of army minister during his term as prime minister, from October 1941 to July 22, 1944. He also served concurrently as home minister from 1941 to 1942, foreign minister in September 1942, education minister in 1943, and commerce minister in 1943. Thus Tojo assumed broad authority and was free to go to the emperor as the head of his government.

With Tojo serving as the government's highest official, the army was fully in control of Japan. He was the military's foremost cheerleader and propagandist, believing passionately in its ability to conquer Asia and control Japan's destiny. Tojo placed very few limits on the armed forces' discretion and judgment, which would later make him accountable for the excesses of Japan's wartime policies.

Tojo's administration was popular early in the war, as Japanese forces claimed a number of battlefield victories. Japanese successes in Singapore, Rangoon, and the Dutch East Indies were trumpeted by Tojo as divine providence. But the Battle of Midway in June 1942 began to turn the tide of war against Japan. By 1943, Tojo faced increasing opposition from within the government and the military.

Tojo the general was forced to become Tojo the politician. And he soon learned just how difficult that was in an environment of supercharged nationalism. Matters were made worse by the structure of the Japanese wartime Cabinet: The military high command enjoyed a great deal of autonomy and was often difficult to manage. His dual roles during the war—as political official and military officer—would later make him a natural target for the Allies in their quest to end the war and hold Japanese officials accountable.

One of the great failures of the Japanese leadership was its faith in a relatively quick military victory, and Tojo was complicit in that policy. When Japan's leaders realized that the war could not be won in the short term, it became clear that there had not been sufficient planning for a long, drawn-out conflict: Materials, supplies, production, troop reserves, and alternative battle strategies were all lacking. When the tide of war began to turn in favor of the Western allies, there was little Japan could do to alter the situation. After the fall of Saipan, Tojo was forced to resign on July 18, 1944. He retired and went into seclusion.

After Japan's surrender in 1945, U.S. General Douglas MacArthur issued orders for the arrest of the first forty alleged war criminals, including Tojo. But before he could be taken into custody, he attempted suicide, shooting himself in the chest. He was rushed to the hospital and doctors were able to save him. "I am very sorry it is taking me so long to die," he murmured.

He was tried by the International Military Tribunal for the Far East for war crimes and found guilty of waging wars of aggression in violation of international law, authorizing the inhumane treatment of prisoners of war, and other charges. He was sentenced to death in November 1948 and executed by hanging on December 23, 1948. In his final statements, he apologized for the atrocities committed by the Japanese military and urged the American military to show compassion toward the Japanese people, who had suffered devastating air attacks, including two nuclear bomb blasts.

⊰ CHAPTER 7 ⊱

THE REBELS

We've looked at the generals—now we'll examine the other side of the coin, the rebels. In most cases, the generals were acting to preserve the political status quo (think Stilicho), or expanding borders and territories (Charles Martel and Hideki Tojo, among them). The rebels, however, were likely to be more interested in the total transformation of their political systems. The generals often came from military backgrounds and traditions, with the idea of national service firmly fixed in their minds. Nation-building, military conquest, and imperialism were often their main goals. But the rebels were more likely to come from civilian life and tended to be motivated by ideals and philosophies. For example, two of the rebels examined

in this chapter were Marxists, while the others were drawn to
internationalism and civil reform.

One of the common threads binding the rebels together is that their
political beliefs and worldviews were shaped largely by threats of foreign
domination. The constant threat, or reality, of foreign power—either from
France, Britain, Japan, or the United States—informed their development
in ways that led them to fight for dramatic political and social change.
Equally important, the rebels were usually fighting against regimes that
were either autocratic and repressive or too incompetent and inflexible to
handle the threats of an increasingly dangerous international system.

Modernization is also a theme prevalent among many rebels. Whereas
the generals often represented tradition, a preference for institutions, and
resistance to change, the rebels wanted to tear down tradition and institute
more modern ways of thinking and acting. This often necessitated a
dramatic departure from the past and the accepted ways of doing things
in order to survive and thrive in a new international order. The rebels,
therefore, were more likely to be influenced by what was occurring in other
countries and political systems, and were more open to seeking change.

The Ronin: Sakamoto Ryoma

At the end of the chapter on the generals, we focused on early twentieth-
century Japan, the rise of militarism, and the influence of Hideki Tojo
and his fellow generals. Now we will look closely at their grandfathers—
the events leading up to one of the most important periods in Japanese
history—the Meiji Restoration (or Revolution). Within this period, we will
focus on the story of Sakamoto Ryoma—a key figure in the political and
military development of Japan—and a born rebel.

The Meiji Restoration of the late 1860s is the signal event in Japanese
political history. It represents a bridge from Japan's feudal past to the
development of a modern state—ushering in an era of industrialization,
international relationships, and Western cultural influence. The late
nineteenth and early twentieth centuries were a time of rapid and intense
political, social, and economic change in Japan, setting the stage for the
rise of imperialism described in the last chapter.

The events leading up to the Meiji period ended more than six hundred years of feudal shogun rule in Japan. The formation in 1866 of an alliance between the leaders of the Satsuma domain and the leaders of the Choshu domain (the two strongest antishogun feudal regions) built the foundation of the Meiji Restoration. These two leaders supported the Emperor Komei (Emperor Meiji's father) and were brought together by Sakamoto Ryoma for the purpose of challenging the ruling Tokugawa shogunate (bakufu) and restoring the emperor to power. On February 3, 1867, Emperor Meiji ascended to the throne after Emperor Komei's death.

Sakamoto Ryoma, one of the agents of this revolution, was born in 1835 in the feudal domain of Tosa, on the island of Shikoku, Japan. His family was from the ranks of merchant samurai, one of the lower ranks in the samurai hierarchy. At that time, there were four distinct social classes, the *shi-nou-kou-sho* (warrior, farmer, artisan, and merchant, in descending order of rank). Ryoma's father ran a successful trade emporium.

At the age of fourteen, Ryoma began to practice traditional kendo, the way of the sword. Some historians say that his older sister enrolled him in fencing classes after he was bullied at school. Through practice and diligent study, he became quite a good swordsman. In 1853, after completing his training, he was sent to Edo (present-day Tokyo) to develop his technique at one of the elite schools of kendo. There he became friends with the nephew of Chiba Shusaku, then the most famous sword master in Japan. Ryoma improved his skills and became the strongest among the students in the school. At the age of nineteen, he received the second rank (*shihan dai*) in his school. He acquired a reputation as one of the strongest sword masters among the many young students who had been sent by their clans to study kendo in Edo.

Ryoma had mastered an ancient tradition at a time when his world was changing. The opening of Japan's ports to Western colonial fleets, coerced by Commodore Matthew Perry and others from 1853 onward, exposed the weakness of the Tokugawa shoguns, and triggered nationalist unrest under the slogan *sonno joi* ("revere the emperor, expel the barbarians"). Ryoma, upon seeing Perry's "black ships" in Edo Bay, was filled with a feeling of dread, but also a feeling of wonder at the power and technology of the foreign fleet. Trained from youth to be a loyalist and a patriot, he was drawn to radical political elements in Edo who wanted to protect Japan from foreign threats at all costs.

Largely influenced by a childhood friend, Takechi Hanpeita, Ryoma became involved in the anti-Tokugawa, pro-emperor movement. Many of these young samurai believed that the Tokugawa shogun was too weak or too corrupt to protect Japan from the foreigners, and they were anxious to see changes take place. He joined a radical movement in his home region of Tosa, but became impatient with its focus on Tosa alone. He aspired to join the broader-based antishogun radicals threatening Tokugawa rule across Japan. Many had come to believe that the greatest obstacle to the salvation of Japan from foreign subjugation was the antiquated Tokugawa system, with its hundreds of feudal domains and repressive class structure.

So in 1862 Ryoma decided to flee Tosa and separate himself from his home clan. Under Japan's feudal hierarchy, one needed permission from the provincial government to leave. But Ryoma decided that asking for official permission would be too risky, so he became a ronin, a samurai with no lord or master, and so was branded a criminal by his home district of Tosa. At that time, there were a number of young samurai across Japan, filled with idealism and ambition, who were willing to break with tradition and obligation, citing a higher duty to country. Like Ryoma, they were willing to sacrifice their status and their safety to safeguard the imperial regime.

Eager to take action, Ryoma, using the simple logic of the swordsman, decided that a campaign of assassination and terror might spur action on the part of others where politics and diplomacy had failed. His next step would change his life. He decided to assassinate a high-ranking official in the Tokugawa bakufu, Katsu Kaishu. Kaishu was a moderate and a supporter of modernization and Western-style progress, so to Ryoma he seemed like a traitor.

Upon his arrival in Edo, Ryoma was likely sheltered by his old sword master Chiba. He became part of an underground network of ronin and various other samurai involved in anti-Tokugawa conspiracies. He recruited an ally, Okamoto Kenzaburo, for his assassination attempt on Kaishu. Arriving at Kaishu's home, they were met at the door by Kaishu himself—he had been forewarned by an informant. Kaishu called out, "Have you come to kill me?" Ryoma and his assassin-comrade froze in astonishment. "Because if you did," continued Kaishu, "you ought to wait until we've had a chance to talk."

Ryoma's political views up to that time had been very narrow; he was trained as a swordsman, not as a prince or a statesman. Kaishu opened his eyes to the wider picture of what was possible with planning and with patience. Ryoma learned that Kaishu was actually just as interested in protecting imperial rule and strengthening Japan as he was. He, too, was resentful of Western demands on Japan, but thought that opening the country up to contact with the West could actually strengthen Japan through modernization, increased economic potential, and the adoption of new technologies. What particularly impressed Ryoma was that Kaishu had a plan of action:

> What we ought to do is send out ships from our country and impress strongly on the leaders of all Asian countries that their very existence depends on banding together and building a powerful navy, and that if they do not develop the necessary technology they will not be able to escape being trampled underfoot by the West. We should start with Korea, our nearest neighbor, and then go on to include China.

Ryoma responded that he had, in fact, come to kill him that night, but "now that I have heard what you have to say, I am ashamed of my narrow-minded bigotry and beg you to let me become your disciple." It was an amazing turnaround in his thinking, but he had now found a leader whose ideas made perfect sense to him. He became a follower and assistant to Kaishu, and introduced his friends and fellow samurai to Kaishu and his ideas for advancement.

The next year, Kaishu persuaded the shogun to allow him to establish a naval school at the coastal village of Hyogo, near modern-day Kobe. He obtained a pardon for Ryoma, still a refugee from Tosa, and named him as an administrator at the new naval training school. Kaishu and Ryoma recruited over three hundred samurai from all over Japan, many of them ronin like Ryoma, who would form the basis of the new naval ranks. The efforts of Kaishu and Ryoma established the institution and training infrastructure that would eventually become the modern Japanese navy.

Katsu Kaishu also introduced Ryoma to Yokoi Shōnan, a loyalist leader of the Fukui clan and a scholar and political reformer. Yokoi shared his vision for the future of Japan, including a complete reform of the Tokugawa bakufu government, a reconciliation between the shogun and the imperial court, the opening of Japan to foreign trade, economic reform, and the establishment of a modern military along Western lines. He also envisioned a national assembly of the major domains, with the shogun evolving into something that resembled a prime minister.

Ryoma became the head of training at the Kobe naval school. During this period, he matured significantly. He retained the confidence and bravado of a master swordsman, but added to that was a more fully developed and strategic political outlook. The increased responsibility at the school and the influential contacts he made as a result also boosted his profile among the political class.

But by 1864, Japan had become unstable. The anti-Tokugawa forces from the Choshu and Satsuma regions had bombed Dutch ships, fought with the British at Kagoshima, and assassinated several key shogun officials. The Choshu clan, in particular, were singled out for punishment by the bakufu. Choshu samurai attempted several coups in 1864, including an attack on the Kyoto Imperial Palace. The Choshu were now branded an "enemy of the court," and all other clans, including the Satsuma, were ordered to attack the Choshu. Katsu Kaishu and Ryoma met with Saigo Takamori, one of leading officials of the Satsuma clan, and convinced him that the opening of Japan to the West was inevitable, and that as the government was unable to deal with this, the only hope for Japan was for a major clan alliance to take power. Taking Kaishu's advice, Saigo decided to refuse to attack the Choshu.

But as the threats to its rule increased, the Tokugawa bakufu became even more authoritarian and clamped down harder on its opponents. Kaishu's naval school had included among its students a fair number of ronin, technically fugitives, and some of these had been implicated in the Choshu attacks on the Tokugawa government. This was used by some of Kaishu's enemies in Edo to convince the bakufu that Kaishu should be replaced. Therefore, he was dismissed from the school and replaced by a bakufu official. This was a significant blow to Ryoma and many of his comrades—they were losing their official protection and a powerful political ally. But Kaishu wasn't quite finished—he wrote to the Satsuma leader, Komatsu Tatewaki, to seek his assistance in supporting Ryoma and his friends. After all, the Satsuma could surely use men of Ryoma's experience and abilities, particularly his naval training. The Satsuma clan became Ryoma's new political and military base of operations. This put him right in the middle of the political developments that would lead to the restoration.

And Ryoma took full advantage of his opportunities. He continued Kaishu's political strategy of seeking the unity of the anti-Tokugawa forces. The Tokugawa war on the Choshu and its strict control of Japanese waterways continued to irritate the Satsuma. But it may have been the bakufu's alliance with France that was the final straw, stoking the antiforeign emotion sweeping through much of Japan. The bakufu's disdainful treatment of Japanese imperial rule and its embrace of foreign power and influence handed Ryoma an opportunity to urge an alliance between the Satsuma and the Choshu.

The Satsuma used Ryoma's naval training by putting him in charge of its shipping. Under their auspices and protection, he established the Kaientai, a shipping company (the forerunner of the Mitsubishi Corporation, the giant Japanese conglomerate of today). Based in the international port city of Nagasaki, the Kaientai was a private navy and shipping firm through which Ryoma and his men ran guns for the Choshu and Satsuma revolutionaries.

The alliance between Satsuma and Choshu meant that the bakufu's chances of retaining national leadership had dwindled. The success of the Kaientai encouraged the imperial court nobles to reach out to the Satusma and Choshu, a very important political development. And this coalition also added the support of Ryoma's home region of Tosa, whose leaders had watched the developing anti-Tokugawa alliance with great interest. The stage was being set for the end of Tokugawa rule and the reemergence of imperial rule in Japan.

Barely thirty years old, Sakamoto Ryoma had become a very important man in the revolutionary movement, but he was also a marked man. To the bakufu, he was a target for assassination. In 1866, there was an attempt on his life, and his escape from certain death has become the stuff of legend. He and a bodyguard were ambushed at an inn on the outskirts of the imperial capital. A young maidservant at the inn, named Oryo, was soaking in a hot bath when she heard the assassins break in. According to the story, she ran from the bathroom stark naked and hurried upstairs to warn Ryoma. What happened next is a very famous scene in Japanese history, and has been re-created numerous times in books, television shows, and movies. Ryoma was armed with two swords and a Smith & Wesson revolver. He and his bodyguard waited quietly for the assailants to enter the room, and then lunged at them. In the ensuing brawl, Ryoma lost part of his thumb when he was hit with a short sword, but not before he emptied his revolver into the assassins and then switched to his swords. Several assassins lay dead or dying as the others fled into the night. Not coincidentally, Oryo, the maidservant who had warned of the attack, later became Ryoma's wife.

Also of note from this period is the development of Ryoma's "Eight-Point Plan" for a new government. It is significant because almost the entire Restoration program is contained within Ryoma's design. It was based on the idea that a peaceful transition of power was possible, which he had first heard from his old mentor Kaishu. It was also based on ideas borrowed from Western parliamentary governments, whose methods of operation the Japanese reformers greatly admired. As regional leaders met in Kyoto to discuss the future shape of politics in Japan, Ryoma showed his ideas to a political ally, Goto Shojiro, who hailed from his home region of Tosa. His plan called for:

1. Political power to be returned to the imperial court.
2. Two legislative bodies, an upper and lower house.
3. Men of ability and experience from the nobility to be used as councilors.
4. Foreign affairs to be conducted in accordance with imperial regulations.
5. Legislation and regulations from earlier times to be set aside and new codes established.
6. The navy to be enlarged.
7. An imperial guard to be established to defend the capital.
8. The value of goods and silver to be brought into line with foreign markets.

Representatives of Satusma, Choshu, and Tosa embarked on a two-track strategy: They would prepare for war against the Tokugawa regime but at the same time advance a proposal for the peaceful transfer of power to the emperor and the formation of a new government, largely along the lines suggested by Ryoma. With the support of the emperor and the threat of war looming, in November 1867 the allies were able to pressure the Tokugawa shogun to relinquish power, effectively beginning the "restoration" period, leading to imperial rule and parliamentary government.

Unfortunately, Ryoma would not live to see the new Meiji government system come into existence. He and his friend and ally, Nakaoka Shintaro, had traveled to Kyoto, where they were planning to meet with several samurai allies the following day for discussions on the Eight-Point Plan. There was still significant pro-Tokugawa sentiment in Kyoto and other major Japanese cities. On the evening of December 10, 1867, they were attacked by bakufu agents, most likely from the ranks of the Shinsengumi, a private police force organized by powerful nobles loyal to the bakufu. This time, there was no maidservant to warn them of the impending attack. Three assassins rushed into the room after overpowering Ryoma's assistant, who was waiting outside. This time, Ryoma was only lightly armed. He and Nakaoka were taken almost completely by surprise and cut down quickly by the three men. Both men were mourned, and the loss of Ryoma was felt by many.

In subsequent years, Sakamoto Ryoma passed into legend. His adventures and his contributions to the liberty and the modernization of Japan were hailed by statesmen, citizens, and schoolchildren. Even today, he is a national hero in Japan. His image and his legacy are indelibly linked to Japan's emergence as a world power. For example, in 2005 executives of two hundred Japanese corporations were asked by *Asahi Shimbun,* a national daily newspaper: "Who from the past millennium of world history would be most useful in overcoming Japan's current financial crisis?" Sakamoto Ryoma received more mention than any other historical figure, topping such giants as Thomas Edison, Leonardo da Vinci, Saigo Takamori, and the founders of the Japanese economic giants NEC and Honda.

The Soul and the Sword: Mazzini and Garibaldi

Around the same time as Sakamoto Ryoma and his allies brought an end to the age of the shoguns in Japan, a nationalistic revolution was also brewing in Italy. Italy was also dominated by a splintered political system of regional powers, rooted in the past several hundred years of its history. Known as *il Risorgimento* (the Resurgence), this decades-long political and social movement had unified the disparate states of the Italian peninsula into a single Italian nation by the 1870s.

After the Congress of Vienna in 1815, Italy was once again divided into a pre-Napoleon patchwork of independent governments. The Habsburg Austrian Empire controlled much of northern Italy and was steadfastly opposed to any changes that would weaken its grip. Another independent state was the Vatican, which vigorously defended its rights to govern the papal states of central Italy. There were also the kingdom of Piedmont-Sardinia, the grand duchy of Tuscany, the duchy of Modena, the kingdom of Naples and Sicily in the South, and the kingdom of Lombardy-Venetia in the North.

The story of the nineteenth century in Italy is largely the story of attempts to unify the Italian kingdom. The idea of a single Italian nation was popular in many quarters, particularly in literature and the arts. But *nationalism* was a dirty word to the monarchs and dukes who controlled regional political systems, particularly the Austrian Habsburgs. The

Vatican also opposed efforts at unification, fearing a loss of power for the Catholic Church. Even those who advocated some type of unified Italian government could not agree on what form it should take. Some suggested a confederation of states under the leadership of the pope; others wanted a republic with Western-style political parties; while still others insisted on a national monarchy.

Under these circumstances, the eventual unification of Italy into a single national state was seen by some as a miracle, or at the very least a result of divine intervention. The reign of the first king of Italy, Victor Emmanuel II, of the kingdom of Piedmont-Sardinia, was largely designed and orchestrated by his chief minister, Count Camillo di Cavour. But much of the credit for Italian unification goes to two other men—Giuseppe Mazzini and Giuseppe Garibaldi. Together with Cavour, they are the founders of modern Italy. To many historians, Cavour is considered the "brain of unification," Mazzini is the "soul," and Garibaldi is the "sword."

No question, the heart and soul of Italian nationalism was Giuseppe Mazzini: He was acknowledged by most nineteenth-century Italians as the spiritual father of modern Italy. He shared with Sakamoto Ryoma a belief that his nation was too weak and splintered to compete in the international arena, and that its people would prosper under a unified political system. But where Ryoma was willing to vest much of the nation's power in an emperor, Mazzini was strictly anti-monarchist: He insisted on a purely republican form of government. Mazzini also shared a strong belief in the virtues of republicanism with that other great Italian thinker, Niccolo Machiavelli. In fact, one could say that Mazzini helped to fulfill Machiavelli's dream of a unified Italy not dominated by foreign powers.

Mazzini was born in Genoa, then part of the Ligurian Republic, under the domination of France. His father was a professor of medicine at the University of Genoa. Although physically delicate as a child, the young Mazzini showed signs of great intelligence, devouring books on a range of subjects. At the age of fourteen, he entered the university and eventually chose to study law. While still in his teens, Mazzini committed himself to the cause of Italian independence and unity. In 1830, he traveled to

Tuscany, where he joined a nationalist group, the Carbonari, a mostly underground organization dedicated to radical political reforms. Forced into exile in 1831 for his revolutionary activities, he began to recruit followers and organize uprisings against the rulers of the various Italian states. His association, *Giovine Italia* (Young Italy), founded in the 1830s, attracted adherents throughout the peninsula and among Italian political exiles everywhere. With the exception of Giuseppe Garibaldi, no other Italian Risorgimento leader enjoyed greater international renown than Mazzini in his time.

Unlike Machiavelli, Mazzini's revolutionary vision extended beyond the limited objective of Italian national unity. His primary goals were the end of Austrian hegemony in Italy and of the temporal power of the pope, overall Italian unity, republicanism, democracy, and the liberation of all oppressed peoples. Imbued with a messianic zeal, he believed that, by banding together under the banner of "God and people," Italians would succeed in ridding themselves of their various rulers and establish a unified, democratic republic with its capital in Rome. This new Italy would lead other subject peoples to freedom and embody a "third" Rome, successor to ancient and papal Rome. A new Europe, controlled by the people and not by sovereigns, would replace the old order.

After founding the revolutionary group Young Italy, Mazzini formed a number of other similar groups, all dedicated to nationalistic movements of liberation—Young Germany, Young Poland, Young Switzerland, and Young Europe. Incidentally, this is where the expression "Young Turks" came from, when Turkish army cadets formed an organization inspired by Young Europe. In the early 1830s, the Austrian government declared membership in Young Italy to be an act of treason, punishable by death. By the 1840s, Mazzini had become the recognized leader of the Italian nationalist revolutionary movement. His revolutionary ideas and calls for Italian nationalism were communicated through letters, essays, and newspaper columns throughout Europe. His appeal to Italians, restive under oppressive governments, was unrivaled, if not unchallenged. Intellectuals and artisans, men and women, all responded to him. Many lost their lives in abortive revolts inspired by his teachings.

The high point of Mazzini's revolutionary activity came in 1848–1849 when revolutions were sweeping through parts of Italy and the rest of Europe. Returning from exile in Switzerland, he traveled to Milan, where he was greeted enthusiastically by revolutionary leaders. But the movement was divided over the issue of accepting help from either the French government or the kingdom of Piedmont-Sardinia and its monarch Charles Albert. Mazzini was steadfastly opposed to foreign intervention, and he argued against inviting the French into his coalition. He believed that in the short term it would be better to work with the Sardinian monarch if it meant the expulsion of the Austrians from within Italy's borders. But he was accused by some of abandoning his commitment to republican principles by agreeing to an alliance, however short, with the Sardinian monarchy. The disagreement became irrelevant that July when the Austrian military reasserted its control over northern Italy, ending the insurrection.

Mazzini had greater success the following year when Pope Pius IX fled from revolutionary mobs and a republic of Rome was proclaimed. Mazzini was invited to join the new government, and he was elected to the Triumvirate, the republic's executive body. However, the experiment in democracy proved brief, as the pope appealed for help from the French, whose forces overwhelmed the republic's defenses in July 1849. The republic dissolved, Mazzini once again went into exile. From that point on, Mazzini would be less directly involved in efforts to nationalize Italy, but he would remain its guiding spirit and prime inspiration.

The failure to drive the Austrians from Italy also had political repercussions in Piedmont-Sardinia. King Charles Albert abdicated in favor of his son, Victor Emmanuel II. In the early 1850s, the new king established a more liberal, Western-style government of ministers, run by his prime minister, Camillo di Cavour. From that point, it was Cavour and the kingdom of Sardinia that became the driving force of unification, assisted greatly by the military exploits of Garibaldi.

If Mazzini was the spiritual father of modern Italy, then Giuseppe Garibaldi was its physical manifestation. The two men are a study in contrasts. Garibaldi was nothing if not colorful and charismatic: He was one of the most dynamic military personalities of the nineteenth century, fighting for independence movements on two continents. Dubbed the "Hero of Two Worlds," he fought not only for Italian nationalism, but also helped lead a rebel army in South America in the 1840s.

Garibaldi would go on to become something of an international celebrity, an early example of image making, which was helpful in efforts to raise money in Europe and gain support for Italian nationalism. He had many admirers, among them the famed French author Alexandre Dumas, who described Garibaldi as "of medium stature, well proportioned, with fair hair, blue eyes, Greek nose, brow, and chin—in other words, as approaching as near as may be to the true type of beauty." He was a dashing figure, very adept at imagery and stagecraft. While in South America, he adopted the red shirts worn by rural gauchos, which became his trademark: He was often photographed or drawn wearing a red shirt with military insignia. Some thought him vain—one wonders if General George Custer studied Garibaldi for dramatic cues.

Garibaldi was from Nice, ruled at the time by the French, as was Mazzini's native Genoa. His father was active in coastal trade; thus Giuseppe was raised to be a merchant seaman, becoming a marine captain in 1832. His life changed in 1833 when he met a political émigré who was active in Mazzini's organization, Young Italy. Inspired by the idea of Italian nationalism and republican government, Garibaldi joined the group. The following year he met Mazzini himself and joined in a popular insurrection against the Sardinian monarchy. The plot failed, and many of its leaders were jailed or exiled. Garibaldi managed to escape, but was sentenced to death in absentia. He fled to Marseilles, then to Tunisia, making his way to Brazil and the beginning of his South American adventures.

There he found a wife, Ana Maria da Silva, and a population in distress. With other Italian exiles and republican émigrés from Europe, he formed the Italian Legion and fought on behalf of the separatists of the Rio Grande do Sul (a former Brazilian province) and the Uruguayans opposed to the Argentine dictatorship. Garibaldi's legionnaires fought under the banner of a black flag, symbolizing Italy in mourning, along with a volcano at the flag's center, representing Italy's dormant power. The Italian Legion attracted followers and grew into a significant fighting force. Garibaldi's mastery of guerrilla warfare and his successful opposition to Brazilian and Argentine imperialism liberated Uruguay in 1846, making Garibaldi a hero in South America and in Europe.

But Garibaldi's heart and mind were focused on his native Italy. He returned in 1848, eager to take part in the revolt against Austrian rule in northern Italy. He agreed with Mazzini's opinion that the republicans should join with the Sardinian monarch, and he offered his services to its king, Charles Albert. But the king knew of Garibaldi's anti-imperialism, both in Italy and in the Americas, and refused to cooperate with him. When the Austrians retook northern Italy, Garibaldi moved his forces to Rome to support Mazzini and the newly formed Roman Republic. Though Garibaldi's Italian Legion won some battles against the numerically superior French, he could not hold out after French reinforcements arrived. He argued in favor of retreating and continuing the resistance from the Apennine Mountains—"Wherever we may be, there will be Rome," he argued. But he was overruled and the Roman government surrendered to the French. Garibaldi fled as he was pursued by Austrian, French, and Spanish troops.

On the run again, Garibaldi stayed briefly in Tangier, then made his way to New York City in 1850. His wife had died in Italy the previous year. He was sheltered by Italian exiles, including the inventor Antonio Meucci, and made a living as a sea captain, recording several voyages to the Pacific and to the North Atlantic. He returned to Italy in 1854 and, using an inheritance from the death of his older brother, bought part of an island north of Sardinia.

His return to prominence came with the Austro-Sardinian War of 1859–1860. Unlike the first war against Austria in 1848, when King Charles Albert turned his back on Garibaldi, Victor Emmanuel II was eager to make use of his military expertise. He was appointed major general and formed a volunteer unit called the Hunters of the Alps. In this capacity, Garibaldi worked as a sort of privateer, allied with the Sardinian armed forces.

Here Garibaldi parted philosophical ways with his mentor, Giuseppe Mazzini: While Mazzini was not opposed to joining forces with Sardinia in 1848 to evict the Austrians, he strongly opposed forming a united Italy behind the Sardinian monarchy—or any monarchy. Mazzini opposed introducing foreign forces, such as France, into the mix. But Garibaldi had come to believe that the only way Italian unification could become a reality was under the banner of Victor Emmanuel II and the political power of the Sardinian monarchy.

The Sardinians joined forces with the French to seize control of much of northern Italy (Lombardy, Parma, and Modena). As Victor Emmanuel and Napoleon III of France marched into Milan, the Austrians eventually withdrew to Venice. As part of the deal with the French, Sardinia ceded to them control of the alpine territories of Nice and Savoy. Garibaldi was angered at the loss of Nice, his birthplace, to the French, and he blamed Cavour for this betrayal. But he had little opportunity to do anything about it. Cavour and Victor Emmanuel II convinced him that there were more important matters to consider—for example, the necessity of bringing southern Italy into the new alliance.

In 1860, Garibaldi led his forces against the kingdom of Naples and Sicily as part of the drive to unify Italy. By May, he had taken the Sicilian capital of Palermo, declaring himself dictator of Sicily in the name of Victor Emmanuel II of Italy. Garibaldi's victory in Sicily gained worldwide attention and made him a hero to many Italians. With the help of the British navy, he and his forces crossed the Strait of Messina and victoriously entered Naples. Together with the Sardinian forces, Garibaldi now controlled most of Italy south of Rome. The big question mark at that point was this: What about Rome?

Garibaldi wanted to finish the job of unification by marching on Rome. But Rome and the pope were still defended by the French army (at the insistence of French Catholics), and Victor Emmanuel was unwilling to jeopardize the gains he had made through his alliance with France by risking a war with the French over Rome. The Sardinian forces had already conquered many of the papal territories in their march south to meet Garibaldi's forces, but had conspicuously avoided Rome. Though

Garibaldi distrusted the pragmatic Cavour, he accepted the authority of Victor Emmanuel II. In October 1860, in a meeting that is now a famous moment in Italian history, Garibaldi greeted Victor Emmanuel at Teano as the undisputed king of all Italy. Only months later (February 1861), the assembled deputies of the first Italian parliament in Turin proclaimed Victor Emmanuel II the king of Italy. Garibaldi then retired to the island of Caprera, while the remaining work of unifying the peninsula was left to Victor Emmanuel.

But it was very difficult for Garibaldi to stay in retirement. His role in the unification of Italy was complete, but the "Hero of Two Worlds" was ready to move on to new battles. At the outbreak of the American Civil War in 1861, he volunteered his services to President Abraham Lincoln. According to historians, Garibaldi was ready to accept a commission in the Union Army, but his condition—that the war's objective be declared as the abolition of slavery—could not be met by President Lincoln at that time for political reasons.

In 1862, believing he would have the support of the new Italian government, he once again raised a fighting force to attempt to seize control of Rome. But the Italian government resisted his efforts, refusing to allow him and his men to attack Rome. There was even a short brawl in the Calabria Mountains as the Italian army took Garibaldi's forces into custody. Garibaldi himself was injured, but he ordered his own men not to fire on their fellow Italians. He was held in custody briefly, while he recovered from his wounds, and then released.

He took part in the Austro-Prussian War in 1866—Italy had allied with Prussia, which allowed the Italians to finally gain possession of Venice. In 1867, Garibaldi renewed his hostilities toward the pope, trying to organize yet another attack on Rome, but was once again frustrated by Italian authorities. In his campaign against Rome, he had sought international support for a proposal that would eliminate the papacy. At a conference in Geneva, he had declared that the papacy was "the most harmful of all secret societies" and should be abolished. The 1870 Franco-Prussian War resulted in French troops being recalled from Rome, allowing the Italian government to finally gain control of the papal city. The war was disastrous for France, but a boon to Italy, which gained control of Venice and Rome, consolidating its national political strength.

Among Garibaldi's final adventures was service to the newly declared Third French Republic—formed after the collapse of the French Empire and the abdication of Napoleon III. Then in 1879 he founded the League of Democracy, an international organization advocating universal suffrage, the abolition of church property, and the emancipation of women.

Garibaldi saw himself as an emancipator. He was dedicated to strengthening Italy as a nation and freeing it from what he saw as regional and foreign dictatorships sapping its liberty. He believed the pope's political authority was an obstacle to Italian nationalism, as evidenced by Garibaldi's multiple attempts to control Rome. But he was also an internationalist: Even though Italy was his main priority, he was passionate about fighting for liberal political progress and anti-imperialism anywhere in the world. He is remembered as an Italian patriot, and a patron saint of nineteenth-century nationalism.

The Perfect Revolutionary: Zhou Enlai

Zhou Enlai, the man who gave a human face to the communist revolution in China, was in many ways the exact opposite of Giuseppe Garibaldi, especially in terms of personal style and approach. Garibaldi was grandiose and theatrical, whereas Zhou was much more reserved and cerebral—more like Mazzini. But Zhou had much in common with both Mazzini and Garibaldi when it came to the political environment of China. As with the two Italian nationalists, Zhou's homeland was dominated by foreign powers—Britain and Japan, for example—and the domestic political system had been fragmented by regional leaders and warlords.

In 1898, Zhou Enlai was born into a dying political system, the Qing Dynasty, the last of the major dynastic empires that ruled China for more than two thousand years. The struggle within China to throw off and replace the dynastic system in the early twentieth century was not unlike the turmoil facing Sakamoto Ryoma and Japanese nationalists several decades earlier in trying to move past the shogun era. One major difference was the emergence in China of the Communist Party, leading Japan and China to move in opposite directions politically—the emerging threat of leftist movements in Asia and Europe helped spur the right-wing militarization of Japan, as noted in the previous chapter.

The Last Perfect Revolutionary is the subtitle of a biography of Zhou Enlai written by Gao Wenqian, a former official of the Chinese Communist Party. Censored in China, this book chronicles the career and the ordeals of Mao Zedong's loyal servant and details how China's survival and emergence as a world power simply would not have happened without Zhou. Wenqian's book is a flattering view of Zhou, building him up as a sort of Chinese Thomas Jefferson. Alternatively, the journalist Jack Anderson, in *Confessions of a Muckraker* (1979), had this to say about Zhou Enlai:

> In his mid-forties, Zhou Enlai had a handsome face, which lingers in my memory for its black eyes and incandescent intelligence. He was slight of build but indefatigable; he affected simplicity but was an elegant man, graceful of movement, accomplished in English and French as well as Chinese dialects, buttressing his arguments with historical and literary allusions that evinced a formidable education. And one caught flashes of a ruthless rationalism that would sacrifice the lives of millions to the triumph of an idea. Walter Robertson, the State Department's Far Eastern expert, described the Zhou Enlai of those years as "one of the most charming, intelligent and attractive men of any race" he had ever known. "But he'll cut your throat."

Some argue that Zhou Enlai was the Chinese Machiavelli. He was a talented diplomat, with a gift for strategic thinking and pragmatic deal making. Very much like Machiavelli, he was greatly concerned with unifying his country as a means of saving it from foreign domination. During Zhou's lifetime, in particular, China was struggling for its very life, not to mention its independence—first from the British, then from the Japanese, and finally from the Soviet Union. But in other ways he was far from Machiavellian: He was willing to surrender power and follow Mao, for example.

Reading Gao Wenqian's work on Zhou Enlai, one is reminded once again of just how demented the Communist Party's supreme leader, Mao Zedong, truly was. In many ways, Zhou was the opposite of Mao. At heart, according to Wenqian, Zhou believed in the "middle way"—the ultimate Confucian ideal. If Mao was by nature a disruptive, provocative personality, Zhou was ever the diplomat, supremely poised, smooth, and charming. But that is part of what makes this story so remarkable: Zhou Enlai had no choice but to work and succeed in an environment where the leader of the country was paranoid and dangerous; no one knew when the slightest wrong move might set him off.

Zhou, along with many other young Chinese, had been drawn to political radicalism partly in response to perceived slights by the West. At the Paris Peace Conference of 1919, the Great Powers all but ignored the Chinese delegates and decided instead to transfer the former German concessions China had been expecting to Japan, which at that time was an ally of the West. This was tantamount to an enormous betrayal by the colonial Western powers, and fomented the political and social revolution of the May Fourth Movement, when students took to the streets protesting Western influence and ideals in China. Many of these would-be reformers gravitated toward socialist and communist ideals.

Zhou emerged soon after as a central figure in student protests. That summer he helped to found a radical publication and he began his career as a political agitator. He was a charter member of an underground group called the Awakening Society, in which he met his future wife, Deng Yingchao. In 1920 he led a large-scale student revolt at Nankai University and was arrested. He spent six months in jail, and emerged a hardened and serious revolutionary. As he became more involved in revolutionary activities, he was increasingly drawn to Marxism. In Beijing, he met a number of political activists who encouraged him to travel to Europe to study Marxist principles and build revolutionary ties.

Zhou spent four years in Europe—first in France, then in Germany. The Marxist training he received there made him valuable to the Chinese communist movement in the 1920s. During the early years of the Chinese Communist Party's struggles for survival, from the Nanchang Uprising in 1927 to the Long March in 1934, Zhou was a crucial party organizer and political strategist.

The key moment in the development of the Chinese Communist Party, and the domination of the party by Mao Zedong, came in January 1935 in the small town of Zunyi. There, at a party conference, party leaders confronted each other over the heavy losses suffered during the Long March. In the midst of factional disputes, in which rival party officials kept trying to gain the upper hand, Zhou threw his support to Mao, thereby ensuring Mao's supremacy in the party and unifying the rank and file behind strong leadership. Ironically, Zhou was ultimately responsible for giving the world Mao Zedong. To historians like Gao Wenquian, this was characteristic of Zhou's philosophy—an unselfish (virtually anti-Machiavellian) view of what was in the best interests of the revolution and, he believed, of the people of China. But it also betrayed a willingness to throw in his lot with tyrants, if that meant securing victory for his Marxist-inspired revolution.

To Zhou, his decades-long relationship with Mao was born of necessity. Zhou sought a unified country that could control its own destiny. For his part, Mao was never warm toward Zhou, but merely saw him as a very useful tool. In fact, Mao resented him, leading to a relationship akin to those some American presidents have had with their vice presidents. It was as if the Soviet dictator Joseph Stalin had kept Leon Trotsky at his side, using his political and organizational talents, as opposed to jettisoning him and eventually ordering his assassination.

The day Zhou died in 1976, Mao was both delighted and worried—delighted because, in truth, he despised him; worried because he was afraid that, in death, Zhou would overshadow the insecure Mao. Mao owed his political survival to Zhou, a bitter pill for him to swallow. But the truth was, he needed him. Zhou's diplomatic skills and his international experience were of great use to Mao and the Communist Party after World War II. So much so that Zhou became premier of the Chinese government, beginning with its inception as the People's Republic of China, in October 1949.

Initially, the Cold War–era international community ostracized China, with the Americans leading a trade embargo and preventing the new People's Republic from taking China's seat at the United Nations. Conflict with the American-dominated UN forces in the Korean War did little to ease the tension. It was Zhou, in April 1954, who made the first steps toward reconciliation at the Geneva conference convened to discuss a solution to the Franco-Vietnamese War. Despite the cold treatment he received, Zhou impressed many with how he dealt with American Secretary of State John Foster Dulles; his skills at mediation gained an international audience.

The following year at an international conference of African and Asian countries, Zhou made his first pitch for Chinese leadership of the developing world claiming that the Americans were the main threat to stability in Asia. Despite ongoing revolutionary rhetoric, this marked the beginning of a process whereby China gradually became more a force for regime stability than for revolutionary insurgency in much of the developing world. Indeed, despite the continued shelling of the offshore islands occupied by Taiwan, Zhou persuaded his colleagues not to invade, and began to use the phrase "peaceful reunification."

Zhou spent much of the 1950s and 1960s traveling the world pressing his diplomatic initiatives. These initiatives came to fruition in the 1970s. The crowning achievement of his career was the dialogue he initiated with the United States, which led to the normalization of relations between the two countries. Most historians and political observers agree that this was a development Mao Zedong could never have achieved on his own.

It was a move orchestrated by Zhou Enlai, again, as with his original alliance with Mao, for the benefit of China's survival. As relations with the Soviet Union grew worse in the 1960s, Zhou knew that China risked being further isolated and marginalized. His solution was to court the United States and bring pressure on the Soviets, fully realizing that China and the United States would essentially be using each other. But he also knew that nothing would happen unless Mao saw the benefits of such a course of action. Zhou, working with top Chinese generals, was eventually able to convince Mao that it was smart strategy to approach the Americans.

Zhou's "ping-pong" diplomacy with the United States, in which he initiated contact with American officials present for the World Table Tennis Championships in Nagoya, Japan, laid the foundation for secret talks with Henry Kissinger in July 1971. This was followed by Nixon's visit to China the following February, and then the Shanghai Communiqué, in which the United States formally recognized the PRC. The world had changed overnight, and Zhou Enlai had given China a front-row seat.

At home, Zhou was a moderating influence on the acerbic and iron-fisted Mao. But even he was unable to prevent implementation of the disastrous Cultural Revolution. Mao defended his actions as a means of preserving true socialism, but in reality it was the product of his paranoia. It was reminiscent of the party purges orchestrated by Stalin in the 1930s. Young, pro-Mao student radicals, the Red Guards, became his storm troopers: Books and art were destroyed, museums were ransacked, temples and shrines were desecrated, and those thought to have counterrevolutionary sympathies (intellectuals, journalists, and others) were assaulted, arrested, and sometimes shot.

The Cultural Revolution was a way for Mao to vanquish his enemies, and Zhou Enlai knew this. In order to survive, he made it clear that he stood firmly behind Mao. To protect himself politically, he publicly praised Mao: "We must raise high the red banner of Mao Zedong Thought and unite with Mao into the eternal future." But at the same time, he worked behind the scenes to hold back Red Guard rioting and push for more leniency to many they had targeted.

Zhou's death in 1976 was a transition of sorts, not only for China, but for Western nations as well. China lost a great revolutionary leader and diplomat. The rest of the world lost a familiar face on the world stage. He was a bridge to the old ways, the revolutionaries of the past, whose intentions and instincts one could understand. After Zhou, relations with China would be altogether different.

The Icon: Ernesto "Che" Guevara

You've seen his image on T-shirts, on posters, on backpacks, in TV ads, in movies, on tennis shoes, tattoos, baseball hats, greeting cards, books, magazines, billboards, and on the Internet. Che Guevara's face may be the most recognized and most reproduced of the entire twentieth century. His image has been commercialized, packaged and sold for untold millions of dollars over the last several decades—which has to be one of the biggest ironies in all of human history. He would hate it; he would absolutely hate it.

He hated the very idea of capitalism—its systemic emphasis on wealth, its inequalities, its excesses. That his face has become a commercialized icon—bought, sold, and traded on the world market— would no doubt be truly revolting to this disciple of Marx and Lenin. He was one of the last—and undoubtedly one of the most committed—true believers in Marxist revolutionary thought. Lenin would have loved this guy; of course, Stalin would have eventually had him shot.

The famous photo of Guevara was taken in March 1960 in Havana by Fidel Castro's official photographer, Alberto Korda. The serious, almost pained expression of Guevara in the photo was no accident: The photo was taken at a memorial service for victims of the explosion of a munitions freighter in Havana harbor. Guevara (a physician by training) had heard the explosion, rushed to the docks, and personally treated some of the blast victims. Korda, who called the photo *Guerrillero Heroico* (Heroic Guerrilla Fighter), said he was drawn to Guevara's facial expression as he walked into view of his camera during Castro's eulogy for the victims.

Korda was a lifelong communist and supporter of the Cuban revolution; he claimed no payment for his picture and has never asked for royalties. He reasoned that Che's image represented his revolutionary ideals; thus, the more his picture was reproduced, the greater the chance that Che's ideals would be adopted as well. "I am not averse to its reproduction by those who wish to propagate his memory and the cause of social justice throughout the world," he said. However, Korda did not intend for the commercialization of the image to sell products he believed Guevara would not have supported. Oh, well.

The photo has become one of the iconic images of the last hundred years, and has been declared by some the "most famous photograph in the world." Versions of it have been painted, printed, digitized, embroidered, tattooed, silk-screened, sculpted, or sketched on nearly every surface imaginable. The Victoria and Albert Museum in London claims that the photo has been reproduced more than any other image in photography. Jonathan Green, director of the California Museum of Photography, marvels that "Korda's image has worked its way into languages around the world. It has become an alpha-numeric symbol, a hieroglyph, an instant symbol. It mysteriously reappears whenever there's a conflict. There isn't anything else in history that serves in this way."

Truly, the photographic image of the man has become larger than the man himself, particularly when one considers that by the mid-1960s Guevara had more or less worn out his welcome in Cuba and was considered by Castro to be something of a loose cannon. His connection to Castro is somewhat similar to Zhou Enlai's ties to Mao Zedong. From 1956 to 1963, Fidel Castro needed Guevara's talents and commitment to revolution, just as Mao needed Zhou's organizational and diplomatic skills. As Marxist revolutionaries, Guevara and Zhou went through similar struggles—years in the mountains organizing resistance to a corrupt regime, eventual victory, followed by civil service to a dictatorship. However, Zhou's government service lasted much longer. Che Guevara was no bureaucrat; he was a jungle fighter. He was restless, always looking for the next fight for freedom.

Ernesto Guevara was from Argentina, born in 1928. His nickname, *Che,* was bestowed on him by his rebel comrades. *Che* is a slang word used by many Argentines as a conversation filler—sort of like "man" or the Canadian use of "eh" at the end of sentences. His frequent use of the word in conversations sounded odd to his Cuban-born comrades; thus, they took to calling him "Che" Guevara. He was the oldest of five children in a family of Spanish, Basque, and Irish descent. His father once explained Ernesto's restless nature by noting that in his "son's veins flowed the blood of the Irish rebels."

Politics was definitely in his blood. His father's family were staunch supporters of antifascist rebels during the Spanish Civil War, and Ernesto was exposed to leftist political thought from an early age. As he grew older, he exhibited a rabid intellectual curiosity as well, devouring books on history, philosophy, great literature, and poetry.

While a medical student at the University of Buenos Aires, he and a friend took a motorcycle trip across South America that changed his life. He was exposed for the first time to the crushing poverty of remote rural areas and to the vast economic differences between wealthy landowners and the poor. He credited this experience with instilling in him a desire to help the poor and downtrodden, remarking on the "stupefaction provoked by the continual hunger and punishment" of those in need. He wrote a book about his experiences on his trip called *The Motorcycle Diaries*, which later became a best seller and then a movie.

The experience influenced his later actions as a revolutionary and as a physician. Cuban rebels routinely recruited doctors and distributed medicine to the rural poor they encountered. It became a policy borrowed by numerous other Latin American leftist revolutionaries of the twentieth century, from Nicaragua to Bolivia. The motorcycle trip also led Guevara to view Latin America as a single political-social entity, not a collection of small nations. He developed a concept of a Hispanic America sharing a common Latino heritage, which would require a continent-wide liberation strategy.

His travels also convinced him that capitalist ideology, the United States' in particular, was inherently unfair and cruel, responsible for much of the suffering and inequality that he saw around him. He often wrote about the U.S.-based United Fruit Company, whose ties to Latin American elites and government officials allowed it to manipulate the agricultural market and control uncultivated land. In 1954, the U.S. government, specifically the CIA, supported a right-wing takeover of Guatemala, whose president had attempted to enact land reform. This cemented Guevara's view of the United States as an imperialist power opposed to any effort to redress the socioeconomic inequality of developing countries. Perhaps coincidentally, the American secretary of state at the time, John Foster Dulles, was a stockholder in and attorney for the United Fruit Company.

Guevara met Fidel Castro's brother, Raul (the current leader of Cuba, as of this writing), in Mexico City in 1955. Guevara then had long conversations with Fidel Castro and agreed to join his fight to topple the government of Fulgencio Batista in Cuba. Guevara was a born revolutionary and a born leader. He quickly learned the tactics of the guerrilla and through rigorous training and instruction became one of the stars of Castro's revolutionary army. He threw himself completely into the revolutionary cause, just as he had approached all his previous endeavors. He became a key lieutenant to Castro and one of his most aggressive and reliable advisors. He set up factories to make explosives, organized production and distribution of food, helped to train new recruits, and even taught some of them to read and write. He also put his medical training to use, establishing health clinics for rebel troops as well as the local population. But during this period his darker side also emerged—he became known for brutality and ruthlessness, summarily executing defectors and organizing execution squads to hunt down those deemed as traitors to the revolution.

In 1958, he was promoted by Castro to the rank of *commandante,* and given command of a rebel division. His command of rebel forces during the Cuban revolution was noteworthy, and became well publicized both during and after the fighting. Working in concert with Castro's main column of troops, Guevara's forces were instrumental in flanking Batista's army and cutting the island in half by taking Las Villas Province in December 1958. As Guevara and his troops came closer to Havana, Batista fled the country. Guevara entered Havana on January 2 and took control of the city; Castro and his forces joined him six days later.

With Castro's victory secure, both he and Guevara became internationally known. In recognition of Guevara's role in the "liberation" of the Cuban people, he was proclaimed a "Cuban citizen by birth." He became a major figure in the Castro regime and also a major figure on the world stage. He had flash and panache, and his travels to foreign conferences and his diplomacy on behalf of Castro and the Cuban revolution drew extensive media attention. He was eagerly sought out by journalists and photographers, and he became a spokesperson for socialist revolutionary causes, as well as a fierce critic of the industrialized West and the United States. He helped make international socialism glamorous.

But revolutions are not pretty. Biographers note that Guevara had become a "hardened" man through the years of sacrifice and warfare. He was charged with purging the old Batista army and imposing revolutionary justice on those responsible for Cuba's misery during Batista's reign. In this capacity, Guevara created military tribunals that imprisoned or executed thousands between 1958 and 1960. This was controversial both within and outside Cuba. But neither Castro nor Guevara was persuaded by humanitarian arguments or calls for civil justice. Guevara insisted that he acted to "defend" the revolution, and that firing squads were a "necessity" for the people of Cuba.

Guevara's role in the successful revolution and his image with the Cuban people made him very useful to Fidel Castro. He was put in charge of a program that was crucial to the new government's economic policies and very near and dear to Guevara's socialist agenda: land reform. As minister of industries, Guevara oversaw the confiscation of thousands of acres of land, much of it owned by American corporations, and the establishment of government-owned cooperative farms. To accomplish this, he formed a 100,000-man militia with the authority to seize farms and enforce the new government policy on land use. When he was given the additional position of minister of finance the following year, he became the "virtual tsar" of the Cuban economy, and the second most powerful person in Cuba.

But revolutionary fervor and ideological passion don't necessarily translate into positive results, and they certainly didn't in this case. As early as 1963, it was clear that far from being the "envy" of the western hemisphere, as Guevara had promised, the Cuban economy was getting worse. His program of incentives for workers led to a steep drop in industrial productivity and a rise in absenteeism among workers. A 1965 CIA report had this to say about Che Guevara's influence on the Cuban economy:

> From the outset Guevara had encouraged the rapid
> nationalization and centralization of the economy, and by the

spring of 1961 the Cuban economy was entirely state owned. Although he was not a trained economist, Guevara convinced Castro, against the objections of Carlos Rafael Rodriguez and the others, that accelerated industrialization was necessary. He maintained that a diversification of agricultural production and increased investment in industry were required to end dependence on sugar and Cuba's "economic enslavement" by the US. By the time Guevara and Castro admitted, in late 1963, that the industrialization plan must be scaled down to reassign resources to sugar production, Guevara's policies had brought the economy to its lowest point since Castro came to power.

Guevara's influence on Castro also began to decline as a result of Che's negative attitude toward, and increasingly strident comments about, Cuba's primary patron, the Soviet Union. Guevara started to sour on the Soviets in response to the withdrawal of strategic nuclear weapons from Cuba after the missile crisis of 1962 and the confrontation with the United States and President John F. Kennedy. He viewed the withdrawal of the missiles as a "betrayal," and he made it clear that if the missiles had been under his control he would have fired them on the United States.

Afterward, Guevara encouraged Fidel Castro to rethink the alliance with the Soviet Union and instead gravitate more toward China. He believed that the Cuban revolution had more in common with "Maoist" philosophy—Guevara's recommendations on industrial policy bore a strong resemblance to China's disastrous "Great Leap Forward." He became almost as critical of the Soviets as he had been toward the United States.

In 1964, his political position began to weaken; he was replaced as minister of industry. Castro was still content to use Guevara's international profile and his fiery revolutionary rhetoric for propaganda purposes. In December 1964, Guevara led the Cuban delegation at the United Nations in New York. His impassioned speech to the UN General Assembly, in which he denounced the United States and its aggressive policies against the people of the world, divided the chamber, much as the UN speech given by Venezuelan President Hugo Chavez would some thirty years later. While in New York, Guevara also took the opportunity to appear on the CBS Sunday news program *Face the Nation.* From there he embarked on an international media tour, which included stops in Paris, Prague, Egypt, China, and Africa.

But at several stops on his media jaunt, he openly and pointedly criticized the Soviet Union, speaking at one point of its "complicity" in the exploitation of the working poor of the world. When he returned to Cuba in March 1965, he was given a cool reception. One can only imagine that Fidel Castro's Russian benefactors had applied not-so-subtle pressure on him to handle the situation. Of course, from Castro's point of view, Che Guevara had ceased to be of use. He then vanished from public life in Cuba.

This marked a major turning point in Che's life, every bit as decisive as the meeting with Fidel and Raul Castro in 1955. His whereabouts were a mystery. Later in 1965, Castro revealed the contents of a letter, purportedly written to him by Guevara, restating his solidarity with the Cuban people, but declaring his intention to renounce his honorary Cuban citizenship, resign his official government positions, and leave Cuba to fight for the revolutionary cause abroad. Apparently, he had decided—or it was decided for him—that he needed to get back to his roots, which were in fomenting revolution and fighting for the poor.

Guevara had recently spent time in Africa, and he decided to go to the Congo and offer his expertise to the rebels in the ongoing conflict. He traveled with a small detachment of Cuban officers, and was later joined by roughly one hundred Cuban soldiers in April 1965. His expedition was a disaster. Unlike the situation in Cuba in the 1950s, the Congo had no popular movement with widespread support. He would later write in his *Congo Diary,* "The human element failed. There is no will to fight, the leaders are corrupt; in a word, there was nothing for me to do."

Next he brought his signature brand of revolutionary zeal to Bolivia. His heart was still firmly fixed on Latin America and the fight to build a more just society there. He went to Bolivia in 1966, at the behest of Bolivian communists, to build a guerrilla army. But he fared little better there than he had in the Congo. His National Liberation Army of Bolivia scored a few successes in minor skirmishes with the Bolivian army, but he was unable to attract a sizable following. Furthermore, the American CIA was on his trail. To hold the line on Marxist-led incursions in the Western hemisphere, the Bolivian army was advised and supplied by U.S. Army Special Forces units.

In October 1967, Guevara was wounded and captured by Bolivian troops. According to biographer Jon Lee Anderson, he shouted, "Do not shoot! I am Che Guevara and worth more to you alive than dead." He was wrong about that. The Bolivian military and its government officials were in no mood to negotiate. They just wanted him gone, and without the international publicity of a trial. Two days later, apparently on the orders of the Bolivian president, Guevara was executed. He was shot several times in the arms, legs, and torso to make it appear as if he had been killed in battle. According to one source who was on the scene, Guevara shouted at his executioner "Shoot, coward, you are only going to kill a man!"

Che Guevara the man died, but Che Guevara the legend, the icon, lives on. Similar in some ways to the sudden loss of John F. Kennedy in 1963, Guevara's killing in the jungle of Bolivia only enhanced the mythical stature of the man. He became a martyr—the patron saint of lost causes and the fight against the world's injustice. His failures as a government official and economic planner in the Cuban government are mostly forgotten, and even his brutal excesses are forgotten by some. Yet some admirers worry that the essence of the man has been lost. "The humanity that worships Che has by and large turned away from just about everything he believed in," according to Ariel Dorfman of Duke University. "The future he predicted has not been kind to his ideals or his ideas." True. But at the close of the twentieth century, *Time* magazine published its list of the one hundred most important figures of the previous hundred years: There were two Latin Americans on the list. One was Che Guevara.

CHAPTER 8

THE TRULY EVIL

Does evil exist? Or does the idea of evil depend on whose side one is on? Is the concept of evil subjective and equivocal, or is it cast in black and white?

For example, a reading of Deuteronomy 2:32 finds God instructing the Israelites to slay their enemies and not worry about the consequences: "When Sihon and all his army came out to meet us in battle at Jahaz, the Lord our God delivered him over to us and we struck him down, together with his sons and his whole army. At that time we took all his towns and completely destroyed them—men, women and children. We left no survivors." They killed all the women and children; was this evil? The ninth Sura of the Koran (9:5 and 9:15) teaches that Allah forgives his followers who slay nonbelievers. Is that evil or just very, very strict?

And were historical figures like Adolf Hitler, Joseph Stalin, and Pol Pot the physical manifestations of a spiritual evil, dedicated to torturing humankind? Were they mentally ill? Or just seriously misguided? Abused children? Ideological sociopaths with a loose grip on reality? Thinkers from Voltaire and Jean-Jacques Rousseau to Hannah Arendt and Elie Wiesel have wrestled with these questions, yet definitive answers are elusive. After all, what kind of political ideology or belief system, or set of

grudges and dislikes, can motivate someone to kill/murder thousands or
even millions of innocent people?

What are the standards for judging evil? What does evil look like?
A 2007 editorial in the *New York Times* pointed out that the very word
evil only came into widespread use as late as the 1500s. "Does it have a
particular smell, like teen spirit? Does it come wearing a hood, as in the
movies? Or, again, does it look like you and me, sitting over dinner and
enjoying a glass of vintage Bordeaux?"

Was Saddam Hussein evil? What about Osama bin Laden? The
president of Iran, Mahmoud Ahmadinejad, has openly spoken of
destroying the State of Israel—men, women, and children. Is he another
Hitler?

And what is the responsibility of those who serve "evil" figures?
As Hannah Arendt pointed out, Nazi official Adolf Eichmann didn't
exhibit or profess anti-Semitism or radical political thought; he was just a
bureaucrat "doing his job." Unfortunately, he did it well. In this way, evil
has been sanctioned and encouraged at the highest levels since the dawn
of the human race. Today, there is no shortage of such cruelty. Just in the
last few years, we have witnessed the barbarism of genocide in Rwanda,
the former Yugoslavia, and Sierra Leone, just to name a few. Sadly, there
will always be those who will carry out orders to maim and murder—
motivated by a combination of hate, misinformation, ideological
blinders, hunger, fear of punishment, or fear of the unknown.

The figures in this chapter were perpetrators of such "evil." They
were in a position to influence those with the political power over life
and death. Some of them pushed for the cruelty and violence that their
times were known for; others committed evil acts as a way to accumulate
power and prestige. We will examine their circumstances, their contexts.
We can try to understand their motivations, their hatreds, and their fears.
But just as numerous scholars and theorists have discovered, satisfying
answers may be in short supply.

The Grand Inquisitor: Tomás de Torquemada

In considering the deeds of people like Tomás de Torquemada, chief administrator of the Spanish Inquisition—responsible for the torture and ritual execution of thousands—one is inexorably drawn to the words of that famous twentieth-century philosopher, the singer/songwriter Jimmy Buffett, whose song "Fruitcakes" asserts that "religion's in the hands of some crazy-ass people." Perhaps there is no greater logic.

But that would be looking at the situation with twenty-first-century eyes. The fact is, the Inquisition, and many similar religious/political crusades of the era, seemed perfectly sensible and appropriate to many, including the government and business elites of Europe. One cannot escape the conclusion that Torquemada was acting primarily out of pure religious faith. Faith that he was right, that the "one true religion" was being undermined by Jews and Muslims. Faith that his actions were sanctioned by God. Faith that he and the church were protecting and serving the righteous. Indeed, his mission was to rid Spain of all heresy; his vigorous efforts earned him the name "the hammer of heretics."

Torquemada was born in Valladolid, Spain, in 1420. His family was very well-connected in the church hierarchy, and Tomás entered the Dominican monastery at a young age. His uncle, Cardinal Juan de Torquemada, was a well-known theologian, and Tomás de Torquemada's superiors took notice of him for this reason. He rose to the position of prior at the Monastery of Santa Cruz in Segovia and held that office for twenty-four years. He accumulated the political power to assume higher church titles, but he preferred to remain a humble friar laboring in the fields of the Lord. Similar to Bernard of Clairvaux, he was an unyielding ascetic who habitually wore a hair shirt under his robes to humble himself.

As outwardly humble as he was, Torquemada managed to amass a personal fortune during the Inquisition, a fortune he used to expand the Monastery of the Holy Cross in Seville and build the St. Thomas Aquinas Monastery in Avila. At the height of his power, he traveled with a detail of 250 armed guards. Toward the end of his life, he grew paranoid and suspicious; he was constantly in fear of assassins. He was known to place a "unicorn's horn" next to his plate when he dined, to ward off the effects of possible poisons placed in his food. Suspicious behavior for a man of the cloth.

Torquemada's principal political supporter was Queen Isabella I of Castile. He had been her confessor since she was a child and remained her closest advisor and confidant throughout her life. This relationship was the source of Torquemada's power. A shrewd political observer, he advised her to marry King Ferdinand of Aragon in 1469 in order to consolidate their kingdoms and form a power base that he could draw on for his own purposes. Thanks to his political and family connections, at age sixty-three, he was appointed to the position of grand inquisitor of the Spanish Inquisition, an office he relished.

The Spanish Inquisition can be seen partly as a reaction to the multireligious nature of Spanish society following the reconquest of the Iberian Peninsula from the Muslims. Roman Catholic officials were gravely concerned that Jewish and Muslim influence was a threat to the authority of the church. Add to this the anti-Jewish hysteria of the previous several hundred years, in which the Jews were blamed for everything from witchcraft and wizardry to the Black Plague, which led to widescale harassment and killing of Jews across Europe.

In some parts of Spain, toward the end of the fourteenth century, there was a wave of violent anti-semitism, encouraged by the preaching of Ferrant Martinez, archdeacon of Ecija. The pogroms of June 1391 were especially bloody: In Seville, hundreds of Jews were killed, and the synagogue was completely destroyed. The number of people killed was also high in other cities, including Cordoba, Valencia, and Barcelona. One of the consequences of these episodes of religious-inspired violence was the mass conversion of Jews in the early 1400s. Jews who converted to Catholicism were known as *conversos* (the converted). There were Muslim converts, too, the *Moriscos,* who would later be targeted by the Inquisition in the early 1500s.

The Spanish Inquisition was distinct in many ways from similar church-sponsored witch hunts, and Torquemada's influence over Queen Isabella enabled him to put his own personal stamp on it. With Torquemada whispering in their ears, the Spanish royal couple lobbied

Pope Sixtus IV to grant their request for a holy office to administer an Inquisition in their kingdoms. The church had established inquisitions in other regions of Europe in the past—for example, in France and Italy—with the Vatican maintaining the ultimate authority over the prosecution of heretics. At Torquemada's urging, however, Ferdinand and Isabella demanded that they, as Catholic monarchs, hold civil authority over the Spanish Inquisition. The pope bowed to their pressure and issued a papal bull on November 1, 1478, granting their request. Quite possibly, the pope did not foresee the hideous results that an Inquisition without papal control would bring.

While Torquemada's religious fervor can hardly be questioned, some historians think it probable that the king, the queen, and the pope had other motives for wanting to stage an Inquisition—financial interests. Sixtus IV needed funds to "subdue rebels in the Papal states and fight a war against Muslims in the east." Ferdinand and Isabella wanted to mount their own war against Muslims residing in Grenada, and they, too, needed money to finance it. According to the rules of the Inquisition, local inquisitors could seize the property of any person accused of heresy, and that property would ultimately fall into the hands of the monarchy. An accused person always had the option of buying a pardon from the Vatican. Both the pope and the Spanish monarchs stood to profit, especially because the heretics targeted by Torquemada, the *conversos,* were for the most part a prosperous lot. A number of *conversos* were leading members of Spanish society, including physicians Andrés Laguna and Francisco Lopez Villalobos (Ferdinand's court physician), writers Juan del Enzina, Juan de Mena, Diego de Valera, and Alonso de Palencia, and bankers Luis de Santangel and Gabriel Sanchez, who financed the voyage of Christopher Columbus.

The focus of Torquemada's obsessive quest to root out heresy in Spain was the *marranos,* Jews who outwardly converted to Catholicism (*conversos*) but secretly continued to observe their original faith. Torquemada and his followers purportedly thought that the *marranos* were undermining the teachings of Jesus Christ and endangering the Catholic Church. Under the tyranny of the Inquisition, all *conversos* were suspect, and Catholics were urged to spy on their neighbors and inform on suspected *marranos*.

What virtually no one knew at the time was that Torquemada himself—the man charged with ridding the Spanish kingdoms of all Jewish influences—was himself the grandson of a *converso*. King Ferdinand also had Jewish ancestors, a fact he did not readily acknowledge either. In ways strangely similar to the Nazis of the twentieth century, the notion of *sangre limpia,* or pure blood, consumed the Spanish nobility. A person with untainted lineage was believed to be closer to God and naturally stood a better chance of entering the kingdom of heaven after death. But many Spaniards, including those in high places, had Jewish ancestors. Jewish communities had thrived in Spain for centuries and there was much intermarriage between Jewish and non-Jewish Spaniards.

The Jewish and *converso* populations were an integral part of the Spanish economy in the fifteenth century. Many Jewish merchants became rich operating on Spanish soil, and Jews profited from money lending, a practice that was forbidden to Catholics. But the Spanish Jews who had not converted to Catholicism presented a thorny political problem to Torquemada. Legally, he could not touch them. His authority from the Vatican was limited to dealing with the *conversos*. His mandate did not permit him to persecute Jews who openly practiced their own faith. So the crafty Torquemada worked around the law—urging Ferdinand and Isabella to issue an edict commanding all Jews to either convert to Christianity or leave Spain. The Jews countered his efforts by offering to pay the sovereigns 30,000 ducats to leave them alone.

Ferdinand was tempted to take their offer, which infuriated Torquemada. The grand inquisitor went to the royal court, carrying a crucifix. "Judas Iscariot sold Christ for 30 pieces of silver," he cried. "Your Highness is about to sell him for 30,000 ducats. Here he is. Take him and sell him." Torquemada slammed the crucifix down on a table and stormed out of the room. Ferdinand decided not take the offer, and in 1492, the year Christopher Columbus set sail from Palos, Spain, to find a new route to the East, Torquemada persuaded the sovereigns to issue an order expelling all Jews from the country. Reportedly, several members of Columbus's crew were Jews, fleeing to beat the deadline set by the government.

A person accused of being a *marrano* immediately forfeited his property to the court. He was also required to walk through the streets wearing a sambenito, a yellow shirt covered with images of the cross that only came to the waist, leaving the rest of the body exposed. A public flogging followed this humiliation. At certain periods during the Spanish Inquisition, accused *marranos* were required to wear red patches on their outer garments to identify themselves—foreshadowing the Nazi policy of the 1930s. They were forced to live in walled neighborhoods called *aljamas* (ghettos), and their doctors were forbidden from practicing medicine. This, of course, was before any of them had been found guilty of anything.

Torquemada's office published a set of guidelines to help Catholics identify practicing Jews in their midst:

- If you see that your neighbors are wearing clean and fancy clothes on Saturdays, they are Jews.
- If they clean their houses on Fridays and light candles earlier than usual on that night, they are Jews.
- If smoke does not emerge from their chimneys on Saturday, they are observing the Jewish Sabbath.
- If they eat unleavened bread and begin their meals with celery and lettuce during Holy Week, they are Jews.
- If they say prayers facing a wall, bowing back and forth, they are Jews.

Torquemada was a methodical man who, according to scholars such as William Thomas Walsh in his book *Characters of the Inquisition*, wanted to improve upon the procedures of previous inquisitions and "mitigate" the use of torture. Suspected heretics were not rounded up and immediately imprisoned and tortured to get them to confess to their sins. The process that brought accused heretics to trial was long and involved— which enriched everyone in the system, particularly the lawyers, judges, and government officials who took bribes.

At the trial, the accused was not assumed innocent until proven guilty. Torquemada felt that if sufficient evidence had already been presented proving the guilt of the accused, torture could be employed as a legitimate tool for ferreting out the truth. Some of the same torture devices and procedures were used a century later in England by Francis Walsingham to squeeze information out of foreign agents. One of the most common methods of torture in the Inquisition was called the water cure—today it is called waterboarding. It became controversial in the United States during the administration of George W. Bush when it was used on suspected terrorists. It is basically simulated drowning, in which the person is tied down with his jaws forced open and water poured into his mouth and nostrils—a historically proven method for eliciting confessions and information.

If the rack or the water cure proved to be ineffective, the accused was then tied with ropes by the wrists and led up to a scaffold. The inquisitor would demand that the accused confess. If the response was not satisfactory, the inquisitor instructed the torturer to shove the accused off the scaffold. The ropes stopped the accused abruptly before his or her feet touched the ground, wrenching the person's joints and producing excruciating pain. This was repeated as deemed necessary under the watchful eye of a physician who checked the accused after each drop to make sure the person did not perish. According to the rules set down by Torquemada, torture was never to result in death.

If, after several rounds of torture, the accused still did not confess, the judges inevitably declared the person guilty of heresy. The penalty was death, and the execution took place at a special public event. The sentence for heresy—burning at the stake—was not formally a part of the ceremony, but it was usually held nearby and conducted by civil, rather than church, authorities. Once condemned by the Inquisition, the heretic was turned over to the local magistrate. The best estimates are that approximately two thousand people were burned at the stake during Torquemada's reign as grand inquisitor.

Even death did not save the accused from execution. If the Inquisition found deceased people guilty, their remains were exhumed and burned. If accused people had fled to escape torture, they were burned in effigy. No one escaped the verdict of the Inquisition. Last-minute confessions sometimes earned suspects a reprieve, but Torquemada and his corps of inquisitors generally distrusted those admissions, suspecting that such confessions were not sincere and were only last-ditch attempts to avoid death. For this reason the condemned were often gagged to keep them from confessing, even though inquisitors continued to demand full confessions for the benefit of the crowd.

In most cases, even if a condemned person managed to confess, the execution was still carried out. A confession could, however, earn a degree of mercy from the authorities. According to author Beth Randall, if condemned heretics "recanted and kissed the cross, they were mercifully garroted before the fire was set. If they recanted only, they were burned with quick-burning seasoned wood." If they refused to recant entirely, "they were burned with slow-burning green wood." Clearly, Torquemada was a man who knew his craft.

Apologists for Torquemada stop short of ranking him with the twentieth-century madmen who used genocide to achieve their aberrant goals. Some scholars argue that Torquemada, unlike Hitler, Stalin, or Pol Pot, was motivated by genuine religious fervor and that he was a humble servant of the Lord who did not seek power for himself. Some also feel that his views and actions are consistent with the pre-Enlightenment age and so he must be judged differently.

But, in fact, Torquemada's persecution of the Jews in Spain bears a remarkable similarity to Hitler's persecution of the Jews throughout Europe before and during World War II. Just as Hitler promulgated the Aryan race as superior, Torquemada believed in the superiority of individuals with "pure blood"—ironic considering that both Hitler and Torquemada had at least some Jewish ancestry. Both ordered Jews to wear identifying markers on their outer clothing. The similarities don't end there. Historian John Edward Longhurst states that Torquemada sponsored "book-burning festivals" in which "Hebrew Bibles" as well as "Arabic books" were destroyed to stem the spread of what he considered heresy.

In Torquemada's case, money may have indeed been at the root of all evil. It seems clear that the grand inquisitor, the Spanish sovereigns, and the pope were all eager to get their hands on Jewish assets in whatever way they could. Torquemada, along with Ferdinand and Isabella, reconciled the blatant seizure of Jewish property as necessary to finance their holy wars against all heathens. In their minds, it was permissible to steal from heretics in order to fight heresy. In this sense, Torquemada's agenda was as cold-blooded as any of the dictators who followed him. Author Simon Whitechapel writes that although Torquemada's death count did not approach that of later mass murderers, "Qualitatively Torquemada stands shoulder-to-shoulder with Hitler and Stalin."

Torquemada died of natural causes at the age of seventy-eight in 1498, but the Spanish Inquisition continued for another 336 years until it was finally abolished in 1834. According to Beth Randall, the apparatus set in motion by Torquemada was ultimately responsible for the murders of thirty thousand Jews. Thus, one of the darkest chapters in human history owed much to the political abilities and persuasive powers of one ambitious cleric.

Machiavelli's Worst Nightmare: "Young" Joe Stalin

June 27, 1907—Tbilisi, Republic of Georgia: The mustachioed man in the red satin shirt and black fedora joked and flirted with the two pretty girls who were carrying parasols and doing their best to hide the Mauser pistols tucked beneath their dresses. A block away, a group of young men wearing bright peasant vests and trousers paced nervously, concealing homemade grenades and pistols, while waiting for the signal. At a nearby tavern, a group of heavily armed gangster types drank and waited. When the stagecoach arrived, carrying the deposits for the new State Bank of Georgia, the dashing man with the mustache, Joseph Djugashvili, gave the signal. Immediately, the waiting men and the two women tossed grenades under the coach. The resulting explosion rocked the entire town. On the street, disemboweled horses lay next to dying soldiers, blood, and innards spread over the street. The waiting gunmen from the tavern rushed into the street, firing their weapons at the remaining soldiers and guards. As onlookers and passersby screamed, Joseph and the girls grabbed the bags of money and rode off on horseback.

Sounds like a scene from the American West in the 1870s, right? The man with the mustache was, of course, Joseph Stalin—much later he would choose the name *Stalin*, which means "man of steel." Before Stalin was the supreme leader of the Soviet Union, he was the primary lieutenant to the heart and soul of the Russian communist movement, Vladimir Lenin. In this position, Stalin influenced some of the more violent and bloody tactics that Lenin and other Bolshevik activists would undertake to assure victory.

The bank job pulled that day in Tbilisi was one of many acts of robbery, terror, and violence that Stalin planned, along with his mentor and protector, Vladimir Lenin, to support the nascent organizational efforts of the Bolshevik Marxists. This opening scene is instructive because the decades-long rise of Joseph Stalin to take over and lead the Soviet government after Lenin's passing is, in large part, a crime story. For Stalin is a great example of what happens when a criminal gains control of a nation—not just any nation, but a nation hundreds of millions strong—with a large military and a philosophy dedicated to conflict. The word *criminal,* as used here, doesn't signal the standard political use of the word, the way that a third-world dictator might refer to the American president or the British prime minister as a "dog" or a "criminal." No, as used here, *criminal* means an actual gun-toting thug.

Without question, Stalin is one of the pivotal figures of the twentieth century. This is the story of his rise to power, and focuses on his early years in the Bolshevik political movement—the years when he developed and honed the bloody skills he would later put to use on a national and international stage.

Most of the speculation surrounding his long political career revolves around two questions: (1) Was he mentally ill? and (2) Just how many millions of his own people did he slaughter?

When considering the "evil" topics of mass murder and genocide, most of the attention goes to Adolf Hitler, which is understandable. But in terms of sheer volume, Hitler wasn't the biggest mass murderer in his lifetime. He isn't even in the top two of the twentieth century!

Mao Zedong, via his Great Leap Forward and Cultural Revolution, takes top billing. But clocking in at number two on the mass murderers list is Stalin. There has actually been quite a lively academic debate over the last twenty-five years as to the number of millions Stalin is responsible for killing. Initial estimates during the Cold War were on the high side, some estimating up to 50–75 million total Soviets killed during the period of forced collectivization and party purges in the 1930s. Stalin apologists countered that those numbers were way too high, that the number he murdered was only around 5–10 million. They added that he also did a lot of really cool things for the Soviet people, so he wasn't such a bad guy. Since the bulk of the Soviet archives have become available after the end of the Cold War in the 1990s, there seems to be a consensus forming around the number 20 million.

Unfortunately for humanity, the kind of barbarism displayed by the likes of Stalin, Hitler, and Mao have been rather commonplace in the last several thousand years. The difference in the cases of Stalin and Hitler was the availability of technology, firepower, administrative apparatus, and transportation to carry out atrocities like these on a massive scale— and, crucially, the existence of twentieth-century observers to document the horrors through news reporting, radio broadcasts, and film.

Acute paranoia, malignant narcissism, sadism, and advanced psychopathic tendencies have all been ascribed to Stalin's behavior over the years by an assortment of psychiatrists, historians, and sociologists. After all, it's easy to believe that someone who committed the atrocities of a Stalin or a Hitler was mad. On some level, it makes these actions easier to accept. "A person would have to be crazy to engage in that kind of wholesale slaughter of human beings," so the thinking goes.

But was Stalin really insane? Probably not, although he did exhibit unmistakable features of paranoid psychopathology, especially in the later part of his life. Yet most eyewitnesses judged him to be mentally competent, meaning he knew right from wrong, he acted with planning and preparation, not hysterical impulse, and he was in control of his actions.

One can even ascribe rational, or at least political, motivations and planning to Stalin's actions. He clearly had no use for the peasant class that populated the agricultural territories his army was converting into collective farms: They were not part of his plans for industrialization; they were merely "in the way." The fact that he intentionally starved to death millions of them is sick, yes, but also part of his larger plan. Russian economist Konstantin Sonin suggests it was comparable to the ethnic cleansing genocides of Rwanda and Bosnia, or the forced emigrations by Fidel Castro in Cuba and Robert Mugabe in Zimbabwe: It is a way to eliminate those who do not support you and to strengthen your hand politically. Sonin and other social scientists refer to this strategy as "trimming your constituency."

It has also been pointed out that Stalin's purges occurred during an economically disastrous period. Some suggest that Stalin was motivated by a desire to divert attention away from the scarcity of food and supplies by blaming particular groups for the state's failings. Though Stalin ruled through fear and terror, he may have also been expressing his own fears of being overthrown. Like most dictators, he was exceedingly careful about his personal safety, keeping bodyguards close and maintaining emergency exits in his private residences. It is true, though, that in his later years his paranoia became excessive, as evidenced by the sadistic treatment of those close to him, including his only legitimate son, Yakov.

One of the most reasonable and comprehensive theories about Stalin's motives lies at the heart of Stalin's personality. A non-Russian from humble beginnings, Stalin was power-hungry and ambitious. He used the Russian Revolution to climb to power, then calculatingly secured his position by purging leaders who had originally been loyal to Lenin. His desire to control who lived and who died may have been part and parcel of this lust for power, or it may have been the most effective way to frighten people into obedience and undermine potential enemies.

In fact, the key to understanding Stalin may be his childhood and youth. As it turns out, he really was an abused child. Not that that excuses his actions any more than does his paranoia or his raging inferiority complex. But the focus of this analysis is his rise to political prominence under the tutelage of Lenin—before Stalin held the reins of government and could use that power to kill and exile at will.

Born to an alcoholic shoemaker in Gori, not far from Tbilisi, the scene of the notorious bank heist described earlier, the young Joseph received savage beatings from both of his parents. Later in life, he asked his mother why she beat him so much. She replied, "It didn't do you any harm." Most psychiatrists would heartily disagree. Domestic violence was his first teacher. His parents separated, but his father would sometimes drunkenly stagger over to Joseph's house and beat his mother. She fought back; Joseph fought back, too, once throwing a knife at his father in an attempt to stop the savage pummeling of his mother.

According to Stalin biographer Simon Sebag Montefiore, Stalin's environment is key to understanding his personal and political development. Montefiore, in his book *Young Stalin,* paints the Republic of Georgia and the Caucasus region as a wild and violent frontier, characterized by high rates of alcoholism, low rates of economic activity, and as a breeding ground for violence and resentment. Street brawling was the principal sport. Organized town brawls, wrestling tournaments, and schoolboy gang warfare were the three traditions the region clung to. Festivals and seasonal celebrations featured a day of heavy drinking, followed by nighttime fights. The "assault of free-boxing," the sport of *krivi,* was a "mass duel with rules." Three-year-olds fought other three-year-olds, then older children, then the teens fought, and finally the adults would go at each other, with the brawling lasting into the next day, even at schools, where students fought in gangs.

But Joseph also received an education—his mother saw to that. His father wanted him to join him in the shoe factory, but his mother steered him toward the seminary, where he became a star student. Montefiore believes Stalin owed his political success to this unusual combination of street brutality and classical education. He was a smart but rebellious student at the several religious schools he attended. He even took up poetry. But his interests shifted away from religion and toward politics. He was inspired by the radicalism of some of the underground political organizations he heard about. He was also shaped in part by the ruthless and draconian administration of the religious schools he attended— "surveillance, spying, invasion of inner life, violation of feelings," he would later say. Taking the name Koba, a fictional Caucasian bandit-hero, he "embarked on a career as an underground political agitator, his life punctuated by multiple arrests and years spent in exile."

As a political radical, Montefiore likens him to a gang leader, documenting his role in bank robberies, protection rackets, extortion, arson, piracy, kidnapping, and murder. Baptized in violence from birth, he thrived on it. He brought to political organizing his penchant for blood, subterfuge, and dark conspiracy. He fully subscribed to the Leninist ideal of the Marxist revolutionary as a man outside normal society and moral law, a pitiless instrument of the working class. It is no surprise that such "black work," as he called it, became standard operating procedure for Bolshevik revolutionaries he worked with, and then later the Soviet government.

Like many Bolshevik activists, Stalin never left behind the "shadow world of spies, double-agents, and criminal conspiracy." To Montefiore, his "Georgian upbringing was the ideal training for the terrorist-gangster." And when Stalin met Lenin in 1905 at a party conference in Finland, Lenin thought him a hothead, but a highly desirable recruit for his central party organization. Here was a man of action, not a "tea drinker," said Lenin. After several meetings with him, Lenin decided that Stalin was "exactly the kind of person I need." Lenin would live to regret it, but just barely.

Stalin was rather short, about 5 feet 4 inches, and his face and hands were pockmarked from a childhood bout with smallpox. In fact, one of the nicknames for him used by the Okhrana, the tsar's secret police, was *Chopura,* the "pockmarked one." In his younger years, he wore his dark hair longish and sported a full beard, as did most revolutionaries. As noted earlier, he liked to dress the part of a revolutionary or a soldier or a brigand, whichever part he was playing at the moment. He would later, of course, adopt the uniform of a Soviet officer, even though he never served in the military. He was definitely attractive to women, not because he was conventionally handsome, but due to his virility and cockiness. He left a trail of lovers and illegitimate children.

In 1902, Vladimir Ulyanov had written his famous essay, "What Is to Be Done?: Burning Questions of Our Movement," in which he had used the alias *Lenin* for the first time. In it he called for an organization of ruthless conspirators who would act at all costs—"Give us an organization of revolutionaries and we shall overturn the whole of Russia!" Joseph Djugashvili was exactly the kind of ruthless conspirator he had in mind. The movement needed cash and leadership, and this Georgian was capable of providing both.

Stalin became a leader of the revolutionaries, but a shadowy figure, operating behind the scenes. Most Communist Party members had not even heard of him until the eve of the October 1917 revolution. The early years of his relationship with Lenin were largely ones of gangster activity, aimed at providing badly needed funds for the movement. Lenin gave him political cover and a shield of secrecy.

And Stalin needed Lenin's protection. At the Communist Party Congress in London in 1907, the Central Committee voted to outlaw the kind of bank robberies and other violent acts of "expropriation" for which Stalin was known. Expulsion from the party was threatened for those found guilty. At the conference, Stalin stayed mostly in the shadows while Lenin nodded in agreement with the condemnations of violence. This was before the Tblisi bank robbery; for years afterward, both Stalin and Lenin were acting in complete defiance of official party policy.

The 1907 London party conference was also where Stalin met his nemesis, Leon Trotsky, for the first time. Trotsky was already famous; he had escaped from Siberia, had written extensively on Marxist revolutionary policy, and had been a featured speaker at a number of meetings and conferences. The two men could not have been more different: Trotsky was "effortlessly brilliant in writing, dizzyingly eloquent in performance, unmistakably Jewish in accent, and shamelessly vain, with his dandyish suits and plumage of mane-like tresses carefully bouffed, possessing the shine of radical celebrity." Stalin hated him instantly.

Stalin's many insecurities fed his anger and paranoia, and would later help explain his obsession with developing a "cult of personality" in the Soviet Union. At his direction, numerous towns, villages, and cities would be renamed after him in the 1930s and 1940s; the Stalin Prize and Stalin Peace Prize were also named in his honor. He accepted grand titles, such as "Coryphaeus of Science," "Father of Nations," "Brilliant Genius of Humanity," "Great Architect of Communism," and "Gardener of Human Happiness." He and his party apparatchiks would rewrite Soviet history to provide him a more significant role in the Bolshevik revolution.

Lenin admired and respected Trotsky, although they disagreed on some aspects of revolutionary policy. Trotsky would go on to become an international star of Marxism for the next decade, while Stalin toiled in the shadows, exiled to Siberia by the Okhrana several times. But it later became clear that Stalin had the inside track over Trotsky. He was personally closer to Lenin. For all his talents, Trotsky was an outsider. He had sided with the Menshevik faction against Lenin, although he later joined the Bolsheviks and became one of its leading voices. Lenin was happy to have Trotsky with him, but when he needed something done, he turned to Stalin—that was the major difference.

Stalin was also a much better politician than Trotsky. They were both ruthless and more than willing to sanction violence, but Stalin knew how to get to people. He understood how to motivate people behind the scenes, when to use fear, when to use flattery, when to pay people off and when to shut them up. Trotsky depended on his flair for persuasion and the power of his ideas. Stalin depended on quiet threats and loud denunciations.

Stalin, Lenin's Frankenstein monster, spent much of the years 1910 through 1917 either on the run and in hiding from the Okhrana, or in exile in Siberia. This contributed to his hardened nature—he brought many of the lessons from prison in Siberia with him to the Soviet government. In 1913, he began to use the alias *Stalin* for the first time. He published several articles for *Pravda* using the byline K. Stalin—the *K* was for Koba, one of his criminal aliases. This was the period when he started to develop his views on the Soviet "nation."

In his writings, it also became apparent that he shared with his fellow mass murderer, Adolf Hitler, a distaste for Jewry. One of the things that bothered him about Trotsky was his membership in the Menshevik faction of the party. Stalin considered the Bolsheviks the "true Russian Faction" and the Mensheviks the "Jewish Faction." For Stalin, the Jews were too independent; they did not easily fit into his vision of a Soviet "nationality."

As observed by Montefiore, the Jews "repelled and titillated Hitler, but irritated and confounded Stalin, who attacked their 'mystical' nature. Too much of a race for Hitler, they were not enough of a nation for Stalin."

Leading up to the Bolshevik Revolution that seized power in 1917, Stalin was in a Siberian prison and Trotsky was in exile in New York City. Lenin was still in Finland hiding from the Tsar's police. But in a matter of months, all three were in Russia working together to topple Aleksandr Kerensky's provisional government. Stalin, in typical fashion, muscled his way into a leadership position, assuming control of *Pravda* from the more junior Vyacheslav Molotov. During the revolution, Lenin and Trotsky led very public roles, while Stalin continued to work behind the scenes. He had been named, along with Lenin, to a seat on the Central Committee, the precursor to the all-powerful Politburo, but he was still relatively unknown to the rank and file of the party. That would soon change.

After the revolution, Stalin used his control of party bureaucracy to outmaneuver Trotsky (as well as other Bolshevik adversaries). As he joined forces with other Central Committee members to marginalize Trotsky, his status as Lenin's number-two man was firmly cemented in the years 1920 to 1923. Then the twisted nature of Stalin's Soviet Union began to take shape. As Lenin grew weaker physically in 1922 and 1923, Stalin began to make his move. At the end, Lenin was taken by surprise at Stalin's raw ambition for power and his dismissive and callous attitude toward him. He should not have been. Dr. Frankenstein could no longer control his monster.

Hitler's Right Hand

For the most part, Hitler was firmly in charge of his maniacal cabal, as was Stalin. But between 1922 and 1945, several ambitious Nazi officials were instrumental in helping Hitler further his dark agenda. Their names are well known to history: Hermann Goering, Joseph Goebbels, Heinrich Himmler, and Martin Bormann, among others. But if one were forced to choose which of these men bore the most responsibility, Hermann Goering would be the likely winner. He was the original commander of Hitler's private army, the *Sturmabteilungen* (SA). He was then Hitler's political commander during the Nazis' rise to power in the Reichstag, and then one of his leading military commanders, with direct control of the Luftwaffe, the German air force. Goering was Hitler's officially designated heir to his authority, should anything happen to the Fuehrer.

Goering was a war hero, a man's man, and to many Germans of the late 1920s and 1930s, he was a living, breathing symbol of the Germanic traditions of bravery, honor, and sacrifice. But by the height of World War II, he had become a study in excess: too much food, too much sexual adventurism, and too much power—too much like the last days of the Roman Empire.

He had been a fighter pilot in World War I—in fact, by the end of the war he was the commander of the famous Richthofen Fighter Squadron, the position once held by the Red Baron himself. The young Goering was said to be dashing, athletic, and handsome —the very picture of German masculinity. He was born into a well-to-do Bavarian family; his father, Heinrich, was a German diplomat, appointed to the consular corps by Otto von Bismarck himself.

Young Hermann Goering came home from the war angry and bitter, as did most Germans. Like many in Germany, Goering believed they had lost the war not because they were defeated in the field, but because they had been stabbed in the back by political and financial leaders. He felt a strong sense of humiliation and he blamed Germany's plight on two elements: the "bad" Germans who had gotten them into this mess; and the victorious Allies, who, through the Versailles Treaty, were grinding the German people into the ground.

He was motivated by a desire to restore the prestige of Germany, to seek retribution against the "traitors" who had lost the war in the first place, and to throw off the "monstrous" terms of Versailles that were strangling Germany. These passions made Goering and thousands of young Germans ripe recruiting targets for the right-wing "patriotic" clubs and societies that were springing up all over Germany in the 1920s, especially in Bavaria.

There were numerous such groups in Munich—Goering would encounter them in beer halls, in street parades, and at civic meetings. In

November 1922, he went to listen to a meeting of the National Socialist German Workers' Party, the NSDAP. It must have been a cathartic experience. Goering would later say that as Adolf Hitler spoke, it was as if Goering himself were speaking. Hitler spoke of Germany's greatness, of the treachery of the financial and social traitors, and of the necessity of forcing Germany back on the right path. Goering felt that at last he had found a man and a cause to which he could fully devote himself. He was so impressed that he went to see Hitler at his headquarters to "see if I could assist him in any way."

Goering was just the kind of person Hitler was looking for. His NSDAP, the Nazis, as they were beginning to call themselves, were growing in number and he needed leaders capable of training and disciplining its recruits. Goering's military experience and his status as a World War I fighter ace were ideal for leading Hitler's SA, which at the time numbered eleven thousand men. Within a year, Goering had transformed the ragtag gaggle of followers into a disciplined paramilitary unit that would later be a key to Hilter's rise to prominence.

The philosophy of the Nazis was one of patriotic nationalism, as opposed to the movement of international socialism that was sweeping parts of Europe and Asia. The fear on the part of many Germans, especially those on the political right, was that the forces of international Marxism would turn Germany into a Soviet client state. Hitler promised to rid Germany of the "criminals" who had given in to the Allies and the "evil Jews" and Marxists who were the real influences behind these traitors. Thus, as in Italy and in Japan, the rise of the militant right was partly a reaction to the growing power of the international socialist left.

But first, the Nazis would have to seize political power in Germany. Then came the famous "Beer Hall Putsch" of November 1923. Hitler and his Nazis attempted a coup d'état. Bavarian government leaders had planned a mass meeting to address its role in the future of Germany at a large beer hall on the outskirts of Munich, the Burgerbrauhaus. Goering led his steel-helmeted SA storm troopers as he, Hitler, and Hitler's assistant, Rudolf Hess, took control of the meeting and announced their radical political program. The Nazi coup was short-lived, however, for the next morning they were confronted by army troops. In the ensuing melee, Hitler and Hess were arrested, and Goering was badly wounded in the leg and hip during gun battles in the street.

SA men carried Goering to a nearby building and hid him there while his men scattered in all directions. The Nazi Party's leaders were now outlaws. Goering's wife Carin and SA supporters managed to get him to Austria, where he went into hiding and began a long, painful process of recovering from his physical wounds. While Hitler was in prison writing his masterpiece, *Mein Kampf,* Goering was becoming addicted to morphine, which he took for pain. He would never be the same again physically. He would eventually overcome his morphine addiction over the next several years, but his health had suffered greatly. His addiction had induced a habit of overeating that would plague him the rest of his life. It had also led to changes in personality and temperament—he was frequently anxious and prone to outbursts of temper. He was no longer the athletic, handsome young fighter pilot.

Hitler was released from prison at the end of 1924 and he was free to resume his maniacal career. But Goering was still an outlaw, due to his role in the Beer Hall Putsch. These were years of frustration and ongoing depression for Goering, as the Nazi movement was gaining strength in Germany without him. He spent time first in Austria, then in Italy, where he had several meetings with Benito Mussolini, and then in his wife Carin's native Sweden. He and his wife were devoted to each other, and her death several years later from illness was a great blow to him, both physically and emotionally.

Goering's official exile ended in 1927 when the German Reichstag approved a petition freeing all political prisoners and pardoning political exiles. He returned to Germany, but things had changed. He had been away for four years. Hitler and the Nazis had moved on. The SA was now commanded by Alfred Rosenberg, and Rudolf Hess was Hitler's main political advisor. (Ernst Roehm would later command the SA until he was shot along with the rest of the SA leadership in the Night of the Long Knives in 1934.) For a time, Goering consoled himself by making money. He went to work as a representative for BMW. His government and business contacts ensured his financial success, and before long he was once again talking to Hitler about a role in the party.

Frustrated in the failed coup of 1923, Hitler, Goering, and Hess decided that the route to power invariably had to run through the political system. Just as he had assisted Hitler in building a physical presence in Bavaria through the SA, Goering set about helping Hitler to build a political presence at the Reichstag in Berlin. No longer mainly a street brawler and paramilitary leader, he became a Nazi political leader, winning a seat in the Reichstag in 1928, along with eleven other Nazis. From 1928 to 1934, Goering was Hitler's driving force in building a political party machine in Berlin.

Goering became Hitler's version of Leon Trotsky—he traveled the country preaching the virtues of national socialism, engaging in debates along the way with socialists, and recruiting Nazi candidates for the Reichstag. With Hitler as his model, he became quite good at public speaking, trading insults with leftist hecklers, and engaging in the worst kind of fascist demagoguery. He could be crude, but he was very effective. As the German economy worsened, right-wing nationalism took hold and the Nazis increased their numbers in the Reichstag, though they did not hold enough seats to gain a majority. It was also a time of intense street fighting among various political organizations, namely the Nazis versus the socialists. Hospitals filled weekly with cracked heads, stab wounds, and broken limbs. It was the physical manifestation of the political battle for the future of the German nation.

Goering also proved to be a very effective tool of public relations with the German president Paul von Hindenburg. The eighty-four-year-old president, a throwback to imperial Germany and the old days, detested Hitler. He saw Hitler as a street thug who had no business at the top levels of government. But he admired Goering's military record and his commitment to Germany's gloried past. By 1932, the Nazis were the single largest party in the Reichstag and Goering, as its leader, held the title of president of the Assembly. The eventual deal between Hindenburg, the Reichstag leader Franz von Papen, and Hitler that brought the Nazis to power would not have been possible without Hermann Goering.

After Hitler was named chancellor in 1933, Goering became Prussian minister of the interior, which gave him control of the police. Now there was little he could not do in the Nazis' push to gain absolute control of the German state. Then began the many purges and mass arrests directed by Hitler and Goering over the next several years that solidified their control of Germany. Under the guise of protecting the German people, Goering openly sanctioned murder:

> Policemen who fire their revolvers in the execution of their duties will be protected by me without regard to the consequences of having fired these weapons. But officials who fail, out of mistaken regard for the consequences, must expect disciplinary action to be taken against them. The protection of the people demands the strictest application of the legal regulations governing prohibited demonstrations, meetings, mass strikes, newspaper offenses, and all other punishable offenses . . . No officer should lose sight of the fact that failure to adopt a measure is more heinous than the making of mistakes in its application.

Though Goering continued to serve in Hitler's inner circle and was one of his top military advisors, his authority declined with the onset of World War II, particularly after the disastrous siege of Stalingrad in 1942. For one thing, Goering was less enthusiastic about all-out war than some of Hitler's other advisors, such as Joseph Goebbels, Joachim von Ribbentrop, and Heinrich Himmler. There were also indications by 1939 that his hold on his offices and his responsibilities was slipping. Due to a combination of Goering's ongoing health issues, the personality and psychological changes he underwent, and his policy differences with other members of the high command, Hitler increasingly turned to others for leadership.

If Hitler was a madman and Goering was a bullying, murderous thug, then Heinrich Himmler was a genocidal lunatic. Sadly, from 1939 to 1944 no one was more influential over German policy than Himmler. He was the prime architect of the Holocaust. This small, bookish, plain-looking man gave a life force to Hitler's dream of Aryan racial superiority and the elimination of "inferior" races, notably the Jews and the Slavs. A participant in the Beer Hall Putsch of 1923, he joined the SS (the *Schutzstaffel,* originally a contingent of the SA) and was instrumental in making that organization Hitler's premier weapon of terror.

His real rise to power in the Third Reich began in 1934 with the Night of the Long Knives. The SA leader Ernst Roehm had overplayed his hand—he wanted the SA to take over many of the functions of the regular army. The military high command, along with Goering and Himmler, convinced Hitler that Roehm and the SA were dangerously out of control and should be eliminated. That paved the way for Himmler and the SS to accumulate sweeping powers within the party.

He shared with Hitler a devotion to building a race-based society of supermen. As Reichsfuehrer of the SS, he introduced the principle of racial selection, in which to be admitted one had to prove racially pure ancestry. He wanted to build a master race of Nordic-looking Aryans (blond hair, blue eyes, fair skin). His earlier experience as a chicken farmer had taught him the rudiments of animal breeding, which he intended to apply to humans. He thought he could genetically engineer a master Nordic race within a couple of generations. Fortunately for Himmler, his theories of racial superiority dovetailed perfectly with Hitler's own racial fantasies and his stated goals of ridding Europe of the Jews, whom the Nazis blamed for Germany's problems.

In 1933, Himmler set up the first concentration camp in Dachau, outside Munich. It was the first in a series of camps designed for mass murder. With Hitler's encouragement, Himmler greatly expanded the range of people who qualified for internment in the camps to include Jews, Slavs, Gypsies, the physically handicapped, the mentally retarded, homosexuals, and others the Third Reich had no use for. In a speech in 1943, Himmler declared that the German people must be true to their own blood "and to no one else. What happens to the Russians, what happens to the Slavs and the Czechs is a matter of indifference to me. Such good blood of our own kind as there may be among the nations we shall acquire for ourselves, if necessary by taking away the children and bringing them up among us. Whether the other peoples live in comfort or perish of hunger interests me only in so far as we need them as slaves for our culture . . ." He then went onto discuss the necessity of "exterminating" all Jewish people. To him the mission of Germany was "the struggle for the extermination of any sub-humans all over the world . . ." Not to put too fine a point on it, Himmler's quest to wipe out half the planet makes Tomás de Torquemada look like a choir boy.

What is truly remarkable about Himmler is how unremarkable he seemed to most who came into contact with him. Those who met him personally were almost unanimous in describing him as utterly mediocre, indistinguishable by any special trait of character, intellect, or physical presence. One British diplomat commented that he had never been able to draw anything from Himmler of the most fleeting interest, and he described Himmler as "normal." It wasn't a compliment.

But this unremarkable man, through his control of the SS and the Gestapo, controlled much of the machinery of Hitler's government. And through the religion of Aryanism and his race-obsessed dedication to terror, he wielded a great deal of psychological power. During the war, Himmler's power in the Third Reich only increased, as Goering's influence was on the decline. By 1943, when he became minister of the interior, he was the second most powerful man in Germany. When in 1944 he obtained command of the newly formed Army of the Upper Rhine (to fight the advancing American and French armies), he gained control of most military transport, censorship, intelligence services, army surveillance, and troop supplies. All the while, his apparatus of death in the concentration camps was working overtime to implement the "Final Solution."

But there was yet another Nazi official who exerted great influence over Hitler, especially in the years from 1943 to 1945. The name Martin Bormann is not as well known to the general public as Goering, Himmler, and Goebbels, yet in the closing years of World War II, no one in Germany had greater influence over Hitler's thinking. He became Himmler's main competitor and antagonist in the battle for power in the Third Reich.

As head of the Nazi Party Chancellery and private secretary to Hitler, Bormann gained Hitler's trust and accumulated immense power by controlling access to him. Many in the Nazi Party overlooked him and underestimated his influence. He had been the chief of staff to Hitler's Deputy Fuehrer, Rudolf Hess. But Hess's ill-fated "peace mission" to Britain in 1941 permanently took Hess out of the picture. From that point on, Bormann worked to make himself indispensable to Hitler, taking personal charge of his paperwork, appointments, personal finances, and policy meetings. A true Machiavellian, he proved to be a master of intrigue, manipulation, and political infighting.

Beginning in 1943, he increasingly controlled policy relating to the security of the regime, legislation, appointments and promotions, and party personnel. He became Hitler's closest collaborator, and showed an uncanny ability to exploit Hitler's personal weaknesses and personality quirks in order to increase his own power. He exerted the kind of influence over Hitler that is only possible through daily personal contact—what might be called the "politics of proximity."

He used that power to tightly control access to the Fuehrer and limit his contact with other party leaders. This relatively unknown Nazi official, in a seemingly minor and unimportant office, was able to systematically undermine his rivals for influence—Goering, Goebbels, and Himmler. Of course, it helped that by 1945 Hitler—deteriorating both physically and emotionally—trusted practically no one.

Goering's influence had been on the decline for some time. Near the end, in April 1945, when the Russians were closing in and Hitler was in the bunker, Goering sent him a message asking if the time was right for him (Goering) to assume command of the Reich. Although Goering had "officially" been designated Hitler's successor (one has to wonder how serious Hitler was about that in the first place), the Fuehrer was infuriated. He ordered Goering's arrest and dismissed him from his government and party posts.

From a military and political standpoint, Himmler had seen the end coming. In early 1945 he attempted to separate himself from Hitler and the rest of the Nazi leadership. He naively thought that he could negotiate with the Allies and be taken seriously. When Hitler learned that Himmler was talking to Allied leaders behind his back, he flew into a rage. As with Goering, he ordered Himmler's arrest and stripped him of his commands. He even had Himmler's SS adjutant, who was there in the bunker, shot immediately.

At the end, Hitler trusted only Martin Bormann and Joseph Goebbels, his propaganda minister. Hitler and Goebbels killed themselves, along with Eva Braun and Goebbels's wife and children, there in the bunker. Himmler committed suicide upon his capture in May 1945, and Goering did the same just before he was to be executed following the Nuremberg Trials in 1946—both of them biting down on cyanide pills.

There were conflicting reports about the fate of Bormann. One escapee from the bunker, Hitler Youth Leader Artur Axmann, said that Bormann was killed by Soviet troops while trying to escape. Other accounts reported that Bormann had committed suicide with Hitler in the bunker. But because his body wasn't found after the war, there were persistent rumors that he had escaped and fled to South America. There were occasional reports of Bormann sightings (as there were for a number of other wanted Nazis) in the 1950s and 1960s, but none were ever confirmed. Finally, in 1972, excavations in Berlin by construction workers found human remains that seemed to corroborate Artur Axman's account of Bormann's death. His body was identified through dental records, created from the memory of a German doctor in 1945. Yet the controversy has never been put to rest—some still insisted that Bormann survived, including famed Nazi hunter Simon Wiesenthal.

➡ CHAPTER 9 ⬅

THE FIXERS

The concept of a political fixer is particularly, almost uniquely, American. It is primarily the U.S. political system that developed partisan political campaigns for elected office, and the United States is most closely associated with both the good and the bad that results from this wide-open, high-stakes public competition.

The *Longman Dictionary of Contemporary English* defines a *political fixer* as "someone who is good at arranging things and solving problems for other people, sometimes by using dishonest methods." As used here, a political fixer is a consultant, advisor, or specialist who works on behalf of a political candidate, or sometimes a political party or interest; largely a behind-the-scenes player who crafts strategy, pulls strings, and troubleshoots. Most often, fixers are political campaign strategists—later in the twentieth century they would likely be referred to as political consultants. But the concept of a political fixer is not limited to elections and political campaign activity. Oftentimes, a fixer is someone in an executive position, a White House staffer, for example, who plays much the same role from the inside—pushing hard for policies and legislation, spinning the media, and putting out fires when needed.

Unsurprisingly (Machiavelli would say "by necessity"), this type of political player exerts great influence on those he works for, often plays fast and loose with the rules and with the facts, and gains a mostly negative reputation with the public, with the media, and with his opponents. In the current climate, almost regardless of country, politicians in general and political consultants in particular are rated by the public very low in trustworthiness and character—down there with used-car salesmen and Wall Street bankers.

This chapter examines the impact of some of the leading practitioners of this kind of political influence. It isn't meant to be an exhaustive list of political fixers, but represents this author's take on some of the leading power players over the last hundred years. Some names are well known; others are not. What they have in common is that they fit the prototype of a King Whisperer: a power behind the throne who made a significant impact on the American political system.

Being a political fixer doesn't necessarily preclude having honorable goals and high moral standards. Many of those who toil in the political trenches have the most noble of goals, and simply want to put people they admire in a position to advocate for policies they believe are important to the country. Ah, but it is the necessity of winning, and the narcotic effects of winning, that drive individuals to take advantage of the process when they do. There may be no finer, more moral person to ever occupy the White House than George Herbert Walker Bush (Bush 41). But in his long career, that didn't stop him from utilizing the talents of people that many observers find, shall we say, ethically challenged. Of course, that could be said of almost any president, whether Republican or Democrat.

A Twentieth-Century Man: "Dollar" Mark Hanna

The roots of modern political campaigning lie in the 1890s and in the mind of Marcus Alonzo Hanna of Cleveland, Ohio. More than any other single person, Hanna was America's first modern campaign manager. His philosophy was simple. He was quoted as saying, "There are two things that are important in politics. The first is money, and I can't remember what the second one is." Today he would be called a political consultant or, worse, a political hatchet man. Newspaper publisher William Randolph Hearst liked to portray him as an overgrown, dollar-hungry, pro-business ogre. For thousands of newspaper readers across America, Hanna was brought to life as "Dollar" Mark Hanna in the eye-catching drawings of Hearst's cartoonist, Homer Davenport.

For a hundred years, Mark Hanna has loomed large in American political mythology. It has even been suggested by some scholars that Hanna was the inspiration for the Wizard in L. Frank Baum's classic children's book, *The Wonderful Wizard of Oz*. Certainly, there has never been a more powerful "behind-the-scenes" operator. In the 1890s and the early twentieth century, he not only became the most powerful political operative the country had ever seen, he revolutionized the way politics and campaigns were practiced.

Hanna's timing was impeccable, and his choice of a hero, William McKinley, was ideal for the climate of the country at that time. The presidential election of 1896 marked a turning point of sorts for America, and for the world. For one thing, it reaffirmed the bond between the Republican Party and big industrial interests, and it also represented a political realignment, ushering in GOP dominance of national government until Franklin Roosevelt and the New Deal. Hanna's campaign strategy also exemplified the professionalization of politics, notably the emerging role of "big money" in presidential campaigns.

After the Civil War, Hanna had gone into the coal and iron business in Ohio. Due to the industrial expansion of the 1870s and 1880s, the demand for coal, iron, and copper skyrocketed, and so did Hanna's fortunes. His talent for sniffing out opportunities and developing new ventures put him on the fast track to becoming one of the richest men in the Midwest. He was known as the "Red Boss," a reference to his coal and iron ventures coloring the skies of northern Ohio. His business success and constant maneuvering brought him into close contact with local and state politicians, and he learned quickly how to get things done. A "regular greasing of the palms for elected officials" was not a problem for Hanna.

Hanna was popular among politicians because of his knack for fund-raising. He not only twisted arms for political candidates among his business associates, he also was known for shaking the money tree in Washington. When he focused his energies on Ohio politics after the election of 1888, Republican candidates there gained access to campaign funds from the Republican National Committee in record amounts.

Although their paths had crossed once or twice before, it was at the 1888 convention that Hanna became highly impressed with William McKinley. To many political observers of the day, and especially to Hanna, the Ohio congressman seemed like a natural politician. He certainly looked the part, with his upright posture, starched white shirts, and handsome, appealing demeanor. He had a natural feel for politics and a reputation for community-minded policies. Most important, he took care of Ohio's best interests. It has also been suggested that politics and policy gave McKinley an escape of sorts from the stress of caring for his wife, Ida, who suffered frequent health problems and bouts of melancholia.

Hanna and McKinley set their sights on the 1891 election for governor of Ohio. Governor Joseph Foraker, a former Hanna ally, had lost to a Democrat in 1889, which he blamed on interference from Hanna's political machine. Hanna's experience in national politics had taught him many lessons about how to exert pressure and reward allies. His contacts in the business community became some of his best field agents, and helped him raise record amounts of cash for a statewide race. By the time of the Ohio State Convention in 1891, McKinley was already the de facto nominee for governor.

McKinley was elected easily, even helping the Republicans take a majority in the Ohio state legislature. He and Hanna were in a position to help the national Republican Party raise money for candidates across the country and win many friends in Washington, D.C. William McKinley, through his experience in Washington, his control of Ohio politics, and the nonstop efforts of Mark Hanna, was becoming a national figure. And Hanna, more quietly, was becoming one of the most powerful men in America.

But there was still work to be done, and a rough road ahead. Many Republicans—Hanna included—saw the train wreck of 1892 coming. Incumbent President Benjamin Harrison had bungled the job to the point that most political observers believed no Republican had a chance of winning against the Democrats, so it wasn't even worth attempting to wrest the Republican nomination away from Harrison. But that didn't mean Hanna wasn't playing power politics and laying the groundwork for the future. At the 1892 convention, he put forth McKinley's name as an alternate candidate for president—not a serious run at the nomination, but a gesture to get McKinley's name known among the party faithful. "McKinley for President" badges were distributed just for show. Hanna had learned how to play the game—it was never too early to start planning for a goal—which, ultimately, was the 1896 presidential nomination.

After the 1894 midterm congressional elections, Hanna retired from his business and devoted himself full time to making McKinley the next president. Using thousands of dollars of his own money, as well as campaign contributions from John D. Rockefeller and J. P. Morgan, Hanna crafted one of the first true "national" campaigns for a presidential party nomination. Though there were few Republicans in the South, Hanna worked them hard for McKinley. One of Hanna's rivals, New York political boss Thomas Platt, said, "Hanna had the South practically solid before some of us waked up."

In building a national following for McKinley, Hanna used both a public strategy and a private strategy. The public efforts included the formation of "McKinley Clubs" in as many states as possible, and a deluge of pro-McKinley advertisements and posters—all of which took money, and lots of it. The private strategy was, of course, working the state delegations and winning over local party bosses. Money was useful there, too.

By the time the convention opened in June in St. Louis, McKinley's nomination was a sure thing. The other top candidates had mostly withdrawn, starting with former President Benjamin Harrison, in January.

Immediately following McKinley's nomination on the very first ballot, deafening cries of "Hanna! Hanna!" were heard throughout the hall. It was Mark Hanna's moment of triumph. Upon his return to Cleveland, he was met by a huge admiring crowd at the train station, and escorted home in a parade as a conquering hero. He remembered it as one of the finest days of his life.

The dominant issue in the 1896 election was the coinage of money, and whether its value should be tied to gold, or silver, or both. At least, that became the symbolic struggle of the campaign. The clash of 1896 was largely about industrial interests versus rural, agricultural interests, the free flow of imports versus high tariffs, and the monied establishment versus the growing populist movement. The Republicans were unified. The cause of "silver" and its perceived threat to the economic health of the commercial and industrial interests scared the pants off the entire business community. That meant they were ready to open their wallets, and Mark Hanna was there waiting for them.

The class warfare the populists were preaching had found an audience, particularly in the South and the West, and the businessmen were nervous, even panicky. But Hanna took charge. While William Jennings Bryan, the Democratic nominee, was crisscrossing the country delivering his *Cross of Gold* speech, Hanna opened two campaign headquarters—one in New York and the other in Chicago. The author and politician John Milton Hay compared Hanna to a general taking command of his troops.

The number-one priority of the Eastern business establishment was to stop this "nonsense" about dropping the gold standard and lowering the tariff. They knew they had to stop the populist movement, and they were prepared to pay to see it happen. Collecting the money was, of course, another matter, and contributions were uneven from business to business. But by the general election, the McKinley campaign reported raising and spending more than $3.5 million—by far a record amount. A number of sources have claimed that the actual amount of money Hanna raised from the business community was almost twice that. If that is true, so the speculation goes, a good bit of the unreported amount was spent on what would now be called "walking-around money."

The money that the campaign did report was spent on an avalanche of pro-McKinley advertising and propaganda, the likes of which had never been seen before. According to the turn-of-the-century businessman and political observer Chauncey Depew:

> The genius of Mark Hanna soon became evident. He organized a campaign of education such as had never been dreamed of, much less attempted. Traveling publicity agents, with wagonloads of pamphlets, filled the highways and the byways, and no home was so isolated that it did not receive its share. Columns in the newspapers, especially the country papers, were filled with articles written by experts, and the platform was never so rich with public speakers.

Depew added that although the campaign was extremely effective, "the expense is so terrific that it will never again be attempted . . . public opinion would never permit it." How quaint.

McKinley's 1896 candidacy is also known for what has come to be called the "front porch" campaign. The decision by McKinley and Hanna to have the candidate campaign from the front porch of his home in Canton, Ohio was strategic. Although most nineteenth-century candidates adhered to the tradition of not "actively campaigning" for the office, it was not unheard of for a candidate to take to the road and make public appearances. If Hanna thought it was in the campaign's interests to go out and actively campaign, then McKinley surely would have. But the nature of their opponent, William Jennings Bryan, led them to adopt a stay-at-home approach. As a candidate, Bryan's greatest strength was his oratorical skill. He embarked on a national speaking tour, traveling by rail, and wowed every audience he spoke to with his riveting style and barn-raising theatrics. The last thing Hanna wanted was a contest over speechmaking between Bryan and McKinley—a competition McKinley was sure to lose.

McKinley agreed with this calculation, famously saying to reporters "unlike my opponent, I have to think when I speak." He was also reluctant to leave his invalid wife for long periods. So the decision was made to create a more statesmanlike and regal atmosphere by bringing citizens to McKinley's home. As the old saying goes, they were bringing "the mountain to Muhammad," and they did it with Hanna's usual flair. In well-scripted "meetings," delegations of Republican supporters flocked to McKinley's home to hear directly from the candidate. Met at the station and shepherded through the streets of Canton, the throngs passed pro-McKinley banners and signs, bought McKinley posters and buttons, and eagerly awaited the nominee's appearance on his front porch. Often, there was a carnival atmosphere to these gatherings. Some delegations marched behind a brass band, singing campaign songs and shouting McKinley slogans. It was classic Hanna. By the time of the election, more than three hundred such delegations had made the pilgrimage to Canton. Farmers, small business owners, factory workers, college students, Civil War veterans, and others came to help usher in the age of "McKinley Prosperity." Through most of this, Hanna had been occupied raising campaign cash to pay for it all.

William McKinley was as close to untouchable as most politicians can ever get. He was a devoted family man, there was not a hint of scandal or any ethical issues in his past, and to many Americans in 1896 he was the very epitome of civic virtue. But Mark Hanna was a different story. Through his close ties to industrial giants, his hard-hitting political style, and his association with gargantuan campaign donations, he presented an appealing target to anyone interested in slinging arrows at McKinley. And William Randolph Hearst was interested.

Hearst is a legend in journalism, and for decades was at the epicenter of American political and social life. In 1896, Hearst supported William Jennings Bryan and his populist calls for the coinage of silver. His strategy was basically to brand McKinley as the unknowing lackey of the capitalist monster Mark Hanna. The best-known images from Hearst's public campaign against Hanna and McKinley are from the *New York World*'s cartoonist, Homer Davenport. His cartoons portrayed Hanna as a grossly overgrown, bull-necked beast with dollar signs all over his clothes, crushing the common man under his feet. One drawing had McKinley dangling on the end of an organ-grinder's string, controlled by Hanna.

In the end, Hearst's efforts were no match for the nationwide media blitz staged by Hanna on behalf of McKinley. But Hearst succeeded in creating an image of Hanna as an evil ogre, an image that lingers to this day. Publicly, Mark Hanna was only too glad to be the lightning rod for McKinley. Privately, though, he confided to friends that the cartoons stung. For his part, Homer Davenport, who later met Hanna, regretted the exaggerated nature of the cartoons he drew for Hearst.

There were many who thought Hanna would continue to pull the strings after McKinley was elected and be the power behind the throne. This belief was no doubt spurred by William Randolph Hearst and his attacks on Hanna. Some, for example, thought Hanna would be offered a Cabinet post. But unlike some leading political strategists today (Karl Rove and David Axelrod, for example), he had little interest in serving in the government bureaucracy. "Me in the Cabinet?" he asked incredulously. But Hanna was a political animal, and there was one office he did covet—senator.

McKinley felt he had to oblige his old friend. After all, he had gotten him elected president. McKinley named Senator John Sherman of Ohio his secretary of state, which opened up a vacancy in the Senate. The Ohio state legislature appointed Hanna to fill Sherman's term. He was later elected to a full term in the Senate, where he served until his death in 1904.

Hanna is known to history as the man who raised heretofore unprecedented amounts of money for a political race, and gave birth to high-dollar political campaigns. But he is also remembered by political and organizational strategists as an innovative problem solver—always thinking strategically for the long term. He galvanized business and commercial interests into a political force, centered around the Republican Party, that lasted several decades, until the Great Depression and the New Deal resulted in a fundamental restructuring of politics, government, and business.

Even after William McKinley's legacy began to fade and subsequent generations were unsure of his place in history, Mark Hanna's contributions were clear. His campaigns and his tactics became textbook materials for future generations of political operatives, from both of the Roosevelts who became president up through George W. Bush and Barack Obama.

Campaigns, Inc.: Clem Whitaker and Leone Baxter

The story of Clem Whitaker and Leone Baxter is an inspiring one. This husband-and-wife team formed the nation's first professional political consulting firm, Campaigns, Inc., managing seventy-five political campaigns from the 1930s to the 1960s (and winning seventy of them). In the process, they pioneered an entire industry and approach to organizing political activity.

Clem Whitaker was a political reporter in Sacramento when, in 1933, he was asked by powerful California State Senator Jack McColl to help the legislature defeat a referendum initiated by Pacific Gas & Electric Company. The legislature had authorized a program creating the Central Valley Project, a flood-control and irrigation development for northern California. But Pacific Gas feared that the program would threaten private power companies in the state, and organized an initiative to defeat it.

Leone Baxter, recently widowed, was a young publicity agent and a booster of the Central Valley Project. She and Whitaker agreed to team up and run a publicity campaign on behalf of the legislature aimed at defeating the referendum organized by Pacific Gas. Working with a budget of just $40,000, Whitaker and Baxter conceived a campaign using family farmers, small-town newspapers, and the emerging tool of radio to handily defeat the referendum. After its defeat, Pacific Gas & Electric was so impressed by their work that they hired Whitaker and Baxter and put them on retainer for the next twenty-five years.

One of their most successful campaigns was also one of their most notorious, and helped establish the art and science of what we know today as "negative campaigning." Fresh off their victory in the Central Valley Project campaign, they were hired by California Governor Frank Merriam in 1934 to beat back an election challenge by renowned muckraking author Upton Sinclair, who had left the Socialist Party and joined the Democratic Party to make a run for governor.

Sinclair's platform, called EPIC (End Poverty in California), was heavy on government spending and government programs, something like a New Deal on steroids. Whitaker and Baxter orchestrated a statewide smear campaign that made Sinclair look like Joseph Stalin. They formed an organization called United for California that was backed by many of the state's leading economic interests, particularly the real estate industry, leading agricultural interests, and the powerful Hollywood-based movie industry.

Whitaker and Baxter executed one of the first large-scale direct mail efforts in American politics, using mailing lists obtained from organizations such as Knights of Columbus, the Boy Scouts, and the American Legion. With headlines such as "The Proof That Upton Sinclair Preaches Revolution and Communism," they created pamphlets and flyers using Sinclair quotes to inspire an anti-Sinclair backlash. They also made use of Hollywood moviemaking. MGM studios, for example, distributed a film called *California Here We Come,* which depicted vagrants and homeless people descending on California by the thousands to take advantage of the "socialist paradise" Sinclair promised. It was effectively brutal, and Governor Merriam defeated Sinclair by more than 300,000 votes.

Whitaker and Baxter married in 1938 and set about creating the premier political consulting service in the land. After their decimation of Upton Sinclair, their operational philosophy was summed up by Clem Whitaker: "The average American doesn't want to be educated, he doesn't want to improve his mind, he doesn't even want to work consciously at being a good citizen. But every American likes to be entertained. He likes the movies, he likes fireworks and parades. So, if you can't put on a fight, put on a show." Today's political consultants couldn't say it better themselves.

Whitaker and Baxter were public relations specialists—that was their training and that was their primary experience. They were simply the first to apply the principles of public relations and advertising in a systematic way to the operation of political campaign activity and make it a successful business enterprise. In short, they made it a profession, and their business model and their successes in the field influenced thousands of political and public relations professionals who would come after them.

A *Time* magazine profile of the pair from 1955 refers to them as a "lanky, gentle-looking white-haired man and uncommonly pretty redhead."

> In private life, Clem, 56, and Leone, a youthful looking 49, are
> Mr. and Mrs. Whitaker. They alternate at being president and
> vice president, switching jobs every year. They hardly know the
> pronoun "I"; almost always they are "we." Usually, they answer
> telephone calls together on two extensions, divide profits
> equally, plot their campaigns together (often in the seclusion
> of an oceanside resort). Clem has a genius for long-range
> planning and Leone tends to defer to his political judgment.
> Leone is a talented writer, a minter of bright ideas, and more
> the day-to-day executive than Clem.

They helped elect governors, lieutenant governors, mayors, state legislators, U.S. senators, and scores of other elected officials and won a number of statewide referenda in California. Though not overtly partisan, they worked primarily for Republican candidates, perhaps because the Republicans were the dominant party in California during their lifetimes.

Their legacy is that they helped to make political campaigning a science. In Whitaker's words, they transformed elections from "a hit and miss business, directed by broken-down politicians" into "a mature, well-managed business founded on sound public relations principles, and using every technique of modern advertising."

Camelot's Merlin: Larry O'Brien

Major changes in the field of political campaigns and consulting occurred in the 1950s and 1960s, some related to the political career of John F. Kennedy. One of the features of the post–World War II American political system was the declining role of the political party organization, culminating in 1972 with the rise of the political primary system for nominating presidential candidates, thereby reducing the domination of party regulars in "smoke-filled rooms." John Kennedy's campaigns for the Senate in the 1950s and the presidency in 1960 were among the first to demonstrate that a political organization run outside the official party structure could be successful. Kennedy's use of independent specialists and advisors to help him develop strategy, perform research, and raise money established a model that other campaigns for national office began to emulate. Kennedy's success, and virtual domination of the Democratic Party, helped solidify the trend away from party resources and toward independently run campaigns.

There were a number of important advisors and counselors Kennedy relied on, beginning with his brother, Robert, and his father, Joseph. Theodore Sorenson, JFK's longtime confidante, was also one of his closest advisors. But when it came to campaign strategy and tactics, no one was more important to Kennedy's political success than a "burly, crew-cut Irishman from Springfield, Massachusetts," Larry O'Brien.

In fact, if John F. Kennedy and his era are remembered as "Camelot," then one might say that Larry O'Brien was Merlin. O'Brien's name may not be as famous as others from that era, but for almost three decades, he was a guiding strategic force behind the national Democratic Party. One of its leading electoral strategists, he helped to reshape American electoral politics from 1946 to 1973.

In a very practical way, O'Brien was himself a bridge of sorts, from the old-style politics of the early and mid-twentieth century to the "New Frontier" (to borrow a Kennedy phrase) of political polling, voter data, and image management. The Kennedy people certainly thought so. It may surprise many people today that O'Brien graced the cover of *Time* magazine on September 1, 1961 as one of the leading lights of the new Kennedy administration:

> To the Kennedy team, O'Brien was and is more than a skillful political organizer. He has the experience and understanding to serve as a bridge between the Democratic Old Guard and the New Frontier. The bright, eager young men around Jack Kennedy have always baffled and often offended the Skeffingtons of Massachusetts; but Larry O'Brien can talk to politicians in their own language and win them over. "He was the essential transition man for us with the Old Guard," says

Bobby Kennedy. At the same time, O'Brien was an invaluable professor of political science for the likes of Bobby, Kenny O'Donnell, Dick Donahue and other young members of the Kennedy group who were rank and file amateurs in Kennedy's successful 1952 senatorial campaign. They have since become a close-knit, highly professional team that is known in Administration circles as "the Irish Mafia."

O'Brien's political experience goes back to 1940s Massachusetts, when as a young law school grad he went to work to elect his friend Foster Furcolo to the U.S. House of Representatives. O'Brien had grown up in politics, the son of a scrappy Democratic Party organizer in Springfield, Massachusetts. His father had experienced firsthand the anti-Irish discrimination still prevalent at the time and the economic and social struggles facing the working class and small businessmen, of which the O'Brien clan were a part. The O'Brien home became a way station for political types, and it gave the young Larry a taste for politics. His experiences in Springfield also gave him an understanding of precinct politics and the importance of getting out the vote.

In his campaign to elect Furcolo to Congress in 1948, O'Brien divided the district into sixty separate units and recruited a corps of campaign workers he called "secretaries" to work the district hard. He kept a steady stream of campaign letters going to voters and businesses, and pushed Furcolo to an unrelenting pace of campaign appearances, community events, and knocking on doors. Many of O'Brien's techniques were later adopted by John Kennedy's state- and national-level campaigns.

The victorious Furcolo brought O'Brien with him to Washington to be his chief of staff. Within a couple of years, Kennedy, also a Massachusetts congressman, had stolen O'Brien away from Furcolo—aided by the fact that O'Brien and Furcolo had a personal falling out and parting of the ways. Kennedy made O'Brien the chief organizer for his 1952 run for the U.S. Senate. O'Brien built a statewide campaign machine for Kennedy outside of the normal state party structure. It was unlike anything that had been seen at the time—consisting of 350 "secretaries," 18,000 volunteers, and a network of committed Kennedy fund-raisers. O'Brien's work helped

Kennedy do what many thought was impossible: He defeated incumbent U.S. Senator Henry Cabot Lodge in a historic upset.

Under O'Brien's direction, Kennedy's Senate campaigns in 1952 and 1958 were a virtual "supermarket of political innovations: the campaign tea parties, with Kennedy's mother and sisters pouring (and an omnipresent guestbook to provide O'Brien with the names and addresses of potential campaign workers); the expanding 'O'Brien Manual,' a handbook of organizational instructions written in language any amateur could understand." He also made extensive use of what he called "womanpower" and the "home telephone technique," enlisting women volunteers to call people listed on a single page in the telephone book, ask for support, and offer transportation to the polls.

Kennedy won reelection to the Senate in 1958 with almost a one-million-vote plurality, a Massachusetts record at the time.

When Kennedy and his brain trust began plotting his 1960 presidential campaign, Larry O'Brien was put in charge of building Kennedy organizations throughout the United States. He brought the same attention to detail and innovation to organizing Kennedy's electoral efforts in the key primary states. He then set about organizing the pro-Kennedy forces at the nominating convention in Los Angeles. Kennedy's efforts were considered a marvel of modern political efficiency and were a testament to the efforts of O'Brien and a host of other Kennedy staffers.

The 1960 general election campaign against Richard Nixon featured many of the same organizational hallmarks that were now standard practice in the O'Brien playbook, and helped Kennedy eke out one of the closest presidential election victories in American history. After his razor-thin win over Nixon, President-elect Kennedy called O'Brien "the best election man in the business."

As Karl Rove and David Axelrod would do decades after him, O'Brien went to work in the administration of the president he had just helped to elect. (By contrast, James Carville in 1992 decided against going to work in the government after helping to elect Bill Clinton.) O'Brien became JFK's special assistant for congressional relations. He was the point man in Congress for many of Kennedy's and Johnson's "New Frontier" programs from 1961 to 1964, and became an invaluable source of political energy and ideas for Kennedy's team.

O'Brien was in the motorcade that fateful day in Dallas in November 1963 when JFK was assassinated. He quickly became a key resource for the new president, Lyndon B. Johnson. Serving in the same capacity for Johnson as he had for Kennedy, O'Brien was largely responsible for the passage of several landmark bills, including those establishing the Peace Corps and the 1964 Civil Rights Act, plus winning congressional approval of the Nuclear Test Ban Treaty. In Johnson's second term, O'Brien served as postmaster general for three years—O'Brien had wanted to leave government for quite some time, but Johnson persuaded him to stay on.

Putting his political experience and strategic skills back to work, he went on to manage Hubert Humphrey's close, but ill-fated, 1968 presidential campaign. Though shackled with the Vietnam War, the assassination of Robert Kennedy, and the memory of the street protests at the nominating convention in Chicago, the Humphrey campaign made it close in the last days of the campaign against Richard Nixon.

O'Brien was then elected chairman of the Democratic National Committee. His experience and his well-known strategic sense had made him invaluable to national Democrats. While in that position, he struggled to unify a shattered party—playing a key role, for example, in the reform of the presidential nominating system that led to the modern-day primary system.

Apparently, Larry O'Brien's office was the prime target of the Nixon White House Plumbers, who broke into Democratic Party headquarters at the Watergate office complex in 1972. According to key sources among those found guilty of criminal conspiracy related to the Watergate break-in, such as G. Gordon Liddy, Nixon's people wanted to bug O'Brien's office in part to learn what he knew about Nixon's ties to Howard Hughes, who had been a key conduit for cash for some of Nixon's campaign and organizational needs.

His last act in politics was as a key advisor to the 1972 Democratic presidential nominee, George McGovern. This was apparently enough to get him out of politics for good. He calls the time spent in the McGovern campaign "the three worst months of my life—a nightmare." McGovern was no JFK. And that 1972 campaign was not Camelot. He left politics and looked for new challenges. From 1975 to 1984, he served as the commissioner of the National Basketball Association. His impact on the NBA was no less powerful than his impact on American politics. He oversaw the merger of the NBA with the American Basketball Association, he negotiated television broadcast agreements with the major networks, and he oversaw this professional sport as it raised its profile significantly by the 1980s. In 1984, the NBA championship trophy was named the "Larry O'Brien NBA Championship Trophy" in recognition of his service to the sport of basketball.

In 1992, the Democratic National Committee created the "DNC Lawrence O'Brien Award," given to recipients who demonstrate commitment to the party and its principles. Thus, Larry O'Brien is unique in American culture: National awards are named after him in basketball and in politics.

The Dark Genius: Roger Ailes

One of the truly fascinating political "fixers" of the modern era has to be Roger Ailes, the Forrest Gump of American politics. There may not be another person in the entire country whose impact on our politics and our culture has been longer or more substantive. He has been a key player in syndicated daytime television, then Richard Nixon's conquest of television in 1968, the birth of the New Right in the 1970s, Ronald Reagan's reelection in 1984, George Bush's 1988 presidential campaign, Rudy Giuliani's first campaign for mayor of New York City, and Rush Limbaugh's television show. He was an NBC network executive for several years, and then the founder of the Fox News Network. And yet, by and large, to the average American he is still relatively unknown.

A graduate of Ohio University, Ailes was the producer of the groundbreaking *Mike Douglas Show* in the 1960s, a landmark in the development of pre-*Oprah* daytime talk/variety television. Richard Nixon was a guest on the show, and he was so impressed with Ailes's grasp of television and modern communication that he brought him onto his 1968 presidential campaign, which launched Ailes's career in political media consulting. Ailes produced the Nixon campaign's series of television programs in key American cities, dubbed the "Man in the Arena" shows. Ailes engineered the broadcasts to help change Nixon's image of cold aloofness into "warmth" and confidence. It worked.

Ailes then founded a media and communications consulting business that included a long client list of corporate executives and political candidates. One of his clients in the 1970s was the fledgling Television News Network (TVN), funded by the right-wing Joseph Coors Foundation. Some consider TVN an early version of Fox News. TVN didn't make it, but some two decades later Fox Television owner Rupert Murdoch would take the idea, hire Ailes, and make it work.

A case study in the art of political fixing is Ailes's contribution to the 1984 Reagan reelection campaign. Ailes had by that time earned a reputation as a guru of communication consulting and media training. Reagan had looked terrible in his first debate with the Democratic presidential nominee, Walter Mondale. Reagan's people brought Ailes in to work with Reagan one-on-one. The feeling of many was that in the first debate Reagan had been so pumped full of statistics and research by his staff that he got confused and gave rambling, unconvincing answers. Ailes encouraged him to forget all the minute policy details and go with his gut when responding to questions.

The elephant in the room, of course, was Reagan's age. At seventy-three, he was the oldest president in American history, which is why his poor performance in the first debate was generating such a buzz. But Ailes worked with him on how to address that issue, too. When in the second debate the age issue was raised by one of the panelists, Reagan sounded much more like the old "Gipper." Without missing a beat, he said he was very much up to the job, and with a big smile added, "and I want you all to know that I will not make age an issue in this campaign. I am not going to exploit for political purposes my opponent's youth and inexperience." The audience erupted in laughter; even Mondale laughed. The debate was over. The election was over. The Gipper was back, and

Ailes had more than earned his place in the history of American presidential debates.

The climax of Ailes's political consulting career came four years later, when he was in charge of media strategy for George H. W. Bush's 1988 presidential campaign. This campaign, in the view of many, exhibited what is best and worst about the impact of professional political consultants. It was an extremely well-planned and well-executed political campaign that met its goals and hit its mark almost perfectly. But it is also considered one of the most negative political campaigns in American history and may have gone a long way toward helping to poison the well between Republicans and Democrats over the last two decades of the twentieth century.

Ailes's GOP consulting colleague, Lee Atwater (himself a legend in political campaign lore), famously announced that the Bush campaign's main goal was to "scrape the bark off" of Michael Dukakis, the 1988 Democratic nominee. They did just that. The Bush campaign went after Dukakis with a vengeance. The '88 campaign is probably best known for the infamous Willie Horton ad, which featured a grainy photo of an African-American prisoner (Horton), who, while on a weekend furlough from a Massachusetts prison, committed violent assaults. The ad was a direct broadside on the "liberal" policies of Dukakis, who was governor of Massachusetts at the time. The ad wasn't created by the Bush campaign, but by an independent group, which gave Ailes, Atwater, and the Bush campaign plausible deniability as to the ad's origins and design. However, doubts persist about the innocence of the Bush forces, particularly because they had made Dukakis and Willie Horton such an issue, and because a longtime colleague of Ailes was the creative director of the group that actually produced the ad.

After the Bush victory in 1988, Ailes was one of the top media consultants in the country. But he was also one of the most controversial consultants in the country; the scorched earth from the Dukakis campaign had followed him. He continued to have success, but also a growing string of high-profile losses—for example, Rudy Giuliani's first run for mayor of New York City in 1989, and former U.S. Attorney

General Richard Thornburgh's bid for a U.S. Senate seat from Pennsylvania in 1991—losses in which Ailes and his reputation for negativity became a campaign issue. By the early 1990s, he was looking to move back to television. He was hired by NBC in 1993 by its cable news division, where he helped develop CNBC into a powerhouse. But when NBC struck a deal with Microsoft to develop MSNBC, Ailes was edged out by network rivals.

Fortuitously, he was already negotiating with Rupert Murdoch to launch an ambitious new cable news network that would compete directly with CNN. Thus, Fox News was born. One could argue that Ailes's political and media influence has only increased since he left active politics to go back into broadcasting. Fox News grew to dominate the cable network news ratings, beginning in 2002, and continues to define the medium, giving Fox, Ailes, and his boss, Rupert Murdoch, enormous political reach in the United States.

The Ragin' Cajun: James Carville

For political watchers and history buffs, there is no state quite like Louisiana—properly pronounced LU-zi-anna. Huey Long, Earl Long, Moon Landrieu, Edwin Edwards, David Duke, and a host of others—it has a long and distinguished history of producing some of the most colorful and interesting characters in American political history. Exhibit A: the Ragin' Cajun, James Carville. Viewers watching political coverage over the years are never quite sure what he's going to say, but it is often memorable. For example, he once notoriously said, "Pennsylvania is basically Philadelphia and Pittsburgh, with Alabama in between." And several weeks before the 2008 presidential election, he quipped, "You can call the dogs in, wet the fire, and leave the house. The hunt's over" (on Barack Obama's likely winning the White House).

Carville became a household name with the election of Bill Clinton as president in 1992. A brilliant strategist and an astute campaign tactician, Carville became known as much for his bombastic and ear-catching presence on television as for his campaign consulting. He remains one of the few examples of premier political consultants who crossed over into the limelight and became a recognizable political figure on his own.

He was one of eight children, the son of a schoolteacher and a postmaster. He served in the U.S. Marine Corps, then graduated from Louisiana State University with a law degree in the early 1970s. Before entering politics, he worked as a litigator at a Baton Rouge law firm. He grew bored with practicing law, and concedes that he wasn't very good at it; instead, he became more interested in politics.

His early years in the political consulting business were humbling. But he was tenacious. He kept at it. And if one can learn from losing, he certainly did; in the 1980s he lost a lot. After being what he called "0-for-life in Louisiana," he went to Virginia and ran a Senate campaign, and lost. In 1984, he first hooked up with his longtime consulting partner Paul Begala and ran Lloyd Doggett's U.S. Senate campaign in Texas, and lost.

Carville credits his turnaround to the 1986 campaign of Bob Casey for governor of Pennsylvania. Casey had run for governor three previous times and lost. His fourth try looked to be a lost cause. But this group of "losers" surprised everyone by winning the Democratic primary and then upsetting the favored William Scranton—scion of the famous political Scrantons of Pennsylvania—in the general election. The Casey campaign had been on the ropes, but campaign officials were able to take advantage of a Scranton pledge to forgo negative campaigning; when an anti-Casey direct mail piece was circulated by Scranton, it handed Casey an opportunity to question Scranton's pledge. The Casey campaign surged at the end, largely on the publicity surrounding Scranton's broken pledge. Carville had been through tough times in politics, but he had learned how to find a way to win; and he had also learned what he deems the most valuable lesson in politics and in life—never give up!

Suddenly, Carville and Begala were in demand. In 1987 Carville scored another huge upset with the surprising win of little-known businessman Wallace Wilkinson as governor of Kentucky. Carville and Begala were on a roll. They were hired to run the gubernatorial campaign of Lieutenant Governor Zell Miller of Georgia in 1990. Miller faced a tough primary, with a field of experienced candidates, including former

UN ambassador and Atlanta mayor Andrew Young. But Miller, Carville, and Begala hung tough, ran a gritty, bare-knuckle campaign, and won a convincing victory.

Carville's leap to national prominence began in the 1991 Pennsylvania race for U.S. Senate with the shocking come-from-behind win of Harris Wofford over the highly favored Richard Thornburgh, who had been President George H. W. Bush's attorney general. Thornburgh's campaign strategist was Roger Ailes. Wofford had begun the campaign down by as much as forty points in some polls. But anxiety over the nation's economy, combined with Carville and Begala's campaign strategy of attacking Thornburgh's record and President Bush's policies, resulted in a surprising win. It was a harbinger of things to come.

James Carville met Bill Clinton in 1991 at a time when the reelection of President Bush seemed like a certainty. Though the economy was heading into a recession, Bush's popularity following the successful Gulf War had scared off most top-name Democrats from seeking the presidential nomination for 1992. Carville took the little-known governor of Arkansas and steered him toward the presidency.

Bill Clinton's win over George Bush in 1992 is a textbook example of Sun Tzu's classic military doctrine: Attack your opponent where he is vulnerable and fight on the terrain that is most advantageous to you. In the Clinton campaign staff's infamous war room, Carville posted what came to be the core of the strategy and the essence of its message: (1) Change versus more of the same; (2) It's the economy, stupid; and (3) Don't forget health care. It was no. 2 that hit the bull's-eye with the American people. The severity of the 1991–1992 recession sneaked up on people, and President Bush didn't seem to have a response. Election over.

Through that campaign, James Carville emerged as a media darling. It's easy to see why: He's a great interview. He's memorable; he's emotional—his face goes into contortions; he speaks plainly, his Southern drawl intoning, "Aw, c'mon, that's nuts" or "Ya gotta dance with the one that brung ya to the party." After the campaign, unlike some other campaign advisors, he chose not to seek an appointed position in the White House or elsewhere in government. It wasn't what he wanted to do; it didn't suit him. He increasingly went into political media punditry, appearing as a regular on CNN's *Crossfire* and other network news programs. And he also switched gears, consulting-wise, going to work for international political campaign clients, including the Greek prime minister, the Brazilian president, and other clients in Argentina, Israel, Panama, Honduras, Great Britain, and a number of other countries.

As his consulting business flourished and his public image grew, he branched out into other activities, publishing several books, appearing in a number of television shows and films, as well as writing and producing, and hitting the lecture circuit. His 1993 marriage to Republican consultant and media commentator Mary Matalin made the pair a highly sought-after combination of he said/she said political analysis. Carville made a name for himself as an aggressive, passionately committed campaign strategist. Among his more memorable and colorful quotes about political campaigning: "It's hard for someone to hit you when you have your fist in their face."

The Architect: Karl Rove

President George W. Bush called Karl Rove "the Architect," while many Bush administration critics called him "Bush's Brain." According to a number of sources, one of Rove's role models is none other than Mark Hanna. Rove claims that the comparison is overstated, yet some who know him say he has always admired Hanna as a strategist and he wanted to emulate his success in helping to engineer a Republican realignment in American politics.

Rove's experience in American politics reaches back much further than many people realize. He rose to national prominence and became a household name with the presidency of George W. Bush, but has been active in national political campaigns since the early 1970s. Like many other well-known Republican Party activists, Rove came up in the ranks of the College Republicans national organization—in fact, he became too busy with College Republicans to actually finish college. While working as the executive director there, Rove was an active participant in the Nixon reelection campaign. Specifically, he is reported to have been a protégé of famous Nixon campaign dirty trickster Donald Segretti, who was later convicted as a Watergate conspirator. It was also there that he first came to the attention of the elder Bush, George H. W. (Bush 41).

In the midst of a rough-and-tumble campaign between Rove and another candidate for the College Republicans chairmanship, someone sent the media a set of recordings of several training sessions Rove had conducted for young Republican activists, in which Rove allegedly encouraged campaign dirty tricks. Rove denied the allegations, claiming the tape had been doctored to exclude a warning to the audience not to try to emulate any of his past misdeeds. Others present simply remember a caution not to get caught. According to a story in the *Washington Post,* Rove openly discusses an incident in 1970 in which he stole stationery from the campaign of Alan Dixon, a Democratic candidate for state treasurer of Illinois. Rove had circulated phony invitations, using Dixon's stationery, to a Dixon campaign event, promising "free beer, free food, girls, and a good time for nothing."

News stories about College Republican activities in August 1973 brought additional unwanted attention to the GOP in the midst of Watergate. But Rove was never the target of federal investigators; according to Watergate figure John Dean, the feds had "bigger fish to fry." George H. W. Bush, chair of the National Republican Committee at the time, was apparently so impressed with Rove's activities that he brought him to the RNC. Rove introduced the elder Bush to Lee Atwater, who had taken over as chair of the College Republicans; and Bush introduced Rove to his son, George W. (Bush 43). American politics would never be the same. Rove recalls his initial meeting with the young Bush: "huge amounts of charisma, swagger, cowboy boots, flight jacket, wonderful smile, just charisma—you know, wow."

In the mid-1970s, Rove became quite close to the Bush family, politically at least. In 1977 he went to work for the elder Bush's Houston-based political action committee, the Fund for Limited Government. That organization was the genesis of Bush's campaign organization for his initial run for the presidency in 1980, in which he lost the nomination to Ronald Reagan. Texas is where Karl Rove found his political home.

In 1978 he worked with the young George W. Bush on his unsuccessful congressional race. But that same year he also helped Republican Bill Clements win the governor's office, breaking a century-long stranglehold the Democratic Party had held on Texas politics. He followed Clements into the Texas governor's mansion and served as his chief of staff.

In the early 1980s, Rove started his own political direct mail firm, and he began to develop a consulting business that helped to reshape Texas politics. He worked for Texas congressman Phil Gramm in 1982 and in 1984 helped him defeat the Democratic candidate for U.S. Senate, Lloyd Doggett. He also did political direct mail for the Reagan reelection campaign. In 1986, the same year that James Carville hit paydirt with Bob Casey in Pennsylvania, Rove helped Bill Clements regain the Texas governorship from Democrat Mark White, who had defeated Clements in 1982. Just before a crucial debate between Clements and White, Rove went public with a claim that his office had been bugged, and he accused the Democrats of political espionage. The charge helped Clements beat White in a close race. An investigation later proved inconclusive; some observers speculate that Rove created the controversy to sway last-minute voters.

By the 1990s, Karl Rove had become one of the nation's premier political consultants, and in the opinion of many was a King Maker in Texas politics. His client list was a virtual *Who's Who* of Texas politics— George H. W. Bush, George W. Bush, Kay Bailey Hutchinson, Bill Clements, Phil Gramm, Rick Perry, and so on. He also worked for clients in other states in some key national races, including U.S. Senator John Ashcroft of Missouri.

But his prize client was, of course, George W. Bush. Rove believed strongly that he was a political winner in the making. He had urged the younger Bush to consider running for governor as early as 1989. In the midst of the anti–Bill Clinton backlash of 1993–1994—remember "angry white males"?—the time seemed right for Bush. At the time, odds makers gave the inexperienced, undisciplined Bush little chance of unseating incumbent Ann Richards. But Rove had been working with Bush. He brought in experts to tutor Bush on policy and politics, and he taught him how to speak to crowds, talk to reporters, and work a room. Bush and Rove ran a very disciplined, very effective campaign. Bush's defeat of Richards in 1994 was one of the many Republican Party victories that year, which included George Pataki's defeat of Governor Mario Cuomo in New York, and Newt Gingrich's Contract with America.

Rove began plotting Bush's presidential run almost immediately, at least on the drawing board in his mind. By the time President Bill Clinton's second term was winding down and Republicans were looking for a leader, Bush seemed like just the ticket. He was from a large Southern state, he had successfully worked with Democrats to pass major legislation, he had been reelected by a large margin in 1998, and for a Republican he had done extremely well among minority voters.

Rove did a masterful job of engineering Bush's path first to the nomination, then to his general election win over Al Gore. But there were a few bumps. One of them was named John McCain, who very nearly stole the GOP nomination with his surprise primary win in New Hampshire and his strong appeal to independent voters. But in the crucial South Carolina primary, according to a number of sources, the ghosts of Dick Nixon and Donald Segretti came roaring back. The Bush forces, backs up against the wall, turned mean. A 2003 article in *Esquire* reported that "Bush loyalists, maybe working for the campaign, maybe just representing its interests, claimed in parking-lot handouts and telephone 'push-polls' and whisper campaigns that McCain's wife, Cindy, was a drug addict, that McCain might be mentally unstable from his captivity in Vietnam, and that the senator had fathered a black child with a prostitute." Since the days of Lee Atwater, South Carolina has been the firewall for the GOP "establishment" candidate for the presidential nomination, and in 2000 that was George W. Bush.

After Bush's election, Rove followed the example of Larry O'Brien and went to work in the White House. As one of President Bush's top advisors, Rove was an extremely powerful force in both domestic and foreign policy. "Little happens on any issue without Karl's OK," said former Bush policy advisor John Dilulio. Rove had reached the apex of his profession. But he was not simply interested in helping Bush have a successful presidency: Rove believed that he could help bring about a political realignment that would make Republicans the majority party in American politics for years to come. Perhaps that is why George W. Bush called him the "architect."

Rove took his role as a political fixer in the White House very seriously, guiding Bush on policy, riding herd on stray Republican members of Congress, and putting out fires where he saw signs of trouble. That tendency may have led to the Bush administration's greatest scandal—the outing of undercover CIA agent Valerie Plame. Though Bush administration officials denied it, sources indicate that Rove and other administration officials wanted to discredit retired ambassador Joseph Wilson, who, after a CIA-authorized trip to Niger, had publicly contradicted President Bush's assertion that there was evidence Saddam Hussein had sought significant amounts of uranium from Africa. Though an investigation found no illegalities on the part of Karl Rove, he allegedly confirmed to columnist Robert Novak that Wilson's wife was a CIA agent. He also reportedly told MSNBC commentator Chris Matthews that Wilson's wife was "fair game." The idea apparently was to punish Wilson for his public comments.

The Plame affair hurt the Bush administration's credibility, though not fatally. Perhaps more important, as far as Rove's plans to achieve a political realignment for the Republicans were concerned, was the declining public confidence in the Iraq War and in the domestic economy. Maybe William McKinley and Mark Hanna had been lucky. Their foreign conflict (the Spanish-American War) actually helped them politically; and, for the most part, the expanding American industrial economy kept humming along until the crash of the stock market and the Great Depression. Bush and Rove weren't so lucky.

⇉ CHAPTER 10 ⇇

SCHEMERS

The schemers are often the "wannabes" of history. Young or old, rich or poor, either well born or from the peasantry, they desperately seek to be in a position of power, and they believe they have found a way to achieve it. Schemers tend to share some traits with Kingmakers from chapter 3. They work behind the scenes to effect a dramatic change in the power structure of the existing government, sometimes not for their own direct benefit but for the benefit of another. Of course, if their schemes are successful, they, too, will benefit in terms of access to power, privilege, and resources. They may try to elevate family members, religious or political allies, or mere puppets into positions of great authority so that they may fulfill aspirations of glory or power.

In contrast to the Machiavellians and the Empire Builders, Schemers often act on impulse and tend not to have well-thought-out, complex plans. Complicating their situation, they may also be working from a position of abject political disadvantage, almost always striving in a hostile environment. Not many of them ever reach the "happily ever after" stage of politics. In fact, more often than not, they meet a premature, sometimes violent, end to their schemes.

Old Testament Values: Haman

Haman represents one of the greatest schemers of all time; the name is often used as an archetype for evil and treachery. The story of Haman and Esther from the Hebrew Scriptures is a harrowing tale of power, jealousy, hatred, revenge, and the plotting of mass murder during the fifth century BC. In the book of Esther, Haman is a powerful court official of the Persian King Xerxes I—yes, the same Xerxes from *The Histories* of the Greek writer Herodotus (and the popular movie *300*). According to the story, Haman, who is descended from the Amalekites (historical enemies of the Jews), is offended because a Jewish official, Mordechai, will not bow down to him. ". . . Haman was filled with fury. But he disdained to lay hands on Mordechai alone. So, as they had made known to him the people of Mordechai, Haman sought to destroy all the Jews, the people of Mordechai, throughout the whole kingdom . . ." (Esther 3:5–6).

Some rabbinical scholars believe that Haman's primary motivation, in addition to his own vanity, was to lead the Jews of the kingdom to violate the Torah. He engineered a trap for them, one that would give him and the kingdom a legal and moral right to eliminate them. He knew that when the children of Israel stray from the Torah, God "hides his face" from them, which allows other nations to oppress them. From the outset, according to this view, Haman intended to attach an idol to his clothing so that when people bowed to him, they were also bowing down to an idol—a serious transgression of Jewish law. When Mordechai did not take the bait, Haman used his court authority and his powers of persuasion to convince King Xerxes that the Jewish people were enemies of the throne:

> There is a certain people scattered abroad and dispersed
> among the peoples in all the provinces of your kingdom; their
> laws are different from every other people, and they do not
> keep the king's laws, so that it is not for the king's profit to
> tolerate them. If it please the king, let it be decreed that they
> be destroyed, and I will pay ten thousand talents of silver into
> the hands of those who have charge of the king's business,
> that they may put it into the king's treasuries (Esther 3:8–11).

King Xerxes had no reason to doubt Haman, so he agreed. But what neither at the time realized was that Mordechai had earlier saved the king's life by informing the court of a plot to assassinate him, as reported in Esther 2:19–23. This would ultimately prove to be Haman's undoing and save Mordechai as well as all the Jews of Persia.

Haman was also an astrologer and a mystic. Together with his wife, Zeresh, he cast lots to determine the most favorable date for the massacres to begin. He found that the middle of the Hebrew holy month of Adar (in March) was most favorable. Haman was so confident of his plotting that he built a gallows outside his home for the public execution of Mordechai.

The heroine of the story is, of course, Esther. While Xerxes was having "fair young virgins" brought before him to choose his next queen, Esther, whose birth name was Hadassah, had been residing in the "house of women" where she was favored because of her beauty. She had begun what was known as the purification process in order to be brought before the king. The "keeper of women" wasn't aware of Esther's Jewish heritage. In most versions of the story, Mordechai is her uncle, who had raised her as one of his own because her parents were dead (Esther 2:7).

When the time arrived for the meeting, Esther was introduced to King Xerxes. He was struck by her beauty and grace, and chose her as his queen. Through Mordechai's instincts of caution and warning, it was not revealed to the king that his new bride was Jewish in origin. Upon hearing of Haman's plot to kill Mordechai and all the Jews, Esther planned a way to save them. She requested that all Jews fast and pray for three days, along with her, and on the third day she sought an audience with Xerxes, during which she invited him to a feast in the company of Haman, then a further feast the following evening. Meanwhile, Haman is again offended by Mordechai, after Haman leaves the feast and Mordechai once again refuses to bow down to him.

That night, Xerxes suffered from insomnia, and when the court's records were read to him to help him sleep, he learned of the services rendered by Mordechai in the previous plot against his life—the records were opened to the place where it was recorded that Mordechai had performed this service. Xerxes was told that Mordechai had not received any recognition for saving the king's life. Just then, Haman appeared, and King Xerxes asked Haman what should be done for a man the king wished to honor. Thinking that the man the king wished to honor was himself, Haman said that the man should be dressed in the king's royal robes and led around on the king's royal horse. To Haman's horror, the king instructed Haman to do so for Mordechai (Esther 6:10).

The next day, Xerxes and Haman attended Esther's second banquet, at which she revealed to Xerxes that she was Jewish and that Haman was planning to annihilate her people.

"If I have found favor in your sight O king, and if it please the king, let my life be given me at my petition, and my people at my request. For we are sold, I and my people, to be destroyed, to be slain, and to be annihilated. If we had been sold merely as slaves, men and women, I would have held my peace; for our affliction is not to be compared with the loss to the king." The king said to Esther, "Who is he, and where is he, that would presume to do this?" And Esther said, "A foe and enemy! This wicked Haman!" (Esther 7:3–6)

Xerxes was taken by surprise, and felt betrayed by Haman. He ordered Haman to be hanged on the same gallows that Haman had prepared for Mordechai. By Persian law, the king's previous decree against the Jews (which sanctioned the massacre of Mordechai's people) could not be annulled, so he allowed Mordechai and Esther to write another decree as they wished. Their new decree in the king's name allowed the Jews to defend themselves during attacks. As a result, 500 attackers and Haman's ten sons were killed in Shushan (Susa). Throughout the empire, an additional 75,000 were slain (Esther 9:16). The next day, another 300 were killed in Shushan. Afterward, Mordechai assumed a prominent position in Xerxes's court, and instituted an annual commemoration of the delivery of the Jewish people from annihilation (Esther 8:2).

The killing of all of Haman's sons is important to note. They were not executed alongside Haman, but were killed in the fighting in Shushan. In Jewish observances of Purim, this is emphasized to underscore the fact that no one was left to carry out Haman's evil legacy.

Purim is a traditional Jewish celebration of the story of Haman and the deliverance of the Jewish people through Esther's bravery. The celebration features songs, feasts, and carnival-like gatherings of celebrants wearing costumes and staging plays. Some have described it as a mix of Mardi Gras and St. Patrick's Day. The primary religious tradition related to Purim is the reading of the book of Esther, commonly known as the *Megillah,* which means "scroll." The reading of the entire book of Esther during the Purim celebration is the origin of the term "the whole megillah." It is customary to boo, hiss, stamp feet, and rattle graggers (noisemakers) whenever the name of Haman is mentioned in the service. The purpose of this custom is to "blot out the name of Haman."

This is an inspiring story—one of barbarism, heroism, and sacrifice. And one of the few things that most modern Christian, Jewish, and Muslim scholars can agree on is that the story of Haman is very likely fictional. Actually, the entire book of Esther is considered to be allegorical by many biblical and rabbinic scholars today. Thus, the extent to which one accepts the validity of Haman as a real historical figure depends a great deal on one's interpretation. There are many Christians who believe that the entirety of the Bible is historically accurate, and, therefore, Haman did exist, he did plan the annihilation of the Jews, and he was executed by King Xerxes I. Likewise, many Orthodox Jews accept the historical validity of the book of Esther, and therefore view Haman as an actual figure in history.

Some scholars, however, trace the history of Esther to a non-Jewish origin entirely; it is, in their opinion, either a reworking of a triumph of the Babylonian gods Marduk (Mordechai) and Ishtar (Esther) over

the Elamite gods Humman (Haman) and Mashti (Vashti), or of the
suppression of the Magians by Darius I, or even the resistance of the
Babylonians to the decree of Artaxerxes II. According to a number of
modern scholars, the story of Purim might be based on Persian legends,
adopted by the Jews of the region for inspiration and guidance.

Author Elaine Rose Glickman has written about the significance of
the Purim story: "In the figure of Haman we have come to see not only
a single person, but a paradigm: Haman as would-be destroyer, Haman
as evil schemer, Haman as merciless enemy." Haman exists today as
an archetype for human evil, not only for Jews, but for all of humanity.
Haman, Mordechai, and Esther are not mere figures in history or in
literature, but represent points of view and violent threats that are all too
real. Writing in 1941, the Brooklyn rabbi and educator Hyman Goldin
reminded readers that "Hamans are found in every land where there are
Mordechais." The reach of Haman may be long and timeless, but so is
the human spirit. Whether Haman was a real flesh-and-blood person, or
was simply a plot device from ancient Persian or Jewish literature, Purim
stands as a celebration of survival; a testament to overcoming one's
torturers and, for many Christians and Jews, a symbol of God's promise
of deliverance.

A Mother's Love: Agrippina the Younger

In Julia Agrippina, historians are much more fortunate than with
Haman. Her exploits have been well chronicled, although accounts vary
as to the extent of her treachery. Easily one of the greatest schemers of
all time, Agrippina routinely pops up on lists of the "most evil women
in history." Her proximity to power in the first century AD Roman
Empire was astonishing, as was the scale of her ambition. Her imperial
family lineage encompasses most of the years of the golden age of the
Roman Empire—running literally from Julius Caesar to Nero. She was
the great-granddaughter of the emperor Augustus, the great-niece and
adoptive granddaughter of the emperor Tiberius, the sister of the emperor
Caligula, the niece and fourth wife of the emperor Claudius, and the
mother of the emperor Nero.

She is remembered by history as ruthless, ambitious, cunning, and dangerous. This was, after all, the sister of Caligula and the mother of Nero—boring she wasn't. Her main claim to fame is that she goaded her husband, the emperor Claudius, into adopting Nero, her son from a previous marriage, making him the royal heir, then poisoning Claudius so Nero could ascend to the throne. Presumably the only reason she wanted her son Nero to rule was that, by Roman law and tradition, women could not wield imperial authority or, surely, she herself would have taken the throne as Empress Agrippina. It seems that poisoning one's enemies was a treasured pastime in imperial Rome, and became quite fashionable through the Dark Ages, into the Renaissance, and beyond. Agrippina was eventually murdered on the orders of her loving son Nero.

Time has certainly not been kind to Agrippina. Most ancient sources on her life hold her in contempt, and modern historians are only slightly more benign. Author Anthony Barrett distills much of the disdain with which investigators have traditionally regarded this "mother" of Rome:

> She plotted against her brother Caligula (as well as sharing his bed), she murdered her husband Claudius with a deadly mushroom, and she tried (unsuccessfully) to cope with a rebellious teenage son, Nero, by sharing his bed too. She was finally eliminated by that same Nero through a scheme as ingenious and outlandish as any in the history of crime—an irresistible combination of treachery, incest and murder.

But the problem with reaching a verdict on her crimes is the differing accounts and interpretations left behind by Rome's chroniclers and by ancient historians. Political and family rivalries tend to muddy the waters and complicate the path to the facts. To historians like Barrett, though, it is worth trying to ferret out the truth because Agrippina represents:

> a political paradox of the early Roman empire, the woman who managed to exercise great power and influence in a society that offered no constitutional role to powerful and

influential women. It is this achievement, to be empress
in an empire that allowed only emperors, that makes her
accomplishments interesting and worthy of serious study.

She and her brother Caligula were victims from early childhood of
the vicious backstabbing and court intrigue that characterized imperial
Rome. Her father Germanicus, the nephew and designated heir of
Emperor Augustus's successor, Tiberius, met an untimely death in AD
20. At the age of thirty-three, Germanicus, a son of Emperor Tiberius's
younger brother, was the most popular member of the imperial family.
When he died after a brief and undiagnosed illness (bad mushrooms?)
while touring the eastern Mediterranean provinces, the Roman people
were convinced that Tiberius had ordered his assassination—another
poisoning, no doubt—out of jealousy and fear. Agrippina the Elder
was also certain that Tiberius was responsible for her husband's death.
The young Agrippina was undoubtedly affected by the subsequent
mistreatment suffered by her mother and brothers at the hands of
Tiberius. Historians have long suspected that a childhood spent steeped
in fear and resentment may have warped Agrippina's brother—the always
colorful and creative Caligula. Perhaps it also turned Agrippina into the
monster that ancient Romans thought her to be.

The four-year-old Agrippina was brought to the village of Tarracina
to meet her mother and accompany her father's ashes on their journey
home. The agonizing public procession to Rome, through crowds
running wild with grief and anger at the death of their favorite, surely
left an indelible impression. Her mother's dignified grief caught the
imagination of the Roman people and won popular esteem for the widow
and her children. If Tiberius had not felt jealous and uneasy earlier, he
now had good cause for worry.

Agrippina the Elder was too ambitious to spend the rest of her life
in quiet widowhood with her children. In fact, more recent historians
are more inclined to see her as giving aid and comfort to the enemies
of Tiberius, and even plotting against him. Her family relationship
to Tiberius had made her and her family targets anyway: As a

granddaughter of Augustus, she was heir to political connections and influence, making any second husband an automatic threat to Tiberius's plans for the succession. Attending state dinners, Agrippina the Elder ostentatiously took precautions against poison in her dishes. In such a politically charged environment, the young Agrippina would surely have been aware of the deepening public hostility between her mother and Emperor Tiberius, who had not even come to the ceremony when the ashes of her father were placed in the tomb of Augustus.

In a move to reduce the family's potential for making alliances, Tiberius decided that the thirteen-year-old Agrippina the Younger would marry the much older Gnaeus Domitius Ahenobarbus in AD 28. Agrippina's new husband was described by the Roman historian Suetonis as a "wholly despicable character" and "remarkably dishonest." Agrippina was only fourteen when her mother and eldest brother were arrested on trumped-up charges in AD 29 and imprisoned. Though her second brother had supplied evidence against them, he was the next to be arrested. In AD 33, Agrippina the Elder starved herself to death, while her son Caligula was left to fend for himself.

According to the first-century Roman historian Tacitus, Tiberius did try to have Caligula killed, but he was unsuccessful. In AD 37 Tiberius died, unable to deny the throne to Caligula. That same year Agrippina gave birth to her only child, Domitius—later to become Nero. Initially, Caligula heaped honors upon his sisters, as only they and he had survived childhood diseases and the hatred of Tiberius. Receiving all the privileges and public honors previously reserved for vestal virgins, Agrippina and her two sisters were included in the annual vows of allegiance to the emperor. Their portraits were also put on coins. Reportedly, the four of them maintained an incestuous relationship. Caligula was especially devoted to his sister Drusilla, who died of fever in AD 38.

But as Emperor Caligula descended into debauchery, depravity, and probable insanity—he wanted to name his favorite horse a consul —he became increasingly paranoid and resentful of his two surviving sisters. Convinced that they were conspiring against him—and they were—he exiled

Agrippina and her sister Livilla to an island prison in AD 39. But Caligula's reign was mercifully short—he was assassinated by his own guards two years later in AD 41. The new emperor was the elderly, infirm Claudius, Agrippina's uncle—her father's brother. Her exile was over.

Nero had been left in near poverty during her exile, when Caligula used the excuse of her husband's death to seize most of their assets. Although Claudius returned the property taken from the two sisters, mere prosperity and imperial connections were not nearly enough to settle the score. Agrippina wanted total control for herself and her son—she believed they were the rightful heirs to the throne, the true progeny of Augustus.

The gossip of the day reported that the first target of her marital ambitions was the wealthy and well-born Servius Galba, but he escaped her matrimonial snares and survived to later succeed Nero as emperor. Her second husband was another rich senator, Gaius Sallustius Crispus, who was quite a bit older than Agrippina, but did much to advance her material and political ambitions. Crispus died in AD 47. Agrippina and Nero were remembered generously in his will, but rumors that she had poisoned him may have been inspired by the later treatment of Claudius and his son Britannicus.

Agrippina's campaign for the throne came closer to fruition with the scandal and suicide of Emperor Claudius's third wife, Messalina, in AD 47. Messalina had favored sending Agrippina and her sister, Livilla, back into exile. Agrippina was thought to have been flirting with her uncle in order to obtain protection against Messalina. Also, Messalina was apparently worried about Nero's popularity as a descendant of both Augustus and Germanicus, who was still fondly remembered. By the time Messalina was apprehended in a plot to put her lover on the throne and murder Claudius, Agrippina had already established key contacts in the court and was ready to make her move.

Claudius's prestige had been badly damaged by the scandal. He desperately needed a public relations triumph. As always in matters of serious business, Claudius consulted his chief executive secretary, a freedman named Pallas who was devoted to Agrippina (many, in fact, believed they were lovers). He and others of Agrippina's party in the court convinced Claudius that what he needed was Agrippina. Marriage between uncle and niece was considered incestuous in Rome, and it took a senatorial decree to legalize the marriage. Still, Agrippina was of the bloodline of Augustus and was popularly idolized as the daughter of Germanicus. Her son Nero could be adopted to secure the survival of the dynasty, since Claudius's own son Britannicus was not past the high mortality years of childhood. In AD 49, Agrippina and her uncle, Claudius, were married. She effected this coup through a tangle of personal alliances, which included Claudius's secretary Pallas; his doctor, Xenophon; and Afranius Burrus, the head of the Praetorian Guard, who owed his promotion to Agrippina.

Neither ancient nor modern historians of Rome have doubted that Agrippina had her eye on securing the throne for Nero from the very first day of the marriage—if not earlier. The Roman historian Dio Cassius's observation seems to bear that out: "As soon as Agrippina had come to live in the palace she gained complete control over Claudius." Agrippina did not, however, concentrate on advancing her son to the point of neglecting herself. She was the only living woman to receive the title "Augusta" since Livia, the wife of Emperor Augustus, and Livia had not been allowed to use the name during her husband's lifetime. Historian Barbara Levick describes Agrippina's conduct in the court of Claudius: "Certainly from 51 onward she appeared at ceremonial occasions in a gold-threaded military cloak, and on a tribunal (distinct from that of her husband, however), greeted ambassadors." Roman men's full nomenclature usually included a reference to their fathers, as in "son of Marcus." One official religious record listed Nero as "son of Agrippina" before putting in the usual reference to his father. According to Tacitus, Claudius's influential secretary Narcissus tried to warn others about Agrippina's plans: "There is nothing she will not sacrifice to imperial ambition—neither decency, nor honor, nor chastity." And Dio Cassius wrote: "No one attempted in any way to check Agrippina; indeed, she had more power than Claudius himself."

In AD 50, Agrippina achieved one of her main goals: Nero became the adoptive son of Claudius. Ultimately, this sealed the fate of Claudius and his son Britannicus, though Agrippina could afford to wait for the most opportune moment. Claudius probably feared a public backlash if he were to exclude Nero, a grandson of Germanicus, from the succession, and he certainly needed loyal military commanders rising through the ranks. While Claudius undoubtedly hoped that the adoption would secure the loyalty of both Nero and those who adored Germanicus, hindsight certainly revealed his error. The last months of his life were characterized by disputes with Agrippina over the advancement of Nero and Britannicus.

But Britannicus would never ascend to the throne. In AD 54, the frail sixty-four-year-old Claudius died. A vigorous debate has long raged over whether Agrippina poisoned him—mushrooms again. She certainly had the motive and the experience. However, there are skeptics who claim that it would have been particularly difficult to poison the emperor in his own household, and ascribe the rumors to anti-Agrippina hysteria among some Roman officials. But the death of Claudius was very timely for Agrippina: He had survived long enough to award formal honors and recognition to Nero, who had used those years to make himself more popular and better known. Yet Claudius died before Britannicus could be set on the same track.

The seventeen-year-old Nero became emperor of Rome, with his mother at first acting as regent. Tacitus claimed that Agrippina foresaw the end to all her plotting. Having consulted astrologers several years before, she had been told that Nero would become emperor but kill his mother. She supposedly replied, "Let him kill me—provided he becomes emperor." Nero tried to justify her subsequent murder after the fact by claiming that she intended to rule Rome, using him as her puppet. His speech to the Senate, as reported in Tacitus, laid out his case: "She had wanted to be co-ruler—to receive oaths of allegiance from the Guard, and to subject Senate and public to the same humiliation [of swearing allegiance to a woman]."

Given those claims, it is ironic that Tacitus and others ascribe the good aspects of Nero's reign to Agrippina. She had Lucius Annaeus Seneca, the noted Stoic rhetorician and philosopher, recalled from exile and made Nero's tutor. After Nero became emperor, she encouraged Seneca and Burrus, the commander of the Praetorian Guard, to function as virtual regents. She may have assumed that she would be able to control them. If so, she was wrong. Seneca and Burrus thought it their duty to act for the good of the emperor, not the emperor's mother. They came to believe it necessary to ease Agrippina out before her blatant attempts to assert power evoked hostility against her son and the dynasty itself. In one dramatic incident at the end of AD 54, she attempted to join Nero on his dais to receive ambassadors from Armenia. Even Claudius had made her sit on a separate throne when receiving visitors. Seneca and Burrus nudged Nero into stepping down to greet her in an apparent gesture of respect, which allowed him to escort her to a separate, lower seat.

The power and influence she had sought for so long continued to wane through the next year. Seneca and Burrus encouraged Nero in an affair with a woman of low birth of whom Agrippina did not approve. They favored anything that reduced his mother's influence over him. They convinced Nero to dismiss his mother's partisan, Pallas, from his powerful administrative post. The mother-son relationship, and the power Agrippina had worked so long to cultivate, teetered on the brink. The teenage Britannicus may have been a victim of this drama. Tacitus reports that Agrippina threatened to switch her allegiance to Britannicus. The result was that Nero had Britannicus poisoned at a formal family dinner—ending once and for all any chance that the real son of Claudius would be a threat to Nero, and sending a signal to the entire family that threats to his reign would be met with violence.

There are even those who accuse Agrippina of trying to seduce Nero in order to hold his loyalty. In any case, Nero understood better than Burrus and Seneca that while Agrippina might be killed, she would never be quietly subdued. Having been separated from his mother in early childhood, as an older child and adolescent Nero had been her partner in deadly conspiracy. He had acquired his political morality from her. Agrippina and her son understood each other well; as her mother had done before her, she began taking preemptive doses of antidotes against common poisons.

When Nero first began to plan Agrippina's death, Burrus kept Nero's confidence by agreeing to carry out his plan if there were actual evidence that she was conspiring against her son. While such evidence did not surface, the issue did not go away. Nero called in Seneca and Burrus for emergency counsel after another plot to kill Agrippina in the preplanned collapse of a pleasure boat failed. Agrippina swam to shore, and Nero was terrified of his mother's wrath. Whereas Burrus and Seneca conceded that an angry Agrippina who knew that her son was her mortal enemy could not safely be left alive, they escaped actual complicity in Agrippina's murder by warning Nero that the praetorians probably would not follow orders to kill her. After all, not only was she descended from Augustus and Germanicus, but she had selected many of the Guard's officers for their positions. Thus, Nero was forced to call in a contingent from the navy to stab his mother in the bedroom of her villa.

Among Agrippina's lasting accomplishments was her recall of Seneca from exile. She provided him with a home in Rome and the financial resources that facilitated his completion of many works of significant influence on the Stoic tradition. She also left her own memoirs and, though they do not survive today, Tacitus used them extensively in constructing his picture of the events of those years.

Nero, who had believed himself incapable of living with Agrippina, found that he was unable to live happily without her. Regardless of her private life and motives, Agrippina tried to ensure that Nero governed well. Tacitus characterized the rest of his reign: "Then he plunged into the wildest improprieties, which vestiges of respect for his mother had hitherto not indeed repressed, but at least impeded." Perhaps Nero's notorious misconduct was an effort to find distraction or a respite from guilt. Dio Cassius reported that he frequently saw his mother's ghost and rarely had a good night's sleep.

The She-Wolf: Isabella of France
Isabella of France was another schemer of pedigree, daughter-in-law to the famously nasty King Edward I (Longshanks) of England, wife of the thoroughly in-the-closet Edward II, and mother of the heroic Edward III;

her father and brothers were also kings of France. She is remembered as a queen who, after suffering countless indignities, took matters into her own hands and guided the future destiny of England. She is important to historians because she was responsible for the movement, that for the first time since the Norman invasion, dethroned a sitting king of England. Though she never poisoned anyone, married her uncle, or slept with her brother, she was as cunning and ruthless as any king or prince of the Middle Ages. In fact, her political judgment and strategic sense were far superior to those of her underachieving party-boy husband, Edward II. As with Agrippina, she could not make it last, and was eventually betrayed by her son. Isabella wasn't stabbed to death, she was imprisoned—exiled to a nearby castle where she was essentially held under house arrest until her death some twenty-five years later. But at least her son, Edward III, went on to do worthwhile things for his country, unlike Agrippina's son, Nero.

Edward I was probably the most successful and certainly the most ruthless medieval monarch between Henry II and Henry VIII. When he wasn't reforming the civil bureaucracy and creating a model English parliament, he was taxing the daylights out of his subjects and expanding his kingdom by subduing Wales and large parts of Scotland. He was no less stern and demanding in his own household. Longshanks had fifteen children, most of them girls. Three of his sons died in childhood, leaving Edward II the heir to the throne. Longshanks did what he could to raise his son Edward to take his rightful place as a man and a king. He involved him in rigorous physical activities and gave him the best military training. But young Edward was more interested in music, acting, and fashion—possibly the effect of having ten or eleven sisters.

Edward II was the very first prince of Wales, born in Caernarfon Castle on the Welsh coast, one of the fortified castles built by his father to conquer Wales. His investiture as prince of Wales was a statement by Longshanks that the rulers of Wales and its royal family were now and forevermore English. But history has cast poor Edward II as a bit of a cream puff. To Longshanks, the "Hammer of the Scots," this must have been crushingly depressing. Yet this was his only surviving male heir. So he brought someone to court to be a good example for the young

Edward—Piers Gaveston, a soldier in the king's service known for his military sense, his wit, and his entertaining manner. Big mistake. Prince Edward adored Gaveston, perhaps a little too much. And the feeling was mutual. Historians have portrayed their relationship as sexual, though there is really no rock-solid proof of that—both men had wives and produced offspring. But the circumstances and records of the time do lend credence to that conclusion.

Piers Gaveston may or may not have been the love of his life, but Edward II's queen was the lovely Isabella. The daughter of King Philip IV of France, she was promised in marriage to the heir of Longshanks, an effort by her father Philip to resolve conflicts between France and England over territorial claims in Gascony, Anjou, and Normandy. Longshanks was wary of the terms of the arrangement, but after his death Edward II jumped at the deal. So the twenty-four-year-old king and Isabella, age twelve, were married in Boulogne in 1308.

Isabella had every intention of being the queen of England and the wife of Edward II. Smart, pragmatic, and good with diplomacy, Isabella was popular with the nobles and with the people. She famously traveled with the king and his troops to war in Scotland. But, to put it mildly, it wasn't a happy marriage. The king seemed more interested in spending time with Gaveston. He lavished him with gifts, lands, and royal favors. He gave Gaveston royal jewelry that had been a gift from Isabella's father, the king of France. He even interceded with Welsh barons and seized property on behalf of Gaveston, breaking his agreement with the nobles. Edward's behavior alienated both his queen and many of the barons who formed the core of the king's power base. Gaveston's arrogance and sense of entitlement only aggravated the situation.

Edward's political situation was weakened by his failure to hold the military ground his father had won and his seeming ambivalence to England's security and prosperity. It was bad enough that the king's behavior toward Gaveston was scandalous, but the fact that it distracted the king from more important business, such as dealing with the Scots, meant that it was affecting the nobles and their ability to protect their lands and property. The feeling was overwhelming that Edward was not serving England well and that part of the problem was Piers Gaveston. Under the authority of Parliament, Gaveston was apprehended in 1312 and taken to Warwick Castle. There, he was beheaded on the orders of the earl of Lancaster. That same year, the sixteen-year-old Isabella gave birth to Edward III, the future king. She would bear her husband three more children, the last in 1321.

Even after Gaveston's death, Edward continued to be a subpar king. In 1314, his army was thoroughly beaten by the Scottish leader Robert the Bruce, negating much of what Longshanks had dedicated his reign to accomplishing. By 1316, Edward had abrogated much of the responsibility for governing to Parliament. Although Isabella had borne him children, the two didn't see much of each other. Edward had a wandering eye. The new object of his affections over the next several years was Hugh Despenser, the son of an influential court advisor. The Despensers, father and son, played the power game very aggressively. The young Hugh had taken the place of the departed Piers Gaveston, and he and his father used their influence at court to shamelessly extend their landholdings and their wealth.

By the 1320s, once again, the barons and many of the nobles were offended and horrified by the outrageous and illegal behavior of the king's favorite. The barons were able to force Edward to exile the Despensers, but it was a very brief exile. Edward gathered an army and went to war on behalf of the Despensers. He forced the execution of the earl of Lancaster (who had beheaded Piers Gaveston nine years earlier), and jailed another leader of the effort to expel the Despensers, the English noble and Welsh land baron Roger Mortimer, in the Tower. The Despensers continued their reign of financial and sometimes physical terror on the English and Welsh countryside. But Roger Mortimer managed to escape from the Tower (by drugging the constable, possibly with the help of Isabella) and escaped to France in 1323.

Isabella had been a victim long enough. She was now an adult—a beautiful, intelligent, and very angry adult. She had acquired in her young life one of the most practical and pointed political educations one could possibly get. She had been taking notes, and soon got an opportunity to act in her own interests.

She is portrayed in the Mel Gibson movie *Braveheart* staring down Longshanks and plotting against him, conspiring with the Scottish hero William Wallace—even conceiving a child with Wallace, which presumably makes him the actual father of Edward III. However, none of that actually happened. Both Longshanks and Wallace were long dead by this time. Wallace was brutally tortured and executed by the English in 1305, when Isabella was ten years old and living in France. Longshanks died two years later in 1307, one year before Isabella was even in the country. Fortunately, it doesn't matter that the Mel Gibson version of events never happened, because what actually did happen is equally dramatic.

Isabella and Hugh Despenser had an especially hostile relationship. They were both seeking the affections of the king, after all. In the mid-1320s, a dispute between France and England broke out over Edward's refusal to pay homage to the French king (who was now Charles, Isabella's brother) for the territory of Gascony. After several failed attempts to regain the territory, Edward sent Isabella to negotiate peace terms, believing that she would have some influence with her family. This was the opportunity she'd been waiting for. She arrived in France in March 1325. She was now able to take advantage of the family connections in her native land and escape the reach of the Despensers and Edward, whom she detested.

In May 1325, Isabella agreed to a peace treaty, favoring France and requiring Edward to pay homage in France to her brother, King Charles; but Edward decided instead to send his son to pay homage. This proved a gross tactical error, and helped to bring about the ruin of both Edward and the Despensers, as Isabella, now that she had her son with her, declared that she would not return to England until the Despensers were removed from power.

Isabella's great ally in France was Roger Mortimer, who became her lover, even though he had a wife back in England. Isabella's presence in France became a rallying point for a number of nobles opposed to Edward's reign. Edward's half-brother, the earl of Kent, married Mortimer's cousin, Margaret Wake; other nobles, such as John de Cromwell and the earl of Richmond, also chose to support Isabella and

Mortimer. An enraged Edward demanded her and their son's immediate return to England; his order was ignored.

With the blessing of her brother, Charles, Isabella and Mortimer went to Holland in the summer of 1326 to prepare an invasion force. William I of Holland, related by marriage to Isabella's family, helped them contract ships and provisions for the invading troops, largely composed of mercenaries. In September 1326, Mortimer and Isabella invaded England, landing at Suffolk. Edward offered a reward for the death of Isabella and Roger Mortimer—Mortimer countered by offering double the amount for the head of Hugh Despenser. But Edward had a problem—a great many nobles and barons had no stomach for a fight to save him. Henry of Lancaster, for example, showed his loyalties by raising an army, seizing a cache of Despenser treasure from Leicester Abbey, and marching south to join Mortimer.

The invasion soon had too much force and support to be stopped. As a result, the army the king had tried to mobilize failed to materialize and both Edward and the Despensers were left isolated. They abandoned London in early October, leaving the city in chaos. The king first took refuge in Gloucester, then fled to South Wales in order to stand and make a defense in Despenser's lands. Once again, Edward was unable to rally an army, and on October 31, he was abandoned by his dwindling number of supporters, leaving him with only the younger Despenser and a few servants.

A couple of days earlier, the elder Despenser had been caught and accused of encouraging the illegal government of his son, enriching himself at the expense of others, despoiling the church, and taking part in the illegal execution of the earl of Lancaster. He was hanged and beheaded at the Bristol Gallows. Henry of Lancaster was then sent to Wales in order to capture the king and the younger Despenser, now largely defenseless. On November 16, Lancaster's forces took them into custody.

Violent reprisals against Edward's allies began almost immediately. Hugh Despenser the younger met an exceptionally violent and graphic end. Guards pulled him from his horse, stripped him, and scrawled biblical verses against corruption and arrogance on his skin. He was dragged into the city square to Queen Isabella, Roger Mortimer, and the Lancastrians, where he was condemned as a thief, castrated (to send a message about his relationship with the king?), and drawn and quartered as a traitor. Despenser's vassal, Simon of Reading, was also hanged next to him on charges of insulting the queen.

One issue remained: What to do with King Edward? Roger Mortimer, now for all intents and purposes the most powerful man in England, pushed the archbishop of York and key parliamentary leaders to depose Edward II as king and enthrone Edward III, who was fourteen years old at the time. Imprisoned at Kenilworth Castle, Edward was informed of the long list of official charges brought against him by Parliament, which included incompetence and "pursuing occupations unbecoming to a monarch." Edward, in a state of shock, reportedly wept while listening. Lamenting that his people had so hated his rule, the king agreed that he would abdicate in favor of his son. He was the first English king to be deposed from the throne. Isabella's son was proclaimed King Edward III on January 25, 1327.

Isabella and Roger Mortimer acted as regents. But the powerful pair were not content to leave Edward II alive, worried that he could be restored to the throne in a coup. Mortimer's agents moved him to Berkeley Castle in Gloucestershire in April 1327. The former king was reportedly kept in vile and unsanitary conditions, near diseased livestock, in the hopes that he would become ill and die. Just because he was a bad king didn't mean he was easy to kill; he survived that plan. But die he did. In October, it was announced at the king's court and at Parliament that he had died of natural causes. Presumably, he was murdered on orders from Isabella and Mortimer. There was even one report that he had been brutally tortured and sodomized with a red-hot poker as means of execution. But that account, by Geoffrey le Baker, was written some thirty years after the fact and is uncorroborated by any other source. Baker and his patron, Thomas de la Moore, are also said to have been opponents of Isabella and Roger Mortimer, so their objectivity is in doubt.

Some modern scholars have put forth the argument that Edward was not killed at all, but escaped, or was helped to escape, and lived out his life in hiding. This view is based on a letter from a Genoese priest, Manuele Fieschi, to Edward III in 1337, in which he claims Edward II escaped and fled to Italy. But this account is also not corroborated by any other source; and someone was buried in Edward II's tomb—almost certainly Edward II himself.

The story doesn't end that happily for Isabella, and certainly not for her lover, Roger Mortimer. For three years, she and Mortimer reigned as regents for her teenage son, Edward III. But they fell victim to that old bit of philosophy: Absolute power corrupts absolutely. Mortimer, in particular, went a little power-mad. Reprisals against allies of Edward II were common. Mortimer seized lands with little or no justification. His hostile and illegal actions were reminiscent of the excesses of the Despensers.

In 1330, when Edward III reached legal age, he asserted his authority as king. Supported by key noble families and their force of arms, he had Isabella and Mortimer taken into custody. Isabella, as Julia Agrippina had done, erroneously assumed that she would either be able to control her son or retain his allegiance. It's unclear as to the feelings of the young king toward Roger Mortimer. Mortimer had helped bring him to power, but had tried to dominate his reign, had acted illegally and selfishly, and was responsible for the murder of his father. Upon seizing the two of them at court, Isabella had cried out to her son, "Fair son, have pity on gentle Mortimer!"

Roger Mortimer was hanged as a traitor in November 1330. Isabella was removed from power and forced into retirement at Castle Rising in Norfolk. She was allowed to live in comfort, but her movements were restricted—not unlike the house arrest imposed on Eleanor of Aquitaine by Edwards's great-great-great-grandfather Henry II two hundred years earlier. Isabella lived another twenty-eight years, dying in 1358. Troubled in his conscience about the part he had been made to play in his father's downfall, Edward built an impressive monument over his father's burial place at Gloucester Cathedral.

What was so remarkable about Isabella was her ability to recognize threats, find coalition partners, and lead a successful coup d'état. Her nickname, the She-Wolf of France, was bestowed by historians to

symbolize what came to be seen as her duplicity and manipulation
in taking Edward II's throne. But modern scholarship has cast new
light on her plight as a wronged queen and the courage, resolve, and
resourcefulness with which she picked up the pieces and changed the
course of European history.

The Mad Monk: Grigori Rasputin

Grigori Rasputin, the mysterious holy man and healer, advisor to the
Russian tsarina, Alexandra Romanov, was murdered almost one hundred
years ago. His murder is still, in the opinion of most, an unsolved
crime. In fact, it is one of the biggest "cold cases" in history. There are
conflicting reports about how he died, who did the killing, and under
what circumstances the killing occurred. The traditional story is that
several Russian nobles, including the tsar's cousin Prince Felix Yusupov,
feared that Rasputin was a dangerous influence on the Romanov family
and had to be eliminated. So, the story goes, they invited him to a lavish
party where they fed him poisoned treats. When this did not kill him,
they shot him. Then they beat him severely. But he was still moving, so
they threw him in the freezing Neva River. Supposedly, when his body was
recovered there was water in his lungs—proof that he was still alive when
he was thrown in the water.

If this sounds like a fairy tale, that's because it surely is. There is little
to no proof of any of it. There are serious holes in the statement given by
Yusupov, and many doubts as to its validity. The story took hold in the
days and months following Rasputin's assassination, partly due to the
messy politics surrounding the Russian monarchy at the time—the events
surrounding Rasputin's life and death were sensationalized by Russian
officials and the media.

There is considerable evidence that Rasputin may have been
killed by the British Secret Service. A BBC investigation in 2004 found
inconsistencies between the forensic evidence and the story of how he
was killed. According to their investigation, a review of the autopsy
photos shows a bullet hole in the center of Rasputin's forehead—surely
enough to stop even the holiest of holy men in his tracks. Investigators

also found a link between Prince Yusupov and a British MI6 agent, Oswald Rayner. The investigation uncovered documents showing that the British government was worried about Rasputin's influence on Russian participation in World War I: "Had he persuaded the Tsar to pull out of the First World War, the Allies would have been overwhelmed on the Western front by German troops no longer needed to fight the Russians in the East."

There has never been credible evidence provided that would substantiate the official story. Was the involvement of Prince Yusupov and his family a cover story to hide the role of the British government? Or did they join forces to lure Rasputin into a death chamber? Much more so than the John F. Kennedy assassination case, there are many unanswered questions and breaks in the chain of evidence.

Perhaps the truly amazing part of the story is that this man—this strange, tattered mystic from Siberia—could rise to such an exalted position in the first place. It was a confluence of events that brought him to St. Petersburg and to the attention of the Romanov family. One can conclude from the histories written of the period that he was a power-hungry, social climbing sex addict. But there is a bit more to the story.

Grigori Yefimovich Rasputin was from the small Siberian town of Pokrovskoye, born into a peasant family who raised horses. Theirs was a family that was better off than most in Pokrovskoye; at least they owned their own land. But Rasputin had a troubled youth. At the age of eight he witnessed his brother's death, which sent him into a two-year depression, during which he rarely left his family's home. An a youth he was constantly getting into trouble with the townspeople because of drunkenness and theft. When he turned eighteen, threatened with jail, he made a public declaration that he would go on a religious pilgrimage to atone for his wrongdoings.

He ended up at the Verkhne-Turski Monastery in central Siberia, where he spent three years. During his time there, he claimed to have had a vision of the Virgin Mary, after which he dedicated his life to God. He also reportedly encountered a radical religious sect called the Khlysty, a group that mingled sexual orgies with religious raptures and which had been emphatically condemned by the Orthodox Church. The unique dogma of the Khlysty taught that one could become closer to God by sinning. For a man who was torn between religious conviction and sins of the flesh, it was a perfect match. After all, if there were such a thing, Rasputin would be a top contender to win the "Caligula" prize. According to multiple sources, he, too, thought himself a demigod, and engaged in sexual degradations that would make a Russian sailor blush.

On his return to Pokrovskoye, he became a *strannik,* or roving man of God. Contrary to popular belief, and inconsistent with the nickname bestowed on him by history—the mad monk—he never took the holy orders to became a monk. He claimed that his was a self-given commission from heaven of the kind that had on occasion appeared in Russian history, sometimes during crisis or war. Meanwhile, according to local sources, he lived so scandalous a life that his village priest investigated claims made against him of sexual depravity. Multiple sources report that throughout the remainder of his life, he alternated freely between sinning and repenting. He once told a priest that "Great sins made possible great repentances."

The Khlysty were also accused by the Orthodox Church of engaging in other heretical practices, such as mysticism and hypnotism. One of the traits Rasputin was said to possess was the unique gift of manipulation through eye contact. It is believed that during his time at the monastery he perfected his talent for hypnosis, which would greatly affect not only his life but eventually all of Russia.

It was also believed that he had healing abilities, another gift he developed under the guidance of the Khlysty. In fact, most of his life he billed himself as a healer, which automatically gave him a certain standing in the remote towns and villages of Siberia. Was hypnotism his secret? Was his famed ability to heal, which made him a close family friend of the tsar through the miraculous effects he had on his son Alexei, the product of hypnosis?

It was during his travels that Rasputin arrived at his most famous and eventually final destination of the Russian capital, St. Petersburg. Rasputin thrived in St. Petersburg. He was such an eccentric character that it did not take long before the nobles of Russia began to take notice of the strange holy man from Siberia. He was invited to the nobility's parties, at first as a novelty. They underestimated Rasputin's power of charm and his magnetic speaking ability. His reputation as a holy man and healer captivated many, particularly the Grand Duke Peter Nikolaevich and Grand Duchess Militsa, who were very close to the tsar's family. Before long, Rasputin had them eating out of his hand. It was through this social network that he was invited to the tsar's court.

Despite his new standing with the Russian nobility, Rasputin continued his life of debauchery. In fact, in St. Petersburg he was rather like the proverbial "kid in a candy store." There were times when he would spend half the night in the tsar's court and finish the night in a dram or brothel. His relationships and liaisons with numerous women in St. Petersburg were common knowledge. These inconsistencies went unnoticed by the Russian populace at first, but as Rasputin became more and more entrenched in the tsar's "inner circle," his actions took on added significance.

One day while at court, the tsar and tsarina stayed in their chambers; the tsarevich, Alexei, was sick. Alexei suffered from hemophilia, a genetic disease in which the blood doesn't clot properly. The royal couple lived in constant fear he would be injured and bleed to death. Alexei was the sole male heir to Nicholas and Alexandra, and thus very precious. His illness was kept secret. Rasputin, who was known in Siberia as a man who healed animals, asked if he could see the boy. Surprisingly, the tsarina granted his wish, beginning his tenure as healer to Alexei and spiritual advisor to Alexandra.

Credible reports indicate that Rasputin was able to stop Alexei's bleeding on multiple occasions. His effect on Alexei, the tsarevich, was such that his overall health did improve (modern studies have shown that hypnosis can indeed be used to slow down bleeding, slow the heart rate, and induce relaxation). Due to his effect on Alexei, Rasputin was invited into the tsar's inner circle, where he was taken in as a savior by the Romanov family. To the tsarina, this "mad monk," as he was soon to be called, was nothing short of a miracle worker.

Tsar Nicholas liked and trusted Rasputin, but it's not clear what effect Rasputin had on political decisions. Reports that he held immense influence over the tsar were overblown, as he was made somewhat of a scapegoat by members of the political class for Russia's problems during World War I. He did gain influence over personnel decisions in the Russian bureaucracy, and shared his political opinions freely with the tsarina. She was of German and English ancestry, and therefore her political loyalties during the war were questioned by some in St. Petersburg. Since Rasputin was known to be firmly against the war, there were concerns that Rasputin and the tsarina were trying to forge a separate peace agreement with the Germans.

Although the "mad monk" may have lacked coercive power over the tsar, the tsarina is a different story. Rasputin clearly had the young queen in the palm of his hand. Although it was claimed by the tsar's enemies that the queen was having sexual relations with Rasputin, contemporary historians have discredited that insinuation. She was fully dedicated to her husband. But Rasputin's influence over her was undisputed, and many assumed that influence extended to the tsar.

The war was extremely hard on the Russian people and on the tsar's military forces. The tsar decided that he should go closer to the front and take a more direct role. This left the tsarina in charge back in St. Petersburg. With the tsarina was Rasputin, who was by this time treated like nobility. The tsarina had a special car to take Rasputin from his apartment to the palace. The car would be seen picking up Rasputin at all hours of the night and returning early in the morning. Russians would see this and think the worst. The rumors of sexual infidelity between the queen and Rasputin were made worse by the man himself. When people asked Rasputin if he were sleeping with the queen, he would not give them a definitive answer. Playing up his image as a power broker and a man of mystery, he wouldn't say yes or no.

What was Rasputin's motivation? Accusations that he was acting as an agent in the employ of the German government have never been proven. He was against the war, but likely for personal reasons, having more to do with his ability to retain his influence at the Russian court.

The government ministers he persuaded the tsarina to appoint to office were incompetent and unthreatening for the most part, which would make them easier for him to manipulate. Rasputin acted to preserve his power base and use that influence to maintain the lavish lifestyle in St. Petersburg to which he had become accustomed.

By 1916, the Russian people's misery was nearing a breaking point. War casualties were enormous, and people were dying at home too. All resources were being sent to the front, while the people of St. Petersburg (renamed Petrograd in 1914) were starving to death. The Romanovs were blamed by many for the widespread suffering, and Rasputin came to be seen as a menacing presence in the government. Socialists and Marxists, who were trying to exacerbate discontent within the Russian capital, used Rasputin as a straw man against the royal family. That December, someone—either the Russian nobles led by Yusupov, or British intelligence (perhaps both)—decided the time had come to act. Rasputin was eliminated as a threat.

Yet it seems that none of those who wanted Rasputin dead got what they wanted. The tsar was forced to abdicate, ending the Russian monarchy and leading to intensive political struggle and bloodshed—so Prince Yusupov and other members of the royal family did not save the monarchy, if that was their intent. And if the British government was behind the killing of Rasputin, Russia pulled out of the war anyway after the Bolsheviks took power, leaving Britain and its allies to face the Germans and their coalition partners on their own.

The urge to save humanity is almost always only a false face for the urge to rule it.

—H.L. Mencken

ENDNOTES

Introduction

2. in its time of great need: Ethan M. Fishman, William Pederson, and Mark Rozell, *George Washington: Foundation of Presidential Leadership and Character* (Westport, Conn.: Greenwood Publishing Group, 2001), p. 33.

2. ". . . to struggle against social injustice": David Garrow, *Martin Luther King, Jr: Civil Rights Leader, Theologian, Orator*, volume 1 (Brooklyn, NY: Carlson Publishing, 1989), p. 712.

Chapter 1: The Machiavellians

9. in a plot to overthrow them: David E. Ingersoll, "The Constant Prince: Private Interests and Public Goals in Machiavelli," *Western Political Quarterly* 21 (December 1968): 588-596.

10. ". . . so much experience at the expense of others": Maurizio Viroli, *Niccolo's Smile: A Biography of Machiavelli* (New York: Hill and Wang, New York, 1998), p. 101.

10. ". . . even the lowliest office . . .": Ibid.

10. stud dogs someone had sent him: Ibid., p. 160.

10. provide prosperity for the citizens: Christian Gauss, *The Prince by Niccolo Machiavelli* (New York: Signet Classics, 1960), p. 59.

11. ethics second: Viroli, p. 180.

11. "Agathocles held rule over the city without any civil strife": Gauss, p. 77.

12. to be destroyed by it: Ibid., p. 46.

12. the power of the people: Ibid., p. 3.

12. ". . . two has to be wanting": Ibid., p. 90.

12. ". . . of punishment which never fails": Ibid.

12. ". . . it more than in war.": Gauss, p. 104.

12. Vatican's list of prohibited books: Leo Strauss and Joseph Cropsey, *History of Political Philosophy* (Chicago: University of Chicago Press, 1987), p. 300.

13. ". . . than of doing something strong": Viroli, p. 206.

13. ". . . from being independent and secure": Ibid.

13. this in the *Catholic Encyclopedia*: Umberto Benigni, "Nicolò Machiavelli." *The Catholic Encyclopedia*, volume 9 (New York: Robert Appleton Company, 1910), p. 346.

13. deviousness and lack of ethics: D. L. Paulhus and K. M. Williams, "The Dark Triad of Personality: Narcissism, Machiavellianism, and Psychopathy," *Journal of Research in Personality* 36 (2002): 556-563.

13. long-term success of a state: Gauss, p. 46.

14. "were simply wrong": Viroli, p. 156.

14. "according to necessity": Ibid.

14. "I must be cruel only to be kind": *Hamlet*, by William Shakespeare, Act 3, Scene 24, Read Books, London, 2010, p. 173-179.

15. all of the Indian subcontinent: B. S. Sihag. "Kautilya on Institutions, Governance, Knowledge, Ethics and Prosperity," *Humanomics* 23, no. 1 (2007): 7.

16. "truly radical Machiavellianism": Ibid.

16. on behalf of the general good: Sihag, p. 9.

17. would return to their posts: Boesche, p. 28.

17. his power safe from within: Ibid.

17. ". . . in riding elephants, horses and chariots": Ibid., p. 31.

18. acquire more to this empire: Ibid., p. 33.

18. ". . . and by going to another": Ibid.

18. ". . . killed by so and so'": Ibid.

18. ". . . lulling the enemy into complacency": Trautman, *Kautilya and the Arthashastra: A Statistical Investigation of the Authorship and Evolution of the Text* (Holland: E.J. Brill, 1971), p. 13.

19. admiration for Machiavelli's political mind: R. J. Knecht, *Catherine de' Medici* (London and New York: Longman, 1998), p. 26.

19. ". . . peculiar to all the Medici": G. F. Young, *The Medici: Volume II* (London: John Murray, 1920), p. 393.

20. an accident foretold by Nostradamus: Ian Wilson, *Nostradamus*: The Evidence (London: Orion, 2003), p. 167.

20. the power of the Catholic nobles: Knecht, p. 39.

21. The conference was a disaster: J. E. Neale, *The Age of Catherine de Medici* (London: Jonathan Cape, 1943), p. 88.

21. would attack: Stephen Budiansky, *Her Majesty's Spymaster* (New York: Penguin, 2005), p. 5.

22. to upwards of thirty thousand: Ibid., p. 8.

22. ". . .the glee of its perverted admirers": Ibid.

23. historian Karl Walling: Karl-Friedrich Walling, *Republican Empire: Alexander Hamilton on War and Free Government* (Lawrence: University Press of Kansas, 1999), p. 16.

23. ". . . intriguer in the United States": John Lamberton Harper, *American Machiavelli: Alexander Hamilton and the Origins of U.S. Foreign Policy* (Cambridge, UK: Cambridge University Press, 2004), p. 199.

23. "first and last Prime Minister": Ibid., p. 64.

23. of French Huguenot descent: Ibid., p. 23.

24. were shunned by James Hamilton: Ron Chernow, *Alexander Hamilton* (New York: Penguin, 2004), p. 27.

24. General George Washington: Harper, p. 23.

24. for personal disenchantment and defeat: Ibid., p. 6.

25. to the national government: Forrest McDonald, *Alexander Hamilton: a Biography* (New York: W. W. Norton and Company, 1982), p. 342.

26. ". . . and less tainted with corruption": Harper, p. 194.

26. ". . . of a Scotch peddler": Ibid., p. 15.

26. ". . . a Bastard": Chernow, p. 397.

27. in the *Albany Register*: Thomas Fleming, *Duel: Alexander Hamilton, Aaron Burr, and the Future of America* (New York: Basic Books, 1999), p. 236.

28. as his assistant: Stephen Hayes, *Cheney: The Untold Story of America's Most Powerful and Controversial Vice President* (New York: HarperCollins, 2007), p. 55.

28. Cheney told his biographer: Hayes, Ibid., p78.

28. "... chief of staff to the President": T. D. Allman, "The Curse of Dick Cheney," Rolling Stone (August 25, 2004) Available at: www.rollingstone.com/politics/story/6450422/the_curse_of_dick_cheney/

29. on November 5, 1975: Hayes, p. 98.

29. "... in his apt": Adam Liptak, "Cheney's To-Do Lists, Then and Now," New York Times (February 11, 2007): [found online http://query.nytimes.com/gst/fullpage.html?res=9D00E6DA1E3FF932A25751C0A9619C8B63.

29. "... what's secret and what's not": Ibid.

30. and the administration: Hayes, p. 190.

31. Chief of Staff Josh Bolten: Barton Gellman, *Angler: The Cheney Vice Presidency* (New York: Penguin Press, 2008), p. 51.

31. were seldom seen: Ibid.

31. "... who must live within it.": Ibid., p. 259.

31. on the battlefield: Ibid, p, 169

32. auditing his compliance: Ibid.

Chapter 2: Empire Builders

35. a chapel and monastery: Norman Cantor, *The Civilization of the Middle Ages* (New York: Harper Perennial, 1994), p. 8

35. "... and an abundance of grace": Piers Paul Read, *The Templars* (Cambridge: Da Capo Press, 1999), p. 98.

35. "... far-reaching and irresistible": Ibid.

35. his mother's side. Gillian R. Evans, *Bernard of Clairvaux (Great Medieval Thinkers)* (New York: Oxford University Press, 2000), p. 87.

35. strongly appealed to Bernard: Cantor, p. 77.

36. to the Pope himself: Read, p. 105.

36. would conquer death: Ibid.

36. "... kings and princes": Marie Gildas, "St. Bernard of Clairvaux," *The Catholic Encyclopedia*, volume 2 (New York: Robert Appleton Company, 1907).

37. the new pope: Evans, p. 149.

37. Lothiar II: Cantor, p. 101.

37. "... of the age": Henry Hart Milman, *The History of Latin Christianity* (Armstrong Publishers, 1903), p. 155.

37. Denmark, Italy, and Austria: Cantor, p. 119.

38. witness to the faith: James Harpur, *Love Burning in the Soul: The Story of the Christian Mystics* (Shambhala Publications, 2005), p. 61.

39. "... are now deserted": Read, p. 119.

39. Knights Templar: Ibid., p. 121.

39. marched through Anatolia: Ibid., p. 123.

40. *De Consideratione*: Ibid., p. 125.

40. sold into slavery: Andre Clot, *Suleiman the Magnificent* (New York: New Amsterdam Press, 1992), p. 46.

41. "... officers of government": Albert Howe Lyber, "The Government of the Ottoman Empire in the Time of Suleiman the Magnificent" (Cambridge: Harvard University Press, 1913), p. 46.

41. an accomplished musician: Clot, p. 48.

41. to go too far: Ibid.

42. jealousy among others: Merriam, Roger Bigelow, *Suleiman the Magnificent: 1520–1566* (New York: Cooper Square Publishers, Inc.), p. 76.

42. sultan's right hand: Lyber, p. 164.

42. in marriage: Merriam, p. 86.

43. officials and dignitaries: Clot, p. 58.

43. sultan's heroes: Joseph Von Hammer-Purgstall, *Geschichte des Osmanischen Reiches* (Vienna: Desbarres, 1827).

43. in contemporary Europe: Ibid.

44. "Sultan" Ibrahim Pasha: Merriam, p. 139.

44. against Suleiman: Ibid.

45. in the sultan's harem: Clot, p. 71.

45. his best friend: Lyber, p. 89.

45. for alleged treason: Ibid.

46. "... God is with us": Jurrien von Goor and Foskelien von Goor, *Prelude to Colonialism: The Dutch in Asia* (Amsterdam: Uitgeverij Verloren, 2004), p. 69.

46. in the East Indies: A. E. Sokol, "Communication and Production in Indonesian History," *Far Eastern Quarterly* 7, no. 4 (August 1948): 339–353.

46. remedy against plague: Giles Milton, Nathaniel's Nutmeg (New York: Farrar, Straus and Giroux, 1999), p. 24.

47. and foreign languages: Milton, p. 247.

47. commerce in Asia: Ibid.

47. arms and battlements: Vincent Loth, "Armed Incidents and Unpaid Bills: Anglo-Dutch Rivalry in the Banda Islands in the Seventeenth Century," *Modern Asian Studies* 29, no. 4 (1995): 710.

48. in Dutch affairs: Ibid., p. 714.

48. at Jakarta instead: George Masselman, "Dutch Colonial Policy in the Seventeenth Century," *Journal of Economic History* 21, no. 4 (December 1961): 465.

49. in East Asia: Loth, p. 717.

49. among the islands: Milton, p. 312.

50. eighty Japanese mercenaries: Ibid., p. 313.

50. an outlaw: Ibid., p. 319.

50. died in Batavia: Ibid.

52. ". . . of the federation": William Sloane, "Bismarck's Apprenticeship," *Political Science Quarterly* 13, no. 3 (September 1899): 421.

52. German Confederation: Erich Eyck, *Bismarck and the German Empire* (New York: W. W. Norton and Company, 1964), p. 21.

52. of Austria: Ibid., p. 33.

53. a decade earlier: E. J. Feuchtwanger, *Bismarck: Routledge Historical Biographies* (New York: Routledge, 2002), p. 100.

53. behind the scenes: Eyck, p. 81.

53. even desirable: Feuchtwanger, p. 105.

53. Austro-Prussian War: Eyck, p. 123.

54. two world wars: Ibid., p. 134.

54. existing estates combined: Sir Charles Grant Robertson, *Bismarck: Makers of the Nineteenth Century* (New York: H. Holt and Company, 1919), p. 311.

55. greedy and untrustworthy: Eyck, p. 165.

55. king of Spain: Ibid.

55. Franco-Prussian War: Werner Richter, *Bismarck* (Los Angeles: Putnam, 1965), p. 173.

56. insulting the king: Eyck, p. 172.

56. of the war: Ibid.

56. England in 1873: Robertson, p. 348.

56. under the king: Eyck, p. 189.

57. threatening to resign: Ibid., p. 277.

CHAPTER 3: **Kingmakers**

59. 16th earl of Warwick: William Safire, *Safire's Political Dictionary* (New York: Oxford University Press, 2008), p. 371.

59. Edward III's youngest son: Charles Oman, Warwick: *The Kingmaker*, reprint ed. (London; New York: Macmillan, 1899), p. 14.

60. "revolted against his own handiwork": Paul Murray Kendall, *Warwick the Kingmaker* (New York: W. W. Norton and Company, 1957), p. 11.

60. featuring red and white roses: Terence Wise and Gary Embleton, *The Wars of the Roses* (Oxford, UK: Osprey Publishing, 1983), p. 5.

61. his chief minister: John Watts, *Henry VI and the Politics of Kingship* (Cambridge, UK: Cambridge University Press, 1996), p. 90.

61. other European power brokers: Ibid., p. 98.

62. wealthiest man in the kingdom: Kendall, p. 36.

62. with the Woodville family: Oman, p. 40.

62. closer ties with the Burgandians: A. J. Pollard, *The Wars of the Roses* (Basingstoke, UK: Macmillan Education, 1988), p. 59.

63. "... if helpless, Edward": Kendall, p. 176.

63. to return to London: Ibid., p. 179.

64. Henry VI's youngest son: Pollard, p. 80.

64. on the continent by bad weather: Kendall, p. 186.

64. attempting to reach his horse: Watts, p. 160.

66. Packard Commercial School of New York City: James A. Farley, *Behind the Ballots: The Personal History of a Politician* (New York: Harcourt, Brace and Company, 1938), p. 8.

66. Democratic Party in upstate New York: Daniel Scroop, *Mr. Democrat: Jim Farley, the New Deal and the Making of Modern American Politics* (Ann Arbor: University of Michigan Press, 2006), p. 19.

67. New York state for years: Farley, p. 51.

67. Tammany Hall political machine: Ibid.

67. regain the Democratic nomination: Scroop, p. 60.

68. replace Smith as New York governor: Farley, p. 58.

69. "... other very necessary activities": Ibid., p. 50.

70. raise a finger to bring it about: Ibid., p. 62.

70. would get the vice presidency: Ibid., p. 71.

71. consult on a range of issues: Scroop, p. 101.

71. "... so goes Vermont.": "The Presidency: Triumph," Time (November 16, 1936): Available at: http://www.time.com/time/magazine/article/0,9171,756871,00.html

71. Thomas Jefferson and James Madison: Farley, p. 243.

72. "... more handshakes than Bennett himself": "The Nation: Farley Wins," *Time* (August 31, 1942): Available at: http://www.time.com/time/magazine/article/0,9171,849988,00.html.

73. in his state more than once: Duncan B. Forrester, "Kamaraj: A Study in Percolation of Style," *Modern Asian Studies* 4, no. 1 (1970): 47.

73. free midday meals in schools: Anthony Lukas, "Political Python of India," New York Times (February 20, 1966): [www.newsanalysisindia.com/114012008.htm].

74. in all forms of political protests: Dennis Templeman, *The Northern Nadars of Tamil Nadu: An Indian Caste in the Process of Change* (Delhi, India): Oxford University Press, 1996), p. 262.

74. eight years in British colonial jails: Forrester, p. 49.

74. dramatically improving employment opportunities: P. S. Subbaraman, "Kamaraj: Symbol of Indian Democracy," *Popular Prakashan* (1966): 23.

74. best managed states in India: Ibid.

75. the party at the grassroots level: Lukas.

75. nation to take such a step: Subbaraman, p. 24.

75. Indian national process into the future: "The Return of the King-Makers," *Commentary, Economic and Political Weekly* 2, no. 9 (March 4, 1967): 498.

76. realistic assessment of human nature: Lukas.

Chapter 4: Spies

78. raspberry reds, canary yellows, and deep blues: Stephen Budiansky, *Her Majesty's Spymaster: Elizabeth I, Sir Francis Walsingham, and the Birth of Modern Espionage* (New York: The Penguin Group, 2005), p. 34.

79. "In my native land of Ethiopia . . .": Ibid., p. 39.

79. belong to Philip and to the pope: Robert Hutchinson, *Elizabeth's Spymaster: Francis Walsingham and the Secret War that Saved England* (New York: Macmillan, 2007), p. 20.

80. ". . . France's five times, Budiansky, p. 58.

80. ". . . keep his own counsel stood out": Ibid., p. 33.

80. ". . . to apply them to his own uses": Ibid.

81. representative of a sovereign government: Ibid., p. 7.

81. playwright Christopher Marlowe: Ibid., p. 93.

82. before choosing a course of action: Vincent Buranelli and Nan Buranelli, *Spy/Counter-Spy: An Encyclopedia of Espionage* (New York: McGraw-Hill, 1982), p. 221.

82. used in a gratuitous manner: Budiansky, p. 115.

82. her "mortal enemy," Secretary Walshingham: Ibid., p. 106.

83. her monitions, mandates, and laws: Ibid., p. 102.

83. the duke of Norfolk was executed: Buranelli and Buranelli, p. 225.

83. wrote Walsingham: Budiansky, p. 81.

84. between Mary and her supporters: Hutchinson, p. 116.

84. put on the rack: Budiansky, p. 134.

85. Catholic spies was Gilbert Gifford: Ibid., p. 151.

85. agents of the Spanish king: Hutchinson, p. 116.

86. it caused some rancor between them: Budiansky, p. 173

86. ". . . with three blows from the executioner's axe": Ibid., p. 170.

86. King Philip's credit with Genoese bankers: Ibid., p. 180.

87. and their intended destinations: Buranelli and Buranelli, p. 302.

88. ". . . English navy fought with their enemies": Budiansky, p. 211.

88. "chief minister" or "first minister": William Robson, *The Life of Cardinal Richelieu* (Oxford, UK: G. Routledge Publishing, 1854), p. 486.

89. to the life of the whole: Anthony Levi, *Cardinal Richelieu: And the Making of France* (New York: Carroll & Graf, 2002), p. 11.

90. ". . . power and the modern secret service": John Ralston Saul, *The Doubter's Companion: A Dictionary of Aggressive Common Sense* (New York: Simon and Schuster, 2002), p. 143.

90. construction of an absolutist state: Robson, p. 366.

91. the dominant voice: Daniel Patrick O'Connell, *Richelieu* (Ann Arbor, Mich.: Weidenfeld & Nicolson, 1968), p. 46.

91. ". . . find something in them to hang them": Sir Richard Lodge, Richelieu (New York: Macmillan and Co., Ltd., 1896), p. 151.

91. his intendants increasingly became spies: Ibid., p. 163.

92. *The Man in the Iron Mask*: Hillaire Belloc, *Richelieu: A Study*, 2nd ed. (New York: J. B. Lippincott Company, 1929), p. 295.

92. Richelieu's administrative talents in 1615: O'Connell, p. 79.

93. French-dominated Catholic Europe: Gustave Charles Fagniez, *Le Pere Joseph et Richelieu (1577–1638)* (Paris: Librairie Hachette, 1894), p. 68.

93. rebellion against the king: Belloc, p. 221.

93. represented by the Habsburg states, Austria and Spain: Robson, p. 179.

93. invade Austria from the north: Fagniez, p. 119.

93. ". . . August 1914 and September 1939": Aldous Huxley, *L'Eminence Grise* (New York: Meridian Books, 1959), p. 18.

94. ". . . pessimism about politics and history. . .": Tenebroso-Cavernoso, "Grey Eminence," Time (October 6, 1941): Available at: http://www.time.com/time/magazine/article/0,9171,790313-2,00.html

94. furthered through countless contacts and intrigues: Ibid.

94. ". . . the charge is not entirely baseless": Huxley, p. 31.

94. as chief minister to the king: Fagniez, p. 156.

95. some circles as the "German" Lawrence: Christopher Sykes, *Wassmuss: The German Lawrence* (London: Longmans, Green, and Company, 1936), p. iii.

95. "The Influence of the Crusades on European Military Architecture": Jeremy Wilson, *Lawrence of Arabia: The Authorized Biography of T. E. Lawrence* (New York: Atheneum, 1990), p. 64.

95. an archaeologist for the British Museum: Ibid, p. 66.

96. ". . . was invaluable throughout the campaign": Jeremy Wilson, *Lawrence of Arabia: A Pocket Biography* (New York: Stroud, Sutton Publishers, 1997), p. 119.

96. to the American journalist Lowell Thomas: Anthony Nutting, *Lawrence of Arabia: The Man and the Motive* (London: Hollis and Carter, 1961), p. 174.

96. ". . . some thought with pleasure": "Tortured Hero," Time (December 1, 1961): Available at: http://www.time.com/time/magazine/article/0,9171,938850,00.html.

97. Sarah Junner: Wilson, *Lawrence of Arabia: A Pocket Biography*, p. 49.

97. he enjoyed being whipped: Harold Orlans, *T. E. Lawrence: Biography of a Broken Hero* (Jefferson, N.C.: McFarland Publishing, 2002), p. 219.

97. discouraging carnal pleasures: Michael Asher, *Lawrence: The Uncrowned King of Arabia* (New York: The Overlook Press, 1998), p. 33.

98. Into his quietness: *T. E. Lawrence, Seven Pillars of Wisdom: A Triumph* (New York: Doubleday and Company, 1966 reprint).

98. archaeological dig before the war: Orlans, p. 255.

98. wrote admiringly of him: *Wilson, Lawrence of Arabia: A Pocket Biography*, p. 58.

98. war aims in support of Germany: Asher, p. 280.

98. of the Middle East: Wilson, *Lawrence of Arabia: The Authorized Biography* of T. E. Lawrence, p. 360.

99. take Jerusalem by Christmas 1917: Ibid.

99. at Damascus, and Feisal as king: Asher, p. 223.

99. worked closely with Feisal: Nutting, p. 218.

100. assumed name of John Hume Ross: Wilson, *Lawrence of Arabia: The Authorized Biography of T. E. Lawrence*, p. 489.

100. political influence of close friends: Ibid.

100. training practices in the RAF: Ibid., p. 708.

101. as part of his cover: Sykes, p. 20.

101. that would threaten British colonial India: Peter Hopkirk, *Like Hidden Fire: The Plot to Bring Down the British Empire* (New York: Kodansha Globe, 1997), p. 111.

101. just held with Kaiser Wilhelm: Sykes, p. 64.

102. possibly shortening the war: Hopkirk, p. 114.

102. belonged to a pro-German skeikh: Ibid.

102. prevent any further pro-German coups: Sykes, p. 119.

102. they were nonetheless decisively defeated: Hopkirk, p. 115.

103. reportedly a broken man: Sykes, p. 160.

103. ensure the president's safety: Yossi Melman, "Israel Pinning Hopes for Hamas Deal in Gaza on Egypt Intel Chief," *Haaretz* (January 23, 2009): Available at: http://www.haaretz. com/print-edition/features/israel-pinning-hopes-for-hamas-deal-in-gaza-on-egypt-intel-chief-1.268496.

103. would offend the conference's Ethiopian hosts: Mary Anne Weaver, "Pharaohs-in-Waiting," *Atlantic Monthly* (October 2003): p. 87. Available at: http://www.theatlantic.com/past/docs/issues/2003/10/weaver.htm.

103. Khalid al-Istanbuli: "Omar Suleiman Pivots from Anti-Terror Fighter to Terrorist Sponsor," DebkaFile (July 27, 2003). Available at: http://www.debka.com/article. phpraid 529.

104. Egypt's main Islamic extremist groups: Melman.

104. ". . . Suleimen tells Mubarak the way it is": Weaver, p. 88.

104. Gamal Abdel Nasser in the 1960s: Ibid.

105. at least not well publicized: Ibid.

105. more than twenty-five years: Issandr Amrani, "Egypt's Next Strongman," *Foreign Policy* (August 17, 2009): Available at: http://www.foreignpolicy.com/articles/2009/08/17/egypts_next_strongman.

105. ". . . position holders in the Arab world": Noam Amit, "The Puppet Master," *Ma'ariv* (May 2, 2003): Available at: http://www.fas.org/irp/world/egypt/sulayman.html.

106. in President Mubarak's Cabinet: Amrani.

106. government-owned daily newspaper *Al-Ahram*: Melman.

106. Egypt's most significant national security priority: Amrani.

106. ". . . protect the life of the president": Melman.

107. valuable as those of Israel's Mossad: Ibid.

107. radical clerics who run contemporary Iran: Amrani.

108. he's a favorite of some Egyptian newspapers: Ibid.

108. long claimed the mantle of Arab leadership: Ibid.

Chapter 5: Silver-Tongued Devils

111. temperament still firmly wedded to Roman tradition: Lawrence Osborne, "Cicero" by Anthony Everitt (Book Review). Salon.com (August 27, 2002). Available at: http://dir.salon.com/story/books/feature/2002/08/27/cicero/index.html.

111. were deemed worthy of preservation and study: Gary Simpson, *War, Peace, and God: Rethinking the Just War Tradition* (Minneapolis: Augsburg Fortress, 2007), p. 40.

111. fledgling city-state on the Tiber River: Anthony Everitt, *Cicero: The Life and Times of Rome's Greatest Politician* (New York: Random House, 2003), p. 21.

111. Senate on Roman policy making: Ibid., p. 14.

112. person with a future in politics: Ibid., p. 59.

112. which was the ultimate prize: T. Brennan, *The Praetorship in the Roman Republic, volume 1* (London: Oxford University Press, 2000), p. 3.

113. set out a comprehensive campaign strategy: Ibid., p. 87.

113. ". . . violated the laws and the courts": Ibid., p. 93.

114. Cherish this pronouncement: Ibid., p. 98.

114. Catiline insulting Cicero as an "immigrant": David Stockton, *Cicero: A Political Biography* (London: Oxford University Press, 1988), p. 218.

115. until the crisis had passed: Frank Cowell, *Cicero and the Roman Republic* (New York: Penguin Books, 1956), p. 201.

116. scornful of his pursuit of power: Everitt, p. 268.

116. ambitious eighteen-year-old adopted son: Ibid., p. 294.

116. one of them was Cicero himself: Marcel Le Glay, Jean-Louis Voisin, and Yann Le Bohec, *A History of Rome* (New York: Wiley-Blackwell, 2005), p. 418.

117. ". . . but do try to kill me properly": Everitt, p. 318.

117. acts of depravity in her youth: Robert Browning, *Justinian and Theodora* (Piscataway, N.J.: Gorgias Press, 2003), p. 18.

118. informant working for Justinian: Edward Gibbon, *The Decline and Fall of the Roman Empire* (New York: Random House, 2003, Modern Library Paperback Edition), p. 706.

118. enter into proper society: Charles Diehl, "Theodora," *Imperatrice de Byzance* (Paris, 1904), p. 44.

118. co-leader of the empire: Ibid.

118. "superior in intelligence to any man": Browning, p. 180.

119. joint names of Justinian and Theodora: Gibbon, p. 706.

119. protecting the status of women: Lynda Garland, *Byzantine Empresses: Women and Power in Byzantium*, AD 527–1204 (New York: CRC Press, 1999), p. 18.

119. stand fast and defend Constantinople: Paolo Cesaretti, *Theodora: Empress of Byzantium* (Paris: Vendome Press, 2004), p. 191.

119. nephew of the former emperor Anastasius: Ibid.

119. "... the loss of dignity and dominion": Gibbon, p. 712.

119. "... the throne is a glorius sepulchre": Ibid.

119. imperial forces were victorious: Browning, p. 172.

120. invite additional rebellions in the future: James Allen Evans, *The Empress Theodora: Partner of Justinian* (Austin: University of Texas Press, 2003), p. 47.

120. at least twenty-five churches: *Procopius, Vol. 7: On Buildings, General Index* (Loeb Classical Library, No. 343). Translated by H. B. Dewing, Cambridge: Harvard University Press, 1940.

120. one of her greatest legacies: Lynda Garland, *Byzantine Empresses: Women and Power in Byzantium, AD 527–1204* (New York: CRC Press, 1999), p. 21.

120. dramatic change due to Theodora's influence: Ibid.

120. condemned by many Orthodox church leaders: James Evans, *Procopius* (New York: Twayne Publishers, 1972), pp. 29–30.

121. even a "traitor": Benjamin Schwarz, "Charm Offensive," *Atlantic* (December 2007): Available at: http://www.theatlantic.com/magazine/archive/2007/12/charm-offensive/6436/.

121. might offer him better opportunities: J. F. Bernard, *Talleyrand: A Biography* (New York: Putnam, 1973), p. 90.

122. appointed bishop of Autun: Ibid.

122. at his seminary about his conquests: Robin Harris, *Talleyrand: Betrayer and Saviour of France* (New York: John Murray Publishers, 2007), p. 19.

122. Declaration of the Rights of Man: Ibid., p. 38.

122. national confiscation of church property: Andrew Roberts, "Talleyrand: The Old Fraud," *Foundation for Cultural Review* (April 1, 2007): page 4.

122. two casinos in Paris: Ibid.

123. "chef of kings and king of chefs": Duff Cooper, *Talleyrand* (Palo Alto, Calif: Stanford University Press, 1932), p. 387.

123. "I have always been rich": David Lawday, *Napoleon's Master: A Life of Prince Talleyrand* (New York: Macmillan, 2007), p. 55.

123. "... everything one had heard against him": Schwarz.

123. its foreign minister: Lawday, p. 134.

123. preserve his political career: Ibid., p. 102.

123. he later wrote: Ibid., p. 42.

123. president of the Assembly in 1790: Roberts.

124. Louis XVI had been executed: Harris, p. 216.

125. notably Madame de Staël: Roberts.

125. suffered politically when that mission failed: Harris, p. 109.

125. led to his resignation in 1799: Lawday, p. 199.

126. an eventual split: Cooper, p. 303.

126. oppose Napoleonic France in the future: Harris, p. 158.

126. captive in his château: Lady Blennerhassett, *Talleyrand*, volume 2. Translated by Frederick Clarke (Whitefish, Mont.: Kessinger Publishing, 2005), p. 382.

126. had entrusted his investments: Harris, p. 199.

126. to destabilize Napoleon: Harris, p. 194.

127. for details of French troop movement: Ibid.

127. reopened a dialogue with the Bourbons: Roberts.

127. with the principal victorious powers: Lawday, p. 274.

128. independent Belgium in the late 1830s: Cooper, p. 358.

128. ". . . as long as it offers shelter": Lawday, p. 338.

130. Marxist principles about society and history: Leon Trotsky, *My Life: An Attempt at an Autobiography* (New York: C. Scribner's and Sons, 1930), p. 112.

130. until his death in 1940: Isaac Deutscher, *The Prophet Armed: Trotsky, 1879–1921* (London: Oxford University Press, 1954), p. 59.

130. behind a common movement: Ibid., p. 44.

130. Lenin's more revolutionary path: Ian Thatcher, *Trotsky* (New York: Routledge, 2003), p. 212.

130. treason against the Russian state: Dmitri Volkogonov, *Trotsky: The Eternal Revolutionary* (New York: Simon and Schuster, 2007), p. 43.

130. Many Other Things, 1901: Deutscher, p. 45.

131. which means "truth": *Trotsky*, p. 220.

131. for their support of the war: Deutscher, p. 181.

131. the following year for revolutionary activities: Trotsky, p. x.

131. the imperial Russian monarchy: Ibid.

132. Military Revolutionary Committee was organized: Deutscher, p. 211.

132. Menshevik faction and other socialist revolutionaries: Volkogonov, p. 79.

133. including Joseph Stalin: Trotsky, p. 436.

133. White armies in 1918 and 1919: Deutscher, p. 274.

133. "What did you promise Comrade Trotsky?": Trotsky, p. 470.

134. Trotsky was disloyal to the party: Deutscher, p. 424.

134. in a move orchestrated by Stalin: Ibid.

134. with Grigory Zinoviev and Levk Kamenev: Volkogonov, p. 140.

135. guaranteeing that he would miss it: Ibid., p. 266.

135. with the rest of Europe: Deutscher, p. 291.

135. a Soviet republic: Volkogonov, p. xvii.

136. into the back of Trotsky's head: Craig Whitney, "The New Trotsky: No Longer a Devil," *New York Times* (January 16, 1989): Available at: http://query.nytimes.com/gst/fullpage.html?res=950DE5D7163EF935A25752C0A96F948260.

136. these two nourished hurts: Trotsky, p. 590.

Chapter 6: The Generals

137. attain to that rank: Niccolo Machiavelli, *The Prince* (New York: The New American Library, 1964), p. 81.

138. the same Germanic tribes: Clive Upton, Stewart Sanderson, John Widdowson, and David Brophy, *Word Maps: A Dialect Atlas of England* (New York: Routledge, 1987), p. 10.

139. an almost thousand-year reign: Edward Gibbon, *The Decline and Fall of the Roman Empire* (New York: Random House, 2003, Modern Library Paperback Edition), p. 563.

139. Nicene Orthodox Christian: M. von Albrecht and G. L. Schmeling, *A History of Roman Literature: From Livius Andronicus to Boethius: With Special Regard to Its Influence on World Literature, Volume 1* (New York: E.J. Brill Publishing, 1997), p. 1340.

139. Maria and Thermantia: Gibbon, p. 564.

140. throne in the East: William Smith, *A Dictionary of Greek and Roman Biography and Mythology: Oarses-Zygia,* volume 3 (Boston: J. Murray, 1890), p. 665.

140. by his own soldiers: Robert Hutchins, *Great Books of the Western World*, volume 40. (Chicago: *Encyclopedia Britannica*, 1952), p. 824.

141. against Alaric's position around Milan: Gibbon, p. 565.

141. of his son Eucherius: Ibid., p. 559.

142. were murdered in Rome shortly afterwards: Ibid.

142. against their cowardly enemies: Hutchins, p. 830.

142. of the imperial West: Gibbon, p. 564.

142. old French word for hammer: John Henry Haaren, *Famous Men of the Middle Ages* (New York: University Publishing Company, 1904), p. 57.

143. ". . . Muslim advance into Europe": Victor Davis Hanson, *Carnage and Culture: Landmark Battles in the Rise of Western Power* (New York: Doubleday, 2001), p. 157.

143. ". . . in the history of the world": Leopold von Ranke and Robert A. Johnson, *History of the Reformation in Germany*. Translated by Sarah Austin (New York: E. P. Dutton, 1905), p. 19.

143. about Valley Forge and Gettysburg: Dexter Wakefield, "An Islamic Europe?" *Tomorrow's World*, volume 8, Issue 3 (May 2006): Available at: http://www.tomorrowsworld. org/cgi-bin/tw/tw-mag.cgi?category=Magazine42&item=1149293702.

143. the Catholic Church: Franco Cardini, *Europe and Islam* (New York: Wiley-Blackwell, 2001), p. 9.

143. during his lifetime: John B. Bury, *The Cambridge Medieval History*, volume 2 (New York: Macmillan, 1913), p. 129.

143. Frankish domination of Gaul: William E. Watson, "The Battle of Tours-Poitiers Revisited," *Providence: Studies in Western Civilization 2*, no.1 (1993): Available at: http://www. deremilitari.org/resources/articles/watson2.htm.

144. often scattered, estates: Bury, p. 131.

144. English slang term *major domo: The American Heritage Dictionary of the English Language*, 4th ed. (Houghton Mifflin Company, 2009).

144. as a strong and capable leader: Gibbon, p. 964.

145. a raid on Autun: Antonio Santosuosso, *Barbarians, Marauders, and Infidels: The Ways of Medieval Warfare* (New York: Westview Press, 2004), p. 126.

145. well prepared for the attack: Ibid.

145. Charles had achieved total surprise: Gibbon, p. 966.

146. stood its ground: Cardini, p. 9.

146. dragged on for seven days: Santosuosso, p. 127.

146. some of his forces: Haaren, p. 59.

146. over the course of his career: Santosuosso, p. 129.

147. as the Battle of Tours: Ibid.

147. ". . . was in his hands": Charles Oman, *The Dark Ages*, 476–918, volume 1 (London: Rivingtons, 1903), p. 297.

147. "the hero of the age": Gibbon, p. 964.

148. Christian chroniclers of the age: Stanley Lane-Pool, *Saladin and the Fall of the Kingdom of Jerusalem* (New York: G. P. Putnam's Sons, 1906), p. 401.

148. virtuous pagan souls in Limbo: Ismael Abaza, "Saladin and His Cairo." Available at: http://www.touregypt.net/featurestories/saladin.htm.

149. under his own command: Piers Paul Read, *The Templars* (Cambridge, Mass.: Da Capo Press, 1999), p. 150.

150. to impart the faith: Lane-Pool, p. 206.

150. by a jihad (holy war): Read, p. 150.

151. ". . . in the Muslim world": Ibid., p. 156.

151. —water: Lane-Pool, p. 207.

152. cut off Raynald's head: Read, p. 160.

152. declared Saladin: Ibid.

153. and the Knights Hospitallers: Ibid., p. 151.

153. by exultant Muslims with clubs: Ibid., p. 161.

154. finance the venture: Lane-Pool, p. 252.

154. Muslim-controlled Acre: Read, p. 163.

154. return to Europe: Thomas Archer, *The Crusade of Richard I, 1189–92* (New York: G. P. Putnam's Sons, 1889), p. 385.

155. to his men: Read, p. 169.

156. ". . . nor yet in obscurity": Ivan Roots, *The Speeches of Oliver Cromwell* (London: Dent, 1989), p. 6.

156. in Cromwell's life and career: Peter Gaunt, *Oliver Cromwell* (New York: Wiley-Blackwell, 1997), p. 217.

156. before the Privy Council in 1630: John Morley, *Oliver Cromwell* (Whitefish, Mont.: Kessinger Publishing, 2005), p. 18.

157. particularly with alcohol: John Morrill, *Oliver Cromwell* (London: Oxford University Press, 2007), p. 9.

157. and openly discussed: George W. Bush, *A Charge to Keep* (New York: HarperCollins, 1999), p. 133.

157. I shall be most glad: Morrill, p. 34.

158. that is how they were known: Frank Kitson, *Old Ironsides: The Military Biography of Oliver Cromwell* (London: Phoenix Press, 2007), p. 163.

159. this gave Cromwell's men an edge: Morrill, p. 117.

159. of certain "chosen people": John Adamson, "Oliver Cromwell and the Long Parliament." In John Morrill, ed., *Oliver Cromwell and the English Revolution* (New York: Longman, 1990), p. 77.

160. after the town's capture: Paul Vallely, "The Big Question: Was Cromwell a Revolutionary Hero or a Genocidal War Criminal?" *The Independent* (September 4, 2008): Available at: http://www.independent.co.uk/news/uk/this-britain/the-big-question-was-cromwell-a-revolutionary-hero-or-a-genocidal-war-criminal-917996.html.

160. to be war crimes: Ibid.

160. "a high act of the Lord's providence": Jane Ohlmeyer and John Kenyon, eds., *The Civil Wars: A Military History of England, Scotland, and Ireland, 1638–1660* (London: Oxford University Press, 2000), p. 66.

161. ". . . to your sitting": W. C. Abbott, ed., *Writings and Speeches of Oliver Cromwell*, 4 volumes., 1937–1947 (Cambridge, Mass.: President and Fellows of Harvard College; reissued 1988), p. 643.

162. in the English-speaking world: Samuel R. Gardiner, *Oliver Cromwell* (London: Longmans, Green and Company, 1901), p. 223.

162. to a bout of malaria: Morrill, p. 105.

162. of a few of his ministers: Morley, p. 413.

162. he had briefly been a student: Gaunt, p. 4.

163. yet he was virulently anti-Catholic: Maurice Ashley, *The Greatness of Oliver Cromwell* (New York: Macmillan, 1958), p. 288.

164. by his samurai father: Robert J. C. Butow, *Tojo and the Coming of the War* (Palo Alto, Calif.: Stanford University Press, 1961), p. 26.

164. ". . . and possessed a quantity of drive": Ian Kershaw, *Fateful Choices: Ten Decisions That Changed the World, 1940–1941* (New York: Penguin Group, 2007), p. 356.

164. and expansionist ideals: Courtney Brown, *TOJO, the Last Banzai* (Cambridge, Mass.: Da Capo Press, 1998), p. 52.

165. ". . . in the Holy War": Address by Hideki Tojo at the opening of the Imperial Diet, Tokyo, May 27, 1942. Foreign Broadcast Monitoring Service, U.S. Federal Communications Commission.

165. of making quick decisions: Butow, p. 7.

165. and even "cowardly": Stanley Karnow, *In Our Image: America's Empire in the Philippines* (New York: Random House, 1989), p. 124.

165. were tried and executed: Chushichi Tsuzuki, *The Pursuit of Power in Modern Japan, 1825–1995* (London: Oxford University Press, 2000), p. 298.

166. as vice-minister of the army: Butow, p. 104.

166. and our control of Korea undermined: Herbert Bix, *Hirohito and the Making of Modern Japan* (New York: HarperCollins, 2001), p. 417.

167. I know much more: Ibid., p. 419.

167. to the imperial institution: Ibid., p. 418.

167. his consent to war: Peter Wetzler, *Hirohito and War* (Honolulu: University of Hawaii Press, 1998), p. 47.

167. the Pearl Harbor attack to Hirohito: Ibid., p. 35.

167. ". . . against the United States, England and Holland": Ibid., p. 30.

168. was often difficult to manage: Butow, p. 423.

169. he murmured: John Toland, *The Rising Sun: The Decline and Fall of the Japanese Empire, 1936–1945*, volume 1 (New York: Random House, 1970), p. 871.

169. including two nuclear bomb blasts: Ibid., p. 873.

Chapter 7: The Rebels

172. of the Meiji Restoration: Marius B. Jansen, *Sakamoto Ryoma and the Meiji Restoration* (New York: Columbia University Press, 1994), p. 222.

172. successful trade emporium: Ibid., p. 78.

172. bullied at school: Ibid., p. 81.

172. ("revere the emperor, expel the barbarians"): Ibid., p. 94.

173. by his home district of Tosa: Ibid., p. 101.

174. ". . . until we've had a chance to talk": Ibid., p. 163.

174. then go on to include China: Jansen, p. 165.

174. ". . . become your disciple": Ibid.

175. attack the Choshu: Hyoe Murakami and Thomas Harper, *Great Historical Figures of Japan.* (Elmsford, NY: Japan Publications Trading Company, 1978), p. 261.

176. by a bakufu official: Jansen, p. 182.

177. fled into the night: Romulus Hillsborough, "Sakamoto Ryoma: The Indispensable Nobody." Reprinted from Romulus Hillsborough, *Ryoma—Life of a Renaissance Samurai* (Ridgeback Press, 1999). Available at: http://www.shotokai.com/ingles/essays/sakamoto_ryoma.html.

177. within Ryoma's design: Jansen, p. 296.

178. with foreign markets: William De Bary, *Sources of Japanese Tradition*, volume 2. Compiled by William De Bary, Carol Gluck, Arthur E. Tiedemann (New York: Columbia University Press, 2006), p. 563.

179. economic giants NEC and Honda: Hillsborough.

179. papal states of central Italy: Lucy Riall, *The Italian Risorgimento: State, Society, and National Unification* (New York: Routledge, 1994), p. 13.

180. Garibaldi is the "sword": W. L. Courtney, ed. *The Fortnightly Review*, volume 111 (New York: Chapman and Hall, 1919), p. 297.

180. of modern Italy: Stringfellow Barr, *Mazzini: Portrait of an Exile* (New York: Henry Holt and Company, 1935), p. 242.

181. among Italian political exiles everywhere: John Gooch, *Unification of Italy* (Lancaster Pamphlets) (New York: Routledge, 2002), p. 5.

181. replace the old order: Emiliana Noether, "Mazzini and the Nineteenth Century Revolutionary Movement," *Consortium on Revolutionary Europe Proceedings* (Athens, Ga.: Consortium on Revolutionary Europe, 1984), p. 277.

181. inspired by Young Europe: John M. Merriman and J. M. Winter, *Europe 1789 to 1914: Encyclopedia of the Age of Industry and Empire* (Scribner Library) (New York: Charles Scribner's Sons, 2006), p. 2514.

182. within Italy's borders: Denis Mack Smith, *Mazzini* (New Haven, Conn.: Yale University Press, 1996), p. 81.

183. in the 1840's: Paul Frischauer, *Garibaldi: The Man and the Nation* (Whitefish, Mont.: Kessinger Publishing, 2006), p. 230.

183. ". . . to the true type of beauty": Alexandre Dumas, *The Memoirs of Garibaldi. Translated by R. S. Garnett.* (Whitefish, Mont.: Kessinger Publishing, 2006), p. 2.

183. his South American adventures: G. Garibaldi and Alexandre Dumas, *Garibaldi: An Autobiography.* Translated by William Robson (New York: Routledge, 1861), p. 50.

184. representing Italy's dormant power: Ibid., p. 55.

184. Austrian, French, and Spanish troops: G. M. Trevelyan, *Garibaldi's Defense of the Roman Republic* (London: Longmans, Green and Company, 1907), p. 227.

184. island north of Sardinia: Garibaldi and Dumas, p. 67.

184. with the Sardinian armed forces: Thayer, William Roscoe, "Cavour's Last Victory," *The Atlantic Monthly*, Volume 108, John Davis Batchelder Collection (Library of Congress), Atlantic Monthly Company, 1911: 514. Available at: http://books.google.com/books?i d=jWoAAAAAYAAJ&pg=PA314&lpg PA514&dq=cavour%27s+last+victory+atlantic+ monthly&source=bl&ots=cKqGdf3mzF&sig=IyETb6skgJGd4Ww50AWunq8XpZY&h l=en&ei=yGeOTLL7DYSKlwfjl-zlAg&sa=X&oi=book_result&ct=result&resnum=1&ved=0 CBIQ6AEwAA#v=onepage&q&f=false.

185. or any monarchy: Garibaldi and Dumas, p. 178.

186. for political reasons: Rory Carroll, "Garibaldi Asked by Lincoln to Run Army," *Guardian* (February 8, 2000): Available at: http://www.guardian.co.uk/world/2000/feb/08/ rorycarroll.

186. should be abolished: Giuseppe Guerzoni, *Garibaldi: Con Documenti Editi e Inediti*, volume 11 (Florence: 1882), p. 485.

187. the emancipation of women: Riall, p. 362.

188. "But he'll cut your throat": Jack Anderson and James Boyd, *Confessions of a Muckraker* (New York: Ballantine Books, 1980), p. 124.

189. ultimate Confucian ideal: Gao Wenquian, *Zhou Enlai: The Last Perfect Revolutionary.* Translated by Peter Rand and Lawrence R. Sullivan (New York: PublicAffairs, 2007), p. 40.

189. was arrested: Chae-Jin Lee, *Zhou Enlai: The Early Years* (Palo Alto, Calif.: Stanford University Press, 1996), p. 141.

190. behind strong leadership: Wenquian, p. 79.

190. insecure Mao: Ibid., p. 306.

191. "peaceful reunification": Ibid., p. 15.

191. achieved on his own: Percy Jucheng Fang and Lucy Guinong Fang, *Zhou Enlai: A Profile* (San Francisco: Foreign Language Press, 1986), p. 116.

192. in July 1971: Fang and Fang, p. 95.

192. sometimes shot: Wenquian, p. 133.

192. Zhou Enlai knew this: Ibid., p. 140.

192. ". . . into the eternal future": Ibid., p. 117.

193. Alberto Korda: "Che Guevara Photographer Dies," *BBC News* (May 26, 2001). Available at: http://news.bbc.co.uk/2/hi/americas/1352650.stm.

193. for the victims: Ibid.

193. ". . . throughout the world," he said: "The Making of an Icon: Forty Years," *Sunday Herald* (Scotland) (October 7, 2007).

194. "most famous photograph in the world": Maryland Institute of Art, referenced at *BBC News*, "Che Guevara Photographer Dies" (May 26, 2001). Available at: http://news.bbc.co.uk/2/hi/americas/1352650.stm.

194. ". . . that serves in this way": Corinna Lotz, "Che as Revolutionary and Icon," *A World to Win*. Available at: http://www.aworldtowin.net/reviews/Che.html.

194. at the end of sentences: Peter McLaren, *Che Guevara, Paulo Freire, and the Pedagogy of Revolution* (New York: Rowman and Littlefield, 2000), p. 127.

194. ". . . of the Irish rebels": I. Lavretsky, *Ernesto Che Guevara*. Translated by A. B. Eklof (Moscow: Victor Kamkin, 1986), p. 17.

195. from an early age: John Lee Anderson, *Che Guevara: A Revolutionary Life* (New York: Grove Press, 1997), p. 22.

195. of those in need: Douglas Kellner, *Ernesto "Che" Guevara* (New York: Chelsea House Publishers [Library Binding edition, 1989]), p. 27.

195. control uncultivated land: Anderson, p. 126.

196. for the United Fruit Company: Kellner, p. 32.

196. as traitors to the revolution: "Castro's Brain," *Time* cover story (August 8, 1960). Available at: http://www.time.com/time/magazine/article/0,9171,869742,00.html

196. joined him six days later: Kellner, p. 13.

197. for the people of Cuba: Anderson, p. 375.

197. second most powerful person in Cuba: Kellner, p. 55.

198. Castro came to power: Brian Latell, "The Fall of Che Guevara and the Changing Face of the Cuban Revolution," CIA Intelligence Memorandum (October 18, 1965). Available at: http://www.gwu.edu/~nsarchiv/NSAEBB/NSAEBB5/.

198. on the United States: Anderson, p. 545.

198. "Great Leap Forward": John Riddell, "Che Guevara's Final Verdict on the Soviet Economy," Center for Research on Globalization (June 13, 2008). Available at: www.globalresearch.ca/index.php?context=va&aid=9315.

199. working poor of the world: Ernesto Guevara, *Che: Selected Works of Ernesto Guevara*. Edited by Rolando E. Bonachea and Nelson P. Valdés (Cambridge, Mass.: MIT Press, 1969), p. 352.

199. ". . . there was nothing for me to do": Kellner, p. 87.

200. U.S. Army Special Forces units: U.S. Army Memorandum of Understanding Concerning the Activation, Organization and Training of the 2d Ranger Battalion—Bolivian Army, April 28, 1967. Available at: http://www.gwu.edu/~nsarchiv/NSAEBB/NSAEBB5/che14_1.htm.

200. ". . . more to you alive than dead": Anderson, p. 733.

200. as if he had been killed in battle: Paco Ignacio Taibo II, *Guevara, Also Known as Che* (New York: St. Martin's Press, 1999), p. 267.

200. ". . . are only going to kill a man!": Juan O. Tamayo, "The Man Who Buried Che," *Miami Herald* (September 19, 1997). Available at: http://www2.fiu.edu/~fcf/cheremains111897.html.

200. ". . . to his ideals or his ideals": "Time 100 Persons of the Century," *Time* (June 14, 1999). Available at: http://www.time.com/time/magazine/article/0,9171,991227,00.html.

Chapter 8: The Truly Evil

201. ". . . We left no survivors": Holy Bible. New International Version, 1984. Deuteronomy Chapter 2, Verse 32.

201. ". . . forgives his followers who slay nonbelievers": Quran, 9:5 and 9:14.

202. ". . . and enjoying a glass of vintage Bordeaux?": Daphne Merkin, "Speak No Evil," *New York Times* (October 21, 2007).

202. "doing his job": Hannah Arendt, *Eichmann in Jerusalem: A Report on the Banality of Evil* (New York: Penguin Classics, 1992).

203. to humble himself: Nancy Rubin Stuart, *Isabella of Castile: The First Renaissance Queen* (Bloomington, Ind.: iUniverse, 2004), p. 205.

204. in his food: Rafael Sabatini, *Torquemada and the Spanish Inquisition a History* (Whitefish, Mont.: Kessinger Publishing, 2003), p. 378.

204. an office he relished: Stuart, p. 205.

204. of the church: John E. Longhurst, *The Age of Torquemada* (Lawrence, Kan.: Coronado Press, 1964), p. 67.

204. was completely destroyed: Deborah Bachrach, *The Inquisition* (Farmington Hills, Mich.: Lucent Books, 1995), p. 49.

204. in the early 1500s: Henry C. Lea, *The Moriscos of Spain: Their Conversion and Expulsion* (Philadelphia: Lea Brothers & Co., 1901), p. 15.

205. granting their request: Simon Whitechapel, *Flesh Inferno: Atrocities of Torquemada and the Spanish Inquisition* (New York: Creation Books, 2003), p. 50.

205. ". . . against Muslims in the east": Ibid.

205. of Christopher Columbus: Beth Tremallo, *Irony and Self-Knowledge in Francisco López de Villalobos* (New York: Garland Publishing, 1991), p. 53.

206. on suspected *marranos*: Whitechapel, p. 56.

206. of a *converso*: Ibid., p. 117.

206. non-Jewish Spaniards: Ibid.

206. leave them alone: Ibid.

206. ". . . Take him and sell him": Charles Herberman, *The Catholic Encyclopedia: an International Work of Reference on the Constitution, Doctrine, Discipline, and History of the Catholic Church*, volume 14 (New York: Robert Appleton Company, 1913), p. 783.

207. they are Jews: Longhurst, p. 122.

207. who took bribes: William Thomas Walsh, *Characters of the Inquisition* (Whitefish, Mont.: Kessinger Publishing, 2007), p. 106.

208. confessons and information: Ibid., p. 347.

208. as grand inquisitor: Michael Ott, "Tomás de Torquemada." *The Catholic Encyclopedia*, volume 14 (New York: Robert Appleton Company, 1912). Available at: http://www.newadvent.org/cathen/14783a.html.

209. ". . . with slow-burning green wood": Beth Randall, "A Regrettable Life: Tomás de Torquemada." Available at: http://www.mcs.drexel.edu/~gbrandal/Illum_html/Torquemada.html.

209. what he considered heresy: Longhurst, p. 78.

210. ". . . with Hitler and Stalin": Whitechapel, p. 7.

210. thirty thousand Jews: Randall, 1996.

210. rode off on horseback: Simon Sebag Montefiore, *Young Stalin* (New York: Alfred Knopf, 2007), pp. 3–9.

212. party purges in the 1930s: Ibid.

212. was only 5–10 million: Glen Garvin, "Fools for Communism." *Reason* (April 2004): Available at: http://reason.com/archives/2004/04/01/fools-for-communism.

212. around the number 20 million: Alexander N. Yakovlev, Anthony Austin, and Paul Hollander. *A Century of Violence in Soviet Russia* (New Haven, Conn.: Yale University Press, 2004), p. 234.

212. of psychologists, historians, and sociologists: Erica Goode, "Stalin to Saddam: So Much for the Madman Theory," *New York Times* (May 4, 2003): Available at: http://www.nytimes.com/2003/05/04/weekinreview/the-world-stalin-to-saddam-so-much-for-the-madman-theory.html.

212. in control of his actions: Roy Medvedev, *Let History Judge: The Origins and Consequences of Stalinism* (New York: Columbia University Press, 1989), p. 544.

213. "trimming your constituency": Konstantin Sonin, "The Dictator's Approach to Electoral Patterns," *Vox Publications* (August 9, 2008). Available at: http://www.voxeu.org/index.php?q=node/1525.

213. undermine potential enemies: Medvedev, p. 545.

214. "It didn't you any harm": William Grimes, "The Dictator as a Young Poet-Thug," New York Times (October 19, 2007): Available at: http://query.nytimes.com/gst/fullpage.html?res=9A02E4DB103DF93AA25753C1A9619C8B63&n=Top/Reference/Times%20Topics/People/G/Grimes,%20William.

214. where students fought in gangs: Montefiore, p. 39.

215. he would later say: Ibid., p. 40.

215. ". . . and years spent in exile": Grimes.

215. of the working class: Ibid.

215. "exactly the kind of person I need": Montefiore, p. 426.

215. the "pockmarked one": Ibid., p. 31.

215. and illegitimate children: Grimes.

216. with the condemnations of violence: Montefiore, p. 174.

216. ". . . of radical celebrity": Ibid., p. 172.

217. of his criminal aliases: Jack Fishman and Bernard Hutton, *The Private Life of Josif Stalin* (London: W. H. Allen, 1962), p. 208.

217. "Jewish Faction": Montefiore, p. 173.

218. "of a nation for Stalin": Ibid., p. 264.

218. more junior Vyacheslav Molotov: Edvard Radzinskii, *Stalin: The First In-Depth Biography Based on Explosive New Documents from Russia's Secret Archives* (New York: Doubleday, 1996), p. 540.

219. Red Baron himself: Robert Wistrich, *Who's Who in Nazi Germany* (The Routledge Who's Who Series) (New York: Routledge, 2001), p. 81.

219. Otto von Bismarck himself: R. J. Overy, *Goering* (New York: Barnes & Noble Publishing, 2003), p. 5.

219. into the ground: Leonard Mosley, *The Reich Marshall: A Biography of Hermann Goering* (New York: Doubleday, 1974), p. 62.

219. that were strangling Germany: Ibid., p. 66.

220. "could assist him in any way": Ibid., p. 69.

220. behind these traitors: Mosley, p. 70.

222. he was very effective: Overy, p. 8.

222. Germany's gloried past: Eberhard Kolb, *The Weimar Republic* (New York: Routledge, 1992), p. 121.

223. in its application: Mosley, p. 165.

223. of the Holocaust: Ben Kiernan, *Blood and Soil: A World History of Genocide and Extermination from Sparta to Darfur* (New Haven, Conn.: Yale University Press, 2009), p. 427.

224. Night of the Long Knives: Gordon Williamson, *The SS: Hitler's Instrument of Terror* (London: Zenith Imprint, 2004), p. 33.

224. a couple of generations: Alan Wykes, *Himmler* (London: Pan Books, 1972), p. 48.

224. had no use for: Jack Fischel, *Historical Dictionary of the Holocaust* (Issue 10 of *Historical Dictionaries of War, Revolution, and Civil Unrest*) (New York: Rowman & Littlefield, 1999), p. 113.

225. ". . . all over the world . . .": Wistrich, p. 113.

225. as "normal": Ernest K. Bramsted, *Dictatorship and Political Police: The Technique of Control by Fear* (New York: AMS Press, 1976), p. 69.

225. most powerful man in Germany: Roger Manvell and Heinrich Fraenkel, *Heinrich Himmler: The Sinister Life of the Head of the SS and Gestapo* (New York: Skyhorse Publishing Inc., 2007), p. 123.

225. over Hitler's thinking: Joachim Fest, *The Face of the Third Reich: Portraits of the Nazi Leadership* (Cambridge, Mass.: Da Capo Press), p. 125.

226. took Hess out of the picture: Ian Kershaw, *Hitler, 1936–45: Nemesis* (New York: W. W. Norton & Company, 2000), p. 378.

226. increase his own power: James McGovern, *Martin Bormann* (New York: Morrow, 1968), p. 63.

226. Goering, Goebbels, and Himmler: Ibid.

226. from his government and party posts: Marshall Dill, *Germany: A Modern History* (Ann Arbor: University of Michigan Press, 1970), p. 421.

227. shot immediately: Peter Calvoressi and Guy Wint, *Total War: Causes and Courses of the Second World War* (New York: Penguin Books, 1972), p. 540.

227. while trying to escape: H. Trevor Roper, *Last Days of Hitler* (London: Pan Books, 1962), p. 245.

227. were ever confirmed: Ladislas Farago, *Aftermath: Martin Bormann and the Fourth Reich* (New York: Simon and Schuster, 1974), p. 43.

227. of Bormann's death: Trevor Roper, p. 246.

227. Nazi hunter Simon Wiesenthal: Charles Whiting, *The Hunt for Martin Bormann* (New York: Ballantine Books, 1973), p. 140.

Chapter 9: The Fixers

228. ". . . sometimes by using dishonest methods": The Longman Dictionary of Contemporary English, available at: http://www.ldoceonline.com/dictionary/fixer.

230. ". . . what the second one is": Bill Moyers and Julie Leininger Pycior, *Moyers on America: A Journalist and His Times*, reprint ed. (New York: Random House, 2005), p. 84.

230. *The Wonderful Wizard of Oz*: Jason Goodwin, Greenback: *The Almighty Dollar and the Invention of America* (New York: Macmillan, 2003), p. 281.

230. not a problem for Hanna: Francis Russell, *The President Makers: From Mark Hanna to Joseph P. Kennedy* (Boston: Little, Brown and Company, 1976), p. 21.

231. bouts of melancholia: Murat Halstead, *The Illustrious Life of William McKinley, Our Martyred President* (New York: American Book & Bible House, 1901), p. 421.

232. ". . . before some of us waked up": Russell, p. 26.

232. in January: Ibid., p. 27.

233. of his life: Ibid., p. 29.

233. of his troops: Howard I. Kushner and Anne Hummel Sherrill, *John Milton Hay: The Union of Poetry and Politics* (New York: Twayne Publishers, 1977), p. 80.

233. was almost twice that: Russell, p. 21.

234. with public speakers: Chauncey Depew, *My Memories of Eighty Years* (Boston: C. Scribner's Sons, 1922), p. 115.

234. ". . . public opinion would never permit it": Ibid.

234. stay-at-home approach: Russell, p. 32.

234. ". . . I have to think when I speak": Ibid.

235. of "McKinley Prosperity": Ibid., p. 33.

235. capitalist monster Mark Hanna: David Nasaw, *The Chief: The Life of William Randolph Hearst* (New York: Houghton Mifflin Harcourt, 2001), p. 154.

235. under his feet: Stephen Hess and Sandy Northrop, *Drawn & Quartered: The History of American Political Cartoons* (New York: Elliott & Clark Publishers, 1996), p. 74.

236. he drew for Hearst: Stephen Scheinberg, *The Development of Corporation Labor Policy, 1900–1940* (Madison, Wisc.: University of Wisconsin Press, 1966), p. 196.

236. he did not covet—senator: Russell, p. 35.

237. approach to organizing political activity: "The Partners." *Time*, December 26, 1955. Available at: http://www.time.com/time/magazine/article/0,9171,807989,00.html.

237. to handily defeat the referendum: Ibid.

238. powerful Hollywood-based movie industry: Greg Mitchell, *The Campaign of the Century: Upton Sinclair's Race for Governor of California and the Birth of Media Politics* (New York: Random House, 1992), p. 86.

238. by more than 300,000 votes: Ibid.

238. "... put on a show": Sheldon Rampton and John Stauber, *Banana Republicans: How the Right Wing is Turning America into a One-Party State* (Tarcher/Penguin, 2004), p. 142.

239. more the day-to-day executive than Clem: "The Partners." *Time* (December 26, 1955).

239. "... of modern advertising": Ibid.

240. Larry O'Brien: Michael O'Brien, *John F. Kennedy: A Biography* (New York: Macmillan, 2006), p. 242.

241. as the "Irish Mafia": "The Man on the Hill." *Time* cover story (September 1, 1961). Available at: http://www.time.com/time/magazine/article/0,9171,939804-1,00.html.

241. getting out the vote: Ibid.

241. parting of the ways: Ibid.

241. committed Kennedy fund-raisers: Ibid.

242. "... any amateur could understand": Ibid.

242. host of other Kennedy staffers: O'Brien, p. 428.

242. "the best election man in the business": *Time* (September 1, 1961).

243. for Kennedy's team: Sally B. Smith, *Grace and Power: The Private World of the Kennedy White House* (New York: Random House, 2005), p. 172.

243. Nuclear Test Ban Treaty: Ed Magnuson, "Honorable Profession," *Time* (January 6, 1975): Available at: http://www.time.com/time/magazine/article/0,9171,912673-1,00.html.

243. persuaded him to stay on: Albin Krebs, "Lawrence O'Brien, Democrat, Dies at 73," *New York Times* (September 29, 1990). Available at: http://www.nytimes.com/1990/09/29/obituaries/lawrence-o-brien-democrat-dies-at-73.html.

243. Watergate office complex in 1972: Stanley Kutler, *The Wars of Watergate: The Last Crisis of Richard Nixon* (New York: W. W. Norton & Company, 1992), p. 204.

243. organizational needs: Ibid.

244. was not Camelot: Magnuson.

244. by the 1980s: David L. Porter, *Basketball: A Biographical Dictionary* (Westport, Conn.: Greenwood Press, 2005), p. 359.

245. into "warmth" and confidence: Joe McGinnis, *The Selling of the President 1968* (New York: Trident Press, 1969), p. 103.

245. Joseph Coors Foundation: Stanhope Gould, "Coors Brews the News," *Columbia Journalism Review* (March/April 1975): 29.

245. when responding to questions: Roger Ailes, *You Are the Message* (New York: Dow Jones-Irwin, 1988), p. 19.

245. "... my opponent's youth and inexperience": Ibid.

246. 1988 Democratic nominee: Thomas Sweitzer, "Kill or Be Killed," *Campaigns & Elections*, volume 17, Issue, 9 (September 1, 1996): 46.

246. actually produced the ad: "Inquiry of Willie Horton Ad Ends without FEC Reaching Judgment," *Los Angeles Times* (January 17, 1992). Available at: http://articles.latimes. com/1992-01-17/news/mn-289_1_willie-horton-political-ad.

247. became a campaign issue. T. R. Reid, "Negative Ad Wizard Becomes Part of the Issue," *Washington Post* (May 9, 1988): page A6. Archived article available here: http://pqasb. pqarchiver.com/washingtonpost/access/8395518.html?FMT=ABS&FMTS=ABS&date=Ma y+9%2C+1989&author=Reid%2C+T+R&pub=The+Washington+Post&startpage=A6&desc= Negative+Ad+Wizard+Becomes+Part+of+the+Issue.

247. edged out by network rivals: Bill Carter, "Ailes Steps Down as Head of CNBC Cable Channel," *New York Times* (January 19, 1996). Available at: http://www.nytimes. com/1996/01/19/business/the-media-business-ailes-steps-down-as-head-of-cnbc-cable-channel.html?scp=1&sq=ailes%20steps%20down%20as%20head%20of%20cnbc%20 cabloe%20channel&st=cse.

247. ". . . Alabama in between": Adam Pertman, "Clinton Hires Key Aide in Pennsylvania Race," *Boston Globe* (December 3, 1991). Archived article available at: http://pqasb. pqarchiver.com/boston/access/59293820.html?FMT=ABS&FMTS=ABS:FT&type=current &date=Dec+3%2C+1991&author=Adam+Pertman%2C+Globe+Staff&pub=Boston+Globe+ %28pre-1997+Fulltext%29&edition=&startpage=69&desc=Clinton+hires+key+aide+in+Pe nnsylvania+race.

247. (on Barack Obama's likely winning the White House): CNN: Election Night in America, October 7, 2008.

248. wasn't good at it: James Carville and Paul Begala, Buck Up, Suck Up . . . and Come Back When You Foul Up: 12 Winning Secrets from the War Room (New York: Simon and Schuster, 2003), p. 21.

248. U.S. Senate campaign in Texas, and lost: Ibid., p. 22.

248. Scranton's broken pledge: Ibid., p. 24.

249. forty points in some polls: Ibid.

250. number of other countries: The Office of James Carville. Available at: http://www. carville.info.

250. ". . . your fist in their face": Sweitzer, p. 47.

250. as a strategist: Ron Suskind, "Why Are These Men Laughing?" *Esquire* (January 1, 2003). Available at http://www.esquire.com/features/ESQ0103-JAN_ROVE_rev_2.

250. in American politics: Jacob Weisberg, "Karl Rove's Dying Dream," Slate.com (November 1, 2005). Available at: http://www.slate.com/id/2129292/.

251. as a Watergate conspirator: James Ridgeway, "Grime Pays," *Village Voice* (July 12, 2005): Available at: http://www.villagevoice.com/2005-07-12/news/grime-pays/.

251. not to get caught: Julian Borger, "The Brains," *Guardian* (March 9, 2004): http://www. guardian.co.uk/world/2004/mar/09/uselections2004.usa1.

251. state treasurer of Illinois: Dan Balz, "Karl Rove the Strategist," *Washington Post* (July 23, 1999): http://www.washingtonpost.com/wp-srv/politics/campaigns/wh2000/stories/ rove072399.htm.

251. ". . . and a good time for nothing": Borger.

251. "bigger fish to fry": David Talbot, "Creepier Than Nixon," Salon.com (March 31, 2004): http://dir.salon.com/news/feature/2004/03/31/dean/index.html.

251. ". . . you know, wow": Borger.

251. to Ronald Reagan: Robert Bryce, "The Can't-Miss Kid," *Austin Chronicle* (June 1, 1999): http://weeklywire.com/ww/06-01-99/austin_pols_feature1.html.

252. his chief of staff: Ibid.

252. sway last-minute voters: Borger.

252. as early as 1989: Bryce.

252. work a room: Ibid.

253. ". . . with a prostitute": Suskind.

253. John Dilulio: Ibid.

254. uranium from Africa: Russ Hoyle, "Foreword: The Niger Affair: The Investigation That Won't Go Away." In Joseph C. Wilson, IV, *The Politics of Truth: Inside the Lies That Put the White House on Trial and Betrayed My Wife's CIA Identity: A Diplomat's Memoir*, rev. ed. (New York: Carroll & Graf Publishers, 2005), pp. xiii–xlix.

254. was a CIA agent: CNN.com, "Novak: Rove Confirmed Plame's Identity" (July 11, 2006): http://articles.cnn.com/2006-07-11/politics/cia.leak_1_robert-novak-randall-samborn-leak-probe?_s=PM:POLITICS.

254. "fair game": Hoyle.

Chapter 10: Schemers

256. will not bow down to him: Emil Hirsch, M. Seligsohn, and Solomon Schechter, "Haman the Agagite," *Jewish Encyclopedia* (New York: Funk & Wagnalls, 1907), pp. 189–190. Available at: http://jewishencyclopedia.com/view.jsp?artid=156&letter=H.

256. serious transgresson of Jewish law: Yassachar Rubin, *Sefer Talele orot*. Translated by Gershon Robinson (Nanuet, NY: Feldheim Publishers, 2003), p. 169.

257. public execution of Mordechai: Ibid.

257. Esther's Jewish heritage: Book of Esther, Chapter 2, Jewish Virtual Library. Available at: http://www.jewishvirtuallibrary.org/jsource/Bible/Esther2.html.

258. how down to him: William Keddie, ed., *The Sabbath* school magazine (Glasgow, Scotland: Glasgow Sabbath School Union, 1875).

259. 300 were killed in Shushan: The Holy Bible, edition 24 (New York, American Bible Society, 1884), p. 426.

259. St. Patrick's Day: Ari Goldman, *Being Jewish: The Spiritual and Cultural Practice of Judaism Today* (New York: Simon and Schuster, 2007), p. 151.

259. "blot out the name of Haman": Stephen Binz, *Feasts of Judaism* (Threshold Bible Study Series) (New London, Conn.: Twenty-Third Publications, 2006), p. 93.

259. very likely fictional: Goldman, p. 149.

259. biblical and rabbinic scholars today: Abraham J. Arnold and Käthe Roth, *Judaism: Myth, Legend, History and Custom: From the Religious to the Secular* (Montreal: R. Davies Publishing, 1995), p. 176.

260. to the decree of Artaxerxes II: Wesley J. Fuerst, *The Books of Ruth, Esther, Ecclesiastes, the Song of Songs, Lamentations: The Five Scrolls* (Cambridge Bible Commentaries on the Old Testament) (London: Cambridge University Press Archive, 1975), p. 38.

260. "Haman as merciless enemy": Elaine Rose Glickman, *Haman and the Jews: A Portrait from Rabbinic Literature* (New York: Rowman & Littlefield, 1999), p. xii.

261. treachery, incest and murder: Anthony Barrett, *Agrippina: Sex, Power, and Politics in the Early Empire* (New Haven, Conn.: Yale University Press, 1999), p. xii.

261. worthy of serious study: Ibid.

262. met an untimely death in AD 20: Robert Ferguson, *Reading the Early Republic* (Boston: Harvard University Press, 2006), p. 184.

262. always colorful and creative Caligula: "Agrippina the Younger," *Encyclopedia of World Biography*, (2004): http://www.encyclopedia.com/topic/Agrippina_Minor.aspx.

262. good cause for worry: Barrett, p. 31.

262. even plotting against him: Miriam Griffin, *Nero: The End of a Dynasty* (Roman Imperial Biographies Series) (New York: Routledge, 2000), p. 25.

263. in her dishes: Seymour Van Santvoord, *The House of Caesar and the Imperial Disease* (Troy, N.Y.: Pafraets Book Co., 1902), p. 145.

263. "and remarkably dishonest": "Agrippina the Younger," *Encyclopedia of World Biography*.

263. incestuous relationship: Barrett, p. 214.

263. name his favorite horse a consul: Anthony Everitt, *Augustus: The Life of Rome's First Emperor* (New York: Random House, 2006), p. 322.

264. two years later in AD 41: Ibid.

264. to later succeed Nero as emperor: Judith Ginsburg, *Representing Agrippina: Constructions of Female Power in the Early Roman Empire* (New York: Oxford University Press, 2006), p. 16.

264. Claudius and his son Britannicus: Ibid.

264. public relations triumph: Barrett, p. 102.

265. Claudius, was married: Ibid.

265. owed his promotion to Agrippina: Griffin, p. 30.

265. ". . . complete control over Claudius": Cassius Dio, *Dio's Rome*, volume 4 (Whitefish, Mont.: Kessinger Publishing, 2004), p. 178.

265. during her husband's lifetime: Barbara Levick, *Claudius* (New Haven, Conn.: Yale University Press, 1993), p. 71.

265. ". . . greeted ambassadors": Ibid.

265. ". . . nor chastity": Levick, p. 75.

265. more power than Claudius himself: Ernest Carey, ed., *Dio's Roman History* (volume 8 of *Dio Cassius Roman History*) (Boston: Harvard University Press, 1982), p. 21.

266. of Nero and Britannicus: Barrett, p. 118.

266. among some Roman officials: Veronika Grimm-Samuel, "On the Mushroom That Defied the Emperor Claudius," *Classical Quarterly* 41 (1991: 178–182).

267. ". . . provided he becomes emperor": Barrett, p. 56.

266. ". . . [of swearing allegiance to a woman]": Ibid.

267. separate, lower seat: "Agrippina the Younger," *Encyclopedia of World Biography*.

267. her allegiance to Britannicus: Griffin, p. 69.

267. hold his loyalty: Barrett, p. 214.

267. against common poisons: Ibid.

268. his mother's wrath: Ibid., p. 187.

268. in the bedroom of her villa: Ibid.

268. the events of those years: Ronald Mellor, *Tacitus* (New York: Routledge, 1994), p. 75.

268. ". . . but at least impeded": David Shotter, *Nero* (New York: Routledge, 2005), p. 53.

269. to the throne: John Carmi Parsons, "The Year of Eleanor of Castile's Birth and Her Children by Edward I," *Medieval Studies XLVI* (1984): 245–265.

269. of a cream puff: P. C. Doherty, *Isabella and the Strange Death of Edward II* (New York: Carroll & Graf Publishers, 2003), p. 98.

270. had wives and produced offspring: Pierre Chaplais, *Piers Gaveston: Edward II's Adoptive Brother* (London: Oxford University Press, 1994), p. 7.

270. in Gascony, Anjou, and Normandy: Doherty, p. 17.

270. only aggravated the situation: Allison Weir, *Queen Isabella: Treachery, Adultery, and Murder in Medieval England* (New York: Ballantine Books, 2005), p. 42.

271. and their wealth: John Sadler, *Border Fury: England and Scotland at War, 1296–1568* (New York: Pearson/Longman, 2005), p. 159.

271. in the Tower: Ian Mortimer, *The Greatest Traitor: The Life of Sir Roger Mortimer, Ruler of England, 1327–1330* (New York: Macmillan, 2006), p. 126.

271. escaped to France in 1323: Ibid., p. 131.

272. in March 1325: Ibid., p. 139.

272. were removed from power: Ronald H. Fritze and William Baxter Robison, *Historical Dictionary of Late Medieval England, 1272–1485* (Westport, Conn.: Greenwood Publishing Group, 2002), p. 177.

273. his order was ignored: Mortimer, p. 146.

273. marching south to join Mortimer: Henry Hartwright, *The Story of the House of Lancaster* (London: E. Stock, 1897), p. 13.

273. make a defense in Despenser's lands: Mortimer, p. 154.

273. took them into custody: Weir, p. 243.

274. insulting the queen: Mortimer, p. 159.

274. ". . . unbecoming to a monarch": Leslie Carroll, *Royal Affairs: A Lusty Romp Through the Extramarital Adventures That Rocked the British Monarchy* (New York: Penguin Group, 2008), p. 36.

274. on January 25, 1327: Ibid.

274. he would become ill and die: *The Medical Times and Gazette*, volume 2 (London: J. & A. Churchill, 1875), p. 180.

274. he had died of natural causes: Weir, p. 285.

274. as means of execution: Dulcie Ashdown, *Royal Murders: Hatred, Revenge and the Seizing of Power* (London: Sutton Publishing, 1998), p. 25.

274. so their objectivity is in doubt: Weir, p. 452.

274. out his life in hiding: Mortimer, p. 255; Weir, p. 290.

275. of the excesses of the Despensers: Sir Charles W. C. Oman, *A History of England* (New York: Henry Holt, 1900), p. 180.

275. taken into custody: Ibid.

275. ". . . on gentle Mortimer!": Jonathan Sumption, *The Hundred Years War: Trial by Battle* (Philadelphia: University of Pennsylvania Press, 1999), p. 115.

275. as a traitor in November 1330: Ibid.

275. at Castle Rising in Norfolk: Ibid.

275. at Gloucester Cathedral: Doherty, p. 215.

276. when he was thrown in the water: Brian Moynahan, *Rasputin: The Saint Who Sinned* (Cambridge, Mass.: Da Capo Press, 1999), p. 340.

276. as to its validity: Ibid., p. 331.

276. how he was killed: "Rasputin Assassinated by British Secret Service—BBC Timewatch Documentary," BBC Press Office (September 19, 2004).

277. Oswald Rayner: Andrew Cook, *To Kill Rasputin: The Life and Death of Grigori Rasputin* (London: Tempus, 2005), p. 79.

277. ". . . the Russians in the East": BBC Timewatch documentary.

277. where he spent three years: Edvard Radzinsky, *The Rasputin File* (New York: Anchor Books, 2001), p. 119.

278. by the Orthodox Church: Ibid., p. 102.

278. during crisis or war: Moynahan, p. 32.

278. "Great sins made possible great repentances": Bernard Pares, "Rasputin and the Empress: Authors of the Russian Collapse," *Foreign Affairs*, volume 6, No. 1 (October 1927): p. 140–154.

278. but eventually all of Russia: Joseph Fuhrmann, *Rasputin: A Life* (Westport, Conn.: Praeger, 1990), p. 28.

279. were very close to the tsar's family: James Minney, *Rasputin* (London: Cassell, 1972), p. 42.

279. were common knowledge: Moynahan, p. 116.

279. spiritual advisor to Alexandra: Colin Wilson, *The Occult: A History* (New York: Random House, 1971), p. 379.

279. on multiple occasions: Moynahan, p. 102.

279. and induce relaxation): Sandra Blakeslee, "This Is Your Brain Under Hypnosis," *New York Times* (November 22, 2005): http://query.nytimes.com/gst/fullpage.html?res=9E06E0DB1F3E F931A15752C1A9639C8B63.

279. of a miracle worker: Minney, p. 46.

280. with the Germans: Mary Priscilla Roberts, *World War I* (Santa Barbara, Calif.: ABC-CLIO, 2006), p. 2376.

280. extended to the tsar: Ibid.

280. say yes or no: Moynahan, p. 116.

281. against the royal family: Jonathan Smele, *The Russian Revolution and Civil War, 1917–1921: An Annotated Bibliography* (Continuum Studies in History). (London: Continuum International Publishing Group, 2006, p. 114).

BIBLIOGRAPHY

Books and Journal Articles

Abbott, W. C., ed. *Writings and Speeches of Oliver Cromwell,* 4 volumes, 1937–1947. Boston: President and Fellows of Harvard College, reissued 1988.

Adamson, John. "Oliver Cromwell and the Long Parliament." In Morrill, John (ed.), *Oliver Cromwell and the English Revolution.* New York. Longman, 1990.

Ailes, Roger. *You Are the Message.* New York: Dow Jones-Irwin, 1988.

Aksan, Virginia, and Daniel Goffman. *The Early Modern Ottomans: Remapping the Empire.* Cambridge: Cambridge University Press, 2007.

Albrecht, M. von, and G. L. Schmeling. *A History of Roman Literature: From Livius Andronicus to Boethius: With Special Regard to Its Influence on World Literature.* London, 1996.

American Heritage Dictionary of the English Language. New York: Houghton Mifflin Company, 2009.

Amrani, Issandr. "Egypt's Next Strongman," *Foreign Policy* (August 17, 2009).

Anderson, Jack, and James Boyd. *Confessions of a Muckraker.* New York: Ballantine Books, 1980.

Anderson, Jon Lee. *Che Guevara: A Revolutionary Life.* New York: Grove Press, 1997.

Archer, Thomas. *The Crusade of Richard I, 1189–92.* New York: G. P. Putnam's Sons, 1889.

Arendt, Hannah. *Eichmann in Jerusalem: A Report on the Banality of Evil.* New York: Penguin Classics, 1992.

Arnold, Abraham J., and Käthe Roth. *Judaism: Myth, Legend, History and Custom: From the Religious to the Secular.* Montreal: R. Davies Publishing, 1995.

Ashdown, Dulcie. *Royal Murders: Hatred, Revenge and the Seizing of Power.* London: Sutton Pub., 1998.

Asher, Michael. *Lawrence: The Uncrowned King of Arabia.* New York. The Overlook Press, 1998.

Ashley, Maurice. *The Greatness of Oliver Cromwell.* New York: Macmillan, 1958.

Bachrach, Deborah. *The Inquisition.* Farmington Hills, Mich.: Lucent Books, 1995.

Barr, Stringfellow. *Mazzini: Portrait of an Exile.* New York: Henry Holt and Company, 1935.

Barrett, Anthony. *Agrippina: Sex, Power, and Politics in the Early Empire.* New Haven, Conn.: Yale University Press, 1999.

Belloc, Hillaire. *Richelieu: A Study,* 2nd ed. New York: J. B. Lippincott Company, 1929.

Benigni, Umberto. "Nicolò Machiavelli," *The Catholic Encyclopedia,* volume 9. New York: Robert Appleton Company, 1910.

Bernard, J. F. *Talleyrand: A Biography.* New York: G. P. Putnam's Sons, 1973.

Binz, Stephen. *Feasts of Judaism* (Threshold Bible Study Series). New London, Conn.: Twenty-Third Publications, 2006.

Bix, Herbert. *Hirohito and the Making of Modern Japan.* New York: HarperCollins, 2001.

Blennerhassett, Lady. *Talleyrand,* volume 2. Translated by Frederick Clarke. Whitefish, Mont.: Kessinger Publishing, 2005.

Boesche, Roger. "Kautilya's Arthasastra on War and Diplomacy in Ancient India." *Journal of Military History* 67, no. 1 (January 2003): 9–37.

Bramsted, Ernest K. *Dictatorship and Political Police: The Technique of Control by Fear.* New York: AMS Press, 1976.

Brennan, T. *The Praetorship in the Roman Republic,* volume 1. London: Oxford University Press, 2000.

Browne, Courtney. *TOJO, the Last Banzai.* Cambridge, Mass: Da Capo Press, 1998.

Browning, Robert. *Justinian and Theodora.* Piscataway, New Jersey: Gorgias Press, 2003.

Buckingham, Peter. *Woodrow Wilson: A Bibliography of his Times and Presidency.* Wilmington, Del.: Scholarly Resources, 1990.

Budiansky, Stephen. *Her Majesty's Spymaster: Elizabeth I, Sir Francis Walsingham, and the Birth of Modern Espionage.* New York: The Penguin Group, 2005.

Buranelli, Vincent, and Nan Buranelli. *Spy/Counter-Spy: An Encyclopedia of Espionage.* New York: McGraw-Hill, 1982.

Bury, John B. *The Cambridge Medieval History,* volume 2. New York: Macmillan, 1913.

Bush, George W. *A Charge to Keep.* New York: HarperCollins, 1999.

Butow, Robert J. C. *Tojo and the Coming of the War.* Palo Alto, Calif.: Stanford University Press, 1961.

Calvoressi, Peter, and Guy Wint. *Total War: Causes and Courses of the Second World War.* New York: Penguin Books, 1972.

Cantor, Norman. *The Civilization of the Middle Ages.* New York: Harper Perennial, 1994.

Cardini, Franco. *Europe and Islam.* New York: Wiley-Blackwell, 2001.

Carey, Ernest, ed. *Dio's Roman History* (volume 8 of *Dio Cassius Roman History*). Boston: Harvard University Press, 1982.

Carroll, Leslie. *Royal Affairs: A Lusty Romp through the Extramarital Adventures That Rocked the British Monarchy.* New York: Penguin Group, 2008.

Carville, James, and Paul Begala. *Buck Up, Suck Up . . . and Come Back When You Foul Up: 12 Winning Secrets from the War Room.* New York: Simon and Schuster, 2003.

Cesaretti, Paolo. *Theodora: Empress of Byzantium.* Paris: Vendome Press, 2004.

Chaplais, Pierre. *Piers Gaveston: Edward II's Adoptive Brother.* London: Oxford University Press, 1994.

Chernow, Ron. *Alexander Hamilton.* New York: Penguin, 2004.

Clot, Andre. *Suleiman the Magnificent.* New York: New Amsterdam Press, 1992.

Cook, Andrew. *To Kill Rasputin: The Life and Death of Grigori Rasputin.* London: Tempus, 2005.

Cooper, Duff. *Talleyrand.* Palo Alto, Calif.: Stanford University Press, 1932.

Cooper, John Milton. *The Warrior and the Priest: Woodrow Wilson and Theodore Roosevelt.* Boston: Harvard University Press, 1983.

Courtney, W. L., ed. *The Fortnightly Review,* volume 111. New York: Chapman and Hall, 1919.

Cowell, Frank. *Cicero and the Roman Republic.* New York: Penguin Books, 1956.

De Bary, William. *Sources of Japanese Tradition,* volume 2. Compiled by William De Bary, Carol Gluck, and Arthur E. Tiedemann. New York: Columbia University Press, 2006.

Deutscher, Isaac. *The Prophet Armed: Trotsky, 1879–1921.* London: Oxford University Press, 1954.

Diehl, Charles. "Theodora," *Imperatrice de Byzance.* Paris: 1904.

Dill, Marshall. *Germany: A Modern History.* Ann Arbor: University of Michigan Press, 1970.

Dio, Cassius. *Dio's Rome,* volume 4. Whitefish, Mont.: Kessinger Publishing, 2004.

Doherty, P. C. *Isabella and the Strange Death of Edward II.* New York: Carroll & Graf Publishers, 2003.

"Esther," *The Universal Jewish Encyclopedia,* volume 4. New York: The Universal Jewish Encyclopedia Inc., 1941.

Evans, Gillian R. *Bernard of Clairvaux (Great Medieval Thinkers).* New York: Oxford University Press, 2000.

Evans, James Allan. *The Empress Theodora: Partner of Justinian.* Austin: University of Texas Press, 2003.

———. *Procopius.* New York: Twayne Publishers, 1972.

Everitt, Anthony. *Cicero: The Life and Times of Rome's Greatest Politician.* New York: Random House, 2003.

———. *Augustus: The Life of Rome's First Emperor.* New York: Random House, 2006.

Eyck, Erich. *Bismarck and the German Empire.* New York: W. W. Norton and Company, 1964.

Fagniez, Gustave Charles. *Le Père Joseph et Richelieu (1577–1638).* Paris: Librairie Hachette, 1894.

Fang, Percy Jucheng, and Lucy Guinong Fang. *Zhou Enlai: A Profile.* San Francisco: Foreign Language Press, 1986.

Farago, Ladislas. *Aftermath: Martin Bormann and the Fourth Reich.* New York: Simon and Schuster, 1974.

Farley, James A. *Behind the Ballots: The Personal History of a Politician.* New York: Harcourt, Brace and Company, 1938.

Ferguson, Robert. *Reading the Early Republic.* Boston: Harvard University Press, 2006.

Fest, Joachim. *The Face of the Third Reich: Portraits of the Nazi Leadership.* Cambridge, Mass.: Da Capo Press.

Feuchtwanger, E. J. *Bismarck: Routledge Historical Biographies.* New York: Routledge, 2002.

Fischel, Jack. *Historical Dictionary of the Holocaust* (issue 10 of *Historical Dictionaries of War, Revolution, and Civil Unrest*). New York: Rowman & Littlefield, 1999.

Fishman, Jack, and Bernard Hutton. *The Private Life of Josif Stalin.* London: W. H. Allen, 1962.

Fleming, Thomas. *Duel: Alexander Hamilton, Aaron Burr, and the Future of America.* New York: Basic Books, 1999.

Forrester, Duncan B. "Kamaraj: A Study in Percolation of Style." *Modern Asian Studies,* 4, no. 1 (1970):43–61.

Frischauer, Paul. *Garibaldi: The Man and the Nation.* Whitefish, Mont.: Kessinger Publishing, 2006.

Fritze, Ronald, and William Baxter Robison. *Historical Dictionary of Late Medieval England, 1272–1485.* Westport, Conn.: Greenwood Publishing Group, 2002.

Fuerst, Wesley J. *The Books of Ruth, Esther, Ecclesiastes, the Song of Songs, Lamentations: The Five Scrolls* (Cambridge Bible Commentaries on the Old Testament). London: Cambridge University Press Archive, 1975.

Fuhrmann, Joseph. *Rasputin: A Life.* Westport, Conn.: Praeger, 1990.

Gardiner, Samuel R. *Oliver Cromwell.* London: Longmans, Green and Company, 1901.

Garibaldi, G., and Alexandre Dumas. *Garibaldi: An Autobiography.* Translated by William Robson. New York: Routledge, 1861.

Garland, Lynda. *Byzantine Empresses: Women and Power in Byzantium, AD 527–1204.* New York: CRC Press, 1999.

Garvin, Glen. "Fools for Communism." *Reason* (April 2004).

Gaunt, Peter. *Oliver Cromwell.* New York: Wiley-Blackwell, 1997.

Gauss, Christian. *The Prince by Niccolo Machiavelli.* New York: Signet Classics, 1960.

Gellman, Barton. *Angler: The Cheney Vice Presidency.* New York: Penguin Press HC, 2008.

Gibbon, Edward. *The Decline and Fall of the Roman Empire* (Modern Library Paperback Edition). New York: Random House, 2003.

Gildas, Marie. "St. Bernard of Clairvaux." *The Catholic Encyclopedia,* volume 2. New York: McGraw-Hill, 1996.

Ginsburg, Judith. *Representing Agrippina: Constructions of Female Power in the Early Roman Empire.* New York: Oxford University Press, 2006.

Glickman, Elaine Rose. *Haman and the Jews: A Portrait From Rabbinic Literature.* New York: Rowman & Littlefield, 1999.

Goldman, Ari. *Being Jewish: The Spiritual and Cultural Practice of Judaism Today.* New York: Simon and Schuster, 2007.

Gooch, John. *Unification of Italy* (Lancaster Pamphlets). New York: Routledge, 2002.

Goodwin, Jason. *Greenback: The Almighty Dollar and the Invention of America.* New York: Macmillan, 2003.

Gordon, C. D. *The Age of Attila: Fifth-Century Byzantium and the Barbarians.* Ann Arbor: University of Michigan Press, 1960.

Griffin, Miriam. *Nero: The End of a Dynasty* (Roman Imperial Biographies Series). New York: Routledge, 2000.

Grimm-Samuel, Veronika. "On the Mushroom that Defied the Emperor Claudius." *Classical Quarterly* 41 (1991, p. 178–182).

Guerzoni, Giuseppe. *Garibaldi: Con Documenti Editi e Inediti.* Florence, 1882.

Guevara, Ernesto. *Che: Selected Works of Ernesto Guevara.* Edited by Rolando E. Bonachea and Nelson P. Valdés. Cambridge, Mass.: MIT Press, 1969.

Haaren, John Henry. *Famous Men of the Middle Ages.* New York: University Publishing Company, 1904.

Halstead, Murat. *The Illustrious Life of William McKinley, Our Martyred President.* New York: American Book & Bible House, 1901.

Hanson, Victor Davis. *Carnage and Culture: Landmark Battles in the Rise of Western Power.* New York: Doubleday, 2001.

Harper, John Lamberton. *American Machiavelli: Alexander Hamilton and the Origins of U.S. Foreign Policy.* Cambridge, UK: Cambridge University Press, 2004.

Harris, Robin. *Talleyrand: Betrayer and Savior of France.* New York: John Murray Publishers, 2007.

Hartwright, Henry. *The Story of the House of Lancaster.* London: E. Stock, 1897.

Hayes, Stephen. *Cheney: The Untold Story of America's Most Powerful and Controversial Vice President.* New York: HarperCollins, 2007.

Herberman. Charles. *The Catholic Encyclopedia: An International Work of Reference on the Constitution, Doctrine, Discipline, and History of the Catholic Church,* volume 14. New York: Robert Appleton Company, 1913.

Hess, Stephen, and Sandy Northrop. *Drawn & Quartered: The History of American Political Cartoons.* New York: Elliott & Clark Pub, 1996.

Hirsch, Emil, M. Seligsohn, and Solomon Schechter. "Haman the Agagite." *Jewish Encyclopedia.*

Hodgson, Godfrey. *Woodrow Wilson's Right Hand: The Life of Colonel Edward M. House.* New Haven, Conn.: Yale University Press, 2006.

———."The Schrippenfest Incident." *History Today* 53, no. 7 (July 2003): p. 47.

Holy Bible containing the Old and New Testaments: translated out of the original tongues and with the former translations diligently compared and revised Edition 24. New York: American Bible Society, 1884.

Hopkirk, Peter. *Like Hidden Fire: The Plot to Bring Down the British Empire.* New York: Kodansha Globe, 1997.

Hoyle, Russ. "The Niger Affair: The Investigation That Won't Go Away," "Foreword" (xiii-xlix). In Joseph C. Wilson, IV, *The Politics of Truth: Inside the Lies That Put the White House on Trial and Betrayed My Wife's CIA Identity: A Diplomat's Memoir,* rev. ed. New York: Carroll & Graf Publishers, 2005.

Hutchins, Robert. "Great Books of the Western World," volume 40. *Encyclopedia Britannica,* 1952.

Hutchinson, Robert. *Elizabeth's Spymaster: Francis Walsingham and the Secret War that Saved England.* New York: Macmillan, 2007.

Huxley, Aldous. *L'Eminence Grise.* New York: Meridian Books, 1959.

Ingersoll, David E. "The Constant Prince: Private Interests and Public Goals in Machiavelli." *Western Political Quarterly* 21 (December 1968): 588–596.

Jansen, Marius B. *Sakamoto Ryoma and the Meiji Restoration.* New York: Columbia University Press, 1994.

Kaid, Lynda Lee. *Encyclopedia of Political Communication,* volume 1. Thousand Oaks, Calif.: Sage, 2008.

Karnow, Stanley. *In Our Image: America's Empire in the Philippines.* New York: Random House, 1989.

Kellner, Douglas. *Ernesto "Che" Guevara.* New York: Chelsea House Publishers, 1989.

Kendall, Paul Murray. *Warwick the Kingmaker.* New York: W. W. Norton and Company, 1957.

Kenyon, John, and Ohlmeyer, Jane, eds. *The Civil Wars: A Military History of England, Scotland, and Ireland, 1638–1660.* London: Oxford University Press, 2000.

Kershaw, Ian. *Hitler, 1936–45: Nemesis.* New York: W. W. Norton & Company, 2000.

———. *Fateful Choices: Ten Decisions that Changed the World, 1940–1941.* New York: Penguin Group, 2007.

Kiernan, Ben. *Blood and Soil: A World History of Genocide and Extermination from Sparta to Darfur.* New Haven, Conn.: Yale University Press, 2009.

Kitson, Frank. *Old Ironsides: The Military Biography of Oliver Cromwell.* London: Phoenix Press, 2007.

Knecht, R. J. *Catherine de' Medici.* London and New York: Longman, 1998.

Kolb, Eberhard. *The Weimar Republic.* New York: Routledge, 1992.

Kushner, Howard, and Anne Hummel Sherrill. *John Milton Hay: The Union of Poetry and Politics.* New York: Twayne Publishers, 1977.

Kutler, Stanley. *The Wars of Watergate: The Last Crisis of Richard Nixon.* New York: W. W. Norton & Company, 1992.

Lane-Pool, Stanley. *Saladin and the Fall of the Kingdom of Jerusalem.* New York: G. P. Putnam's Sons, 1906.

Lavretsky, I. *Ernesto Che Guevara.* Translated by A. B. Eklof. Moscow: Victor Kamkin, 1986.

Lawday, David. *Napoleon's Master: A Life of Prince Talleyrand.* New York: Macmillan, 2007.

Lawrence, T. E. *Seven Pillars of Wisdom: A Triumph.* New York: Doubleday, 1966.

Lea, Henry C. *The Moriscos of Spain: Their Conversion and Expulsion.* Philadelphia: Lea Brothers & Co., 1901.

Lee, Chae-Jin. *Zhou Enlai: The Early Years.* Palo Alto, Calif.: Stanford University Press, 1996.

Le Glay, Marcel, Jean-Louis Voisin, and Yann Le Bohec. *A History of Rome.* New York: Wiley-Blackwell, 2005.

Levi, Anthony. *Cardinal Richelieu: and the Making of France.* New York: Carroll & Graf, 2002.

Levick, Barbara. *Claudius.* New Haven, Conn.: Yale University Press, 1993.

Levin, Phyllis Lee. *Edith and Woodrow: The Wilson White House.* New York: Simon and Schuster, 2001.

Lodge, Sir Richard. *Richelieu.* New York: Macmillan and Co., Ltd., 1896.

Longhurst, John E. *The Age of Torquemada.* Lawrence, Kan.: Coronado Press, 1964.

Loth, Vincent. "Armed Incidents and Unpaid Bills: Anglo-Dutch Rivalry in the Banda Islands in the Seventeenth Century." *Modern Asian Studies* 29, no. 4 (1995): 705–740.

Lyber, Albert Howe. *The Government of the Ottoman Empire in the Time of Suleiman the Magnificent.* Cambridge, Mass.: Harvard University Press, 1913.

Manvell, Roger, and Heinrich Fraenkel. *Heinrich Himmler: The Sinister Life of the Head of the SS and Gestapo.* New York: Skyhorse Publishing Inc., 2007.

Martindale, John R., ed. *The Prosopography of the Later Roman Empire,* volume II, A.D. 395–527. Cambridge, Mass., 1980.

Masselman, George. "Dutch Colonial Policy in the Seventeenth Century." *Journal of Economic History* 21, no. 4 (December 1961): 455.

McDonald, Forrest. *Alexander Hamilton: A Biography.* New York: W. W. Norton and Company, 1982.

McGinnis, Joe. *The Selling of the President 1968.* New York: Trident Press, 1969.

McGovern, James. *Martin Bormann.* New York: Morrow, 1968.

McLaren, Peter. *Che Guevara, Paulo Freire, and the Pedagogy of Revolution.* New York: Rowman and Littlefield, 2000.

Medical Times and Gazette, volume 2. London: J. & A. Churchill, 1875.

Medvedev, Roy. *Let History Judge: The Origins and Consequences of Stalinism.* New York: Columbia University Press, 1989.

Mellor, Ronald. *Tacitus.* New York: Routledge, 1994.

Merriman, John M., and J. M. Winter. *Europe 1789 to 1914: Encyclopedia of the Age of Industry and Empire.* New York: Charles Scribner's Sons, 2006.

Merriman, Roger Bigelow. *Suleiman the Magnificent: 1520–1566.* New York: Cooper Square Publishers, 1966.

Milton, Giles. *Nathaniel's Nutmeg.* New York: Farrar, Straus and Giroux, 1999.

Minney, James. *Rasputin.* London: Cassell, 1972.

Mitchell, Greg. *The Campaign of the Century: Upton Sinclair's Race for Governor of California and the Birth of Media Politics.* New York: Random House, 1992.

Montefiore, Simon Sebag. *Stalin: The Court of the Red Tsar.* New York: Random House, 2005.

———. *Young Stalin.* New York: Alfred Knopf, 2007.

Morgan, David. *The Mongols.* New York: Wiley-Blackwell, 1990.

Morley, John. *Oliver Cromwell.* Whitefish, Mont.: Kessinger Publishing, 2005.

Morrill, John. *Oliver Cromwell.* London: Oxford University Press, 2007.

Mortimer, Ian. *The Greatest Traitor: The Life of Sir Roger Mortimer, Ruler of England, 1327–1330.* New York: Macmillan, 2006.

Mosley, Leonard. *The Reich Marshall: A Biography of Hermann Goering.* New York: Doubleday, 1974.

Moyers, Bill, and Julie Leininger Pycior. *Moyers on America: A Journalist and His Times,* reprinted. New York: Random House, 2005.

Moynahan, Brian. *Rasputin: The Saint Who Sinned.* Cambridge, Mass.: Da Capo Press, 1999.

Murakami, Hyoe, and Thomas Harper. *Great Historical Figures of Japan.* Elmsford, NY: Japan Culture Institute, 1978.

Nasaw, David. *The Chief: The Life of William Randolph Hearst.* New York: Houghton Mifflin Harcourt, 2001.

Neale, J. E. *The Age of Catherine de Medici.* London: Jonathan Cape, 1943.

Noether, Emiliana. "Mazzini and the Nineteenth Century Revolutionary Movement," Consortium on Revolutionary Europe Proceedings. Athens, Ga.: Consortium on Revolutionary Europe, 1984.

Nutting, Anthony. *Lawrence of Arabia: The Man and the Motive.* London: Hollis and Carter, 1961.

O'Brien, Michael. *John F. Kennedy: A Biography.* New York: Macmillan, 2006.

O'Connell, Daniel Patrick. *Richelieu.* Ann Arbor, Mich.: Weidenfeld & Nicolson, 1968.

Oman, Charles. *Warwick, the Kingmaker,* reprint ed. London, New York: Macmillan, 1899.

———. *The Dark Ages, 476-918,* volume 1. London: Rivingtons, 1903.

———. *A History of England.* New York: Henry Holt, 1900.

Orlans, Harold. *T. E. Lawrence: Biography of a Broken Hero.* Jefferson, N.C.: McFarland Publishing, 2002.

Ott, Michael. "Tomás de Torquemada." *The Catholic Encyclopedia,* volume 14. New York: Robert Appleton Company, 1912.

Overy, R. J. *Goering.* New York: Barnes & Noble Publishing, 2003.

Pares, Bernard. "Rasputin and the Empress: Authors of the Russian Collapse." *Foreign Affairs,* volume 6, No. 1 (October 1927): 140–154.

Parsons, John Carmi. "The Year of Eleanor of Castile's Birth and Her Children by Edward I." *Medieval Studies* XLVI (1984): 245–265.

Paulhus, D. L., and Williams, K. M. "The Dark Triad of Personality: Narcissism, Machiavellianism, and Psychopathy." *Journal of Research in Personality* 36 (2002): 556–563.

Pollard, A. J. *The Wars of the Roses.* Basingstoke, UK: Macmillan Education, 1988.

Porter, David L. *Basketball: A Biographical Dictionary.* Westport, Conn.: Greenwood Press, 2005.

Procopius. *Buildings,* Book 1, Chapter 2 1940. Translated by H. B. Dewing.

Quran, 9:5 and 9:14.

Radzinskii, Edvard. *Stalin: The First In-Depth Biography Based on Explosive New Documents from Russia's Secret Archives.* New York: Doubleday, 1996.

———. *The Rasputin File.* New York: Anchor Books, 2001.

Rampton, Sheldon, and John Stauber. *Banana Republicans: How the Right Wing is Turning America into a One-Party State.* New York: Tarcher/Penguin, 2004.

Read, Piers Paul. *The Templars.* Cambridge, Mass.: Da Capo Press, 1999.

Riall, Lucy. *The Italian Risorgimento: State, Society, and National Unification.* New York: Routledge, 1994.

Richter, Werner. *Bismarck.* Los Angles: G. P. Putnam's Sons, 1965.

Roberts, Andrew. "Talleyrand: The Old Fraud." *Foundation for Cultural Review* (April 1, 2007): p. 4.

Roberts, Priscilla Mary. *World War I.* Santa Barbara, Calif.: ABC-CLIO, 2006.

Robertson, Sir Charles Grant. *Bismarck: Makers of the Nineteenth Century.* New York: H. Holt and Company, 1919.

Robson, William. *The Life of Cardinal Richelieu.* Oxford, UK: G. Routledge Publishing, 1854.

Roots, Ivan. *The Speeches of Oliver Cromwell.* London: Dent, 1989.

Rummel, R. J. *Death By Government.* New Brunswick, N.J.: Transaction Publishers, 1994.

Russell, Francis. *The President Makers: From Mark Hanna to Joseph P. Kennedy.* Boston: Little, Brown and Company, 1976.

Sabatini, Rafael. *Torquemada and the Spanish Inquisition a History.* Whitefish, Mont.: Kessinger Publishing, 2003.

Sadler, John. *Border Fury: England and Scotland at War, 1296–1568.* New York: Pearson/ Longman, 2005.

Safire, William. *Safire's Political Dictionary*. London: Oxford University Press, 2008.

Santosuosso, Antonio. *Barbarians, Marauders, and Infidels: The Ways of Medieval Warfare*. New York: Westview Press, 2004.

Santvoord, Seymour Van. *The House of Caesar and the Imperial Disease*. Troy, N.Y.: Pafraets Book Co., 1902.

Saul, John Ralston. *The Doubter's Companion: A Dictionary of Aggressive Common Sense*. New York: Simon and Schuster, 2002.

Saunders, John. *The History of the Mongol Conquests*. Philadephia: University of Pennsylvania Press, 2001.

Scheinberg, Stephen. *The Development of Corporation Labor Policy, 1900–1940*. Madison: University of Wisconsin Press, 1966.

Schoen, Robert. *What I Wish My Christian Friends Knew about Judaism*. Chicago: Loyola Press, 2004.

Scroop, Daniel. *Mr. Democrat: Jim Farley, the New Deal and the Making of Modern American Politics*. Ann Arbor: University of Michigan Press, 2006.

Shakespeare, William. *Hamlet,* Act 3, Scene 24. Read Books, London, 2010, 173–179.

Shotter, David. *Nero*. New York: Routledge, 2005.

Sihag, B. S. "Kautilya on Institutions, Governance, Knowledge, Ethics and Prosperity." *Humanomics* 23, no. 1 (2007): 7.

Simpson, Gary. *War, Peace, and God: Rethinking the Just War Tradition*. Minneapolis: Augsburg Fortress, 2007.

Sloane, William. "Bismarck's Apprenticeship." *Political Science Quarterly* 13, no. 3, (September 1899): 421.

Smele, Jonathan. *The Russian Revolution and Civil War, 1917–1921: An Annotated Bibliography* (Continuum Studies in History). London: Continuum International Publishing Group, 2006.

Smith, Denis Mack. *Mazzini*. New Haven, Conn.: Yale University Press, 1996.

Smith, Sally B. *Grace and Power: The Private World of the Kennedy White House*. New York: Random House, 2005.

Smith, William. *A Dictionary of Greek and Roman Biography and Mythology: Oarses–ygia,* volume 3. Boston: J. Murray, 1890.

Sokol, A. E. "Communication and Production in Indonesian History." *The Far Eastern Quarterly* 7, no. 4 (August 1948): 339–353.

Sonin, Konstantin. "The Dictator's Approach to Electoral Patterns." *Vox Publications*. (August 9, 2008). Available: http://www.voxeu.org/index.php?q=node/1525

Stockton, David. *Cicero: A Political Biography*. London: Oxford University Press, 1988.

Strauss, Leo, and Joseph Cropsey. *History of Political Philosophy*. Chicago: University of Chicago Press, 1987.

Stuart, Nancy Rubin. *Isabella of Castile: The First Renaissance Queen*. Bloomington, Ind.: iUniverse, 2004.

Sumption, Jonathan. *The Hundred Years War: Trial by Battle*. Philadelphia: University of Pennsylvania Press, 1999.

Sun Tzu. *The Art of War*. New York: Courier Dover Publications, 2002.

Sykes, Christopher. *Wassmuss: The German Lawrence*. London: Longmans, Green, and Company, 1936.

Taibo II, Paco Ignacio. *Guevara, Also Known as Che*. New York: St. Martin's Press, 1999

Templeman, Dennis. *The Northern Nadars of Tamil Nadu: An Indian Caste in the Process of Change*. Delhi, India: Oxford University Press, 1996.

Thatcher, Ian. *Trotsky*. New York: Routledge, 2003.

Toland, John. *The Rising Sun: The Decline and Fall of the Japanese Empire, 1936–1945,* volume 1. New York: Random House, 1970.

Trautmann, Thomas R. *Kautilya and the Arthashastra: A Statistical Investigation of the Authorship and Evolution of the Text*. Leiden, Holland: E.J. Brill, 1971.

Tremallo, Beth. *Irony and Self-Knowledge in Francisco López de Villalobos*. New York: Garland Pub., 1991.

Trevelyan, G. M. *Garibaldi's Defense of the Roman Republic*. London: Longmans, Green and Company, 1907.

Trevor-Roper, H. *Last Days of Hitler*. London: Pan Books, 1962.

Trotsky, Leon. *My Life: An Attempt at an Autobiography*. New York: C. Scribner's Sons, 1930.

Tsuzuki, Chushichi. *The Pursuit of Power in Modern Japan, 1825–1995*. London: Oxford University Press, 2000.

Upton, Clive, Stewart Sanderson, John Widdowson, and David Brophy. *Word Maps: A Dialect Atlas of England*. New York: Routledge, 1987.

Viroli, Maurizio. *Niccolo's Smile: A Biography of Machiavelli*. New York: Hill and Wang, 1998.

Volkogonov, Dmitri. *Trotsky: The Eternal Revolutionary*. New York: Simon and Schuster, 2007.

Von Goor, Jurrien, and Foskelien von Goor. *Prelude to Colonialism: The Dutch in Asia*. Amsterdam: Uitgeverij Verloren, 2004.

Von Hammer-Purgstall, Joseph. *Geschichte des Osmanischen Reiches*. Vienna: Desbarres, 1827.

Von Ranke, Leopold, and Robert A. Johnson. *History of the Reformation in Germany*. Translated by Sarah Austin. New York: E. P. Dutton, 1905.

Walling, Karl-Friedrich. *Republican Empire: Alexander Hamilton on War and Free Government*. Lawrence: University Press of Kansas, 1999.

Walsh, William T. *Characters of the Inquisition*. Whitefish, Mont.: Kessinger Publishing, 2007.

Watson, William, E. "The Battle of Tours-Poitiers Revisited." *Providence: Studies in Western Civilization* 2, no.1 (1993).

Watts, John. *Henry VI and the Politics of Kingship*. Cambridge, UK: Cambridge University Press, 1996.

Weir, Allison. *Queen Isabella: Treachery, Adultery, and Murder in Medieval England*. New York: Ballantine Books, 2005.

Wenquian, Gao. *Zhou Enlai: The Last Perfect Revolutionary*. Translated by Peter Rand and Lawrence R. Sullivan. New York: PublicAffairs, 2007.

Wetzler, Peter. *Hirohito and War*. Honolulu: University of Hawaii Press, 1998.

Whitechapel, Simon. *Flesh Inferno: Atrocities of Torquemada and the Spanish Inquisition*. New York: Creation Books, 2003.

Whiting, Charles. *The Hunt for Martin Bormann.* New York: Ballantine Books, 1973.

Williamson, Gordon. *The SS: Hitler's Instrument of Terror.* London: Zenith Imprint, 2004.

Wilson, Colin. *The Occult: A History.* New York: Random House, 1971.

Wilson, Ian. *Nostradamus: The Evidence.* London: Orion, 2003.

Wilson, Jeremy. *Lawrence of Arabia: The Authorized Biography of T. E. Lawrence.* New York: Atheneum, 1990.

———. *Lawrence of Arabia: A Pocket Biography.* New York: Stroud, Sutton Publishers, 1997.

Wilson, Joseph C. IV. *The Politics of Truth: Inside the Lies That Put the White House on Trial and Betrayed My Wife's CIA Identity: A Diplomat's Memoir,* rev. ed. New York: Carroll & Graf Publishers, 2005.

Wise, Terence, and Gary Embleton. *The Wars of the Roses.* Oxford, UK: Osprey Publishing, 1983.

Wistrich, Robert. *Who's Who in Nazi Germany* (The Routledge *Who's Who* Series). New York: Routledge, 2001.

Wykes, Alan. *Himmler.* London: Pan Books, 1972.

Yakovlev, Alexander N., Anthony Austin, and Paul Hollander. *A Century of Violence in Soviet Russia.* New Haven, Conn.: Yale University Press, 2004.

Young, G. F. *The Medici: Volume II.* London: John Murray, 1920.

Newspapers, Magazines, and Online Media

The Atlantic

The Austin Chronicle

BBC.com (UK)

The Boston Globe

Campaigns & Elections

CNN.com

Columbia Journalism Review

The Economic and Political Weekly (India)

Esquire

Fighting Arts

The Guardian (UK)

Haaretz (Israel)

The Los Angeles Times

Ma'ariv (Israel)

The Miami Herald

The New York Times

Popular Prakashan (India)

Rolling Stone

The Sabbath (Scotland)

Salon.com

Slate.com

The Sunday Herald (Scotland)

Time

Tomorrow's World

TourEgypt.net

The Village Voice

The Washington Post

Center for Research on Globalization (online)

Foreign Broadcast Monitoring Service, U.S. Federal Communications Commission

George Washington University National Security Archive (online)

ACKNOWLEDGMENTS

I'd like to express my appreciation to Iris Blasi and the good folks at Union Square Press, as well as my agent, Scott Mendle of Mendle Media Inc. Thanks also to my colleague Mark Kramer for his thoughts on Niccolo Machiavelli and political theory. The scope of research on this project was daunting, and my research assistant, David Anderson, was extremely helpful. Justin Hayes and John Ashley also provided research assistance. Work like this would not be possible without the support and encouragement of my academic home, Kennesaw State University, and its faculty and administrators. Finally, I'd like to thank my family, especially my wife, Sandy, for their patience and support during the many months of research and writing.

INDEX

ABOUT THE AUTHOR

Kerwin Swint is an author, a tenured professor at Kennesaw State University, and an internationally known expert in politics, history, and media. Most recently, he is the author of *Mudslingers: The 25 Dirtiest Political Campaigns of All Time* and *Dark Genius: The Influential Career of Legendary Political Operative and Fox News Founder Roger Ailes.* His media appearances include CNN, Fox News, MSNBC, ABC's *The View,* C-Span, BBC Radio, National Public Radio, the *Wall Street Journal,* the *Los Angeles Times,* and London's *Daily Mail* and *Guardian.*